082431

Reinforcement and Behavior

Contributors

D. E. BERLYNE

PETER L. CARLTON

KEITH N. CLAYTON

VERNE C. COX

W. K. ESTES

JAN W. KAKOLEWSKI

IRVING KUPFERMANN

CARL PFAFFMANN

HAROLD PINSKER

DAVID PREMACK

LARRY STEIN

JACK T. TAPP

ELLIOT S. VALENSTEIN

EDWARD L. WALKER

HARDY C. WILCOXON

REINFORCEMENT AND BEHAVIOR

EDITED BY

JACK T. TAPP

DEPARTMENT OF PSYCHOLOGY
VANDERBILT UNIVERSITY
NASHVILLE, TENNESSEE

ACADEMIC PRESS

New York San Francisco London 1969

A Subsidiary of Harcourt Brace Jovanovich, Publishers

ACADEMIC PRESS, INC.
111 Fifth Avenue, New York, New York 10003

United Kingdom Edition published by
ACADEMIC PRESS, INC. (LONDON) LTD.
24/28 Oval Road, London NW1

LIBRARY OF CONGRESS CATALOG CARD NUMBER: 68-59166

PRINTED IN THE UNITED STATES OF AMERICA

List of Contributors

Numbers in parentheses indicate the pages on which the authors' contributions begin.

D. E. BERLYNE* (178), University of Toronto, Toronto, Canada

PETER L. CARLTON (286), Department of Psychiatry, Rutgers Medical School, New Brunswick, New Jersey

KEITH N. CLAYTON (95), Department of Psychology, Vanderbilt University, Nashville, Tennessee

VERNE C. COX (242), Department of Psychophysiology-Neurophysiology, Fels Research Institute, Yellow Springs, Ohio

W. K. ESTES† (63), Department of Psychology, Stanford University, Stanford, California

JAN W. KAKOLEWSKI (242), Department of Psychophysiology-Neurophysiology, Fels Research Institute, Yellow Springs, Ohio

IRVING KUPFERMANN (356), Department of Psychiatry and Neurology and Department of Physiology and Biophysics, New York University Medical School, New York, New York

CARL PFAFFMANN (215), The Rockefeller University, New York, New York

*Present address: Institut d'Estetique et des Sciences de l'Art, Paris, France
†Present address: The Rockefeller University, New York, New York

HAROLD PINSKER (356), Department of Physiology and Biophysics, New York University Medical School, New York, New York

DAVID PREMACK (120), University of California, Santa Barbara, California

LARRY STEIN (328), Wyeth Institute for Medical Research, Radnor, Pennsylvania

JACK T. TAPP (146, 387), Department of Psychology, Vanderbilt University, Nashville, Tennessee

ELLIOT S. VALENSTEIN (242), Department of Psychophysiology-Neurophysiology, Fels Research Institute, Yellow Springs, Ohio

EDWARD L. WALKER (47), Psychological Laboratories, University of Michigan, Ann Arbor, Michigan

HARDY C. WILCOXON (1), Department of Psychology, George Peabody College for Teachers, Nashville, Tennessee

Preface

Over half a century of research on the principles of learning and reinforcement has resulted in the development of a technology which is having considerable impact on the control of behavior. The personnel of numerous schools and hospitals are being trained in the effective use of rewards to reinforce and, consequently, modify behavior. Such programs are the hope of the future and will, perhaps, markedly change the management of undesirable behavior patterns.

The series of papers in this volume brings together the research findings and views of a number of investigators whose work has challenged the more traditional interpretations of the nature of the reinforcement process. Within the book, the chapters are organized from a molar level of analysis to a molecular one, not only to reflect the diversity of strategies that are being brought to bear on the problem, but also to show that the research on the nature of reinforcement transcends lines of scientific disciplines and that many different levels of analysis contribute to our understanding of the phenomenon.

The first and last chapters give historical perspective to the remainder of the book by reviewing the contributions of a number of individuals who have dealt with the problem in their own work and by pointing out some of the major issues on the molar level that are still unresolved. The remaining chapters can be roughly divided into two categories, both of which reflect reconceptualizations of the problem but which employ somewhat different strategies. One examines the consequences of rewards on behavior in order to specify the limits of their operations and the variables which predispose organisms to be responsive to the consequences of rewards. The other deals with the neural mechanisms which underlie reinforcement and learning. This volume presents a more extensive analysis of the process by which rewards influence behavior than has previously been published elsewhere and new experimental data are presented in support of the views of the various authors. The ideas and experimental findings contained in these papers will serve as a challenge for further investigations of the nature of the reinforcement process.

The work developed from a series of colloquium addresses, by the contributors, to the Departments of Psychology at Vanderbilt University and George Peabody College for Teachers. The historical chapter by Hardy Wilcoxon and the chapter by Irving Kupfermann and Harold Pinsker are exceptions. Dr. Wilcoxon agreed to write an introduction when the book was conceived in order to place the contributions of the other authors in historical perspective. The chapter by Dr. Kupfermann and Dr. Pinsker was conceived after the colloquium series was planned, as a result of a discussion in which the implications of their work for this problem became apparent. The senior authors of the remaining papers gave oral presentations to the Vanderbilt and Peabody Joint Colloquium Series in Psychology during the academic year 1966-1967. The final manuscripts based on their research were submitted at a later date to keep material commensurate with the most recent research findings.

I am indebted to Professor Gilbert Meier, who was the colloquium coordinator for Peabody College, for his encouragement and cooperation in pooling the resources of our respective institutions, and for his assistance in working out a mutually beneficial colloquium schedule. I am also grateful for the support and encouragement of the members of the Department of Psychology at Vanderbilt, particularly Professors Donald L. Thistlethwaite and Jum C. Nunnally, who, respectively, served as Chairman of the Department during the inception and conduct of the colloquium series. A special note of thanks is due to the various agencies of the federal government who have supported the research activities of the contributors and who provided funds which supported the colloquium series. These include the National Institutes of Mental Health, the National Science Foundation, the Office of Naval Research, the Veterans Research Administration, the National Aeronautics and Space Administration, and the National Research Council of Canada.

I would also like to express my gratitude to several individuals who assisted in various stages of this project. Most importantly, I thank the contributors for their willingness to participate in writing chapters for this volume and for their patience and cooperation. I would also like to thank Mr. Michael Spiegler for his assistance in the conduct of the colloquium series, and Mrs. Vance Bradley for her assistance in the composition of the final product. I am particularly grateful to my wife, Dona, for the encouragement, assistance, and forbearance she has provided, not only on this project, but in all of my endeavors throughout the years.

JACK T. TAPP

Nashville, Tennessee
February, 1969

Contents

2. Reinforcement—"The One Ring"

EDWARD L. WALKER

3. Reinforcement in Human Learning

W. K. ESTES

4. Reward and Reinforcement in Selective Learning: Considerations with Respect to a Mathematical Model of Learning

KEITH N. CLAYTON

8. Taste Preference and Reinforcement

CARL PFAFFMANN

9. The Hypothalamus and Motivated Behavior

ELLIOT S. VALENSTEIN, VERNE C. COX,
AND JAN W. KAKOLEWSKI

10. Brain-Acetylcholine and Inhibition

PETER L. CARLTON

11. Chemistry of Purposive Behavior

LARRY STEIN

12. Plasticity in *Aplysia* Neurons and Some Simple Neuronal Models of Learning

IRVING KUPFERMANN AND HAROLD PINSKER

13. Current Status and Future Directions

JACK T. TAPP

Reinforcement and Behavior

CHAPTER 1

Historical Introduction to the Problem of Reinforcement

HARDY C. WILCOXON

... we must regard the processes of learning as wholly automatic.
Clark L. Hull (1943, p. 69)

The "problem of reinforcement" is the admittedly vague and general question of how certain behaviors get strengthened in relation to others as an organism learns. Historically, the term reinforcement has had many different meanings. A history of the problem, therefore, must reflect that diversity and some of the controversy surrounding the attempts to give the term more definite meaning. This introductory chapter is an attempt to provide a historical background for those

1

that follow, each of which represents a new effort to achieve a better understanding of the problem of reinforcement.

I. PHILOSOPHICAL ANTECEDENTS

It is difficult to find a legitimate ancestor to the modern problem of reinforcement in the long philosophical prehistory of psychology. Although many of the problems dealt with by philosophers before the rise of modern science were similar to the modern one, their similarity is at best analogous, and not homologous. Hedonism, as developed in Greek philosophy, may be taken as an example to illustrate this difference. For Epicurus (341-270 B.C.) pleasure was an ultimate good and, in a sense, the determinant of behavior. In contrast with contemporary views, pleasure determined behavior in a teleological sense; that is, pleasure was the goal toward which rational men strived. Thus, man's reason was the determinant of his behavior, if we subscribe to the modern view that causes must be prior to their effects. But since no account was given of how prior events brought about changes in the choices made by reason, man's behavior was, in the last analysis, indeterminate. This kind of "determination" of man's behavior by some indeterminate entity such as reason or "free will" was characteristic of prescientific philosophy and is the basic reason that it contains little, if anything, of direct relevance to the modern problem of reinforcement.

II. EARLY EVOLUTIONISM

Only when biological scientists began to view behavior in the context of the natural sciences did the problem of reinforcement arise in acute form. So long as animals did what it was "in their natures" to do and man did what his reason dictated, there was little cause to worry over a problem such as reinforcement. Thus, the history that is relevant to our purpose began around the time of Charles Darwin in the nineteenth century, when the biological sciences were at last ushered into the realm of true natural science.

A. Charles Darwin (1809-1882)

Two aspects of Darwin's achievement were especially critical in determining the course that behavioral science took and in shaping the intellectual climate in which the question of what we now call reinforcement arose as a serious scientific problem. His principle of natural selection made teleological explanations in biology unnecessary and at the same time demanded that reason be considered in a new light.

Darwin (1859) was the first to give a nonteleological explanation of how species could evolve through increasingly adaptive and complex stages. Lamarck (1744-1829), whose views on evolutionary theory were published in the year of Darwin's birth, had already expressed many of the ideas which Darwin was later to incorporate into his own theory. Indeed, Darwin differed radically from Lamarck on only one major issue, the crucial one of teleology. For Lamarck, adaptive change and speciation came about through the directed adaptive efforts of organisms. In his view, inheritable variation occurred as a result of purposeful striving. Darwin, on the other hand, was able to show convincingly that organisms could be expected to evolve toward better and more complex adaptations to their environment through the unguided operation of principles of natural selection that involved no teleological notions whatever. His theory assumed that inheritable variation occurred spontaneously or by chance rather than by the adaptive effort of the organism, and it recognized that selection was natural to the struggle for existence in which all animals engage. In substituting chance variation and the grim criterion of survival for Lamarck's teleological idea of individually directed adaptive effort, Darwin gave a fresh perspective to the biological sciences. Many biological problems were brought into sharper focus, either immediately or eventually, as a logical consequence of the wholly natural science approach which Darwin showed was possible in the study of living things. If natural selection could account for the evolution of species with no recourse to teleological striving, perhaps similar principles of natural science could explain adaptive changes in the behavior of individual organisms during the course of their lives, regardless of whether such changes could be passed on through inheritance.

The second critical feature of Darwin's theory, for our purposes, was the new perspective in which it put reason. In Darwin's time the prevalent view was that only man possessed reason. Now, with man on the same continuum with other animals, he could no longer be considered so unique as to possess a capacity totally lacking in other creatures. This led first to a search for evidence of reason in animals, as seen in the well-known work of Romanes (1848-1894). But it led, also, and more importantly, to a reassessment of the way in which reason might legitimately function in a science of behavior. Reason could no longer be regarded as the "unguided guide" which led man, and perhaps even animals, inexorably toward goals not yet experienced. If man and other animals possessed reason, then reason was a part of nature and must conform to natural laws. Reason as the "indeterminate determiner" was by no means expelled immediately, but its popularity as an explanatory concept began to wane as the implications of Darwin's great generalization came to be explored.

Among those who explored some of the behavioral implications of the theory of natural selection was Darwin himself. His *Expression of the Emotions in Man and Animals* (1872) was an effort to show evolution in behavior that paralleled evolutionary changes in structure. Although he did not do much with the topic of learning, its study was greatly stimulated by the emphasis he had placed upon adaptation in evolutionary theory. Romanes, a friend and supporter of Darwin, did study learning and problem solving in animals, but in a loose and methodologically unsound way. His reliance upon anecdotal evidence prevented his views from attaining wide acceptance among scientists. Further, from the standpoint of our present interest, he attempted no theory of the learning process that would subsequently influence reinforcement theory. Another associate and follower of Darwin did, however, and to his views we now turn.

B. Herbert Spencer (1820-1903)

Herbert Spencer was a contemporary of Darwin and one of the more notable of those friends and fellow scholars who stood up for him after publication of *The Origin of the Species* caused a storm of protest (Boring, 1950). Spencer was a man of wide interests and was a prolific writer. He saw principles of evolution[1] at work everywhere he looked, and he looked in many directions. The world knows him best as the proponent of "Social Darwinism," the view that social structures and

---

[1]According to Boring (1950), Spencer claimed to have anticipated Darwin's evolutionary views in the first edition of his *Principles of Psychology* published in 1855 and actually did more specifically anticipate Darwin by a year or so. Certainly, a great deal of thought had been given to evolution much earlier, not only by Lamarck, but also by the German poet Goethe and by Charles Darwin's grandfather, Erasmus Darwin. In Greek philosophy, both Empedocles and Aristotle developed theories of evolution, but with strong teleological tinges. The most exact anticipation, if it can be called that, was in the paper of Darwin's friend, Alfred Russell Wallace, which Wallace sent to Darwin for his opinion. Darwin published it and an abstract of his own views almost immediately, and followed with the publication the next year of his great classic for which he had been systematically gathering and revising notes for over 20 years.

cultures evolve in a way that parallels the evolution of organisms. His most significant contribution to reinforcement history, however, was his authorship of an influential, though highly speculative, theory of learning.

Spencer's theory of learning (1870) embodied the first really systematic attempt to give scientifically plausible explanations of the differential strengthening of the actions of organisms. Consequently, his is the first theory of reinforcement in the modern pattern. It deserves more attention than it has received, as Cason (1932) pointed out long ago, if for no other reason than that it bears such a close resemblance to Thorndike's famous Law of Effect. Thorndike's law was formulated 30–40 years later, embodied essentially the same ideas, and dominated discussions of learning theory for over half a century.

Spencer's central argument is that during the course of evolution, the principle of natural selection works to produce a correlation between feelings of pleasure and actions that are beneficial to survival, on the one hand, and feelings of pain with actions that are injurious, on the other. The organism that experienced pleasure as a consequence of actions that were detrimental to its survival and pain in consequence of actions that were beneficial would not long survive. By the same reasoning, those organisms so constituted as to experience pleasure while performing beneficial actions and pain in those actions which were injurious would obviously remain in better health, have longer reproductive lives, and eventually populate the world with creatures similarly constituted. "In other words, those races of beings only can have survived in which, on the average, agreeable or desired feelings went along with activities conducive to the maintenance of life, while disagreeable and habitually avoided feelings went along with activities directly or indirectly destructive of life; and there must ever have been, other things equal, the most numerous and long-continued survivals among races in which these adjustments of feelings to actions were the best, tending ever to bring about perfect adjustment (Spencer, 1870, p. 280)."

Spencer took it as obvious that an organism would tend to repeat actions that brought pleasure and desist from those which brought pain. Such an assumption is implicit in the above argument and necessary for its logical validity. Spencer was aware that the "obvious," common sense assumption needed a scientifically respectable explanation; he attempted to give it one in highly speculative, neurological terms. His general argument was that feelings of pleasure were accompanied by an increase in activity in the nervous system, while feelings of pain were accompanied by a corresponding decrease. The increased nervous activity accompanying pleasure somehow found its way to those parts of the body which had just been active, thereby increasing the probability that they would become active again in a similar situation. This crucial idea, along with most of the other features of his theory of learning, is revealed in the following passage:

> Suppose, now, that in putting out its head to seize prey scarcely within reach, a creature has repeatedly failed. Suppose that along with the group of motor actions approximately adapted to seize prey at this distance, the diffused discharge is, on some occasion, so distributed throughout the muscular system as to cause a slight forward movement of the body. Success will occur instead of failure; and after success will immediately come certain pleasurable sensations with an accompanying large draught of nervous energy towards the organs employed in eating, etc. This is to say, the lines of nervous communication through which the diffused discharge happened in this case to pass, have opened a new way to certain wide channels of escape; and, consequently, they have suddenly become lines through which a large quantity of molecular motion is drawn, and lines which are so rendered more permeable than before. On recurrence of the circumstances, these muscular movements that were followed by success are likely to be repeated: what was first an accidental combination of motions will now be a combination having considerable probability. For when on such subsequent occasion the visual impressions have produced nascent tendencies to the acts approximately fitted to seize the object, and when through these there are nascently excited all the states, sensory and motor, which accompany capture, it must happen that among the links in the connected excitations there will be excitations of those fibres and cells through which, on the previous occasion, the diffused discharge brought about the actions that caused success. The tendency for the diffused discharge to follow these lines will obviously be greater than before; and the probability of a successfully modified action will therefore be greater than before. Every repetition of it will make still more permeable the new channels, and increase the probability of subsequent repetitions; until at length the nervous connexions become organized (Spencer, 1870, p. 545).

Clearly, Spencer was trying to give a mechanistic account of the learning process, and his theory, although wildly speculative and based largely on casual observation and logic rather than experiment, nevertheless had tantalizing appeal for those looking for a way to explain behavior deterministically. Although implausible in some respects, it yet has a modern ring.

Spencer recognized that the correlations he described between feelings and actions were not perfect, but he felt them to be generally true and under constant improvement through successive generations. He further recognized that anomalies sometimes exist because of changes in environment to which animals have not had time to adapt.

"How then, it will be asked, does it happen that animals sometimes die from eating poisonous plants, or surfeit themselves fatally with kinds of food which, though wholesome in moderate quantities, are injurious in large quantities? The reply is that, by natural selection, the guidance of pleasures and pains can be adjusted only to the circumstances of the habitat within which the special type has been evolved. *Survival of the fittest cannot bring the inclinations and aversions into harmony with unfelt conditions* (Spencer, 1870, p. 281, italics added)."

Spencer also recognized that the complexity of certain organisms sometimes obscured the natural correlations which resulted from selection. For simple organisms there were consistent correlations between feelings of pleasure and beneficial actions and feelings of pain and actions which were injurious. They were sometimes difficult to see in higher organisms.

"This is illustrated most clearly among ourselves. There are so many kinds of superiorities which severally enable men to survive, notwithstanding accompanying inferiorities, that natural selection cannot by itself rectify any particular unfitness. . . . Indeed, the imbecile and idle are artificially enabled to multiply at the expense of the capable and industrious (Spencer, 1870, p. 284)."

He saw the complexity of man as being so great that the outlook for his further improvement by evolutionary mechanisms is not optimistic, especially since many seem to believe that painful actions are beneficial and pleasurable actions detrimental. This common notion "has been, and still is, upheld by creeds which present for the worship of men a Being who is supposed to be displeased with them if they seek gratifications, and to be propitiated by gratuitous self-denials and even self-tortures (Spencer, 1870, p. 284)."

This theory of Spencer provides the real starting point for what we now call theories of reinforcement. Several of his contemporaries held similar views. Alexander Bain (1818-1903) had a related theory (1888) but gave a slightly more subjective interpretation to animal learning. Also, the pleasure-pain theory of J. M. Baldwin, 1861-1934 (1895), bore a strong resemblance. The interpretations of animal learning by C. Lloyd Morgan, 1852-1936 (1894), one of the great pioneers of experimental, as opposed to naturalistic, studies of animal learning, also drew heavily upon Spencer's ideas. Thus, Spencer's influence was very great, whether acknowledged, as it sometimes was, or unacknowledged, as came to be the case.

Baldwin, who freely acknowledged Spencer's influence, had this to say about the "grudging payment" psychology made of its debt to Spencer:

"It is strange, but it is true, that many British writers find it impossible to do any sort of justice to Spencer. And yet where is there the British writer, save Darwin, whose name and theories are to be found in the whole world's literature of a half-dozen great subjects, since 1850, as Spencer's are? We hear it said that half the world nowadays thinks in terms of Darwinism: but it is truer to say, 'in terms of evolutionism'; for half of the half thinks its evolutionism in terms, not of Darwinism, but of Spencerism. Moreover, in the Latin countries and in the United States, it was the leaven of Spencer's evolutionism that first worked its way through the lump. Why not, then, recognise Spencer as what he was, one of the greatest intellectual influences of modern times, a glory to British thought? In psychology this is specially worth insisting upon, since Spencer came just at a time of surprising barrenness in this department in England (Baldwin, 1913, pp. 98-99)."

Even William James was at first strongly attracted to Spencer's psychology, but later repelled by it. In 1876 he offered an "elective" in Spencer at Harvard which he launched with enthusiasm, only to tire of it before it was finished. In a letter to a friend in December of that year he said, ". . . I have some bright boys in my Spencer class, – but I am completely disgusted with the eminent philosopher, who seems to me more and more to be as absolutely worthless in all *fundamental* matters of thought, as he is admirable, clever and ingenious in secondary matters. His mind is a perfect puzzle to me, but the total impression is of an intensely two and sixpenny, paper-collar affair . . . (Perry, 1954, p. 144)."

Years later, after he had left psychology for philosophy, he made the following characteristic remarks about Spencer in the first of his *Pragmatism* lectures:

. . . Rationalists feel his fearful array of insufficiencies. His dry schoolmaster temperament, the hurdy-gurdy monotony of him, his preference for cheap makeshifts in argument, his lack of education even in mechanical principles, and in general the vagueness of all his fundamental ideas, his whole system wooden, as if knocked together out of cracked hemlock boards – and yet the half of England wants to bury him in Westminster Abbey.

Why? Why does Spencer call out so much reverence in spite of his weakness in rationalistic eyes? Why should so many educated men who feel that weakness, you and I perhaps, wish to see him in the Abbey notwithstanding? Simply because we feel his heart to be *in the right place* philosophically. His principles may be all skin and bone, but at any rate his books try to mould themselves upon the particular shape of this particular world's carcase. The noise of facts resounds through all his chapters, the citations of fact never cease, he emphasizes facts, turns his face towards their quarter; and that is enough. It means the right *kind* of thing for the empiricist mind (James, 1907, pp. 39-40).

James' opinion of Spencer's views is especially interesting for the possible bearing it might have had on Thorndike's attitude toward Spencer. James attracted Thorndike to psychology, befriended him when he was a graduate student at Harvard—even to the point of housing his chickens in the basement of his home during one term— and remained a lifelong friend (Thorndike, 1936). It seems certain that Thorndike was aware both of Spencer's theories and of James' attitude toward them, although it is difficult to find evidence of such awareness in Thorndike's writings. A secondary source (Pax, 1938, p. 120) mentions that Thorndike once invited a comparison of his own views with those of several earlier writers, including Spencer.

It seems probable that Spencer's views fell into disfavor because he espoused an evolutionary theory that was more Lamarckian than Darwinian. He did explicitly endorse the doctrine of inheritance of acquired characteristics, but he need not have done so. Darwin's idea of natural selection could have served just as well to achieve the same result. For example, Spencer's argument for the development of correlations between actions and feelings over successive generations is just as valid under the Darwinian principle of natural selection as it is under the doctrine of the inheritance of acquired characteristics. This, indeed, seems to be true in the case of any argument for a structure or behavioral tendency seen in any living organism. The existence of a structure or a behavior pattern can be accounted for by either the Lamarckian or the Darwinian view.

Thus, science drifted away from Spencer primarily for the irrelevant reason that he espoused the more and more doubtful doctrine of the inheritance of acquired characteristics. What does not seem to have been generally recognized is that the theory of learning, in contrast to some other parts of Spencer's psychology, did not require the doubtful doctrine.

There were, of course, other criticisms of Spencer's works. Some did not like their irreligiousness and rejection of rationalism (e.g., James, 1890; James, 1907). Others had factual sorts of criticism, both behavioral and physiological, as additional facts became known. Cason (1932) has given an extensive summary of these arguments, which are essentially the same as those that were leveled against Thorndike's Law of Effect.

III. THE LAW OF EFFECT

A. Edward L. Thorndike (1874-1949)

The general outline of Thorndike's position on reinforcement,[2] a position he was to maintain without essential modification for more than three decades, was fairly explicit in his doctoral dissertation (1898). But he did not name it the Law of Effect there, nor was his main interest at that time in formulating new laws of learning. His main thesis, which was more iconoclastic than constructive, was that animals did not utilize ideas in solving problems.

An attacker, to be effective, needs a good target, and Thorndike chose a prominent one in C. Lloyd Morgan. He showed that Morgan, whose famous law of parsimony had earned him the reputation of being the most hardheaded and objective of the world's comparative psychologists, was actually guilty of a certain amount of anthropomorphism himself. He turned Morgan's canon against its author, not because Morgan was the worst, but because he was the best.

Thus entered the swashbuckling young "upstart," as some of his elders considered him (Jonçich, 1968). His was a battle against "mentalistic" explanations of behavior, and his zeal never abated during the remaining 51 years of his life.

His major weapon quickly came to be the Law of Effect, although the Law of Exercise was paired with it from the beginning, and many other laws, both major and minor, were added as his vigorous research program developed. The Law of Effect was first given that name in *The Elements of Psychology* (Thorndike, 1905), while the first attempt to give it a physiological basis is found in an infrequently cited paper that appeared three years later (1908) under the fascinating title "A Pragmatic Substitute for Free Will." This paper deserves more exposure than it has recently received because it tells us so much about what Thorndike thought he had in the Law of Effect, and where he thought it could take us.

[2]For those who might wish to see more extended and detailed treatments of Thorndike, many excellent ones are available. Waters' early review (1934) of the literature on the Law of Effect was followed by a much more extensive review by Postman (1947). For the early history, the best single source is Pax (1938). Perhaps the most widely read account is that by Hilgard in his *Theories of Learning* (Hilgard & Bower, 1966). Thorndike's own compilation, *Selected Writings from a Connectionist's Psychology* (1949), is also valuable but necessarily limited to a few selections from the hundreds of articles and many books that he published during his career.

The paper is one of the *Essays Philosophical and Psychological in Honor of William James* published by Columbia University the year after James had visited the institution to deliver his lectures on pragmatism. In keeping with the occasion, Thorndike chose to deal with a topic bearing upon James' philosophy—the topic of meliorism, or the belief that the world tends to become better and better and that man can aid its betterment. Thorndike's opening paragraph shows clearly where he stands:

"In his recent lectures on Pragmatism Professor James emphasizes the fact that the only issue of consequence in the free-will controversy is meliorism, for which indeterminism gives possibility. It has perhaps not been clearly understood that meliorism is possible without the presupposition that the result of any condition of nature is indeterminate,—without any need of our going against, or even beyond, the scientific, matter-of-fact point of view and habit of interpreting the universe. It seems worth while, then, to show that the natural constitution of the world makes meliorism possible, and, in fact, necessary (Thorndike, 1908, p. 587)."

The crux of Thorndike's argument is that the nervous system is so constructed as to lead to the survival and strengthening of those connections which have been active just prior to a satisfying event and to the weakening and eventual disappearance of those connections which have been active prior to annoying events. Thus, the nature of the nervous system makes us do more things that bring satisfaction, and fewer that bring annoyance. If one means by meliorism ". . . that the world can *increase in satisfyingness* or *decrease in annoyingness* or *both* to the individual or group in question" (Thorndike, 1908, p. 588), then we have no reason to desert natural science in order to maintain our faith that we can make the world better. "What free will offers is the right to believe that human behavior may, so far as it itself goes, possibly change the world for the better. What our substitute for the freedom of the will offers is the surety that it does (Thorndike, 1908, p. 606)."

His speculations about the physiological basis for this natural action of the nervous system, while interesting, are too lengthy and involved for detailed presentation here. In general, however, he sees it as "a struggle for existence amongst neurone connections. The formation of a habit means the survival of one connection, the elimination of a futile response to a given situation means the death of another (Thorndike, 1908, p. 591)." One of the more interesting specific hypotheses is that the neuron is capable of a kind of ameboid movement at its end processes, which would make changes in the strength of connections possible. When neurons conduct with the moderate intensity thought to be characteristic of satisfying states, the connections then active become stronger through movement of the end processes. Annoyance, he thought, has the opposite effect on neuron movement, bringing a weakening of the active connections.

Thorndike did not present his neurological speculations with the confidence that they were right, but rather with the vigorous insistence that they *could be right*; thus, he saw no need to abandon a deterministic approach. He insisted, also, that his point of view applied equally to thought as well as to action. "For the word 'response' anywhere in this paper, *idea* may be substituted on the same terms as *act*. The beliefs of a man of science or a philosopher are selected in just the same way as the movements of his play at billiards or golf (Thorndike, 1908, p. 608)." The true causes in the development of belief, reasoning, and knowledge are the same satisfying and annoying states as those responsible for alterations in acts. "The history of intellect and morals, is as 'natural' as the history of the backbone (Thorndike, 1908, p. 610)."

In Thorndike's early writings, there is evidence that he gave considerable thought to the mind-body problem, something that every psychologist of the day tussled with to some degree. His concern is seen in several papers that appeared around the turn of the century (Pax, 1938, p. 122). He seems never to have resolved, even in his own mind, the dilemma that he saw between the two contentions, (1) that feelings cause changes in bodily processes, a view which seems to lead to philosophical absurdities, and (2) that they do not, which seems equally absurd from a naive, empiricist viewpoint. At any rate, during this early period he began to paraphrase what he meant by satisfaction and discomfort, putting their meanings in behavioral terms. It was not a solution that calmed his critics, as we shall later see, but he stuck by it to the end and never again ventured very far into the entangling thicket of mind-body arguments. The following statement in his autobiography is perhaps revealing: "Under no circumstances, probably, could I have been able or willing to make philosophy my business (Thorndike, 1936)."

Although he used the words Law of Effect in 1905, he referred in 1908 only to "our law." But by 1911, when his dissertation was republished along with additional studies under the title *Animal Intelligence*, the law was going by its familiar name and was stated concisely in a section toward the end of the book:

"The Law of Effect is that: Of several responses made to the same situation, those which are accompanied or closely followed by satisfaction to the animal will, other things being equal, be more firmly connected with the situation, so that, when it recurs, they will be more likely to recur; those which are accompanied or closely followed by discomfort to the animal will, other things being equal, have their connections with that situation weakened, so that, when it recurs, they will be less likely to occur. The greater the satisfaction or discomfort, the greater the strengthening or weakening of the bond (Thorndike, 1911, p. 244)."

Already sensitive to the criticism that "satisfaction" and "discomfort" are subjective terms, he quickly added, "By a satisfying state of affairs is meant one which the animal does nothing to avoid, often doing such things as attain and preserve it. By a discomforting or annoying state of affairs is meant one which the animal commonly avoids and abandons (Thorndike, 1911, p. 245)."

Spencer, too, had felt the need to clarify what he meant by pleasure and pain, and he did so in a way that is strikingly parallel to the above: ". . . substitute for the word Pleasure the equivalent phrase – a feeling which we seek to bring into consciousness and retain there, and . . . substitute for the word Pain the equivalent phrase – a feeling which we seek to get out of consciousness and to keep out . . . (Spencer, 1870, p. 280)."

Spencer's and Thorndike's paraphrases of their key terms, while similar in form, are different in content. Spencer defined the troublesome words pleasure and pain in terms of equivalent conscious feelings which the individual would seem, *a priori*, to retain or expel. Thorndike, on the other hand, defined feelings of satisfaction and discomfort in terms of behavior which could be seen either to persist or to be cut short. Thus, although Cason (1932) and Pax (1938) consider these paraphrases as essentially identical, they are, in fact, different in a rather important way. Both definitions can lead to circularity, to be sure, but Spencer had two invisible riders on his merry-go-around, "pleasure" and "feeling," while Thorndike had only one, "satisfaction." Thorndike's definition, then, did represent an improvement over Spencer's.

A unique feature of Thorndike's theory, as compared to earlier associationist theories, is its emphasis on *connections* between *situations* and *responses* (S-R connection). Spencer, Bain, and Baldwin, as well as the philosopher John Locke (1632–1704) much earlier, had thought pleasures and pains primarily strengthened or weakened the tendency for an idea or a response to be aroused. Their views, in this particular respect, were closer to Skinner's current conception of the strengthening of an operant than to Thorndike's conception of the

strengthening of an S-R connection. It was Thorndike's theory, therefore, that set the pattern for the S-R interpretation of learning.

Much has been made of Thorndike's insistence upon the automatic
action of effect, and of how this feature of his theory made it objective
and scientific in contrast to earlier theories and some contemporary
rival ones that were held to be subjective and indeterminate. Thorndike certainly did insist upon automatic action, that is, action which is
unmediated by ideas or other "mentalistic" entities. But from the beginning, he also insisted upon a number of other things that had to be
taken into account before the automatic action of effect could be seen
clearly. These "other things being equal" made the theory indeterminate from the start and to a large extent incapable of disproof, which
no doubt contributed enormously to its longevity.

The situation in 1911 was as follows (it got worse later): "The other
things that have to be equal in the case of the law of effect are: First,
the frequency, energy and duration of the connection, — that is, the
action of the law of exercise; second, the closeness with which the satisfaction is associated with the response; and, third, the readiness of
the response to be connected with the situation (Thorndike, 1911, p.
248)."

He specifies what he means by the first qualification reasonably
well, but note how he elaborates the meaning of the second. "The
second is most clearly seen in the effect of increasing the interval
between the response and the satisfaction or discomfort (p. 248)." So
far, so good; psychologists can measure time to their satisfaction, although theoretical physicists sometimes have trouble with it. However, Thorndike goes on to say:

"Close temporal sequence is not the only means of insuring the
connection of the satisfaction with the response producing it. What is
called *attention to the response counts also*. If a cat pushes a button
around with its nose, while its main occupation, the act to which its
general 'set' impels it, to which, we say, it is chiefly attentive, is that of
clawing at an opening, it will be less aided in the formation of the
habit than if it had been chiefly concerned in what its nose was doing
(p. 249)."

He does not say that the Law of Effect fails altogether when the
animal is not attending to the response, but only that it works better
when the subject is "paying attention." Nevertheless, he has provided
a good-sized loophole. His later Law of Belongingness (Thorndike,
1935a) seems to have evolved from this early notion, and it enjoyed
the same extremely loose relationship to the Law of Effect.

Thorndike also elaborates on the third qualification that must be made in order for the Law of Effect to operate in pure form. "The third factor, the susceptibility of the response and situation to connection, is harder to illustrate. But, apparently, of those responses which are equally strongly connected with a situation by nature and equally attended to, some are more susceptible than others to a more intimate connection (p. 249)." This notion was elevated to the status of the Law of Readiness two years later in the first volume of *Educational Psychology* (1913). Hilgard and Bower (1966, pp. 18-19) present a good summary of Thorndike's treatment of it, pointing out that although his physiological explanation of its action has many objectionable features, the law does have important psychological meaning as a law of preparatory adjustment.

The purpose here in presenting Thorndike's various qualifications to the unmitigated action of the Law of Effect is not to suggest that the qualifying statements were unnecessary, but to emphasize that the claim that the action of effect is automatic, which he and his followers so often made, is true only in a limited sense. Within the framework of the theory, it is true only in the sense that the action of effect is stoutly held to be independent of any mediation by conscious experience or ideas.

The Law of Effect per se retained its essential form from the time of its original formulation until about 1930. By that time Thorndike had become doubtful of the validity of the part having to do with the weakening effect of "annoyers," "discomforts," etc. Some of his studies with both human and animal subjects were convincing him that "punishment" was much less effective in weakening connections than "reward" was in strengthening them. As a result the Law of Effect was radically revised; the part dealing with the weakening effects of punishment was eliminated, and attention was drawn to the rather complex consequences of punishment, one of which was that in some situations the cessation of punishment could be considered a reward. In such cases the rewarding effects of cessation of punishment were simply a special case of the first half of the Law of Effect, which had said all along that rewards strengthened connections.

Much of the experimental work and revised theory is to be found in the two compilations published as *The Fundamentals of Learning* (1932) and *The Psychology of Wants, Interests and Attitudes* (1935b). The best condensed statement of the revisions of the reinforcement theory alone, however, is the article, "A Theory of the Action of the After-Effects of a Connection Upon It (Thorndike, 1933)."

Here Thorndike describes a hypothetical neural mechanism called the "ok reaction," or "confirming reaction," which he believes can account for his long-standing position that a satisfying aftereffect of a connection works back to strengthen it. But backward action is only one of many powers that he hypothesizes for this remarkable mechanism. He considers it capable of selecting from among several contemporaneous actions the particular one to be strengthened by a satisfier. Also, and this may be the most radical change in the theory, the confirming reaction is said to be independent of sensory pleasures. Even a pain may set it in action, with the result that a connection active just prior to a pain may be strengthened.

Curiously, Thorndike is less explicit about how his new mechanism works backward to strengthen connections, even though he gives that as his main reason for introducing it, than he is about its various other powers. Presumably, however, it strengthens those connections which have recently brought overt action by working upon their traces which are still active at the time the mechanism gives its "ok."

Here is an example of what he means by selective action: "When an animal that runs about seeking food attains it, the strengthening will be more likely to influence the [activity, state, or condition of the neurons] concerned with its locomotion, its hunger, and its ideas about food and eating, than those concerned with contemporaneous casual scratchings of an itching ear, or stray thoughts about Shakespeare's sonnets or Brahms's symphonies (p. 435)."

He is careful to point out that there is nothing mysterious about all this. "Its influence will not, however, pick out the 'right' or 'essential' or 'useful' [activity, etc.] by any mystical or logical potency. It is, on the contrary, as natural in its action as a falling stone, a ray of light, a line of force, a discharge of buckshot, a stream of water, or a hormone in the blood (p. 435)."

There is no elaboration upon the statement that even a pain may set off the confirming reaction to strengthen a just prior connection; there is only the citation of the Tolman, Hall, and Bretnall study (1932), which he says demonstrated the phenomenon "in a striking experiment."

There is one further important modification of the theory. In earlier versions of the Law of Effect, the greater the satisfaction or discomfort, the greater is the strengthening or weakening of the connections involved. But now, "The potency of a confirming reaction may bear little relation to the intensity of the satisfier. A 'want' or 'purpose' or 'self' may be as well satisfied, and so issue as full and adequate a confirming reaction, by a moderate reward as by one much larger (p. 438)."

Although Thorndike says his "ok" reaction is activated by a satisfying aftereffect of a response, he considers the satisfaction to be independent of sensory pleasures. Even a pain may serve as the "satisfying aftereffect" that triggers the ok reaction and, once triggered, its strengthening action is independent of the intensity of the satisfying state. Where, now, is the "automatic action" of effect? What really governs whether the confirming reaction will occur, and the strength with which it will occur? He tells us: "The confirming reaction seems often to issue from some overhead control in [the neurons], the neural basis of some want or 'drive' or purpose or then active self of the animal. This overhead control may be rather narrow and specific, as when a swallow of liquid satisfies thirst, and the satisfaction confirms the [activity, state, or condition of the neurons] which caused the swallowing, and makes the animal continue or repeat that [activity, etc.]. This may happen while the main flow of his purposes concerns the work he is doing or the game he is playing or the book he is reading. It may be very broad and general, as when the purpose is to do well and win a game or to pass the time pleasantly, and is satisfied by any one of many movements in response to some play of one's adversary or by attentiveness to any one of many sights and sounds. It may be stimulated to send forth its confirming reaction by a rich sensory satisfier, such as freedom, food, and companionship for an animal escaping from a cage, or by a purely symbolic satisfier, such as the announcement of 'Right' in an experiment in learning. If *what the overhead control wants* is the announcement of 'Right,' that *is what will most surely lead it to make the confirming reaction* (p. 437, italics added)."[3]

Clearly, the Law of Effect had come upon troubled times. Otherwise its author, the foremost champion of tough-minded, deterministic explanations of behavior, would never have relinquished the control of learning to an "overhead" neural mechanism which, given the

[3]The reference to the announcement of "Right" in the quotation derives from Thorndike's extensive work in verbal learning on the so-called Spread of Effect. Although Thorndike regarded his findings as conclusive evidence for an automatic strengthening effect upon the S–R connection that received an announcement of "Right" (as opposed to "Wrong," which seemed to have a much less powerful weakening effect) and the automatic spread of the effect to neighboring associations, the studies had many methodological defects and do not allow clear-cut interpretation. For a review of the problem, see Estes' chapter (Chapter 3) in the present volume and the chapter on Thorndike's connectionism in Hilgard and Bower (1966).

prevailing ignorance of such things at that time, could only be viewed as a 1933 model of the ancient homunculus, capable of making up its own mind.

B. Criticisms of the Law of Effect

As the Law of Effect received increased emphasis in Thorndike's writings and as those writings came to have wider and wider influence, it is no surprise that the law attracted the critical attention of a number of psychologists. Since the criticisms have been dealt with in detail by Cason (1932), Waters (1934), Pax (1938), and Postman (1947), only the major ones will be briefly summarized here.

1. The Backward Action of Effect

One of the classic criticisms was that the alleged backward action of effect was logically indefensible. How could a satisfier that came after a response cause the strengthening of a connection that had already occurred? Although Boring (1950, pp. 562–563) belittles this objection, saying that Thorndike had always meant that the strengthening was of the neural traces of connections just made, a number of prominent psychologists made the criticism. They included Carr (1925), Peterson (1927), and Dashiell (1928), all of whom were shortly to serve terms as president of the APA. Yet it was not until 1932 that Thorndike explicitly gave a trace interpretation as a solution to the dilemma (Thorndike, 1932, p. 481). The basic idea was later worked out more rigorously by Hull (1943).

Those who objected to backward action on logical grounds, and who probably would not have liked the trace solution even if it had occurred to them, had another way of accounting for the everyday fact that organisms often do seem to repeat actions that bring satisfaction and desist from those that bring pain. Carr (1925) and Hollingworth (1928), for example, use an argument which Baldwin (1895) had developed fully, and which is also implicit in Dewey's classic paper "The Reflex Arc Concept in Psychology" (1896). The central idea is not that the strength of the S-R connection changes, but that the stimulous itself changes as a result of the things that are experienced contiguously. When the stimulus recurs, it is different from what it was before. To the naive child the candle flame as a stimulus is only a flame, a flickering light. Such a stimulus could easily be the occasion for a reaching response. After such a response, the burnt child sees not just a flame, but flame plus pain. It is not a weakening of the just prior, S-R connection that prevents another reaching response after the burn; it is the changed stimulus — changed in the sense that what first was only flickering light is now flickering light plus pain. Thus, their emphasis was placed on the sensory side, and their explanation seems to require some kind of mediation in order for the changes in the stimulus to have any influence upon movement. Mediation by ideas was anathema to Thorndike, of course, but so was his "simple" connectionism to many of his critics. His preference for the trace solution is easy to see: it preserved the relation that he considered vital — namely, the direct connection between stimulus and response.

2. Effect, or Affect?

Another criticism voiced by many was that the Law of Effect was really a law of *affect* in which conscious feelings determined whether actions would be repeated or abandoned. These critics converged on the Law of Effect from two quarters: the rationalist camp, in which the governance of behavior by something as crude as "feeling" was viewed as demeaning, especially to man; and the behavioristic camp, in which the notion was intolerable that consciousness of anything, even feelings, could be a causal determinant in behavior. Thorndike did, of course, give behavioral definitions of satisfaction and annoyance, and he repeated them year in and year out with only minor changes in wording. His critics, however, never really accepted them (Cason, 1932), and Thorndike never seemed to understand why.

Hull (1935), in a special review of Thorndike's *The Fundamentals of Learning* (1932), analyzed this and other problems in the theory in meticulous detail. He said: "The results from the experiments concerned with the 'law of effect' appear so obvious to Thorndike that he occasionally seems a trifle mystified that any informed person should fail to accept it as a plain matter of fact. A careful examination of the formulation . . . may somewhat clarify the mystery (Hull, 1935, p. 818)."

In Hull's critical examination of Thorndike's latest statement of the law, he suggests that Thorndike face up to whether he really means that "a satisfying state of affairs" is exactly the same thing as a state of affairs "which the animal does nothing to avoid, often doing such things as attain and preserve it." Thorndike had said that the first "roughly" means the second. If they are not fully equivalent statements, Thorndike should have told us in what way they are different and, above all, which one is the ultimate criterion in determining whether a connection will be strengthened. (It will be remembered that at this point the Law of Effect applied only to the *strengthening* of connections, the *weakening* effect having been dropped.) If the law is not to be mysterious, Hull argued, we must know which of the two states of affairs is the critical one if they are in any way different. If the two are really identical, Hull said, ". . . why complicate the situation with the entanglements of the subjective feelings of 'satisfyingness' at all (p. 820)?"

Although Hull was not yet committed to the drive-reduction interpretation of "effect" for which he is now best known, he was clearly dissatisfied with Thorndike's formulation of the law; he was actively searching for an alternative that would be less ambiguous and less open to the criticism that it was subjective.

3. *Circularity*

Another early and persistent criticism of the Law of Effect was that it is circular. From the time that Thorndike began to use behavioral definitions of satisfyingness and annoyance, there were critics who claimed that such definitions made the law meaningless. They argued that Thorndike's alleged explanatory law says no more than that organisms do what they do because they do it. Others have argued in Thorndike's defense that the law is not circular, and the controversy is still going on (Hilgard & Bower, 1966, p. 20). The reason, of course, that the argument can stay alive is that Thorndike's law is really quite vague. On the question of circularity, one can say in fairness to Thorndike that it is not completely circular and, in fairness to the critics, that the only reason it is not is that it was not stated clearly enough. As the general ideas embodied in the Law of Effect evolved in the work of others who sought greater clarity, it did indeed become circular. Such workers, however, were able to find a way out of the circularity, as we shall see later.

Sometimes Thorndike's Law of Effect is defended against various logical and terminological shortcomings on the ground that it is, after all, empirically valid. Hilgard and Bower (1966, p. 20) reflect this view when they comment, "Some of his statements were indeed objectionable, but the objectionable statements never did express the essence of the law of effect, which is essentially an empirical matter." Such a view is hardly fair to Thorndike's many distinguished critics. Primarily, it does not distinguish between matters of fact and matters of theory. It is possible to be right for the wrong reasons. The being right (or wrong) is a matter of fact, while the reasons are a matter of theory. Thorndike never intended for his discussions of learning to be taken as descriptive, empirical accounts; he meant them as explanatory, theoretical efforts. Consequently, he was fair game for other theorists who could find fault with his theoretical explanations and at the same time agree, as many of them did, that the effects of responding influenced the tendency to respond in the future. To Thorndike's great credit he fostered acceptance of this "matter of fact" in spite of his inability to formulate an acceptable theory. Also to his great credit, he resolutely kept the faith that such facts were capable of "natural" explanation.

The situation is reminiscent of how William James saw Spencer's place in the history of psychology. Spencer was useful, he said, because "'He left a Spencer's name to other times, linked with one virtue and a thousand crimes.' The one virtue is his belief in the universality of evolution—the 1000 crimes are his 5000 pages of absolute incompetence to work it out in detail (as quoted in Boring, 1950, p. 243)."

In these lines one can substitute Thorndike for Spencer and "natural laws" for "evolution" to achieve a result that is not only interesting, but also reasonably close to the historical truth.

IV. NONEFFECT THEORIES

During the 30-odd years that Thorndike's Law of Effect was under development, a number of other important learning theories were being advanced, some of which specifically denied the influence of any kind of "effect" in the strengthening or weakening of learned behavior. Whether they are considered reinforcement theories depends of course on what is meant by reinforcement. In the broadest view, they do deserve a place in a history of reinforcement, because they say something about how associations are formed, how behavior is strengthened, etc. The theories of Pavlov, Watson, Guthrie, and Tolman are the most prominent examples. The first three are clear-cut instances of noneffect theories; the last is a mixed example since Tolman admitted the importance of effect in some types of learning, but denied it in others.

A. Ivan P. Pavlov (1849–1936)

Although the widespread use of the term reinforcement in learning theory is traceable to Pavlov's influence (1927), he was not himself a reinforcement theorist in the sense that came to be accepted in American psychology. Pavlov identified reinforcement with the occurrence of the unconditioned stimulus and its elicited response. He conceived of the association that was formed between the conditioned stimulus and the response as resulting from the contiguity of the conditioned stimulus with the response elicited by the unconditioned stimulus. Reinforcement was merely a way of getting the response and its accompanying cortical excitation to occur contiguously with the conditioned stimulus and its accompanying cortical activity. It was not thought to have any *additional* strengthening effect upon the S-R association that developed between the conditioned stimulus and the conditioned response.

Pavlov's theory concerning the actions in the brain that were held to be the physiological basis of conditioning was not influential among psychologists. Although based on sounder knowledge of the nervous system than Thorndike's early neurological speculations, it was still highly speculative — in contrast to his method and the many lawful relationships that the method produced. The method and the empirical "laws," therefore, came into the mainstream of learning theory along with the word reinforcement,[4] but Pavlov's physiological theory did not.

Although his physiological theory of the reinforcement process was virtually ignored and his term "misused," Pavlov exerted a powerful influence upon learning theory in general, and reinforcement theory in particular. Many psychologists saw him as the paragon of scientific objectivity in the study of behavior. He equated mind with brain ac-

---

[4]Reinforcement is a term which can mean many things in both its technical and nontechnical usages. It always has something to do with strengthening, of course, but even in lay language it can legitimately mean either the act of strengthening, the state of being strengthened, or the thing that strengthens. When we turn to its technical use in psychology, we find that it has been used in all of the above senses as well as many other more specialized ones. For example, in the dictionary of psychological terms compiled by English and English (1958), two and one-half pages are required to list and describe the various usages. They deal with nine different psychological meanings of the single term, reinforcement, and 32 separate entries of its various combined forms, such as aperiodic reinforcement, primary reinforcement, and serial reinforcement. The usage they prefer is the one that is based on the Pavlovian paradigm, "the natural occurrence or the experimental presentation of the *unconditioned stimulus* along with the *conditioned stimulus*; or the strengthening of the *conditioned response* relationship thereby." For the remaining special meanings that have enough operational specificity to be useful, English and English advocate the use of alternate words that are synonyms for the specialized meanings: facilitation, reward, drive or tension reduction, confirming reaction, and goal attainment.

The situation has not changed appreciably since English and English recommended that "reinforcement" be restricted to the Pavlovian meaning. If anything, its meanings have proliferated even more. In "reinforcement theory," it is rarely used in the Pavlovian sense.

tivity; he could reveal lawful behavioral relationships through his methods without reference to such terms as consciousness, ideas, purposes, wants—terms which psychologists had struggled with rather unsuccessfully for years. What psychologists called association, habit, and learning could be dealt with as conditioned reflexes in a thoroughly objective way. The train of thought about the "why" of behavioral change had been put back on the deterministic track, and many psychologists welcomed the opportunity to get on board.

B. John B. Watson (1878-1958)

The most influential of the psychologists who, as the graduate students always say, "saw salvation in salivation" was John B. Watson, the founder of behaviorism. Actually, he had decided his course (Watson, 1913) before he learned about Pavlov and merely used Pavlov's work to shore up his own position that the study of behavior could be made thoroughly objective. Consciousness not only was ruled out as a causal influence in behavior, but also was denied any real existence, a step now generally regarded as philosophically naive and unnecessary. The only admissible datum was behavior, by which he meant the action of muscles and glands.

On the question of reinforcement, Watson's position was similar to Pavlov's. The Law of Effect was intolerably subjective, and the only necessary laws of learning were the laws of frequency and recency. Mere repetition of responses in the presence of given stimuli increased the likelihood that the responses would be made to the same stimuli in the future, with a tendency for the more recently formed associations to be stronger. Reinforcement was not necessary in ordinary habit formation, such as in maze learning, and was thought in Pavlovian conditioning to serve only as a means of eliciting the response to be learned.

Watson was disturbed that some of his colleagues failed to see that the laws of frequency and recency were adequate explanations of learning. "Most of the psychologists, it is to be regretted, have even failed to see that there is a problem. They believe habit formation is implanted by kind fairies. For example, Thorndike speaks of pleasure stamping in the successful movement and displeasure stamping out the unsuccessful movements. Most of the psychologists talk, too, quite volubly about the formation of new pathways in the brain, as though there were a group of tiny servants of Vulcan there who run through the nervous system with hammer and chisel digging new trenches and deepening old ones (Watson, 1930, p. 206)."

As for the fundamental basis of habit formation, Watson thought that it might eventually be discovered in physiological terms, but that physiologists were a long way from being able to explain what was already known about behavior. "Fortunately," he said, "we can continue our work in behavior without awaiting the true explanation of these biological phenomena couched in physiochemical terms (Watson, 1930, p. 210)."

C. Edwin R. Guthrie (1886-1959)

Guthrie's theory is the purest one we have yet encountered, since it relies much more on the logic of the learning situation than upon the laboratory. It was not born of a research program, nor did Guthrie initiate a large one to test its implications. However, a number of his students became active in research and have put many of Guthrie's theoretical ideas, as well as their own extensions of them, into conjunction with data (e.g., Lumsdaine, 1964; Sheffield, 1961; Sheffield, 1966a; Sheffield, 1966b; Voeks, 1950).

The theory was first presented in Smith and Guthrie's *General Psychology in Terms of Behavior* (1921) and did not change in any fundamental way for over 30 years. For Guthrie there was only one law of learning: the principle of association of stimulus and response through their contiguous occurrence. His view was in the S–R tradition set by Thorndike but, like Watson, Guthrie thought the Law of Effect too subjective and, in any event, unnecessary to account for the facts of learning. He was an avowed behaviorist, in contrast to Thorndike, and his views were greatly influenced by both Pavlov and Watson. He differed from Pavlov primarily in his insistence that Pavlov's conditioning situations were only special cases of the operation of the law of contiguity (Guthrie, 1934). The Pavlovian paradigm, far from being the fundamental model from which all learning could be derived, was itself derivable from the more general associationist principle of contiguity.

Where Guthrie's associationism departed from many earlier associationist theories was in his belief that the principle of contiguity was not just a necessary condition for the formation of associations, but a sufficient condition as well. Nothing other than a single pairing in time of a stimulus and a movement was necessary for associative learning. Guthrie's word for such learning was "conditioning." He made no distinction between the kind of conditioning Pavlov dealt with and the kind which Thorndike had called trial-and-error learning; both, he thought, conformed to the single, sufficient principle of association by contiguity. He stated the rule as follows in the last edition of his text on learning: "A combination of stimuli which has accompanied a movement will on its recurrence tend to be followed by that movement (Guthrie, 1952, p. 23)."

However simple in statement, the principle requires considerable elaboration when applied to concrete learning situations. The typical problems in applying the rule are those of accounting for apparent exceptions. What other theorists had seen as obvious and powerful influences upon the formation, strengthening, and weakening of associations, Guthrie saw as derivable from his single principle of one-trial learning by mere contiguity of stimulus and response. Unconditioned stimuli, rewards, incentives, punishments, etc., that others had given prominent causal roles in the formation of associations, Guthrie saw only as arrangements of conditions that influenced what the subject did, to be sure, but that had no further influence upon what associations were formed, strengthened, or weakened.

The function of food reward in Thorndike's problem-box experiments with cats, for example, was simply to lure the animal through the doorway of the box once a movement by the cat opened it. The reward in no way strengthened the S–R association between the cues arising from the interior of the box and the "successful" response. That association was formed the instant the cat made the movement in the presence of the cues. All the "reward" did was to make it likely that the animal would immediately leave the box upon occurrence of the "successful" movement, and thereby protect the association that had already been formed at full strength. The arrangement, therefore, of dealing with a hungry cat that could see food outside was simply a way of increasing the likelihood that the last movement made while inside the box would be the successful one. When it was, which nearly always came to be the case after a few trials, the problem was solved, not because the S–R connections had been stamped in by the effect of reward, but merely because the "correct" response was the last one that had occurred to the cues of the interior of the box. It could, thereafter, be expected to recur when the animal was again placed in the presence of those cues.

That several trials were often required before smooth performance was attained was not seen as anything requiring a law of "exercise," "frequency," or "practice." If the animal dallied in the box after making the movement that unlatched the door, whatever response he did make just before leaving the box would be the one expected to occur first on the next trial. But given the conditions, the animal before very long would likely leave the box immediately when the correct movement was made.

Guthrie also called attention to the complexity of the stimulus situation to which the correct response must get attached. This stimulus situation consisted not only of all the cues arising from the interior of the box, but also of cues arising from the interior of the cat! A sudden gas pain, for example, might be a part of one stimulus situation, but not the next. More generally, Guthrie argued that the total stimulus situation as sensed by the animal could be expected to vary from trial to trial, so that practice allowed the conditioning of the response to more and more of the stimuli that could possibly occur in the situation. This basic notion has been formalized by others and incorporated into mathematical models of the learning process (e.g., Estes, 1950).

The supposed weakening of response tendencies through the effect of punishment (early Thorndike), or continued elicitation of the conditioned response without reinforcement (Pavlov), Guthrie saw as merely the replacement of one response by another. Both the original learning of the response and the learning of its replacement manifested the same principle of association by contiguity.

Guthrie's theory, then, although extremely simple in basic principle, became complicated in accounting for the facts of learning. Yet, it was a theory which purported to account for the formation of association "automatically," that is, without reference to mediation by ideas, purposes, goals, etc.

In Guthrie's final statement (1959) of the theory, however, he made a major concession to the importance of "attention" in learning that, for the time being at least, destroyed the "automaticity" that the theory appeared to have. The earlier, simple statement that a movement would tend to be followed by recurrence of the stimulus combination that had last accompanied it was modified to read: "what is being noticed becomes a signal for what is being done (Guthrie, 1959, p. 186)." Clearly, until the determinants of attention can be specified independently of the learning process, Guthrie's theory in its final form is incapable of predicting whether learning will occur in any particular instance.

The historical parallel with Thorndike is interesting. Both Thorndike and Guthrie held throughout the major part of their careers that their respective principles could account for the "automatic" formation of associations. Neither really ever gave up the "faith" that such was the case. Nevertheless, each in his final theoretical statement was unable to handle the facts of response selection without reference to some factor which, at the present time anyhow, is incapable of being specified deterministically.

D. Edward C. Tolman (1886-1959)

The theory of learning that Tolman outlined in his *Purposive Behavior in Animals and Men* (Tolman, 1932) differed in several respects from those we have already considered. Tolman's was not a stimulus-response theory, as the others were, for he considered the learning process as one in which associations are formed between "signs" and their "significates." Thus, it was a cognitive theory, emphasizing what amounted to the acquisition of knowledge, rather than the acquisition of response tendencies. Further, it specifically denied that Thorndike's Laws of Exercise and Effect were necessary for such learning to take place.

As the theory developed over the years, several different kinds of learning were recognized, some of which appeared to conform to the Law of Effect (e.g., the learning of cathexes and equivalence beliefs), while others did not. The kind of learning that came to be stressed most, the learning of expectancies, was held not to require reward, or reinforcement.

The best-known studies which seem to disprove the operation of the Law of Effect are those on latent learning. Tolman apparently first saw these studies as a disproof of Thorndike's Law of Exercise, although they are invariably cited nowadays as evidence against the Law of Effect and similar "reinforcement" theories of learning. This interesting historical point is made by Tolman in a footnote: "Acknowledgment is to be made to Dr. H. C. Blodgett for first having pointed out to us this fact that the latent learning experiments really disprove the Law of Effect as well as the Law of Exercise (Tolman, 1932, p. 344)."

This is better understood if we remember that when Tolman's book was in preparation, Thorndike's Law of Exercise was of almost parallel importance with the Law of Effect, and Tolman went to considerable trouble to disprove it. But, in the meantime, Thorndike himself had disproved it to his own satisfaction (i.e., exercise without effect did not bring learning) and published the retraction in his *Human Learning* (Thorndike, 1931). Another footnote reveals Tolman's thinking on this point, as well as his view of Thorndike's "Connectionism" and Law of Effect: "The present chapter and the next were both almost completed before the appearance of Thorndike's *Human Learning* . . . . The reading of the latter has proved tremendously stimulating and important. And, if it could have been done sooner, would have led us to a somewhat different organization and emphasis in the presentation of our own argument. We should have made greater use than we have here of Thorndike's present attack upon the 'Law of Exercise' and of the many interesting experiments which he has presented for substantiating this attack.

"Our position, however, would not have been altered as regards his 'Law of Effect.' And we would have continued to reject the too simple S–R 'connectionism' to which even in this last presentation he still seems to cling (Tolman, 1932, p. 339)."

For Tolman, rewards and punishments served as "emphasizers" rather than as strengtheners and weakeners of S–R connections (Tolman *et al.*, 1932). Thus, they could lead to changes in expectation of "what-leads-to-what," and equally to the strengthening of expectations, whether of desirable or of undesirable outcomes. But they did not strengthen S–R associations. Tolman insisted on a distinction between learning and performance, and he steadfastly refused to make a direct tie between stimulus and response. Even Pavlovian conditioning was thought of in expectancy terms. As a result he was frequently criticized by S–R theorists for not providing an adequate explanation of how "knowledge" got translated into "behavior." The most succinct is Guthrie's jibe that Tolman's theory left the rat "buried in thought" at the choice point (Guthrie, 1952, p. 143).

V. THE EMPIRICAL LAW OF EFFECT

From the swirl of controversy that surrounded the Law of Effect over the years, there emerged a generalization that nearly all psychologists were willing to accept: the consequence of a response is an important determiner of whether the response will be learned. This generalization, along with its many variations, came to be called the empirical law of effect.

According to McGeoch (1942), Carr (1938) first suggested the name for this point of view that agrees to the importance of response consequences, yet does not attempt to give theoretical reasons for their importance. The position is reasonably close to the one Carr had adopted earlier in his influential text (Carr, 1925), in which he proposed that the fixation and elimination of acts are explained in terms of their consequences.

There are, however, many different versions of the "so-called" empirical law of effect, and they are not all equally empirical. The reason for this diversity is that Thorndike's law involved not one, but several theoretical assumptions. For example, it assumed that learning consisted in the strengthening of S-R connections, that such strengthening resulted from the "effect" of the response, that effect was "a satisfying state," etc. Adoption of a noncommittal stance on any one, or any combination of these assumptions could give rise to a new version of the Law of Effect that would be empirical to some extent. McGeoch (1942, p. 574) gives three statements of the empirical law of effect that illustrate a progression from the purely empirical law to a final statement that is almost as theoretical as Thorndike's original: "Other things being equal, acts leading to consequences which satisfy a motivating condition are selected and strengthened, while those leading to consequences which do not satisfy a motivating condition are eliminated."

The meaning most often intended, however, is the purely empirical one that learning is influenced by the consequences of responding. Empirical observation can then allow the cataloging of such consequences into those that promote learning, impede it, or have relatively neutral effects.

B. F. Skinner (1904-   )

The first and best systematic treatment of the empirical law of effect was given by Skinner (1938) before the law had been named. It issued from his general analysis of the requirements for an objective science of behavior and was not, therefore, a special effort to improve upon Thorndike's law. The position he adopted on reinforcement was only a part, albeit an important one, of his overall descriptive empiricism.

Because Skinner was impressed with Watson's insistence that an independent science of behavior was possible (Skinner, 1959), he set himself the goal of constructing a framework for it. By an "independent" science of behavior Skinner meant, as Watson had, that behavior should be studied in its own right. He saw no place in such a science for fictional, explanatory entities of either the "mental" or the "neurological" kind. The scientific goal was to discover the empirical variables of which behavior is a function and to relate them to behavior through descriptive laws. He advanced the idea, therefore, that psychologists should give up the search for the internal, physiological reasons for changes in response strength, and look for direct relationships between the occurrence of observable events and changes in the probability that a given response would occur.

Pavlov's work was seen as important and admirable, but rather limited. Skinner particularly admired Pavlov's careful control of experimental conditions. As he put it years later, "Pavlov had shown the way; but I could not then, as I cannot now, move without a jolt from salivary reflexes to the important business of the organism in everyday life (Skinner, 1959, p. 362)." Skinner dealt with Pavlovian conditioning, therefore, as a limited kind of learning—the learning of elicited, or "respondent" reflexes. He designated it Type S to emphasize the importance of the stimulus in eliciting the reflexes. The unconditioned stimulus in such situations was viewed as a reinforcing stimulus in much the same way that Pavlov had conceived of it.

A far more important class of behavior, in Skinner's view, was the one he designated "operant." Behavior of this type, called Type R, operated upon the environment, often producing changes in it that affected the strength of the behavior. Operants were not to be thought of as elicited by stimuli because such stimuli could not be observed to precede the behavior in a lawful way. Instead, they were to be conceived of as "emitted," that is, as occurring without a known stimulus. This concept of the emitted operant is the most novel feature of Skinner's system and has provided the basis for most of his work on reinforcement.

Skinner's (1938; 1953) approach to the problem of reinforcement is through definition and empirical observation. It is a fact, not a theory, he says, that some events which follow responses have the effect of increasing the likelihood that the response will be repeated. Such events are defined as reinforcers, not in terms of any effect they might have upon the internal mechanisms of the organism, but strictly in terms of the effect that they have in increasing the probability of response. Of those events found through observation to be reinforcers, some are called positive and some negative. Positive reinforcers are those events whose presentation strengthens the response, while negative reinforcers are those whose removal strengthens the response. Punishment is the presentation of a negative reinforcer, or the removal of a positive.

Although reinforcers are defined by their strengthening effects, Skinner does not see the definitions as circular. "There is nothing circular about classifying events in terms of their effects; the criterion is both empirical and objective. It would be circular, however, if we then went on to assert that a given event strengthens an operant *because* it is reinforcing (Skinner, 1953, p. 73)."

Thus, Skinner's treatment of reinforcement is purely empirical and descriptive, implying no theory. This does not mean that he has ignored why some events have the effect of strengthening behavior. He deals with the question of why a reinforcer reinforces in *Science and Human Behavior* (1953, pp. 81-84) at some length. The obvious relationship between reductions in states of deprivation and many of the events that are known to be reinforcing is acknowledged. Such relationships, however, are not reliable predictors of whether an untried event will be reinforcing, although they obviously have great biological significance. The process of evolution has no doubt resulted in a fairly strong correlation between the event that is reinforcing and the event that is satiating. But while the correlation has obviously been strong enough to insure the survival of present-day organisms, Skinner maintains it is not strong enough to insure an accurate prediction of whether an untried stimulus will be reinforcing. "We must therefore be content with a survey in terms of the effects of stimuli upon behavior (Skinner, 1953, p. 84)."

Such a survey is not ordinarily very difficult in any situation the experimenter wishes to analyze. Since reinforcing events can easily be found for a given organism in a given situation, they can be made contingent upon the emitted response one wishes to strengthen, with the result that control is efficiently achieved. The problem is not comparable to the formidable one faced by the investigator who regards all behavior as elicited, and who sets as his goal, as Watson apparently did, the wholesale prediction of the response to every possible stimulus, and the inference of the eliciting stimulus for every possible response (Skinner, 1938, pp. 10-12). Skinner regards such a goal as unrealistic not only because of differences among organisms, but also because the reflexive repertoire of even a single organism must be expected to change over time as a result of learning. At best, the approach could achieve only a "botanizing" of reflexes which, however complete it might become, would not be likely to show general, lawful relationships.

The concept of the emitted operant resolves this problem since it sharply delimits the number of relationships that require investigation. There is no need to attempt inferences to unobserved eliciting stimuli; nor is there a need to find all possible stimuli that can serve as reinforcing events—a few will do and in general are easily found. Thus, in operant conditioning, Skinner argues that control can be achieved and order can be obtained, but it is probably a hopeless task to try to do so within the conceptual framework that regards all behavior as elicited. Control, therefore, becomes the primary goal of a science of behavior, with prediction following easily once control has been attained.

An emitted operant can be brought under the control of a stimulus by arranging for the emission and reinforcement of the operant in the presence of the stimulus. The stimulus is then the occasion for emission of the operant but does not elicit it in the sense that a conditioned stimulus (CS) elicits a conditioned response (CR) in Type S conditioning. Operants that are emitted upon the presentation of their controlling stimuli are shown to obey different laws from those of elicited reflexes.

In Skinner's system, reinforcement is automatic, almost by definition. Perhaps the most convincing demonstration of the automatic effect of a reinforcer is what Skinner (1948) has called "superstitious behavior." In this situation, an event known to be reinforcing is presented intermittently without respect to what the subject is doing. But if it is doing anything (and this can be made likely through deprivation, etc.), the response just prior to the delivery of the reinforcer is strengthened, as evidenced by an increase in its rate of emission. The subject comes to "act as if" the response that has been fortuitously strengthened somehow produces the reinforcement. This occurs even though the reinforcer is actually delivered by a mechanical device that is in no way responsive to the subject's behavior.

The automatic effect of reinforcement is also illustrated in Skinner's effective techniques of shaping behavior. These procedures could hardly have sprung from a point of view that regarded all behavior as elicited. But with the organism viewed as "emitting" the varied responses already in his repertoire, it was an easy step to conceive of shaping. If the observer simply controlled the quick presentation of a reinforcer, then he could strengthen any behavior the organism happened to emit. Responses not in the subject's repertoire could then be built into it by appropriate arrangements of environmental conditions and the successive approximation technique.

Given the view that operants are emitted, adoption of response rate as the measure of operant strength was virtually required. With no eliciting stimulus or CS as a starting point, two of the measures commonly used in Type S conditioning were obviously ruled out. That is, neither latency nor probability of occurrence could be measured if no eliciting stimulus was under observation. It was possible to measure response rate, however, and Skinner has been able to show that this convenient and objective index is a very useful one.

Perhaps the most powerful variables that affect operant strength are those having to do with schedules of reinforcement. Skinner outlined the basic schedules and showed many of their effects in *The Behavior of Organisms* (1938). Since then, schedules (Ferster & Skinner, 1957) and many other features of the system have been extensively investigated and applied to an impressive variety of problems. But that work belongs to the present rather than the past, since it is a dominant part of contemporary psychology.

VI. DRIVE REDUCTIONISM

As we saw in the noneffect interpretations of reinforcement, a number of Thorndike's contemporaries developed ways of dealing with the strengthening of behavior that either denied the validity of the Law of Effect, or relegated it to a minor role. The theory of reinforcement we shall consider next, however, bears a strong, acknowledged relationship to Thorndike's.

A. Clark L. Hull (1884-1952)

Clark L. Hull breathed new life into the theoretical Law of Effect at a time when it might otherwise have expired. For although it was coming to be accepted by behaviorists in its empirical form (e.g., Skinner, 1938), it was under heavy attack as a theoretical, explanatory principle. Hull was among those who believed that Thorndike's formulation of the Law of Effect fell short of the clarity and objectivity required of a scientific principle. Nevertheless, his criticisms were constructive, and he suggested many possibilities for improvement of the law (Hull, 1935). The research program he carried out in the 1930's showed the gradual development of a general theory of behavior that eventually included a revised theoretical Law of Effect at its core. First stated in complete form in *Principles of Behavior* (Hull, 1943), the theory unquestionably stimulated more concentrated research on learning during the decade following its publication than psychology had ever seen before.

1. Hull's First Complete Statement of the Theory

Hull, following in the behavioristic tradition, insisted upon a natural science approach to the study of behavior. He chose as his theoretical model the hypothetico-deductive approach exemplified by Newtonian mechanics. Newton's *Principia*, liberally sprinkled with Hull's own marginal notes, was made available to his students as background reading. The notes ("Exactly!" "Psychology must have such laws," etc.) and the structure of his theory leave no doubt as to the source of his inspiration or of his devotion to the ideal of making psychology a

deductive science. His statement of the requirements for an acceptable principle of learning is found in an early chapter of *Principles of
Behavior*: "In accordance with the objective approach outlined earlier
we must regard the processes of learning as wholly automatic. By this
it is meant that the learning must result from the mere interaction
between the organism, including its equipment of action tendencies
at the moment, and its environment, internal as well as external.
Moreover, the molar laws or rules according to which this interaction
results in the formation or strengthening of receptor–effector connections must be capable of clear and explicit statement. Recourse cannot
be had to any monitor, entelechy, mind, or spirit hidden within the
organism who will tell the nervous system which receptor–effector
connection to strengthen or which receptor–effector combination to
connect *de novo*. Such a procedure, however it may be disguised,
merely raises the question of the rule according to which the entelechy or spirit itself operates; this, of course, is the original question all
over again and clarifies nothing (Hull, 1943, p. 69)."

Hull wanted to account for selective learning with a principle or
rule that could be clearly and objectively stated, and that was not itself
under the direction of some indeterminate, "higher" control, as was
the case with Thorndike's confirming reaction. At the same time, he
wanted the rule to be explanatory. He offered the following: "The
most plausible statement of this rule at present available is: *Whenever
a reaction takes place in temporal contiguity with an afferent receptor
impulse resulting from the impact upon a receptor of a stimulus energy, and this conjunction is followed closely by the diminution in a
need (and the associated diminution in the drive, and in the drive receptor discharge), there will result an increment in the tendency for
that stimulus on subsequent occasions to evoke that reaction. This is
the 'law' of *primary reinforcement* (Hull, 1943, p. 71, his symbolic
notation deleted)."

Having stated his law, Hull acknowledged its similarity to Thorndike's and indicated that it was a "law" only in the same loose sense
that the Law of Effect was. Both, he said, might better be called hypotheses. Perhaps the greatest similarity between Hull's principle of
reinforcement and Thorndike's is in the idea that some biologically
relevant consequence of response strengthens the S–R relationship.
Hull, however, was somewhat more explicit and objective than
Thorndike had been about the nature of "effect." For Hull it was reduction in a biological need and its associated drive, things that
seemed more capable of objective, independent measurement than
Thorndike's "satisfyingness." Thorndike's treatment of effect had led

to nearly circular definitions in terms of the behavior it was said to explain. Hull's interpretation of effect as drive reduction, on the other hand, was not circular provided independent measures of biological need or drive could be obtained.

Although both theories were in the S-R framework, there was a noticeable difference in the meaning of S-R connections. Thorndike referred to "intimate connections of neurones," while Hull referred to "receptor-effector connections." Hull's terms reflect a deliberate ef-' fort to emphasize the functional character of S-R associations. Though the choice of words did move the elements that entered into association a bit more to the periphery of the organism, it did not get them outside the skin. As a result, many persons never took Hull's disavowals of physiological intent seriously. Historically, this parallels, with a kind of "reverse English," the fact that few persons really took Thorndike seriously when he disavowed any subjective intent with the words satisfaction and annoyance.

In general, however, Hull's theory was somewhat more functional than Thorndike's. Thorndike repeatedly gave hypothetical physiological reasons for the strengthening of S-R bonds, but Hull never did. There never was in his theory any attempt to explain how a reduction in a drive could strengthen a receptor-effector connection.

Both Thorndike's Law of Effect and Hull's law of primary reinforcement were statements about motivation as well as explanations of the strengthening of S-R connections. In Thorndike's law the motivational idea resides in his definition of a satisfying state as one that the subject will do things to attain or preserve; in Hull's law it is the concept of drive. Throughout Thorndike's writings motivation assumes first importance in learning (wants, interests, attitudes, zeal, attentiveness, and striving were some of the motivational terms), but it is not possible to say exactly what he thought motivation was, or exactly how he thought it contributed to effect. The motivational influence in learning is sharply focused in Hull's law of primary reinforcement: motivation is drive, and the strengthening of an S-R connection depends upon drive reduction.

Hull was also clearer than Thorndike on the role of noxious stimuli in reinforcement. They were treated as drives, and their reduction, like that of any other drive, was reinforcing. Thus, punishment did not weaken S-R connections; its termination strengthened them. Thorndike's revised Law of Effect had given punishment a comparable role, but his position was never stated as explicitly as Hull's.

The major variables affecting habit strength in Hull's 1943 theory were (1) the number of reinforced trials, (2) the amount of reinforcement per trial, (3) the delay of reinforcement, and (4) stimulus-response asynchronism, i.e., the interval between the occurrence of the stimulus and the response. All resemble one or another of Thorndike's earlier statements, but the amount of reinforcement variable deserves special attention. In the early 1930's Thorndike gave up the idea that amount of satisfaction affected the strengthening of S-R bonds; yet in 1943 Hull incorporated the same basic idea in his theory. He was not to give it up until his own theory underwent major revision several years later.

Another difference was the way the two theories accounted for Pavlovian conditioning. Thorndike considered it a special type of learning, "associative shifting," in which the response originally connected to one stimulus (the UCS, unconditioned stimulus) shifts to another (the CS). He did not believe that the Law of Effect operated in such instances. Hull, on the other hand, interpreted Pavlovian conditioning as falling under the drive-reduction principle as a special, rather artificial case. He argued that the unconditioned stimulus, such as shock to a dog's paw or acid placed in its mouth, induced a biological need to avoid tissue injury. The response, then, reduced a need and its accompanying drive, thereby producing a reinforcing state of affairs. But Hull chose his examples carefully and, in general, did not make a convincing case.

Essentially the same difficulty that confronted Hull in fitting Pavlovian conditioning into a drive-reduction scheme cropped up in his treatment of secondary reinforcement and, later, secondary drive. The central question, of course, is whether the major claim of the theory is really tenable: Does all reinforcement, and hence all learning, actually depend on "diminution in the receptor discharge characteristic of a need," as stated in the law of primary reinforcement?

Hull was not unaware of the problems. *Principles of Behavior* has an entire chapter devoted to them, including several pages of detailed terminal notes. He accepted as fact that neutral stimuli acquire the power to reinforce when they accompany the reinforcement of responses. But how are we to understand the facts theoretically? Primary reinforcement appears to depend upon a reduction in drive and its accompanying stimuli; yet once a secondary reinforcing stimulus acquires strengthening power, the *presentation* of it reinforces. Does this mean that secondary reinforcement works on a stimulus-increase principle, whereas primary reinforcement works by stimulus reduction?

Pavlov had stressed the importance of stimulus presentation, but

Hull had tried to reinterpret Pavlov in drive-reduction terms, as we have seen. And although Hull seemed confident about reinterpreting Pavlov's basic conditioned response, he was unsure about solving the problem of secondary reinforcement. Nevertheless, after lengthy speculation, he leaned toward the hypothesis that secondary and primary reinforcement could eventually be shown to conform to the same principle, i.e., drive reduction. Here is how he put it: "So far as our present knowledge goes, the habit structures mediated by the two types of reinforcement agents are qualitatively identical. This consideration alone constitutes a very considerable presumption in favor of the view that both forms are at bottom, i.e., physiologically, the same. It is difficult to believe that the processes of organic evolution would generate two entirely distinct physiological mechanisms which would yield qualitatively exactly the same product, even though real duplications of other physiological functions are known to have evolved (Hull, 1943, pp. 99–100)."

2. Revisions in the Theory

Hull always insisted that his theory was sensitive to empirical test and that its basic assumptions should be modified when they were in conflict with data. But whether a conflict between theory and data is real or apparent may be difficult to decide, especially if the theory is at all loose, as Hull's and all previous learning theories were, and the theorist tenacious, as Hull was. Yet, he did change some of the basic principles radically in the late 1940's to conform to the facts as he then saw them. The modifications first appeared in a *Psychological Review* article (Hull, 1950) and in the small book, *Essentials of Behavior* (Hull, 1951); the final statement of the theory is found in the posthumous volume, *A Behavior System* (Hull, 1952).

Of the changes that appeared in the final theory, two bear importantly on the problem of reinforcement. One was essentially a clarification of what Hull meant by drive reduction. In *Principles of Behavior* he had used several different phrases when he discussed the effective conditions for reinforcement. Biological-need reduction, reduction in the drive arising from biological need, and reduction in the stimulation characteristic of a biological need were phrases he had used almost interchangeably. He resolved the inconsistency in 1952 by adopting the position that drive reduction is a decrease in the intensity of the drive stimulus. This is the view that Neal Miller had advocated for several years (Miller & Dollard, 1941), and it was a badly needed step toward making the theory more testable.

The other change had to do with the influence of amount of reinforcement. Instead of influencing the strength of association (i.e., habit strength) as it had since 1943, it now influenced a new intervening variable, Incentive Motivation, christened with a new symbol, K. Kenneth W. Spence undoubtedly influenced Hull's thinking on this point, as even the symbol suggests. Spence had never committed himself to the drive-reduction theory of reinforcement, although he had been closely associated with the development and advocacy of Hull's theory for almost 20 years. For example, he participated prominently in the latent learning controversy, always on the side of the argument that Hull's type of theory could account for the facts.

The above modification certainly made it easier for Hull's theory to deal with latent learning, but at great cost to the importance of drive reduction as a learning variable. Although habit strength was still a function of the number of reinforced trials, any degree of drive-stimulus reduction brought about the same degree of strengthening of the S-R connection. Incentive Motivation (K), now an important determinant of performance, was a function solely of the quantity of incentive given as reinforcement. Whether an incentive had to reduce a drive stimulus in order to be effective was not clear.

What then is the status of the drive-reduction principle of reinforcement in Hull's final theory? The power it previously enjoyed in determining what would be learned is present in name only. Even its power over performance is in doubt. Nevertheless, the drive-reduction principle was left in the theory, perhaps out of respect for the past, to serve forever as a kind of honorary chairman of the board.

B. Neal E. Miller (1909-   )

Neal E. Miller participated importantly in the development and application of the Yale learning theory that bore Hull's name. He and John Dollard boiled the theory down to its essentials in *Social Learning and Imitation* (Miller & Dollard, 1941). By emphasizing an even more functional approach than Hull, and by steering clear of premature efforts at exact quantification of the variables, Miller and Dollard outlined a theory that has stood up very well.

The major elements of the theory are Drive, Cue, Response, and Reward. Both Drive and Cue are functions of stimulation, Drive being a function of stimulus intensity and Cue a function of stimulus "distinctiveness." A stimulus is a drive to the extent that it is intense and a cue to the extent that it is distinctive. Rewards strengthen the functional connection between cues and responses and are defined in terms of such strengthening. That is, anything that strengthens an association between a cue and a response is a reward. It is assumed that the underlying principle at work is drive-stimulus reduction, but the assumption is regarded as a tentative hypothesis, albeit the best one available.

Their position on reinforcement is summarized: "Any event known to strengthen stimulus–response connections may be called a reward. The term 'reward' will be used hereinafter to refer to drive reduction, to events (such as eating when hungry) from which drive reduction may be reliably predicted, to the object (such as food) producing the drive reduction, and to other events empirically found to have the effect of strengthening cue–response connections. In the last instance, the definition is not circular so long as the fact that the event . . . found to strengthen one connection is used to predict that it will strengthen others (Miller & Dollard, 1941, pp. 29–30)."

This theory, then, accepts the empirical law of effect *and* the drive-stimulus reduction principle as its provisional foundation. The definition of reward is not circular so long as drive reduction can be demonstrated. It is circular in the absence of an independent measure of drive reduction *unless* the event shown to be a reward by its strengthening effect alone can then be shown to strengthen other cue-response connections. This way out of the circularity of the Law of Effect was also suggested several years later by Meehl (1950), who gave the idea a name, "transituational reinforcer."[5]

In evaluating their various assumptions on motivation and reward, Miller and Dollard conclude that some of them are more firmly grounded than others. They believe that it is "almost certain that drives and rewards play an important role in the performance of learned responses. . . . Two more specific hypotheses seem quite probable: namely, that drives and rewards are essential to the occurrence of any learning, and that all drive reduction acts as a reward. Finally, and least certainly established, is the hypothesis that reduction

[5]The reader will recall that Skinner takes a slightly different approach in avoiding circularity of his definition of a reinforcer. He avoids saying that a reinforcer is a reinforcer *because* it strengthens, saying only that an event is a reinforcer *if* it strengthens. He is not constrained to predict that an event that reinforces in one situation will do so in another, although he finds this generally to be true. His descriptive approach is in no trouble, however, if contrary cases occur.

in the strength of stimulation is the only source of reward (Miller & Dollard, 1941, p. 35, footnote 8)."[6]

Miller and Dollard make it quite clear, as Hull was less successful in doing, that the connections they refer to are purely functional. The terms cue and response usually refer to observable features of the environment or the behavior of the organism; but in cases where they do not, as in some "response-produced cues" and all "perceptual responses," Miller and Dollard deal with them functionally and assume that they follow the same laws as other cues and responses. They specifically disclaim any assumptions about a physiological mechanism to account for the correlation between reward and strength of connection.

The position on reinforcement outlined in 1941 was the one Miller adhered to consistently for more than 20 years of his remarkably productive research career. That he accepted the drive-stimulus reduction principle as only tentative did not prevent a vigorous and persuasive espousal of it; and he frequently reminded the critics of drive reduction that his advocacy was based only on his belief that it was the best single principle available. Although seemingly wedded to it, he was able to entertain the idea of divorce. Frequently he challenged those who disagreed to suggest a better, equally general alternative (e.g., Miller, 1959). In contrast to Thorndike and Hull, Miller seems to have enjoyed answering the critics. On several occasions when the hypothesis appeared at last untenable, he published an answering experiment (not just an argument) that showed it was still viable. Unquestionably, also, he helped to reveal the basic weaknesses in the point of view. For by sharpening the idea to "stimulus reduction" from the vaguer "drive reduction" and by pushing it to the experimental limits of testability, he revealed weaknesses that less ingenious experimenters would never have found.

VII. INADEQUACIES OF DRIVE REDUCTIONISM

Although there were those who objected to the Yale learning theory from its inception, it was undoubtedly the best *theory* of learning available for many years. The success of the theory, however, did not much depend on whether the drive-reduction principle per se was correct. Spence, as we have seen, never adhered to it, and Miller's theory of learning was never critically dependent upon whether drive-stimulus reduction was the basis of the empirical law of effect.

---

[6]Notice that what appears most certain is the importance of drives and rewards in the *performance* of learned responses.

Nevertheless, the drive-reduction hypothesis was there, and it invited attack. In the decade of the 1950's a rapid accumulation of evidence indicated that it was probably wrong. Miller estimated its chances of being correct as "considerably less" than 50–50 (Miller, 1959). Many of the difficulties came from the research of psychologists working outside the framework of the theory, but others were uncovered by persons working within, mainly Miller himself.

A. Difficulties Arising outside the Theory

Many psychologists had never thought it reasonable to conceive of all unlearned motivation as noxious (as implied by the drive-stimulus reduction principle) or of all reinforcement as dependent upon reduction in stimulation (e.g., Troland, 1928; Young, 1936; Young, 1952). Was there not unlearned motivation of a positive kind and unlearned reinforcement that depended upon increases in certain kinds of stimulation? The drive-stimulus reduction principle accounted for striving, but derived it as a learned phenomenon based on drive reduction. Secondary reinforcement, which to Hull had appeared to depend upon stimulus increase, was nevertheless derived from prior association with drive reduction.

The work on sensory reinforcement began to show that there were indeed types of motivation that were not noxious and reinforcement that could not be considered reduction in stimulation except by rather wild stretches of the imagination. Sheffield and Roby (1950), working from the Guthrian contiguity point of view, demonstrated that ingestion of saccharin, although non-nutritive and stimulating, nevertheless reinforced behavior. Sheffield, Wulff, and Backer (1951) showed that male rats were reinforced by copulation short of ejaculation. For Sheffield, the vigor of the consummatory response accounts for conditioning by contiguity. More recently, Sheffield (1966a; 1966b) has proposed a challenging "drive induction" view of reinforcement in sharp contrast to "drive reduction."

In a separate line of attack, Harlow and his associates (Harlow, 1953; Harlow, Harlow, & Meyer, 1950; Harlow & McClearn, 1954) demonstrated the existence of exploratory and manipulatory drives in the monkey. These drives were convincingly interpreted as motivation that led the animal to do things that increased, instead of decreased, his overall level of stimulation. Similarly, Harlow's studies (1958) established that the affectional attachment of the infant rhesus monkey to its mother surrogate was best understood as based on "contact comfort," rather than upon the concept of secondary reinforcement.

The publication of Hebb's stimulating book, *The Organization of Behavior* (1949), also contributed to the growing dissatisfaction with the drive-stimulus reduction principle of reinforcement. If to Freud the brain was an enlarged appendage of the gonads, to learning theorists of the 1930's and 1940's it was no more than a knot to keep the spinal cord from unraveling. But during the 20-year vacation psychologists had taken from the nervous system, it had become a much more interesting structure. Perhaps most significantly, it was now active, not merely reactive. Not only did incoming stimuli affect its operation, but also its activity affected incoming stimuli by influencing which ones would be responded to and in what ways. Furthermore, now that neurophysiologists had an active brain under study, psychologists could probably benefit from their knowledge.[7]

Although Hebb proposed no neurological mechanism for reinforcement in 1949, he influenced others to probe the brain for behavioral effects, and dramatic ones were soon discovered. The most exciting was the discovery of the "reward center" by Olds and Milner (1954). Though the discovery raised more questions than it answered, as seems typical of important discoveries, a drive-stimulus reduction interpretation of the reinforcing effect of septal stimulation seemed unlikely.

Other theoretical developments (e.g., Berlyne, 1960; Helson, 1964; Spence, 1956) and experimental results too numerous to mention were making the drive-reduction principle a very doubtful comprehensive explanation of reinforcement.

B. Difficulties within the Theory

Thorndike broadcast seeds of future difficulties for drive reductionism when he gave up the two-valued Law of Effect, and Hull planted them when he followed in the same path with a reinforcement theory that relied on the single principle of drive reduction. For although this tactic solved one problem elegantly, it created others which remain.

---

[7]Interestingly, Skinner, who thinks that the science of behavior can contribute to neurology but that psychologists should study only behavior, included the idea of a spontaneously active nervous system in a discussion of 12 contributions of the science of behavior to neurology. He said, "The notion of conductivity as the essential function of a center must be supplemented with a state of excitation in which impulses are simply emitted (Skinner, 1938, p. 430)."

The idea that cessation of noxious stimulation reinforces the response just made was a good one, so far as it went. But Hull went on to view all motivation as essentially noxious, inasmuch as drive was said to give rise to stimulation, only the reduction of which was reinforcing. This was a reasonable solution for the puzzling failure of punishment to show weakening effects equal to the strengthening effects of satisfaction (Thorndike) and drive reduction (Hull). At the same time, however, it made Pavlovian conditioning, secondary reinforcement, and secondary drive impossible to understand in any straightforward way. None of them fitted into the drive-reduction mold easily; they had to be forced into it by tedious, roundabout, and often unconvincing arguments.

Miller, the author and foremost advocate of the drive-stimulus reduction principle, has been as aware of the problems as anyone, if not more so. His extensive research program, especially that part concerned with the acquisition of fear and its functioning as a drive, helped to sharpen the issues, if not to solve the inherent problems. His contention has always been that seemingly attractive solutions to some of the problems create others that are equally grave, and that the drive-stimulus reduction principle is the best *single* hypothesis available to account for the diversity of data. In his most complete statement of the theoretical position and the findings it has generated (Miller, 1959, pp. 256-257) he says, "Therefore, I feel that it is worthwhile to try out applying it consistently, if only to highlight the obstacles and infuriate others into devising superior hypotheses and the experimental programs to support them."

Twenty-two years and hundreds of experiments after the original statement of his theory, Miller took what he called "a tentative fling" at devising a superior hypothesis of his own (Miller, 1963, p. 65). In this tightly packed, though sizeable chapter written for the annual Nebraska Symposium on Motivation, he reviews all the major existing alternatives and finds them wanting. He then proposes a new alternative, the key concept of which is a hypothetical brain process called the "go mechanism." The notion bears some resemblance to Thorndike's ok reaction, as Miller himself points out. The go mechanism does not, however, appear to be capable of making up its own mind, although Miller does not bother to mention this deficiency. It is activated, or triggered, by the occurrence of things now known empirically to be reinforcing, as well as by a number of others which may be. Its effect is "to intensify ongoing responses to cues and the traces of immediately preceding activities, producing a stronger intensification the more strongly the 'go mechanism' is activated (Miller, 1963, p. 95)." All responses, including the activation of the "go mechanism," require only contiguity for their conditioning to cues. Additional assumptions about its function appear to handle the problems of strict drive reductionism without raising new ones of equal or greater difficulty.

Thus, the divorce Miller had entertained is final. In his view, the "go mechanism" looks like a good replacement for the drive-stimulus reduction principle. But it is difficult to see why. The "go mechanism" is by no means the slim, attractive thing we had been led to expect Miller was holding out for. It is a complex, hypothetical neural mechanism requiring six major, detailed assumptions and a seventh minor one for its explication.

Perhaps Miller decided that we had better try to live with complexity after all. The choice of complexity is not simple — but the search for simplicity in reinforcement theory still goes on.

REFERENCES

Bain, A. *The emotions and the will.* (3rd ed.) New York: Appleton, 1888.

Baldwin, J. M. *Mental development in the child and the race.* New York: Macmillan, 1895.

Baldwin, J. M. *History of psychology.* Vol. 2. New York: Putnam, 1913.

Berlyne, D. E. *Conflict, arousal, and curiosity.* New York: McGraw-Hill, 1960.

Boring, E. G. *A history of experimental psychology.* (2nd ed.) New York: Appleton, 1950.

Carr, H. A. *Psychology: A study of mental activity.* New York: Longmans, Green, 1925.

Carr, H. A. The law of effect. *Psychol. Rev.,* 1938, **45,** 191-199.

Cason, H. The pleasure-pain theory of learning. *Psychol. Rev.,* 1932, **39,** 440-466.

Darwin, C. *On the origin of species by means of natural selection, or the preservation of the favoured races in the struggle for life.* London: 1859.

Darwin, C. *Expression of the emotions in man and animals.* London: Murray, 1872.

Dashiell, J. F. *Fundamentals of objective psychology.* Boston: Houghton, 1928.

Dewey, J. The reflex arc concept in psychology. *Psychol. Rev.,* 1896, **3,** 357-370.

English, H. B., & English, Ava C. *A comprehensive dictionary of psychological and psychoanalytical terms: A guide to usage.* New York: Longmans, Green, 1958.

Estes, W. K. Toward a statistical theory of learning. *Psychol. Rev.,* 1950, **57,** 94-107.

Ferster, C. S., & Skinner, B. F. *Schedules of reinforcement.* New York: Appleton, 1957.

Guthrie, E. R. Pavlov's theory of conditioning. *Psychol. Rev.,* 1934, **41,** 199-206.

Guthrie, E. R. *The psychology of learning.* (Rev. ed.) New York: Harper, 1952.

Guthrie, E. R. Association by contiguity. In S. Koch (Ed.), *Psychology: A study of a science.* Vol. 2. New York: McGraw-Hill, 1959. Pp. 158-195.

Harlow, H. F. Learning by rhesus monkeys on the basis of manipulation-exploration motives. *Science,* 1953, **117,** 466-467.

Harlow, H. F. The nature of love. *Amer. Psychologist,* 1958, **13,** 673-685.

Harlow, H. F., Harlow, M. K., & Meyer, D. R. Learning motivated by a manipulation drive. *J. exp. Psychol.,* 1950, **40,** 228-234.

Harlow, H. F., & McClearn, G. E. Object discrimination learned by monkeys on the basis of manipulation motives. *J. comp. physiol. Psychol.*, 1954, **47**, 73-76.

Hebb, D. O. *The organization of behavior.* New York: Wiley, 1949.

Helson, H. *Adaptation-level theory.* New York: Harper, 1964.

Hilgard, E. R., & Bower, G. H. *Theories of learning.* New York: Appleton, 1966.

Hollingworth, H. L. *Psychology, its facts and principles.* New York: Appleton, 1928.

Hull, C. L. Thorndike's fundamentals of learning. *Psychol. Bull.*, 1935, **32**, 807-823.

Hull, C. L. *Principles of behavior.* New York: Appleton, 1943.

Hull, C. L. Behavior postulates and corollaries – 1949. *Psychol. Rev.*, 1950, **57**, 173-180.

Hull, C. L. *Essentials of behavior.* New Haven: Yale Univer. Press, 1951.

Hull, C. L. *A behavior system: An introduction to behavior theory concerning the individual organism.* New Haven: Yale Univer. Press, 1952.

James, W. *The principles of psychology.* New York: Holt, 1890.

James, W. *Pragmatism: A new name for some old ways of thinking.* Cambridge, Mass.: Riverside Press, 1907.

Jonçich, G. E. L. Thorndike: The psychologist as professional man of science. *Amer. Psychologist*, 1968, **23**, 434-446.

Lumsdaine, A. A. Educational technology, programmed learning, and instructional sciences. In E. R. Hilgard (Ed.), *Theories of learning and instruction.* Chicago: Univer. of Chicago Press, 1964. Pp. 371-401.

McGeoch, J. A. *The psychology of human learning.* New York: Longmans, Green, 1942.

Meehl, P. E. On the circularity of the law of effect. *Psychol. Bull.*, 1950, **47**, 52-75.

Miller, N. E. Liberalization of basic s-r concepts: Extensions to conflict behavior, motivation and social learning. In S. Koch (Ed.), *Psychology: A study of a science.* Vol. 2. New York: McGraw-Hill, 1959. Pp. 196-292.

Miller, N. E. Some reflections on the law of effect produce a new alternative to drive reduction. In M. R. Jones (Ed.), *Nebraska symposium on motivation.* Lincoln, Nebr.: Univer. of Nebraska, 1963. Pp. 65-112.

Miller, N. E., & Dollard, J. *Social learning and imitation.* New Haven: Yale Univer. Press, 1941.

Morgan, C. L. *An introduction to comparative psychology.* London: W. Scott, 1894.

Olds, J., & Milner, P. Positive reinforcement produced by electrical stimulation of septal area and other regions of rat brain. *J. comp. physiol. Psychol.*, 1954, **47**, 419-427.

Pavlov, I. P. *Conditioned reflexes.* London and New York: Oxford Univer. Press, 1927.

Pax, W. T. *A critical study of Thorndike's theory and laws of learning.* Washington, D. C. Catholic Education Press, 1938.

Perry, R. B. *The thought and character of William James.* (Briefer version) New York: George Braziller, 1954.

Peterson, J. Forced adjustment versus association in constructive learning and thinking. *Amer. J. Psychol.*, 1927, **39**, 264-282.

Postman, L. The history and present status of the law of effect. *Psychol. Bull.*, 1947, **44**, 489-563.

Sheffield, F. D. Theoretical considerations in the learning of complex sequential tasks from demonstration and practice. In A. A. Lumsdaine (Ed.), *Student response in programmed instruction.* Washington, D. C.: National Academy of Sciences-National Research Council, 1961. Publ. 943, pp. 13-32.

Sheffield, F. D. A drive-induction theory of reinforcement. In R. N. Haber (Ed.), *Current research in motivation.* New York: Holt, 1966. Pp. 98-110. (a)

Sheffield, F. D. New evidence on the drive-induction theory of reinforcement. In R. N. Haber (Ed.), *Current research in motivation.* New York: Holt, 1966. Pp. 111-121. (b)

Sheffield, F. D., & Roby, T. B. Reward value of a non-nutritive sweet taste. *J. comp. physiol. Psychol.*, 1950, **43**, 471-481.

Sheffield, F. D., Wulff, J. J., & Backer, R. Reward value of copulation without sex drive reduction. *J. comp. physiol. Psychol.*, 1951, **44**, 3-8.

Skinner, B. F. *The behavior of organisms; an experimental analysis.* New York: Appleton, 1938.

Skinner, B. F. Superstition in the pigeon. *J. exp. Psychol.*, 1948, **38**, 168-172.

Skinner, B. F. *Science and human behavior.* New York: Macmillan, 1953.

Skinner, B. F. A case history in scientific method. In S. Koch (Ed.), *Psychology: A study of a science.* Vol. 2. New York: McGraw-Hill, 1959. Pp. 359-379.

Smith, S., & Guthrie, E. R. *General psychology in terms of behavior.* New York: Appleton, 1921.

Spence, K. W. *Behavior theory and conditioning.* New Haven: Yale Univer. Press, 1956.

Spencer, H. *The principles of psychology.* Vol. 1. (2nd ed.) New York: Appleton, 1870.

Thorndike, E. L. Animal intelligence: An experimental study of the associative processes in animals. *Psychol. Rev., Monogr. Suppl.*, 1898, **2**, No. 8.

Thorndike, E. L. *The elements of psychology.* New York: Seiler, 1905.

Thorndike, E. L. A pragmatic substitute for free will. In *Essays philosophical and psychological in honor of William James.* New York: Longmans, Green, 1908. Pp. 587-610.

Thorndike, E. L. *Animal intelligence.* New York: Macmillan, 1911.

Thorndike, E. L. *Educational Psychology.* Vol. 1. *The original nature of man.* New York: Teachers College, 1913.

Thorndike, E. L. *Human learning.* New York: Century, 1931.

Thorndike, E. L. *The fundamentals of learning.* New York: Teachers College, 1932.

Thorndike, E. L. A theory of the action of the after-effects of a connection upon it. *Psychol. Rev.*, 1933, **40**, 434-439.

Thorndike, E. L. The influence of relevance and belonging. *J. exp. Psychol.*, 1935, **18**, 574-584. (a)

Thorndike, E. L. *The psychology of wants, interests and attitudes.* New York: Appleton, 1935. (b)

Thorndike, E. L. Edward Lee Thorndike. In C. Murchison (Ed.), *A history of psychology in autobiography.* Vol. 3. Worcester, Mass.: Clark Univer. Press, 1936. Pp. 263-270.

Thorndike, E. L. *Selected writings from a connectionist's psychology.* New York: Appleton, 1949.

Tolman, E. C. *Purposive behavior in animals and men.* New York: Appleton, 1932.

Tolman, E. C., Hall, C. S., & Bretnall, E. P. A disproof of the law of effect and a substitution of the laws of emphasis, motivation and disruption. *J. exp. Psychol.*, 1932, **15**, 601-614.

Troland, L. T. *The fundamentals of human motivation,* Princeton, N. J.: Van Nostrand, 1928.

Voeks, Virginia W. Formalization and clarification of a theory of learning. *J. Psychol.*, 1950, **30**, 341-362.

Waters, R. H. The law of effect as a principle of learning. *Psychol. Bull.*, 1934, **31**, 408-425.

Watson, J. B. Psychology as the behaviorist views it. *Psychol. Rev.*, 1913, **20**, 158-177.

Watson, J. B. *Behaviorism.* (Rev. ed.) New York: Norton, 1930.

Young, P. T. *Motivation of behavior.* New York: Wiley, 1936.

Young, P. T. The role of hedonic processes in the organization of behavior. *Psychol. Rev.*, 1952, **59**, 249-262.

CHAPTER 2

Reinforcement— "The One Ring"[1]

EDWARD L. WALKER

I. INTRODUCTION

Those who are devoted to J. R. R. Tolkien's furry-footed halflings, the hobbits, will have no difficulty discerning the meaning of the title of this paper. Those who are about to read this trilogy in four volumes by a professor of medieval literature at Cambridge University may welcome an explanation.

"The One Ring" is a master ring of 20 magic rings made by Sauron, the embodiment of evil power. The possessor of the One Ring could exercise mastery over every living creature, but use of the ring inevitably corrupted the person who used it.

The story of *The Lord of the Rings* (Tolkien, 1964) concerns the efforts of an assortment of hobbits, a dwarf or two, a number of elves, a troop of ents, one wizard, and a number of men to achieve destruction of the ring by casting it into the fiery crack of doom in the side of Mount Orodruin, otherwise known as Mount Doom, in the Land of Mordor where the shadows lie. These white hats were opposed in this

[1]Preparation of this paper was supported by grants from the U.S. Public Health Service of HEW, numbers K6 MH 21, 868 and HD 00904.

effort by Sauron, the maker of the ring, Saruman, a bad wizard, nine Ringwraithes, and assorted orcs and trolls. There were also a few men in black hats.

It has become a game in some quarters to identify certain prominent psychologists with some of the characters in The Lord of the Rings. Thus, those who are already Tolkien fans are invited to speculate on the identities of such characters as Bilbo, Frodo, Samwise Gamgee, Gimli, Gandalf, and Aragorn among the white hats and Sauron, Saruman, Smeagol or The Gollum, the Ringwraithes, or nameless orcs and trolls among the black hats.

My thesis is fairly simple. In the general task of explaining behavior, the concept of reinforcement is redundant; it constitutes overdetermination of behavior, and its necessity and operation have not been demonstrated. In short, like the ring, it is pure magic with great but destructive power.

II. CLASSIFICATION OF LEARNING-THEORY CONCEPTS

To simplify the problem, one can divide theory construction strategies into single-concept and multiconcept approaches. In single-concept strategies, such as those of the various operant conditioners, the concept of reinforcement is the sole term used to account for arousal, control, modification, and extinction of behavior. In multiconcept strategies, such as those of Hull (1943; 1952) and Tolman (1932), as many concepts are developed as the theorist can discriminate properly. The problems posed by the reinforcement concept can be seen most clearly in the multiconcept setting, but whatever conclusion one reaches with respect to it is applicable to both.

Within the multiconcept setting, let us ignore the problems of generalization and discrimination, as well as the concept of inhibition, since they are not particularly germane to the present problem. The remaining concepts of a number of behavior theories can be reduced to four classes which I shall label Push, Structure, Pull, and Glue. I am going to try to develop the argument that what we know about acquisition of behavior can be accounted for with three concepts rather than four. More precisely, I am going to argue that a Pull concept, such as Incentive, is wholly sufficient, and that the added contribution of a Glue concept, such as Reinforcement, has the status of a magic incantation and the functional usefulness of snake oil. In order to clarify the nature of this glue property of reinforcement, let us examine each of the four classes of concept in turn.

The most commonly employed Push concepts are drive, motive, arousal, and tension, although there are others. All are efforts to take into account manipulable or assessable variations in the readiness of the organism to react or to behave that are attributable to differences in the *state* of the organism. Depending on how they are defined and used, they refer to generalized readiness to behave or delimited readiness to react to a subclass of stimuli. The defining dependent variable is differential vigor of reaction in response to modifications of the state of the organism through push-related manipulations or operations. For example, the organism has been without food for 3 or 30 hours; the organism has had 0 or 10 hours of experience with the stimulus pattern; the organism has had early independence training or late independence training. Vigor of reaction is usually measured in terms of time, speed, force, or amplitude of response. It is the state of the organism that is indexed, and the measurement is taken with the stimulus situation held constant or unvaried.

While the capacity to be pushed is a native characteristic of the organism, it is worthy of note that there are such things as learned drives and acquired motives.

The most common Structure concepts are cognitive organization, knowledge, hypothesis, and hobbit strength.[2] While they vary with respect to the terms used in describing the structure, they all have one thing in common — they all refer to information stored in the organism relevant to the situation. Learning is usually described as being a change in structure that occurs through the medium of experience. Hull (1943; 1952) talks about $_sU_R$ as a native structure and $_sH_R$ as a learned structure. Tolman (1932) endowed the rat with hypotheses as initial structure, and described learning as the selective development of an expectancy as a result of confirmation of one or more of them.

An important characteristic of structural concepts is that once a structural organization has been acquired through learning, it remains somewhere in the organism permanently. It is not totally forgotten, and except under unusual circumstances, the acquired structure is essentially unmodified in subsequent experience. New learning provides new structure. Any consideration of the necessity for a concept of reinforcement hinges on these characteristics.

The dependent variables used to index the acquisition of structure are frequently the same as those used to index push concepts — time, speed, vigor, force, or amplitude of response. There is, however, one

[2]*Hobbit Strength* is a new term in psychology. It was suggested by Kenneth Abrams of the University of Michigan as a replacement for *Habit Strength*.

additional class that is applicable to structure more particularly than to push concepts. This is the class of choice behavior measured in terms of number or percentage of errors or correct responses.

The most common Pull concepts are reward and punishment, sometimes described in terms of positive or negative valence or incentive value. An *incentive* is defined as something that incites or has a tendency to incite to action. It is unfortunate for psychology that the term incentive does not normally have the full range of forms as does reinforcement. Somehow the set *to incent, incentive,* and *incentment* has a ring of illiteracy about it. We might have been better off to have chosen *to incite, inciter, and incitement.* I am aware that it is a bad choice, but I think we should be using one or the other of these sets in most instances in which we now use *to reinforce, reinforcer,* and *reinforcement.*

An incentive or inciter is something, usually external to the organism, that has a special capacity to interact with the push state. The push state arouses to action, and the incentive focuses that action on itself or on behavior leading to itself.

Incentives or inciters may be involved in at least two kinds of learning, only one of which is a major concern of this paper. It appears true that some stimuli, such as food, may be assumed to have incentive value without learning. Whether this statement is true or not, stimuli without incentive value can acquire it through consistent association with incentives. This property is, according to my argument, inappropriately called *secondary reinforcement.* This is the K value in Hull (1943; 1952) and Spence (1956), and it is the concept of *Equivalence Beliefs* in Tolman (1949). Incentive value is indexed by the same set of dependent measures used to index structural changes — time, speed, force, vigor, amplitude, and errors.

The second kind of learning in which incentives may be involved and the one that concerns us in dealing with the glue property of the reinforcement concept involves the removal of an incentive from immediate sensory detection. A paradigmatic study would be one of diet selection. An animal, made deficient in a given vitamin, may be given two sources of food which are identical except for the presence of the missing vitamin in one of them. The difference between the two foods is not obvious, but the animal comes slowly to choose the vitamin-rich food. In some manner, the differential properties of the two foods come to act on future choices in a situation in which it could not act on the first choice. The animal has learned something, and that learning is usually described as a change in structure — possibly in hobbit strength. If we translate this incentive study into a T-maze in which food is placed in one nonvisible goal box, we have the simple paradigm for simple learning as a change in habit strength, or structure.

Glue is reinforcement. As employed, the reinforcement concept encompasses all of the characteristics of the Pull concepts, but it has an additional property. That property is variously defined as the strengthening of the connection between a stimulus and a response, the reinforcement of a bond. A reinforcer, in addition to forcing the response (the incentive function), reinforces the response (phraseology attributable to Kenneth Spence). Let me restate my argument. In Fig. 1 I have used a convention of metatheory to focus the issue. The Behavior is determined by three intervening variables (those inside the box). The three intervening variables are ordinarily manipulated through push-inducing operations (e.g., time of deprivation, Td), through the manipulation of pull-inducing operations (S), and through experience (N). The arrow running from the Pull concept through the Glue to the Structure concept is the effect of reinforcement that is at issue. If that effect cannot be demonstrated, then the concept should be dispatched forthwith.

In the case of the Push and Pull concepts, the question of whether reinforcement is a necessary or sufficient condition for the acquisition of a secondary push or a secondary pull is entirely academic. By definition, behavior cannot be manipulated or measured meaningfully in the absence of either. If both drive and incentive are always present

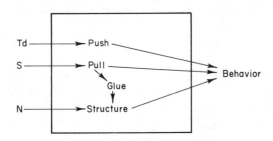

FIG. 1. Organization of concepts.

Concept class	Concepts
Push	Drive, motive, arousal, tension, etc.
Structure	Cognitive organization, knowledge, hypothesis, habit strength, etc.
Pull	Incentive, inciter, positive and negative valence, etc.
Glue	Reinforcement

during both acquisition operations and test operations, then the issue is moot, fictitious, and without hope of meaningful resolution. The issue upon which meaningful argument might be brought to bear is the question of whether reinforcement is necessary to produce a change in structure or whether behavior followed by reinforcement reveals more change in structure than behavior not followed by reinforcement. I am arguing that the relevant properties of behavior can be accounted for as well with three concepts — Push, Pull, and Structure, or Drive, Incentive, and Habit — as they are with four, including the Glue of Reinforcement. Therefore, the employment of the concept of Reinforcement is unnecessary.

If the case can be made that reinforcement is an indefensible concept for use in multiconcept strategies, the same argument, that the glue properties of reinforcement cannot be demonstrated, is applicable to the use of reinforcement in single-concept strategies. The only counter argument posed to me so far is that one can choose to define the word reinforcement in any way one chooses. I am reminded by this argument of an interchange between Alice and Humpty Dumpty from Lewis Carroll (1871). Humpty Dumpty has just been explaining to Alice why it is better to celebrate 364 *un*birthdays each year rather than only one birthday.

"There's glory for you!" he says, referring to one birthday and one present.

"I don't know what you mean by 'glory.' " Alice said.

Humpty Dumpty smiled contemptuously.

"Of course you don't — till I tell you. I meant 'there's a nice knock-down argument for you.' "

"But 'glory' doesn't mean 'a nice knock-down argument.' " Alice objected.

"When *I* use a word," Humpty Dumpty said, in a rather scornful tone, "it means just what I choose it to mean — neither more nor less."

"The question is," said Alice, "whether you *can* make words mean so many different things."

"The question is," said Humpty Dumpty, "which is to be master — that's all."

III. THE SUPERFLUOUS NATURE OF GLUE

If I may return from Carroll to Tolkien, throwing the magic ring into the crack of doom was no easy task for Frodo and his company. Exorcising reinforcement from psychology is likely to be equally difficult.

My thesis is based on two arguments. (1) A review of the results of experiments in relevant problem areas in learning fails to reveal a single demonstration of the reinforcement (Glue) effect over and above the incentive effect of rewards. (2) If there is a reinforcement effect, traditional procedures could not be expected to yield a demonstration of the effect because there is too little information in the usual measurements taken in learning experiments.

The statement of the reinforcement principle can be made in two forms. In the strong form, the assertion is made that all learning occurs as a function of reinforcement. In the second and weaker form, the assertion is made that while learning can occur in the absence of reinforcement, more learning occurs with reinforcement than without, or that the greater the amount of reinforcement the greater the learning. The two forms raise different issues and are attacked with different types of experiments. Let us consider the evidence for each in turn.

The core postulate of reinforcement theory is that habit strength increases as a function of the number of reinforcements. I have pointed out elsewhere that this foundation stone is cracked, at least, and may have crumbled (Walker, 1964). I would argue that the standard effect of the application of a reward, or the presentation of an unconditioned stimulus, over a long series to trials is a performance curve that rises and *falls*. A search of the literature reveals a very large number of such curves, and a search of the unpublished results of a great many experimenters would yield literally thousands more. Let me cite a few examples which have been chosen almost at random but with some effort to sample the range of experimental paradigms of human and animal subjects.

Figure 2 contains data on human eyelid conditioning reported by Hilgard (1933). Under continued application of the CS-UCS with an interval of 300 msec between them, the amplitude of the CR increased and then decreased over an eight-day period with 50 trials per day. It is worthy of note that the data of Fig. 2 were reported as an afterthought at the suggestion of Clark L. Hull. In a study by Walker and Earl reported in Walker (1964), the performance of a head-lifting avoidance response in rats also showed a similar pattern. The CS was a tone, and the UCS a bright light in the animal's eyes which he could avoid by lifting his head.

I believe that similar results typify instrumental reward learning. In a previous article (Walker, 1964), I cited several sets of instrumental learning results showing this pattern. For example, in a study by Ashida (1963) in which he was investigating learning and extinction with various amounts of reward, a group with a large reward showed first an

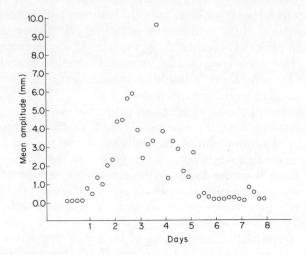

FIG. 2.   Performance of Subject B in a human eyelid conditioning study during 400 trials of pairing of a light as CS and a tone as UCS. The CS–UCS interval is 300 msec. Each point is a mean performance on 10 trials. Redrawn from Hilgard (1933) with permission of the author and publisher.

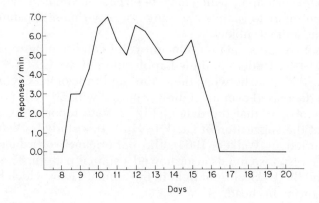

FIG. 3.   Operant record of one subject, Jimmy D, showing performance on a 10-second DRL schedule. S is an eight-year-old mentally retarded boy. The operant conditioning sessions scheduled twice a day were the only sources of food for the subject. Redrawn from Longfellow (1967) with the permission of the author.

increase and then a decrease in speed in a straight alley with continued reward, both in original learning and in relearning after extinction.

A dramatic instance of recent origin may be seen in Fig. 3. Longfellow (1967) applied operant conditioning techniques to mentally retarded children. He arranged that the children receive their total food supply in the operant situation which was carried out twice a day with intervals of 9 and 15 hours between the beginnings of the sessions. The reward was a carefully constituted complete and balanced diet most nearly resembling fudge with coconut in taste and appearance. All three of his subjects showed at least some evidence of learning a 10-second DRL schedule, and all gained weight. Jimmy D, whose performance record is shown in the figure, produced the most efficient performance of the three before his operant behavior began to fall off. It fell to zero, and his participation in the study had to be terminated to prevent harm to the child through starvation.

I believe that the pattern of increase and then decrease in performance is general and that the problem faced by people who are learning is one of explaining the limited conditions in which performance can be maintained under unvarying reward patterns. If what is glued comes unglued without modifying the "reinforcement" process, then it is not habit strength or the structural concept that is being manipulated. These results suggest that the major determiner of the performance is the incentive and the learned incentive rather than modification in the structural concept. In Hullian terms, it is K that is relevant to these modifications, not $_sH_R$.

The latent-learning studies have faded from favor, but they made a point. There are several reviews of these studies by Thistlethwaite (1951), Kimble (1961), and Walker (1967). A summary of 50 or more studies will show fairly clearly that a structural change, learning, can occur in the absence of discernible reinforcement and then be activated when an incentive is provided. They seem to offer the conclusion that reinforcement is not necessary for learning to occur.

Thus, if reinforcement is not necessary for learning, and if reinforcement often leads to first an increase and then a decrease in performance, the basic postulates (1) that reinforcement is necessary and (2) that learning increases as a function of the number of reinforcements must be wrong.

Contemplation of extinction phenomena offers little support for the current conception of reinforcement theory. The most rational stance is to think of simple extinction occurring as a function of the change in incentive conditions. Omitting the incentive removes the pull in the situation, and the gradual nature of the extinction process should reflect the reduction in learned incentive value of associated stimuli. This interpretation is supported by the mass of latent extinction data. Exposure to the empty goal box provides information on the absence of the incentive, and the gradualness of the remaining performance curve reflects extinction of learned incentive value of associated stimuli. It is also true that if one cares to look upon extinction as the learning of a new response, one has learning in the absence of palpable reinforcement, since reinforcement is operationally absent. Thus both interpretations of extinction appear to reflect performance changes in the pull concept, incentive, and not in the structural concept.

I should also like to point out that the data on the effect of overlearning on extinction generally fail to confirm the core postulates of reinforcement theory. For example, Ison (1962) varied the number of reinforcements in a simple runway from 10 to 100 in six different groups of animals. He found that the greater the number of reinforcements, the faster the extinction occurred. These results confirm the general conclusion that performance tends to increase and then decrease under continued reinforcement.

I should also like to invite your attention to a set of curious results with an implication that is usually overlooked. The implication arises from relating findings from three seemingly unrelated studies. The first of these is a study of sensory preconditioning reported by Kendall and Thompson (1960). They varied the number of CS–CS pairings from 0 to 800 in 12 different groups of cats and found essentially no difference as a function of trials and certainly none above four pairings. This result suggests that the structural change involved in conditioning might occur in a single trial, while the development of the performance curve in a normal conditioning study requires many trials.

The second study is that of Goldstein (1960) on acquired drive. He paired a CS with unavoidable shock and varied the intensity of the shock as well as the number of pairings. He then offered the animals an instrumental hurdle-jumping response to turn off the CS that had acquired push or drive properties. He found differences in speed of jumping as a function of shock intensity, but *not* as a function of the number of pairings or the order of stimuli, for that matter. Thus whatever structure is required to associate a CS with shock did not increase with N and did not obey the principle that backward conditioning cannot occur.

In a third study, Miles (1956) investigated the secondary reinforcing properties of a dim light and a click paired with food reward in a lever-pressing situation. He found that the number of prior pairings of the light and click with food *did* vary the number of trials to extinction.

The conclusion cannot be strongly held, but at least can be tentatively stated, that of the three concepts, Push, Pull, and Structure, the one that varies normally as a function of the number of reinforcements is the Pull, while neither the Push nor the Structure follow reinforcement postulates.

The data on acquisition and extinction of conditioned responses in the absence of the occurrence of the response are also probably relevant to the issue. For example, Lauer (1951) carried out acquisition procedures in a dog under curare. When the dog was tested after recovery, the conditioned response could be demonstrated without prior performance. Likewise, Black (1958) demonstrated partial extinction, without performance, by carrying out extinction trials while the dog was immobilized by curare. Both results seem to support the hypothesis that it is the development and demise of learned incentive that occurs in simple conditioning situations, not a change in the value of the structural concept, for the reinforcement conditions necessary for a change in structure did not occur in these studies.

One might think that the problem that is discussed in textbooks, such as Kimble's version of Hilgard and Marquis (1961), as "The Nature of Reinforcement" would be relevant to this issue, but it is not. If I may summarize briefly the results of a very large body of some of the most significant studies in the field of experimental psychology, they add up to a fairly simple statement. Food in the mouth, food placed directly into the stomach, food injected directly into the bloodstream, non-nutritive saccharin, coitus without ejaculation, and simple stimulus change can serve as *incentives*. There is *not* in that literature, despite its name, any effort to establish the glue character of reinforcement.

Let us turn to the weak form of the reinforcement postulate — that the greater the reinforcement, the better the learning. The cleanest and most straightforward study that is relevant is that of Bower, Fowler, and Trapold (1959). They motivated rats to run down a runway by placing 250 V of current on the grid floor. They varied the amount of reinforcement by varying the amount of voltage reduction in the goal box. The voltage dropped 50, 100, or 200 V for three different groups. Running speed varied as a function of the amount of incentive, the greater the amount of drop in voltage the faster the running speed. Following this phase of their experiment, they shifted the amount of shock reduction for subgroups and found fairly rapid shift in performance to match that of animals that had been continuing on the same amount of reduction. The absence of semipermanent effects of the prior reinforcement history is strong evidence that it is the Pull construct that has been manipulated, not the Structure$-K$, not $_sH_R$. While earlier findings such as those of Crespi (1942) are somewhat different in detail, they do not appear to require alteration of the conclusion.

Let me summarize. What evidence I can find suggests that learning, in the sense of modification in the structural concept, can occur in the absence of reinforcement, and the amount of such structural change does not seem to differ with different amounts of reinforcement. Thus the reinforcement concept appears entirely superfluous.

IV. ALTERNATIVE EXPERIMENTAL STRATEGIES

If both forms of the reinforcement postulate could be considered to have been demolished, we could turn to the possibility that there is a defect in experimental strategy which effectively prevents the possibility of demonstrating the glue effect of reinforcement even if there were one. Most learning theorists have chosen to limit their measurements to a restricted class and range of dependent variable. Hull (1943; 1952) dealt with four performance measures: latency, amplitude, number of trials to extinction, and probability of response. Tolman chose to deal only with probability of choice (1932). Skinner (1938; 1953) chose to deal almost exclusively with rate of responding.

I shall not attempt to review the whole area of interrelations of response measures, but a few examples of the problem might serve. Estes (1944) reported that the rate of responding but not the number of responses was affected by punishment. Hillman, Hunter, and Kimble (1953) reported that drive strength influenced speed of maze performance but not the number of errors. Cotton (1953) counted the number of irrelevant responses on each trial and found that when he examined speed as a function of drive strength and looked only at those trials on which irrelevant responses did not occur, speed did not vary with drive strength. This small set out of a very great number of possible citations suggests one form of the problem—that there are only two measures but that there are three concepts. Thus (see the following tabulation):

Concept	Typical measure
Push	Vigor
Structure	Vigor and number
Pull	Vigor and number

The question of the role of reinforcement in learning and performance, assuming that it has a role, is to be resolved in terms of differential measurement. Two simple measures for three complex concepts may be logically inadequate.

Suppose that I were wholly dedicated to the efficacy of reinforcement in producing structural changes and wanted to demonstrate that effect. How would I start to do it?

The first step, I should think, would be to find some way to increase the amount of information in the output of the organism. If present measures were too few, too simple, and contained too little information to permit the kinds of discriminations required by the reinforcement concept, and I thought this were the heart of the problem, then I would seek measures that contained more information.

In an abstract sense, let me suggest the pattern. Suppose we construct stimulus situations, the complexity of which we can measure or quantify with some precision. Let us permit the organism a response that can be highly complex in the same terms. With a potentially high information output, the organism could index the complexity of the structure within the organism produced by its experience with the stimulus. *Then* it might be possible to discriminate between different amounts of structural change — habit strength, if you will — produced by different amounts of reinforcement. I know of no such enterprise.

Structural changes of the kind I am suggesting are barely approximated in the literature of learning to learn. A small sample of this area to make my suggestions concrete would include the following. North (1950) carried rats through a series of reversals of a discrimination problem. He found first slower and then more rapid learning or relearning of successive reversals. Mackintosh (1962) showed that overlearning of the first problem speeded reversal learning but slowed the learning of a new problem. However, Harlow's work (1949; 1959) shows that over many such shifts, learning sets develop until "no trial learning" can be demonstrated. These are structural changes of a magnitude and complexity that hold some potential for discrimination between the effect upon structural change of different amounts of reinforcement. However, the measurement problem, as I have posed it, has not been solved in these studies since they were devised for other purposes.

V. SUMMARY

The behavior of organisms in simple learning situations does not support the core postulates of reinforcement theory. No reinforcement effects, as opposed to incentive effects, have yet been demonstrated.

Nor are such effects likely to be demonstrated without more complex
and information-rich dependent variable measures. The glue of reinforcement is The One Ring that gives its user apparent mastery over
all living creatures. Unfortunately, it is a power of evil that corrupts
the user, as does all magic. The laws of association existed for some 23
centuries at least before the magic of reinforcement was forged by
Sauron.

The only task that remains is to complete the analogy and assign
roles from *The Lord of the Rings* to various pertinent psychologists in
the light of their history of involvement with the concept of reinforcement. Basically, who is Sauron, or Frodo, or The Gollum? Figure 4
will give you an opportunity to do your own matching. To interpret
the roles of the names in the legend, read J. R. R. Tolkien. To read the
names of psychologists who might be assigned roles, either turn cryp-
tologist or learn the Angerthas, for the letters are elvish runes, suitable
for incising on stone.

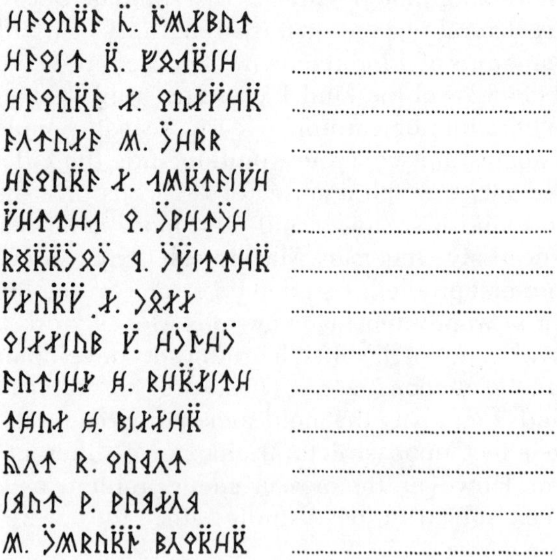

ᚻᚦ�995ᛆᚼᚠ Ｋ̈. Ｆ̈ᛗᚴᛒᚼ↑   ....

ᚻᚦ95↑ Ｋ̈. ᚠᚱ↑Ｋ̈ᛁᚻ   ....

ᚻᚦ95ᚼᚴᚠ ⳤ. 9ᚼⳤᚠ̈ᚺᚼᛆ   ....

ᚠᚪ↑ᚼⳤᚠ ᛗ. ⳤᚻᚱᚱ   ....

ᚻᚦ95ᚼᚴᚠ ⳤ. ⳽ᛗᚴ↑ᚼᚠ̈ᚺ   ....

Ｖ̈ᚻ↑↑ᚻᛁ 9. ⳽ᛈᚻ↑⳽ᚻ   ....

ᚱᚷᚴ̈ᚴ̈⳽ᚷ⳽ ⳽. ⳽Ｖ̈ᛁ↑↑ᚻᚴ̈   ....

Ｖ̈ᛈᚼᚴ̈Ｖ̈ ⳤ. ⳾ᚷ↑ᚠ   ....

9ᛁᚴᚠᛁᚼᛒ Ｖ̈. ᚻ⳽ᛗᚻ⳽   ....

ᚠᚼ↑ᛁᚻ⳽ ᚻ. ᚱᚻᚴ̈ᚠᛁ↑ᚻ   ....

↑ᚻᚼⳤ ᚻ. ᛒᛁⳤᚻᚴ̈   ....

ᚼ̈ᚪ↑ ᚱ. 9ᚼⳤᚪ↑   ....

ᛁⳤᚼ↑ ᛈ. ᛈᚼ⳥ⳤᛁ⳥   ....

ᛗ. ⳽ᛗᚱᚼᚴ̈Ｆ̈ ᛒᚪ9ᚴ̈ᚻᚴ̈   ....

FIG. 4. The roles in *The Lord of the Rings* to be assigned to various psychologists
who have had something to say about reinforcement are: Frodo Baggins, Bilbo Baggins,
Aragorn, Samwise Gamgee, Gandalf, Gimli, Legolas, Elrond, Sauron, Saruman, Worm-
tongue, The Gollum, Ringwraithes (9), and Orcs (any number).

REFERENCES

Ashida, S. Theoretical and experimental analysis of incentive motivation. Unpublished doctoral dissertation, Univer. of Nebraska, 1963.

Black, A. H. The extinction of an avoidance response under curare. *J. comp. physiol. Psychol.*, 1958, **51**, 519-524.

Bower, G. H., Fowler, H., & Trapold, M. A. Escape learning as a function of the amount of shock reduction. *J. exp. Psychol.*, 1959, **58**, 482-484.

Carroll, Lewis. *Through the looking-glass, and what Alice found there.* London: Macmillan, 1871.

Cotton, J. Running time as a function of the amount of food deprivation. *J. exp. Psychol.*, 1953, **46**, 188-198.

Crespi, L. P. Quantitative variation of incentive and performance in the white rat. *Amer. J. Psychol.*, 1942, **55**, 467-517.

Estes, W. K. An experimental study of punishment. *Psychol. Monogr.*, 1944, **47**, 1-40 (Whole No. 263).

Goldstein, M. L. Acquired drive strength as a joint function of shock intensity and number of acquisition trials. *J. exp. Psychol.*, 1960, **60**, 349-358.

Harlow, H. F. The formation of learning sets. *Psychol. Rev.*, 1949, **56**, 51-65.

Harlow, H. F. Learning set and error factor theory. In S. Koch (Ed.), *Psychology: A study of a science.* Vol. 2. New York: McGraw-Hill, 1959. Pp. 492-537.

Hilgard, E. R. Modification of reflexes and conditioned reactions. *J. gen. Psychol.*, 1933, **9**, 210-215.

Hillman, B., Hunter, W. S., & Kimble, G. A. The effect of drive level of maze performance in the white rat. *J. comp. physiol. Psychol.*, 1953, **46**, 87-89.

Hull, C. L. *Principles of behavior.* New York: Appleton, 1943.

Hull, C. L. *A behavior system.* New Haven: Yale Univer. Press, 1952.

Ison, J. R. Experimental extinction as a function of number of reinforcements. *J. exp. Psychol.*, 1962, **64**, 314-317.

Kendall, S. B., & Thompson, R. F. Effect of stimulus similarity on sensory preconditioning within a single stimulus dimension. *J. comp. physiol. Psychol.*, 1960, **53**, 439-443.

Kimble, G. A. *Hilgard and Marquis' conditioning and learning.* (revised) New York: Appleton, 1961.

Lauer, D. W. The role of the motor response in learning. Unpublished doctoral dissertation, Univer. of Michigan, 1951.

Longfellow, L. A. Effects of food deprivation on temporally spaced responding in moderately retarded children. Unpublished doctoral dissertation, Univer. of Michigan, 1967.

Mackintosh, N. J. The effects of overtraining on a reversal and non-reversal shift. *J. comp. physiol. Psychol.*, 1962, **55**, 555-559.

Miles, R. C. The relative effectiveness of secondary reinforcers throughout deprivation and habit strength parameters. *J. comp. physiol. Psychol.*, 1956, **49**, 126-130.

North, A. J. Improvement in successive discrimination reversals. *J. comp. physiol. Psychol.*, 1950, **43**, 442-460.

Skinner, B. F. *The behavior of organisms.* New York: Appleton, 1938.

Skinner, B. F. *Science and human behavior.* New York: Macmillan, 1953.

Spence, K. W. *Behavior theory and conditioning.* New Haven: Yale Univer. Press, 1956.

Thistlethwaite, D. A critical review of latent learning and related experiments. *Psychol. Bull.*, 1951, **48**, 97-129.

Tolkien, J. R. R. *The lord of the rings,* Part 3. *The return of the king.* New York: Ballantine Books, 1964.

Tolman, E. C. *Purposive behavior in animals and men.* New York: Century, 1932.

Tolman, E. C. There is more than one kind of learning. *Psychol. Rev.,* 1949, **56**, 144-155.

Walker, E. L. Psychological complexity as a basis for a theory of motivation and choice. In D. Levine (Ed.), *Nebraska symposium on motivation.* Lincoln, Nebr. Univer. of Nebraska Press, 1964. Pp. 47-95.

Walker, E. L. *Conditioning and instrumental learning.* Belmont, California: Brooks/Cole, 1967.

CHAPTER 3

Reinforcement in Human Learning[1]

W. K. ESTES

I. INTRODUCTION

Although the interpretation of reinforcement in animal learning has been a focus of theoretical controversy for many decades, the corresponding issue as it arises in experimentation on human learning has been strangely quiescent for a very long period. Perhaps the reason is in part that much of the research on human learning, at least in this

[1]Preparation of this article was supported by contract Nonr 225(73) between the Office of Naval Research and Stanford University. Experimental research reported herein was supported in part by a grant from the National Science Foundation.

I am indebted to Alexander M. Buchwald for his painstaking criticisms of a preliminary draft of the article.

country, has been conducted by investigators in the functionalist tradition. Although functionalism entails no necessary commitment to any particular theory of reinforcement, its representatives seem usually to have proceeded on the assumption that the nature of reward is captured in essentials by Thorndike's Law of Effect, according to which the action of reward is a direct and automatic strengthening of the stimulus-response association.

Following Thorndike's systematic studies of "aftereffects" (1931; 1935), the problem of reward in human learning received little explicit attention until the recent burgeoning of research on verbal behavior by means of operant conditioning techniques. The wave of these studies, which followed Greenspoon's original experiment (1955), appeared uniformly to support an operant conditioning interpretation essentially equivalent to the Law of Effect (see, e.g., Salzinger, 1959). It appeared that suitably programmed rewards controlled the occurrence of verbal behaviors in a manner predictable from analogous studies of operant behavior in animals, and, in particular, that effects of rewards were independent of the subjects' awareness of relationships or contingencies between their responses and reinforcing operations.

In a major review of the literature on verbal rewards and punishments Postman and Sassenrath (1961) concluded that (1) the Law of Effect was on the whole well supported by a variety of evidence; (2) of the various types of evidence that other investigators had thought brought the principle in question, only that having to do with the necessity of awareness of response-reinforcement contingencies on the part of the learner was truly germane to the issue; and (3) owing to methodological and logical difficulties having to do with criteria of awareness, the studies purporting to relate effectiveness of rewards to the subject's awareness of contingencies cannot provide a source of critical evidence regarding tenability of the Law of Effect.

In his own theoretical writings, Thorndike (1931) recognized and attempted to refute an alternative type of theory in which rewards and punishments might function as determiners of choices but without any direct influence on learning. According to this conception, the learning which occurs in a standard human learning experiment would be a matter of the subject's acquiring information concerning relationships between stimuli and responses in the material to which he is exposed and relationships between these and rewarding or punishing outcomes. The learning would simply be a function of such variables as contiguity, frequency, and recency. The values of rewards and punishments would be relevant only insofar as they determined the subject's choice of responses on a given trial once he had recalled the relevant events that had occurred on the preceding trials of an experiment. This alternative viewpoint has received little attention in the literature on human learning, perhaps partly because Thorndike did not favor it himself and perhaps more importantly because no explicit and detailed theory of this type has been formulated.

More recently, two research developments have lent new interest to the desirability of formulating a theory of the second type. First, with regard to the operant conditioning situation, studies by Dulany (1962) and by Spielberger (1962) and his associates (Spielberger, Bernstein, & Ratliff, 1966) have cast considerable doubt upon the conclusion that verbal response tendencies are systematically modified by the effects of rewards when the subjects are unaware of relationships between the rewarding events and their responses. Second, with regard to the more classic types of human learning experiments involving the paired-associate or Thorndikian paradigms, a series of studies by me and my associates (Estes, 1966; Humphreys, Allen, & Estes, 1968; Keller, Cole, Burke, & Estes, 1965) has provided considerable evidence that the function of reward in these situations can be experimentally decomposed into what may be termed informational and motivational components.

In the remainder of this chapter I propose, first, to review a sample of earlier findings from the rather extensive series of studies done in my laboratory leading to an interpretation of reinforcement in human learning that does not assume the Law of Effect; second, to outline the theory that has taken form; and third, to present one of the relatively novel experiments we have contrived to put this formulation to an exacting test.

II. INFORMATION VERSUS EFFECT

When a reward is presented following a response, there are at least two distinct ways in which the reward might affect learning of the response. First, there is the possibility that the reward exerts a direct strengthening effect upon the associative connection between the response and the stimulus which evoked it, this being of course the conventional Law of Effect interpretation. Second, there is the possibility that the subject simply learns the relationships between the preceding stimulus and response and the reward as a result of having experienced them in temporal contiguity. A long-term experimental program in my laboratory has been directed toward the problem of separating these two possible functions of reward.

The first set of data relevant to this issue comes from two groups included in a larger experiment that was conducted by a group of graduate students in my advanced laboratory methods course at Indiana University in 1957. The purpose was to ascertain the extent to which learning of a paired-associate item could be influenced by reward in the sense of an indication of correctness of response when opportunities for acquiring information about stimulus-response-reward relationships were strictly equated. For brevity let us denote the two conditions as being the Effect and the Information conditions. Twenty-four college student subjects were run under each condition, learning 12-item lists of double letter, double digit pairs. Subjects in the Effect condition received first a cycle through the list on which each of the stimulus–response pairs was presented once, then a series of cycles under a conventional anticipation procedure, continuing until the subject met a criterion of all 12 responses correct through a single cycle.

Under the anticipation procedure of the Effect condition, each trial began with a 3-second exposure of the stimulus member of an item during which the subject attempted to give the correct response from memory, then a 2-second blank interval, then a 3-second presentation of the stimulus together with its correct response. A 60-second rest interval intervened between successive cycles through the list, and, of course, the order of items was randomized anew for each cycle.

For the Information group, odd-numbered cycles through the list involved only paired presentations of the stimulus–response members of the items; and even-numbered cycles comprised recall test trials on which the stimulus members were presented alone, with the subject attempting to give the response from memory but with no feedback of any kind from the experimenter indicating correctness or incorrectness of the response. Under this procedure, on any one trial of the paired presentation cycle the subject received the 3-second presentation of the stimulus–response pair, then a 2-second blank interval, then a 3-second presentation of the next scheduled pair, and so on; a 30-second rest interval intervened between the end of this cycle and the following test cycle. On a test trial each stimulus member appeared alone for 3 seconds, during which the subject responded, with 2 seconds between successive trials and a 30-second rest at the end of a cycle before initiation of the following paired presentation cycle. Thus, within a margin of error of 2 seconds per cycle on the average, the interval between a paired presentation of any item and the next subsequent recall test on that item was strictly equated for the Effect and Information conditions. The distinctive difference between the procedures was that under the Effect condition subjects received immediate reward, in the sense of an indication of correctness, following every correct response; under the Information condition a subject's correct response on a recall test could have received no reward until that item came up on the subsequent paired presentation cycle, in general more than a minute later and after a large number of intervening items had been presented. Whereas both groups received exactly the same amount of information concerning correct stimulus–response relationships between successive recall tests, the Effect group should have had an advantage if an immediate indication of correctness exerts a strengthening effect on stimulus–response association in the manner assumed by the classic Law of Effect.

TABLE I

Trials and Errors to Criterion under Information and Effect Conditions

Condition	Trials		Errors	
	M	SE_M	M	SE_M
Information	7.71	0.64	37.79	3.81
Effect	8.96	0.48	45.83	3.05

The principal results are presented in Table I in terms of mean numbers of trials and mean numbers of errors to criterion for the two conditions. Clearly the Effect condition yielded no advantage, and in fact resulted in slower learning according to both measures, though in neither case was the difference statistically reliable. The lack of any advantage for the group receiving immediate knowledge of results is evidently not peculiar to our conditions, for it has subsequently been replicated several times (e.g., Battig & Brackett, 1961). This finding, rather unexpected from the viewpoint of Law of Effect theory, could perhaps be explained in various ways, but the simplest interpretation would seem to be that learning of the correct stimulus–response relationships in this situation depends simply upon contiguous experience of the corresponding events and not upon rewarding consequences following correct responses.

Having failed to detect any strengthening effect of immediate knowledge of results when information presented was held constant across conditions, we turned next to the mirror image, that is, a comparison with reward value held constant while information was allowed to differ. In a study by Keller *et al.* (1965), subjects learned a 25-item paired-associate list; all items had different stimulus members, but there were only two response alternatives, one or the other of which was correct for each item. On each trial of the experiment the stimulus member of an item appeared on a screen, then the subject chose one of the two possible responses and, following this, received the reward assigned to that stimulus-response combination. Rewards were given in "points," the numerical values of which were presented visually immediately following the response; the number of points received over a series of trials was directly related to the subject's monetary payoff for participating in the experiment.

For each stimulus in the list a pair of reward values, for example 1 point vs. 8, 2 points vs. 4, was assigned to the two possible responses, and the assignment did not change for the given subject throughout the experiment. However, the conditions of presentation of the rewards differed for two groups, one group being run under what we shall call the Correction and the other the Noncorrection procedure. The Noncorrection condition corresponded essentially to that of the Thorndikian trial-and-error experiments; that is, on each trial a subject made his choice of responses following presentation of the stimulus and then was shown the reward value given for that response. Under the Correction condition, once the subject had made his choice on each trial, *both* assigned reward values were shown, the one which the subject received for the response he had made and also the one associated with the response not made on that trial. Thus, the rewards actually received for each stimulus-response combination were exactly the same for the two groups, but the amount of information given per trial concerning stimulus-response-reward relationships was twice as large for the Correction as for the Noncorrection condition.

With an error on any item defined as a choice of the response carrying the lower reward value, mean errors per item to a criterion of five consecutive correct responses were compared for items having different reward combinations within each of the training conditions. For the Noncorrection condition, the overall picture was essentially as one would anticipate on the basis of classic conceptions of reward, the rate of learning being higher the greater the difference between the reward values assigned to the two response alternatives of an item; a similar ordering appeared with respect to mean trial of the last error. In each case the variation over reward combinations was highly significant, the mean value for the item with the largest reward differential (1 point vs. 8) being less than half that for the slowest learned item (2 vs. 4). For the Correction condition, in contrast, there was no significant variation in either of these statistics over items with different reward combinations and no consistent ordering of items with respect to reward differentials. For example, the fastest learned item was 4 vs. 8 with 1.84 errors and the slowest 1 vs. 4 with 3.07 errors, with such extreme differential items as 1 vs. 8 and 1 vs. 2 falling in between.

The first of these sets of findings fits in with the notion that a larger difference between the reward values for an item leads to a drawing apart of associative strength for the two response alternatives simply because of the different increments in strength produced by the two rewards. However, the correction procedure involved the same reward contingencies, yet led to no significant variation of learning rate with reward differentials, thus casting doubt upon that interpretation. When full information was given on each trial for each item, the relationship between learning rate and reward differential disappeared.

If learning rate were a function purely of information received by the subject per trial, we should expect the rate to be approximately twice as great for the Correction as for the Noncorrection condition, since in the former information concerning both of the response-reward relations of an item was given on each trial but in the Noncorrection condition only one of the two was available to the subject on any one trial. Interestingly, the rate of learning as measured by the slope constant of the learning curve was almost exactly twice as large for the Correction as for the Noncorrection condition (.21 vs. .10). If learning is actually a function only of information transmitted, then the variation among observed learning curves for the Noncorrection condition must be attributed simply to a performance difference, expected on the ground that in the case of partially learned items, subjects will tend to make fewer errors if the reward differentials are large. When only one alternative has been learned for a given item, that choice will tend to be made if the learned reward is large; that choice will tend to be avoided if the learned reward is small.

Additional data of considerable value both for evaluating the classic interpretation and for pointing the way to desirable modifications are available in the response latencies of the study by Keller *et al.* Considering mean latencies over the entire series as a function of reward combinations, for the Correction condition there were only slight differences, and the only noticeable systematic trend was a slight tendency for latencies to decrease as the sum of the reward values per item increased. For the Noncorrection condition, however, a much steeper function emerged, with mean latency decreasing as the higher reward value of a pair increased, and when the higher value was held constant, decreasing as the sum of the reward values increased.

Some points of special interest with respect to the Noncorrection data are brought out in Fig. 1, in which mean correct response latencies are plotted for the first block of 10 trials in the upper two panels and for the final block in the lower two panels. On the left-hand side, latencies are plotted as a function of reward differential per item. A significant, though modest correlation is apparent, but the correlation decreases somewhat from the first block to the last; in fact, if the point for the reward differential of 1 (the 2 vs. 1 item) were deleted, the correlation would be virtually 0 in the last block.

On the right-hand side, latencies are plotted as a function of the value of the higher reward per item. The two significant findings which emerge from the latter are that the correlations of latency with the independent variable are higher in both instances on the right than on the left, and that the correlation increases from the first block to the last, the function being virtually linear in the final block.

Evidently, the higher the reward value a subject has learned to expect following a given response, the more probable is that response to occur and the lower is its latency on the average when it does occur.

Still more direct demonstrations of the establishment of learned associations between originally neutral stimuli and rewards, and of

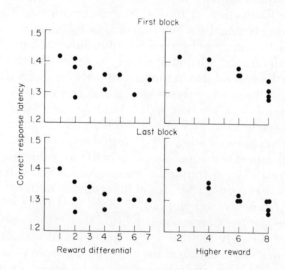

FIG. 1. Mean correct response latency as a function of reward differential (left-hand panels) and of value of the higher reward per item (right-hand panels) at early and late stages of learning. Data are for Noncorrection Group. From Keller *et al.* (1965).

the effects of this learning upon performance in new situations are provided by several recent studies conducted with children. For example, Nunnally, Duchnowski, and Parker (1965a) gave children in the second grade experience with an apparatus constructed somewhat like a roulette wheel except that the wheel was bordered with nonsense syllables rather than numbers. When the wheel stopped with the pointer on a particular one of the syllables, the positive stimulus, the subject received a two-cent reward; when it stopped on a second syllable, the negative stimulus, the subject was punished by loss of one cent; and when the wheel stopped on the third syllable the outcome was neutral, that is, neither gain nor loss. After a series of training trials, tests were given in a "treasure hunt" situation in which the subject was confronted with a set of white boxes, identical except that each had one of the nonsense syllables printed on the top, and was given a series of opportunities to find the box which contained a 25-cent reward. The subjects exhibited a significant tendency to select boxes labeled with the previously positive stimulus as compared to the previously negative or neutral stimuli. Further, when in another test the subjects were simply allowed to look at cards containing the various nonsense syllables in a view box with their eye movements being photographed, they exhibited a greater tendency to look at the positive than the neutral stimulus and longer at the neutral than the negative stimulus. Similar results concerning "looking time" were obtained in a related series of experiments reported by Nunnally, Stevens, and Hall (1965b).

In a study of somewhat different design Witryol, Lowden, and Fagan (1967) gave children training intended to establish associations between stimulus dimensions and reward values. During a training series the child made a choice and then received a reward. When two stimuli from one dimension, say color, were presented, the child received a high reward regardless of his choice, and when stimuli from the other dimension were presented the child received a low reward regardless of his choice. Following this training, the children were given a series of trials on a discrimination problem in which one of the formerly presented dimensions was relevant and the other irrelevant with a light now serving as the reinforcing stimulus indicating correctness of response. Discrimination learning was more rapid when the formerly high reward dimension was relevant, and this finding, together with other aspects of the data, indicated that the children had developed an increased tendency to attend to the dimension associated with high reward.

III. PROVISIONAL INTERPRETATION OF THE FUNCTIONS OF REWARD

The findings just reviewed are representative of the series of studies which appears to be converging in a rather direct way upon a particular set of assumptions regarding the functions of reward. The ideas involved are applicable to animal as well as human learning and can be cast in mathematical form up to a point (see Estes, 1967; Humphreys *et al.*, 1968), but for present purposes it will suffice to develop them informally in the context of standard human learning situations.

Any one trial of a simple trial-and-error learning experiment, such as that by Keller *et al.*, involves presentation of a stimulus, a choice of response by the subject, and finally presentation of a rewarding outcome. For brevity we shall denote these three components by S, R, and O. The principal assumption to be made concerning learning is that associations between any two of these components may be formed simply as a function of contiguous experiences of them. Thus, on a trial in which a stimulus S is followed by a response R and outcome O, associations of the form S–R, S–O, and R–O may be established. It is assumed that learning in this sense occurs on an all-or-none basis, with a constant probability over trials that an association will form upon the contiguous occurrence of the appropriate members. The term association is being used simply in the sense of memory storage such that in the case of an S–R association, the presentation of S evokes a representation of R, in the case of an S–O association the presentation of S evokes a representation of O, and so on. This learning is assumed to occur purely as a function of contiguity and independently of reward values of outcomes.

One aspect of this last assumption requires clarification. What is proposed is that, once two stimuli are sampled, or perceived contiguously, there is some probability that an association will form, this probability being independent of associated reward values. It is not implied, however, that the probabilities of sampling particular stimuli may not change over a series of trials. In fact, application of the present theory to the learning of perceptual, or orienting responses leads to the prediction that subjects' selective sampling of stimuli may be systematically modified by a learning series in which different cues are associated with different rewards.

The principal function of rewards in this theory is to modify response selection in any given state of learning. If learning has occurred with respect to a particular item, then when the item is presented the stimulus members are scanned and their learned associations are activated, that is, brought into the subject's immediate memory. It is assumed that recall of a rewarding or punishing outcome carries what may be termed facilitatory or inhibitory feedback. The effect of modulation by feedback is that when the scanning process moves from a recalled response with anticipated outcome of higher to one of lower reward value, feedback becomes inhibitory and the latter response does not occur overtly. When the process moves from a lower to a higher recalled reward, the latter response–reward association carries facilitatory feedback, and there is some probability, directly related to reward value, that the response will occur overtly.

Thus, when an item is in the fully learned state, that is, both alternative responses and their associated rewards have been learned, then upon each presentation of the stimulus, the correct response is chosen, and the latency of the response is shorter the higher the associated reward value. When an item is completely unlearned, no representations of previous responses or rewards are brought into memory when the stimulus is presented, and the subject simply must choose at random between the available alternatives. When an item is partially learned, so that upon occurrence of the stimulus only one of the associated response–reward combinations can be recalled, the outcome is not fully determinate. Presumably the feedback associated with the response whose reward value is unknown would be equal to the average of that generated by choices of responses with unknown rewards during the preceding trials of the experiment. Since this value would fluctuate somewhat from trial to trial, all that can be assumed is that for any given known reward value there is some probability that it would carry higher positive feedback than that of the unknown reward value associated with an alternative response to the same stimulus, and this probability would be higher the higher the value of the known reward.

Even if our assumption that associative learning of a stimulus–response relationship depends solely upon the contiguous experience of the two members by the learner were correct, it must be recognized that other factors influence performance under various test conditions. There is considerable reason to believe that, for recognition of learned stimulus–response relationships, the contiguity assumption is for all practical purposes sufficient as well as necessary (see, e.g., Estes & Da Polito, 1967). By contrast, any type of recall test involving determination of the subject's tendency to give the response upon presentation of the stimulus alone is sensitive to variables influencing covert or overt rehearsal. In the study by Estes and Da Polito, for example, introduction of an instructional condition intended to reduce the subject's tendency to rehearse stimulus–response relationships during training had virtually no effect upon subsequent recognition performance but was severely detrimental to subsequent recall.

Within stimulus sampling theory (Estes, 1959) there are several reasons for expecting this dependence of recall performance upon rehearsal. First, the repetition involved provides repeated opportunities for elements of the stimulus to become associated with the response. Second, during rehearsal the stimulus member occurs out of the context of the training trial, which might be expected to promote transfer to later tests in which the stimulus appears in different contexts. Third, in rehearsal the stimulus and the response members of the association will frequently be brought into closer temporal contiguity than was the case under conditions of a training trial.

The pertinence of these observations for the present discussion is that, in adult human subjects at least, it must be expected that motivational variables and, in particular, rewards and punishments will influence rehearsal. The effects may be expected to be manifest in at least two ways. First, if one compares conditions for different groups of subjects which differ with respect to reinforcing conditions, we must expect an overall difference in performance, other things equal, in favor of the group receiving the greater rewards or punishments, since either would lead to increased tendencies to rehearse and thus to an improvement in performance which would be nonspecific with respect to items. Second, in experiments in which reinforcing conditions vary from item to item, we should expect greater tendencies to rehearse on items involving larger reward values. However, it should be noted that the essential relationship here is between the stimulus members of the item and the associated rewards, not the specific relations between responses and rewards. Thus, for example, in the Correction condition of the study by Keller *et al.* (1965), an overall tendency was manifest for response latencies to decrease as a function of the sum of the reward values associated with the stimulus member of an item. This effect was slight, however, in conformity with a large amount of experience indicating that when adult human subjects participate in experiments under instructions to learn, sufficient rehearsal occurs so that differences attributable to this factor are very hard to demonstrate. When, however, the learning task is masked in some fashion from the subjects, as in many studies of operant conditioning of verbal behavior, of incidental learning, or of learning without awareness, differential rehearsal becomes a major variable and must be taken into account.

IV. AN EXPERIMENTAL TEST OF THE THEORY

The distinctive feature of the interpretation just outlined is that a reward is assumed to exert no direct effect upon associative connections at the time of its occurrence, but to exert its effects upon performance only upon later occasions after the relationships between stimuli and reward have been learned. That is, rewards do not influence learning, but rather information concerning rewards must be acquired before rewards can influence performance. This conception accounts for the experimental findings mentioned in preceding sections of this paper, but we should like to see the central assumptions put to a more direct test. An example of the type of experiment which seems to be called for is the following, hitherto unpublished study conducted at Indiana University in 1961.

In all traditional trial-and-error learning experiments, rewards are presented immediately following stimulus-response occurrences, and thus the opportunity for any strengthening effect of the reward upon the stimulus-response association and the opportunity for the learning of relationships between the stimulus-response combination and reward are inextricably confounded. What I wished to accomplish in this study was to separate these two possible aspects by contriving a situation in which the subject could learn relationships between stimulus-response combinations and reward values without any possibility of a direct strengthening effect of the latter upon the former. This end was accomplished by the following procedure.

The task was a modification of the verbal discrimination experiment which has been used previously by Bower (1962), Estes (1966), and others. During the training phase subjects were exposed to repeated cycles through a set of pairs of stimulus cards. Reward values were assigned to the cards, and on each trial the subject was to choose the card of the pair which he thought carried the larger reward value. Up to this point the procedure is the same as that of previous studies of two-choice, differential reward learning with the Noncorrection procedure (Estes, 1966; Keller *et al.*, 1965). However, in the present experiment the subject's task was complicated in that, in order to receive the reward, he had not only to choose the correct card of a pair but also to guess correctly the precise reward value assigned to that card. In all cases the incorrect card of a pair had reward value zero. For some pairs some single reward value was assigned to the other card and did not change over the series of trials. For the items of the type just described, belonging to what we shall term the Uniform condition, whenever the subject made a choice of a card together with his guess at the reward value, he was then shown the assigned reward value and, if he had both chosen and guessed correctly, was given that reward.

For the set of items belonging to what we shall term the Random condition, one card of a pair carried zero reward and the other either of two values, for example 1 or 2 units. For these items, upon correct choices the reward value displayed by the experimenter at the end of the trial was chosen randomly from the two assigned values; hence, when the subject had learned the values assigned to the card he would on the average guess the value correctly and thus receive the reward on only half the trials.

For a third set of items, belonging to what we shall term the "Never-right" condition, the assignment of rewards to the two cards of a pair was identical to that of a corresponding item in the Random condition. But the procedure differed in the following way. Whenever the subject chose the correct card of a pair and guessed a reward value belonging to the assigned set, for example, 1 if the pair was 1 or 2, the reward value displayed by the experimenter was always the one not guessed by the subject. Thus, on these items the subject could learn the pair of reward values assigned to the correct card of a pair, but he could never actually receive any reward for his choice. Since the three types of items were mixed together and given in new random order on each cycle during the training phase of the experiment, it was expected that the subjects would be able to learn the various stimulus-response-reward relationships but would not be able to perceive the overall structure of the experiment and, in particular, would not be aware that they never actually received rewards on some particular items.

After the subjects had learned the correct responses to all items, in the sense of always choosing the correct member of each pair and always guessing a reward value which belonged to the assigned subset, test trials were given in which the nonzero cards from the training pairs were recombined in various ways. By means of these tests it was hoped that we could determine whether a subject's tendency to choose one card over another in a new combination would be determined by the rewards actually received for choices of these cards during previous training, or simply by the reward values previously assigned to the cards, which the subject had had opportunity to learn even though he might never have received the given rewards. The following is a more detailed exposition of the methodology of the experiment.

A. Method

1. Subjects and Materials

The subjects were 40 undergraduate students at Indiana University who received $2.00 each for participation in the experiment. The stimuli were presented on 3 × 5 inch cards, each of which contained a nonsense syllable, that is, a consonant-vowel-consonant combination printed in capital letters on the face and the assigned reward values on the back. During the experiment the cards were kept in a rack behind a shield and were presented in pairs by the experimenter, the subject seeing the stimulus sides of the cards but never being shown the sides of the cards containing the reward values. Behind the shield was also a bank of electric counters. A set of 16 nonsense syllables was used as stimuli, with a different random assignment of syllables to reward values for each subgroup of 10 subjects.

2. Stimulus-Reward Conditions

The 16 stimulus cards used for a given subgroup of subjects were assigned to reward values and to conditions of informational and rewarding feedback according to the schedule shown in Table II. For convenience, the stimuli here and elsewhere are denoted by small letters. In this notation, stimuli i-p were all assigned the reward value 0 and served as the incorrect members of the eight training pairs. Four of the stimuli, e-h, belonged to the Uniform condition and were assigned the reward values of 1, 2, 3, or 4 units. On the occurrence of Uniform items, the associated reward value was always displayed by the experimenter at the end of the trial and was the amount received

TABLE II
Design of "Never-Right" Experiment

Stimulus	Value assigned	Informational condition	Reward on correct
a	1,2	Random	1,2
b	3,4	Random	3,4
c	1,2	Never-right	0
d	3,4	Never-right	0
e	1	Uniform	1
f	2	Uniform	2
g	3	Uniform	3
h	4	Uniform	4
i-p	0	Uniform	0

by the subject as his reward. The items of the critical Never-right
condition, denoted c and d in the table, were assigned the reward values 1, 2, or 3, 4, respectively. When the item c–k, for example, occurred, if the subject chose card c and guessed any reward value other
than 1 or 2, the experimenter displayed 1 or 2 at random; if the subject
chose card c and guessed value 1, the experimenter displayed 2, and if
the subject guessed 2 the experimenter displayed 1, in either case the
subject receiving no reward on the trial. Conditions were analogous
for card d with reward values 3 and 4. Cards a and b belonged to the
Random condition, for which one or the other of the assigned reward
values was displayed whenever the given card was chosen regardless
of the subject's guess, so that on the average once the subject had
learned the values assigned to the stimulus he received reward on half
the trials.

3. *Training Procedure*

At the beginning of the training series the subject was instructed as
to how trials would be run; he was told that his task was to attempt to
choose the correct card of each pair and to guess the associated reward
value, and that he would receive the reward displayed if he chose a
correct card and had guessed the correct reward value. His objective
was to attain as large a total of reward points as possible during the
experiment. It was explained that the reward he received on each correct trial would be entered in his account by means of the electric
counters and that he would know when he received a reward because
he could hear the counter operate. On each trial when the subject did
in fact choose the correct card and guess the correct reward value, the
counter was operated with a clearly audible buzz, though actually no
point totals were reported to the subject. The trials were subject-
paced, with exposures of stimuli lasting until the subject responded,
and with no intervals between trials or cycles except the time required to change cards. On any one trial the two cards of an item were
presented, the left–right order being determined randomly; the subject chose a card and guessed a reward value; the experimenter displayed the reward value called for by the procedure on that trial; if the
subject was correct in both his choice and his guess the counter was
operated to indicate that the subject received the reward displayed.
Training continued until the subject went through an entire cycle of
16 items (each of the eight items appearing in each of the two
left–right arrangements), with correct choices and correct guesses of
reward values on all trials of the cycle, the correct guess for a Random
or a Never-right item being defined as either of the reward values assigned to that stimulus.

4. Test Procedure

After the training criterion had been met, it was explained that the subjects would now be given a series of trials in which the cards involved in the preceding series would be recombined in various ways but without any other change except that the subject would no longer be shown the reward values at the end of the trial. The counter was operated on all test trials. The subject was given to understand that reward contingencies would be the same as before but that the information was being withheld for purposes of the test. The test series comprised two cycles; during the first cycle all eight of the correct stimuli of the training series occurred in all possible pairs with one left–right orientation and during the second cycle all of these pairs occurred with the other left–right orientation. Thus, there was a total of 80 observations for each test.

B. Results

1. Training Data

To be credited with a correct response on any trial during the training series, the subject had to choose the correct card of the pair and to guess the correct reward value, in the case of Uniform items, or a value belonging to the assigned pair for the Random or Never-right items. Mean errors to criterion, with errors scored according to this definition, were computed for each item type. It will be recalled that according to the theory under test the speed of learning should not be significantly related to the reward value, or mean reward value, assigned to the correct alternative of an item.

Within the set of Uniform items, no systematic relationship between mean errors and reward value was observed, the means being 9.45, 7.40, 9.05, and 5.35, for items with correct reward values of 1, 2, 3, and 4, respectively. Similarly, errors were not related systematically to mean reward value within either the Random or the Never-right condition; in the former instances mean errors were 5.62 and 6.70 for the 1, 2 and 3, 4 items and in the latter 6.92 and 5.88 for the 1, 2 and 3, 4 items, respectively. No direct comparison can be made between the Uniform items and the others since the likelihood of guessing the reward values within the assigned subset would be different in the two cases. It is of special interest to note, finally, that there was no appreciable difference in rate of learning, as measured by errors to criterion, between the Random and Never-right conditions, indicating that the rate of learning was a function primarily of the information given regarding associations between stimuli and reward values rather than by reward actually received for correct responses.

2. Test Data

The principal results of the test series are summarized in Table III in terms of the proportion of times that a card belonging to any given condition was chosen over cards belonging to each of the other conditions. The values are presented in terms of the proportion of choices of the row entry over the column entry for each cell, with the marginal proportion of times that each type of card was chosen over all competitors indicated in the column of mean proportions at the right.

When the marginal proportions are considered, for the Uniform items the marginals line up monotonically and almost linearly with reward value. Further, the marginals for the Random and Never-right conditions fall between the corresponding pairs of the Uniform conditions (for example, the marginal mean for Random 1, 2 falling midway between the values for Uniform 1 and Uniform 2) and in fact very close to the values that would be predicted by interpolation if the 1, 2 items were assigned values of 1.5 and the 3, 4 items values of 3.5. When the Random and matched Never-right conditions are compared, there is virtually no difference for the 3, 4 items and a small difference in favor of the Random condition for the 1, 2 items (probably reliable in view of the quantity of data, though no simple statistical test is available).

When the interior of the table is considered, within the Uniform condition accuracy of the pair-wise choices is extremely high, indicating that the learning criterion was effective and that there was negligible retention loss between the training and test series. It will be noted that virtually all of the few errors occurring within the Uniform condition involved items with adjacent reward values.

Proportions of choices of a given Random item over the different

TABLE III
Choice Proportions on Test Series of
"Never-Right" Experiment

Stimulus	Condition[a]	a	b	c	d	e	f	g	h	ave.
a	R; 1,2	—	.02	.61	.05	.85	.19	0	0	.25
b	R; 3,4	.98	—	1.00	.44	1.00	.95	.79	.05	.74
c	NR; 1,2	.39	0	—	.01	.76	.04	0	0	.17
d	NR; 3,4	.95	.56	.99	—	.95	.92	.74	.01	.73
e	U; 1	.15	0	.24	.05	—	.04	0	0	.07
f	U; 2	.81	.05	.96	.08	.96	—	0	.01	.41
g	U; 3	1.00	.21	1.00	.26	1.00	1.00	—	.02	.64
h	U; 4	1.00	.95	1.00	.99	1.00	.99	.98	—	.98

[a]R, random; NR, never-right; U, uniform.

Uniform items yield steep and monotonic functions, with the 50% point crossed in each instance between the two Uniform values corresponding to those of the given Random item and with a mean difference of about 70 percentage points across these two items. Choices of Random 3, 4 over Random 1, 2 are comparable to those for Uniform 3 over 1 or 4 over 2.

The Never-right items behaved precisely like the Random items in all of these respects, yielding a similar function versus the Uniform items, with crossovers at the same places and an average of about 72 percentage points difference at the crossover. Similarly, choices of Never-right 3, 4 over Never-right 1, 2 (.99) are virtually identical to those of Random 3, 4 over Random 1, 2, Uniform 3 over Uniform 1, and Uniform 4 over Uniform 2.

Finally, with regard to a direct comparison of Random versus Never-right items with matched reward pairs, the mean preference was only .52 for the former over the latter, the Random condition having a small advantage at 1, 2 and the Never-right condition at 3, 4.

3. Conclusions

It seems clear, from the tests involving pairs of Uniform items especially, that the reward values used were extremely effective in producing significant and systematic effects upon performance. Thus, the detailed similarity in patterns of test results for the Random and Never-right conditions and the small differences between the two, wherever matched comparisons were possible, would seem to be of some import regarding one's interpretation of the manner of action of rewarding aftereffects. For items in the Never-right condition, the subjects had opportunity to learn relationships between stimuli and sets of reward values. Clearly this learning occurred and is sufficient to account for the performance on test combinations involving stimuli from Never-right items. On these items the subjects had never received rewards for correct responses during training, and thus there was no opportunity for direct strengthening of associative connections in the manner assumed in the traditional Law of Effect. Evidently the lack of such opportunity was no appreciable handicap to either learning or test performance. While a strengthening effect cannot be ruled out, the absence of positive support for it in our data is rather striking.

V. INTERPRETATIONS OF STANDARD LEARNING EXPERIMENTS

A review of some of the well-established findings of the standard types of human learning experiments may be useful, not so much for the purpose of testing the present theory, which is better accomplished by specially designed new experiments, but for elucidating the intended meaning and mode of application of the concepts more adequately than can be done in a brief summary statement of assumptions.

A. Thorndikian Experiments

The interpretation of Thorndike's lengthy series of trial-and-error learning experiments involving various manipulations with rewards and punishments is a particularly natural first exercise since Thorndike, in effect, began the task himself, discussing a number of his results in terms of what he called the "representational" theory. This theory, which Thorndike believed he was able to refute on the basis of his data, conforms quite closely to the present formulation up to a point. By a "representational" or "ideational" conception, Thorndike referred to the possibility that an image or similar central representation of the rewarding or punishing event might become associated with the stimulus and response terms of an item occurring in an experimental situation. Then, upon later trials, presentation of the stimulus would call up representations of the response and aftereffect previously associated with it, thus putting the learner in a position to choose the response leading to the more desirable outcome. Of the three sources of evidence that Thorndike thought to weigh against the representational theory, two are largely matters of conjecture and even to the present can scarcely be evaluated except as a matter of opinion based on intuition or common sense observation. The first of these is the fact that questioning of his subjects did not evoke many verbal reports that they had experienced images of the outcomes of previous trials during the course of his experiments. In view of the notorious fallibility of an individual's verbal accounts of his experiences, this source of evidence needs to be supplemented by experimental tests of the learner's ability to recall rewarding and punishing outcomes in order to be taken at all seriously. This task Thorndike seems not to have undertaken.

Results of a recent study conducted in my laboratory are of some interest in this regard, however (Estes, 1966). Following a series of learning trials in which rewards, calibrated in terms of point values, were given for differential responses to a number of stimulus combinations and a subsequent series of transfer tests, subjects were presented with the stimuli singly and asked to report the previously associated reward values from memory. From the data of this final test it was apparent, first, that not only could the subjects recall the reward values with considerable accuracy, but also there was a gradient of uncertainty, much like the generalization gradient associated with conditioned stimuli. Thus, it is clear that subjects can retain considerable information concerning associations between stimuli and rewards without necessarily manifesting the veridical recall that might be expected if presentation of stimuli on the recall tests evoked images of previously experienced outcomes.

Thorndike's second objection to representational theory seems scarcely open to experimental attack at all. He identified the recall or reinstatement of an associative connection between previously experienced events with the occurrence of an image, as the term is commonly understood, then argued that in everyday life situations, such as the performance of skilled athletes, responses follow one another too rapidly to be mediated by images.

The third point involves the empirical generalization established by numerous of Thorndike's researches that an announcement of "right" is a more effective modifier of response repetition than an announcement of "wrong," together with the argument that according to a representational theory there should be no difference since announcements of "right" and "wrong" should be equally likely to be recalled on later occasions. The empirical facts on this matter seem beyond serious question, but the inference drawn from them is not. The weakness in the latter has been clearly exposed by Buchwald (1967), who has analyzed the use of "right," "wrong," and nothing (i.e., neither "right" nor "wrong") as reinforcers following verbal responses in terms very close to those of the theory presented in this paper. If a learner's performance on a given trial in this type of experiment is determined by information concerning stimulus-response-outcome relationships of previous trials involving the same item, then it can readily be seen that two of these factors work together to produce repetitions on "right" items but tend to cancel each other on "wrong" items.

When a subject makes a given response to a stimulus and this event is followed by "right," he has opportunities on that trial to learn the correct stimulus-response relationship and also the relation between these and the outcome, both of which contribute to the repetition of the response upon later occurrences of the stimulus. On a trial when the subject makes a given response and it is followed by "wrong," he has opportunity to learn the stimulus-response relation, which, other things equal, increases the likelihood of making that response to the stimulus, and the relation of these to the outcome "wrong," which would lead him to avoid repetition. In the former case neither of the learned relationships would oppose repetition of the response that had been followed by "right," whereas in the latter case recall of the response without the outcome would tend to lead to increased repetition, and only simultaneous recall of the previous response and outcome would lead to an avoidance of repetition. This analysis appears to meet Thorndike's most substantial objection to the representational theory, and we shall see in a later section that the analysis receives independent support from experiments involving novel manipulations of stimulus–response–outcome relationships.

An experimental relation which emerged as a major variable in Thorndikian experiments, and which kept Thorndike himself and later Law of Effect theorists continually skating on the edge of self-contradiction, is that of "belongingness." As used by Thorndike (1931; 1935) this term referred to two different empirical phenomena. The first was that, if during the learning of a task, such as a list of paired-associate items, the learner were suddenly given a monetary reward with some such comment as, "This is a bonus for faithful work," but with no indication that the reward was related to the response of the preceding trial, the reward would have little or no effect upon the probability that the preceding response would be repeated upon the next occurrence of that item.

The other manifestation of belongingness has nothing special to do with reward or punishment but rather concerns the conditions used to test for learning following presentation of a given set of material. Suppose, for example, that a subject were presented with a series of pairs of letters and digits, then at the end were tested for recall. He would be much more likely to be able to give the correct digit when presented with a letter from the preceding list than he would be to give the letter belonging to the pair which occurred at position N if presented with the digit member of the pair that occurred at the position $N - 1$.

Thorndike proposed to account for these findings in terms of a principle of belongingness, according to which rewarding aftereffects are more influential in strengthening preceding stimulus–response associations if both the stimuli and responses, and responses and rewards are related in a way that is meaningful to the subject. His principle seems most foreign in spirit to a theory which depends heavily for its support upon the contention that rewards exert their effects automatically upon preceding stimulus–response associations independently of the learner's awareness of the contingencies involved. Within the present theory, both aspects of the phenomena subsumed under belongingness are special cases of the general principle that later recall of a stimulus–response relationship is facilitated by any conditions leading the learner to perceive the constituent stimulus–response–outcome relationships contiguously and to rehearse these during the interval between training and testing.

Another principal source of support for the classic interpretation of Thorndikian experiments was the phenomenon of "spread of effect," that is, the observation that occurrence of a reward following a particular response pair in a series of items frequently led to increased probability of repetition of the responses belonging to neighboring items in the series. The theoretical notion was that the strengthening effect of the reward spread from the rewarded connection to others that were active contiguously in time whether before or after the occurrence of the reward. However, since the concept of spread of effect was an independent assumption developed expressly to account for the phenomenon in question, it scarcely seems logical that the occurrence of the phenomenon can be taken as independent evidence for the Law of Effect.

The somewhat tortuous literature concerning the spread of effect (see, e.g., reviews by Postman, 1962; Postman & Sassenrath, 1961) leaves one with the net impression that after various artifacts in the earlier studies have been eliminated there remains a genuine effect, though not as large or pervasive a one as assumed by Thorndike. Within the present formulation the observed phenomenon of "spread" has nothing to do with the action of aftereffects, but rather is to be interpreted as a manifestation of stimulus generalization. When the reward occurs at a given point in a list of items, there is opportunity for the learning of relationships between the stimulus member of the item and the reward and also between contextual cues associated with the given position in the list and the reward. The result of this learning will generalize to temporally contiguous items which share contextual cues with the rewarded one. According to the present theory, learning of the neighboring items will be unaffected, but performance will be modified on a subsequent trial when the common contextual cues have increased probabilities of evoking anticipation of reward.

B. Operant Conditioning of Verbal Behavior

The extensive literature concerning modifications of verbal behavior by techniques analogous to those of operant conditioning has gone through two principal phases. In the first, it was initially demonstrated by Greenspoon (1955) that rate of occurrence of verbal responses could be modified if, during the flow of spontaneous speech, words having certain common properties were followed by events which might be expected to have rewarding properties, for example, the utterance of "good" by an experimenter. Following this demonstration a large number of studies sought to show that procedural manipulations, for example, use of fixed ratio or fixed interval reinforcement schedules, discriminative relationships between stimuli and reinforcements, and the like, would produce effects on human verbal behavior similar to those already well documented with respect to the control of bar-pressing behavior in rats and key-pecking in pigeons by scheduling of food rewards. A measure of success attended these efforts, and reviews of the literature by Krasner (1958) and Salzinger (1959) provided some basis for the conclusion that the processes involved might be basically similar in the human and animal cases.

The assumption that the reinforcements in these experiments exerted their effects via a direct strengthening of response tendencies, as assumed in Skinner's (1938) principles of operant conditioning and in Thorndike's Law of Effect, depended primarily upon the observed similarities in some phenomena between human and animal experiments and, perhaps more importantly, upon the fact that in some earlier studies questioning of subjects failed to yield evidence that they were aware of the response-reinforcement contingencies. As in the Thorndikian situation, however, later studies (e.g., Spielberger *et al.*, 1966) approached the question of awareness with more exacting methods and yielded rather clear evidence of strong correlations between indications of awareness of reinforcement relationships and effects of these reinforcements upon response tendencies.

Within the present theory, the operant conditioning experiments are to be interpreted in much the same way as the Thorndikian variety. Rewarding aftereffects should be expected to produce changes in rate of occurrence of verbal utterances in a free responding situation only to the extent that associations between the verbal utterances and the rewarding consequences are learned by the subjects. Although awareness of the constituent relationships on the part of the subjects would not be a necessary condition for this learning, it would be expected to be a correlated variable since the conditions which give rise to awareness are in general the same as those which tend to lead subjects to attend to stimulus-outcome relationships and thus to be in a position to learn them. In the free responding situation, even though the rewarding event may follow a certain verbal response closely in time, since the activity continues without interruption, conditions are not favorable for the subject to perceive the response-reinforcement relation and even less favorable for rehearsal of this association. Thus, it is not surprising that studies using the free responding procedure have generally found the effects of rewards to be slight and unreliable.

By contrast, in a procedure introduced by Taffel (1955) the experiment is divided into discrete trials with a stimulus presented at the

beginning of each trial; the subject chooses a response from a specified set of alternatives, and the rewarding event follows the response
which is scheduled for reinforcement. Changes in relative frequency
of responding as a function of reward are much larger and more repro-
ducible than in the free responding situation. The change in conditions from the less to the more effective procedure, it will be noted,
involves little if any change in the temporal relation of response to
reward, but major changes in the likelihood that the subjects will perceive the constituents of the stimulus–reward relationship and in the
opportunity for rehearsal of this association between trials.

C. Magnitude of Reward

Within the present theory rewards enter into learning simply as associative elements or, in other terms, as items of information. After
such learning has occurred, associations between stimuli, responses,
and rewards are an important determiner of performance, as discussed
in previous sections of this paper. It should be noted, however, that
we have been concerned in this discussion only with specific effects
of reward. Although it is scarcely feasible at this stage to incorporate
them into a formal theory, there are well-known nonspecific effects of
rewards which must be taken into account in designing and interpreting experiments concerned with this variable.

In particular, when comparisons are made between different subjects or groups of subjects who learn under different reward conditions, one must recognize the possibility that rewards, like any other
motivational condition, may influence subjects' tendencies to attend
to material presented and to rehearse stimulus–response relationships. Thus, when Thorndike (1935) gave his subjects periodic
sums of money which were not associated with particular stimulus-
response associations, there was no differential strengthening of
the responses which had happened to precede these unexpected
rewards, but in some instances there was a modification of behavior
over the experiment as a whole in comparison to other experiments
which did not involve monetary rewards. A better controlled comparison was provided in a study by Thorndike and Forlano (cited
in Thorndike, 1935) in which different groups of subjects learned sets
of trial-and-error items with, for one group, monetary reward being
associated with correct responses versus none for incorrect responses.
Some increase in rate of learning was observed for the group receiving
monetary rewards. However, when similar comparisons were made
between different items for the same subject, the outcome was quite
different. In a study by Rock (cited in Thorndike, 1935), subjects ex-

hibited no differences in learning rates among items of a set of trial-and-error problems when the amount of monetary reward for correct responses, in each case paired with zero reward for incorrect responses, varied over items for each subject.

This negative result led Thorndike to the postulation of a threshold of what he termed the *confirming reaction* of a reward. According to this notion any reward sufficient to exceed the threshold would produce a facilitating effect upon learning, but further variations in reward value above the threshold would have no differential effects. Although this ad hoc notion could accommodate the results of Rock's study, it would be quite out of line with data of studies such as that of Keller *et al.* (1965). In this study, the rates of approach of learning curves to their asymptotes were found to depend strongly upon reward magnitude when different items in a set had different combinations of reward for the correct and incorrect responses (this result, as noted above, holding only under a Noncorrection procedure).

Taking all the various types of experiments into account, one is led to the view, not that each involves some threshold, but rather that effects of reward magnitude are qualitatively different for different combinations of dependent variables and experimental arrangements. As predicted by the present theory, variations in reward magnitude, entailing variation in facilitative feedback, quite uniformly generate corresponding variation in response speeds or reaction times. However, this appears to be strictly an effect on performance, for as seen in the data of Keller *et al.* cited above, the relationship is as pronounced at asymptote as at earlier stages of learning. In contrast, variations in reward magnitude affect relative frequency of correct responding only under conditions such that different amounts of reward convey different amounts of information regarding correctness of response. The accumulating support for this last generalization is by no means limited to my own series of studies. One recent example arising in a quite different context is a study of verbal conditioning by Farley and Hokanson (1966). Rewards varying in monetary value from zero to one cent were assigned orthogonally, by instructions, different information values relative to correctness of response. Steepness and terminal levels of acquisition curves were directly related to the latter variable but were independent of the former.

D. Delay of Reward

The interval between the occurrence of a response and the following reward has been one of the most conspicuous experimental variables in the study of reinforcement. In view of the very extensive literature upon this variable in animal learning and conditioning, it was only natural that attention should turn at an early stage to attempts to reproduce some of the classic animal findings with human subjects. Further, since the classic Law of Effect is defined in terms of proximity of response and reward, one of the principal consequences of that conception is a gradation in learning rate as a function of delay of reward.

Within the present theory, the interval between the response per se and subsequent rewards is immaterial, although delay of reward may under some circumstances exert effects on rate of learning by modifying the opportunity for learning of associations between the reward and either the stimulus which evoked a given response or stimulus characteristics of the response itself. In experiments conducted according to the classic "simultaneous" paradigm, that is, with two or more stimuli presented on a trial and the subject required to select one of these, the interval between response and reward may modify learning rate indirectly if activities occurring during the delay interval lead to the learning of interfering associations. In experiments conducted according to the "successive" paradigm in which, for example, response 1 is correct for stimulus A and response 2 for stimulus B, with only one stimulus or the other occurring on any one trial, it is the stimulus compound including elements of the presented stimulus A or B and the correct response to it which must enter into a learned association with the rewarding event. Thus, in these experiments and also in experiments on motor skill and the like where the task is primarily one of response selection to a constant stimulus, the degree of discriminability between the stimulus aspects of the alternative responses will be an important variable.

To the extent that the subject can hold representations of the relevant stimuli and responses in immediate memory during the interval of delay, the length of delay interval before occurrence of the reward should be immaterial. Thus, we are prepared for the ineffectiveness of delay generally found for simple motor learning tasks with adult human subjects (Bilodeau & Bilodeau, 1958). More importantly, the present interpretation fits well with the finding of Saltzman (1951) that with the same stimuli, responses, and intervals, delay of reward had no effect under conditions which made it easy for subjects' immediate memory to span the delay interval, but produced a significant decremental effect when the load on immediate memory was increased.

In the recent very extensive and carefully controlled study of paired-associate learning in adults by Kintsch and McCoy (1964), conditions were arranged so as to permit delays of 0, 4, or 8 seconds, while insuring adequate opportunity for the subject to associate the

stimulus and response members. On each trial the subject was presented with a nonsense syllable stimulus, made a choice of a right or
left response key, and then after an interval observed a reinforcing
light above the correct key. In Experiment 1 the stimulus was repeated at the time of the feedback light; in Experiment 2 the stimulus
was not repeated but was originally presented for a sufficiently long
interval to provide the subjects adequate opportunity to encode the
stimulus in immediate memory and maintain it over the delay interval. In both cases errors to criterion of learning *decreased* slightly as a
function of the delay of reinforcement.

In studies conducted with children, delay of reward has usually
been a more effective variable, though with the conditions of substantial effects generally pointing to the importance of stimulus rather
than response-reward relationships. For example, in a study by Brackbill, Bravos, and Starr (1962) children were shown a picture at the beginning of each trial, made a choice of key-pressing responses, then
were presented with a light over the correct key after a delay interval.
However, no measures were taken to insure that the children observed the picture at the end of the delay interval when the reinforcing light appeared, which may well account for faster learning with
shorter delays. Even so, retention of the learned relationships was
poorer after shorter delays, which is scarcely in line with any theory
requiring greater strengthening of associations with shorter delay of
reward. Again, in a study by Hockman and Lipsitt (1961), children
were presented with a stimulus light on each trial and had to select
the response button to turn off the light, then receive information as to
correctness or incorrectness after a 0-, 10-, or 30-second delay interval.
When there were only two alternative stimuli, orange versus green
lights, corresponding to the two response alternatives, there was essentially no effect of delay upon rate of learning. When the number of
stimuli was increased to 3, a red or an orange light corresponding to
one response and a green to the other, but with no change in the response alternatives, learning was somewhat retarded by the 10- and
30-second delays. As implied by the present theory, the effects of the
same delays upon the same responses differed in accordance with the
discriminability of the stimuli and, therefore, with the difficulty of
maintaining distinctive representations of the stimuli in memory over
the delay intervals.

Perhaps of more diagnostic value with respect to alternative formu-
lations than any of the standard experiments is a recent study by Buchwald (1967), designed especially to demonstrate clearly that delay of
reward or of punishment produces effects simply according as the delay entails changes in correlated variables which modify the probabil-

ity of associative learning. In particular, Buchwald deduced from his analysis of the Thorndikian situation, in which the rewarding or punishing events are indications of right or wrong following the subject's response, that it should be possible to contrive a situation in which delay of reinforcement would actually facilitate learning.

College student subjects were given two trials on each of several lists of common English words with instructions to attempt to learn the responses which went with them. The subject was required to choose a digit as his response each time the stimulus was presented. Under an Immediate condition, the experimenter said "right" immediately after the subject's response on a Right item and "wrong" immediately after the subject's response on a Wrong item; then on trial 2 the subject attempted to give the correct response immediately upon presentation of the stimulus member of each of these items. Under the Delay condition, the experimenter said nothing following the subject's response on trial 1 but said "right" immediately after presenting the stimulus for a Right item on trial 2 and said "wrong" immediately after presenting the stimulus for a Wrong item on trial 2.

From the standpoint of Law of Effect theory, the relevant variable is delay of reward and punishment, with the Immediate condition being favorable for learning and the Delay condition involving a very large delay of reward or punishment by ordinary standards and thus being presumably exceedingly unfavorable. According to the present theory, which in application to this situation corresponds in essentials to Buchwald's interpretation, the subject's performance on trial 2 is a function of his ability to recall relationships between the stimulus member of the item and the response which he made to it on trial 1 and between the stimulus member and the rewarding or punishing outcome, if any, given by the experimenter. In the Immediate condition, the subject's response and the experimenter's indication of right or wrong occur immediately following the stimulus on trial 1, and the subject will be in a position to repeat the response if it is correct and suppress it if it is wrong on trial 2 if he remembers both of the constituent relationships. Under the Delay condition, the subject again must recall his previous response to a given stimulus when it occurs on trial 2 in order to behave appropriately, but the experimenter's indication of right or wrong is supplied at the beginning of trial 2, thus eliminating any necessity for the subject to have learned and recalled this constituent relationship. The principal results were that repetition of a trial 1 response was increased slightly for the delayed over the immediate right condition and was reduced substantially more by the delayed wrong than by the immediate wrong condition. Further, in a follow-up study with some modifications in procedure, both results were replicated, but with a substantially greater advantage for delayed right over immediate right in the second experiment.[2]

VI. SUMMARY

A review of the literature on reward in human learning reveals major inadequacies in the Law of Effect interpretation which become accentuated as experimental designs depart from classic paradigms. Although it is indeed the case that, in many everyday life situations and in many standard experiments, subjects come with experience to select responses which lead to reward over those which do not, the conclusion does not follow that there is a direct and fundamental connection between the occurrence of the reward and the establishment of a learned association between previous stimuli and responses. New types of experiments contrived to bear especially upon this issue indicate, in fact, that the associative learning process is independent of rewarding or punishing aftereffects. Further, the increasingly complex pattern of empirical relationships involving such major variables as delay and magnitude of reward is not satisfactorily interpreted by any extant theory cast in the Law of Effect framework.

The alternative theoretical framework outlined in the present paper embodies the following principal assumptions.

1. Associative learning is a function solely of conditioning by contiguity. When any two behavioral events (whether they are termed stimuli or responses is immaterial) occur in succession, there is some probability that an association between the two members will form on an all-or-none basis. The result of formation of an associative linkage is that on a later occasion the occurrence of the first event calls into memory a representation of the second.

2. Recognition performance depends solely upon this learning by contiguity.

3. If the second member of an association is a response which has occurred on the previous occasion, the overt occurrence of this response upon a later test requires not only activation of the association but also facilitative feedback, which arises as a function of anticipation of reward.

4. Modification of learned performance by rewards involves two stages. First, an association must be established between the stimulus member of a stimulus-response event and the reward. Second, upon the subsequent occurrence of the stimulus member, the representation of the reward must be brought into memory by activation of the learned association. This anticipation of reward generates facilitatory

[2] A. M. Buchwald, personal communication, 1967.

feedback. If at the same time the previous response is recalled, the effect of the feedback is to cause the recalled response to be made overtly.

5. The immediate effect of facilitatory feedback following presentation of a stimulus is to increase the probability that the associated response will be made overtly during any given interval of time, and thus on the average to reduce the reaction time.

6. In a choice situation, in which the subject must select the stimulus to which to respond from a set of two or more, the subject is assumed to scan the available stimuli and, in general, to respond overtly to the one with which the highest reward has been associated during previous learning experiences. Thus, in selective learning situations, the function of rewards may be characterized as one of stimulus amplification. Different stimuli become associated with different rewards, and the consequence is that the stimuli then carry differential weights in the determination of response, either in the same or in new situations.

This theoretical schema has received relatively direct support from an experiment designed to permit the learning of stimulus–reward associations in the absence of any opportunity for the direct strengthening of stimulus–response associations by the rewards. Further, the consideration of several major areas of research on human learning indicates that effects of major variables such as delay and magnitude of reward, as well as information value (relative to correct versus incorrect responding), can be organized and interpreted within this framework. This is not to say, however, that the theory is complete and satisfactory in all respects. In fact, it is definitely limited as presently formulated in that the task remains to develop an adequate conceptualization of motivational conditions in human learning and their relationships to rewards and punishments.

REFERENCES

Battig, W. F., & Brackett, H. R. Comparison of anticipation and recall methods in paired-associate learning. *Psychol. Rep.*, 1961, 9, 59-65.

Bilodeau, E. A., & Bilodeau, I. McD. Variation of temporal intervals among critical events in five studies of knowledge of results. *J. exp. Psychol.*, 1958, 55, 603-612.

Bower, G. H. A model for response and training variables in paired-associate learning. *Psychol. Rev.*, 1962, 69, 34-53.

Brackbill, Y., Bravos, A., & Starr, R. H. Delay improved retention of a difficult task. *J. comp. physiol. Psychol.*, 1962, 55, 947-952.

Buchwald, A. M. Effects of immediate vs. delayed outcomes in associative learning. *J. verb. Learn. verb. Behav.*, 1967, 6, 317-320.

Dulany, D. E., Jr. The place of hypotheses and intentions: An analysis of verbal control in verbal conditioning. In C. W. Eriksen (Ed.), *Behavior and awareness*. Durham, N. C.: Duke Univer. Press, 1962. Pp. 102-129.

Estes, W. K. The statistical approach to learning theory. In S. Koch (Ed.), *Psychology: A study of a science*. Vol. 2. New York: McGraw-Hill, 1959. Pp. 380-491.

Estes, W. K. Transfer of verbal discriminations based on differential reward magnitudes. *J. exp. Psychol.*, 1966, 72, 276-283.

Estes, W. K. *Outline of a theory of punishment*. Stanford, Calif.: Stanford Univer. Press, 1967. Tech. Rep. No. 123. To appear in R. M. Church and B. A. Campbell (Eds.), *Punishment and aversive behavior*. New York: Appleton, 1969, in press.

Estes, W. K., & Da Polito, F. Independent variation of information storage and retrieval processes in paired-associate learning. *J. exp. Psychol.*, 1967, 75, 18-26.

Farley, J. A., & Hokanson, J. E. The effect of informational set on acquisition in verbal conditioning. *J. verb. Learn. verb. Behav.*, 1966, 5, 14-17.

Greenspoon, J. The reinforcing effect of two spoken sounds on the frequency of two responses. *Amer. J. Psychol.*, 1955, 68, 409-416.

Hockman, C. H., & Lipstitt, L. P. Delay-of-reward gradients in discrimination learning with children for two levels of difficulty. *J. comp. physiol. Psychol.*, 1961, 54, 24-27.

Humphreys, M. S., Allen, G. A., & Estes, W. K. Learning of two-choice, differential reward problems with informational constraints on payoff combinations. *J. math. Psychol.*, 1968, 5, 260-280.

Keller, L., Cole, M., Burke, C. J., & Estes, W. K. Reward and information values of trial outcomes in paired-associate learning. *Psychol. Monogr.*, 1965, 79 (Whole No. 605).

Kintsch, W., & McCoy, D. F. Delay of informative feedback in paired-associate learning. *J. exp. Psychol.*, 1964, 68, 372-375.

Krasner, L. Studies of the conditioning of verbal behavior. *Psychol. Bull.*, 1958, 55, 148-170.

Nunnally, J. C., Duchnowski, A. J., & Parker, R. K. Association of neutral objects with rewards: Effect on verbal evaluation, reward expectancy, and selective attention. *J. Pers. soc. Psychol.*, 1965, 1, 274-278. (a)

Nunnally, J. C., Stevens, D. A., & Hall, G. F. Association of neutral objects with rewards: Effect on verbal evaluation and eye movements. *J. exp. child Psychol.*, 1965, 2, 44-57. (b)

Postman, L. Rewards and punishments in human learning. In L. Postman (Ed.), *Psychology in the making*. New York: Knopf, 1962. Pp. 331-401.

Postman, L., & Sassenrath, J. The automatic action of verbal rewards and punishments. *J. gen Psychol.*, 1961, 65, 109-136.

Saltzman, I. J. Delay of reward and human verbal learning. *J. exp. Psychol.*, 1951, 41, 437-439.

Salzinger, K. Experimental manipulation of verbal behavior: A review. *J. gen. Psychol.*, 1959, 61, 65-94.

Skinner, B. F. *The behavior of organisms*. New York: Appleton, 1938.

Spielberger, C. D. The role of awareness in verbal conditioning. In C. W. Eriksen (Ed.), *Behavior and awareness*. Durham, N. C.: Duke Univer. Press. 1962. Pp. 73-101.

Spielberger, C. D., Bernstein, I. H., & Ratliff, R. G. Information and incentive value of the reinforcing stimulus in verbal conditioning. *J. exp. Psychol.*, 1966, 71, 26-31.

Taffel, C. Anxiety and the conditioning of verbal behavior. *J. abnorm. soc. Psychol.*, 1955, 51, 496-501.

Thorndike, E. L. *Human learning*. New York: Appleton, 1931.

Thorndike, E. L. *The psychology of wants, interests, and attitudes*. New York: Appleton, 1935.

Witryol, S. L., Lowden, L. M., & Fagan, J. F. Incentive effects upon attention in children's discrimination learning. *J. exp. child Psychol.*, 1967, 5, 94-108.

CHAPTER 4

Reward and Reinforcement in Selective Learning: Considerations with Respect to a Mathematical Model of Learning[1]

KEITH N. CLAYTON

[1]The research reported here was supported, in part, by U.S. Public Health Service Grant HD 00924. The author is grateful to James Brophy, who ran the Ss of Exps. I and III, to Gary Waller, who ran the Ss of Exp. II, and to Paul Schmidt, who wrote the computer program to provide the "stat-rat" data described in the text. The final draft of this paper was prepared while the author was visiting the Department of Psychology, University of California, Berkeley.

95

I. DISTINCTION BETWEEN REWARD AND REINFORCEMENT

Most psychologists, and all parents, are acutely aware of the fact that rewards may or may not modify behavior. Another truism is that some rewards are more likely to affect behavior than others. For example, a food pellet will probably have a greater influence on the bar-pressing behavior of a hungry rat than the parent's verbal approval will have on a child's reactions toward his sibling. What is perhaps less obvious, however, is the full significance of the observation that rewards differ in their effectiveness. The observation has important implications for the discussion of the nature of reinforcement. As an illustration of the implications, suppose an experimenter states that the correct response was followed by a "reinforcer." Does "reinforcer" refer to the observable operations (e.g., dispensing a pellet of food) or to some inferred event which changes response probability? If it is the latter, to what extent does the experimenter thereby commit himself to a specific theory of reinforcement? The major point here is that the language of the reinforcement issue must be clarified so that a distinction between observable events and inferred processes is constantly apparent. In the first part of this chapter an attempt will be made to sharpen this distinction. In the second and larger part of the article, the distinction will be illustrated within the framework of a particular model of discrimination learning.

A. Definition of Reinforcement

The term "reinforcement" will be used with reference to the *consequence* of the experimental operation. More specifically, it will be assumed that if learning takes place, reinforcement has occurred. Thus, reinforcement is an event which is *inferred* from relatively durable changes in behavior (changes not due to sensory loss, drugs, etc.). The use of such terminology is familiar; it amounts to the adoption of the "empirical Law of Effect" (Spence, 1956, p. 33), although to refer to a "law" serves to confuse the primarily definitional status of the term. It should be stressed that this empirical definition of reinforcement is totally neutral with regard to precisely what has occurred when reinforcement is inferred. *Something* has to occur, it is assumed, in order for a relatively durable change in behavior to take place, but no specific hypothesis is implicated.

B. Definition of Reward

When reinforcement is defined so as to designate inferred events, it is semantically confusing to use the term additionally to signify the observed operations or procedures of the learning situation. For example, if a pellet of food is dispensed to a rat when the rat presses a bar, it would be incorrect to state that the rat was *reinforced* if the term were used to refer to the observable event of the dispensing of the food. To refer to these observed operations, in contrast to the inferred events, the term "reward" will be used in this paper.[2] Several comments are required in order to clarify the selection and recommended use of this term. First, the selection of "reward" to refer to the observed events in instrumental learning is an adoption of the common, or vulgar, meaning as distinguished from the traditional technical sense. A paraphrase of the typical dictionary definition of reward is exemplified in the phrase "something given for something done," and this is the definition taken here. A pellet of food for a bar-press is a reward. A drop of water at the end of a runway is a reward. So also are the electrical stimulation of the brain and the presentation of a light for a bar-press. Whether these observable events produce reinforcement is an empirical question.

It is important to stress that reward, so defined, is as theoretically neutral as the definition of reinforcement. Since Thorndike, reward has connoted "satisfaction" in the technical literature, and this is unfortunate, because it is too restrictive. Perhaps the intent here can best be appreciated if reward were defined as *"anything* given for something done." Note that the definition includes no reference to the motivational state of the learner. Of course, the experimenter usually selects a reward which is appropriate to the S's drive state, but to insist the term reward be applied only to those rewards known to modify a drive state is to edge too close to a theoretical position. An additional clarification gained from stripping consideration of the learner's motivational state from the definition of reward is an increased recognition that a learning trial typically terminates with several outcomes. For example, a rat trained to traverse a maze for a pellet of food is also rewarded by being removed from the maze. Within this context, the fundamental issue of the nature of reinforcement boils down to a consideration of which, if either, of these two rewards (pellet vs. removal) is responsible for, or related to, reinforcement.

Reward and reinforcement may also differ in the variety of ways they may occur. For example, rewards can differ in quantity (e.g., number of food pellets), quality (type of pellet), probability

[2]The distinction between reward and reinforcement made here for instrumental learning closely parallels the distinction recently made by Sheffield (1965) for classical conditioning.

(percentage of rewarded trials), delay of presentation, etc. Reinforcement, in contrast, might be considered an either-or event, that is, one which either occurs during a trial or does not. Thus, attempts to relate rewards and reinforcements take the form of the question: How does this particular aspect of reward affect the *probability* that reinforcement will occur? Estes and Suppes (1959, p. 145) have treated amount of reward in this manner, and as will be seen, the models of learning considered below assume that reinforcement occurs probabilistically. At any rate, the distinction may now be amplified another way: The probability of reinforcement may not necessarily be, indeed probably is not, the same as the probability of reward. For example, to return to the initial illustrations of "ineffective" rewards, reinforcement may not occur on every trial even when reward does occur on every trial. Similarly, in view of the complexity of the events terminating a trial, reinforcement may occur even when a particular reward (food pellet) is absent.[3]

On the following pages, three experiments will be described in which an attempt was made to examine the relationship between rewards and reinforcement. However, this was done within the context of a specific model of discrimination learning. Thus, the purpose of the experiments was twofold. They sought first of all to provide a test of the mathematical model; second, since the model assumes that learning, hence reinforcement, is probabilistic, an attempt was made to determine how some characteristics of reward affect the probability that reinforcement takes place. The model will first be described, and then the implications of the reward-reinforcement distinction for the model will be discussed.

II. A MARKOV MODEL FOR SIMPLE SPATIAL DISCRIMINATION

A. Assumptions of the Model

The proposed model, which has been studied by Greeno and Stei-

[3]It is probably apparent that the class of observable events which constitute reward as defined here ("anything given for something done") include the presentation of noxious and painful stimuli. Since reinforcement is inferred from a *change* in behavior, it is convenient to distinguish between *positive* reinforcement, which is inferred from a durable increase in the measured behavior, and *negative* reinforcement, inferred from a decrease. The question therefore arises: Should not the terms referring to *observable* events be sensitive to this potential difference in outcome? Terminological convenience demands an affirmative answer and a reasonable candidate for *observable* events which are expected to be related to negative reinforcement as "punishment."

ner (1964), is presented schematically in Fig. 1. Three states of the learning process are assumed: a permanent learned state, State L, and two temporary unlearned states, State E and State S. It is also assumed that on any trial the S is in one and only one of the states, and that after a trial the S moves in an all-or-none manner among the states. Since the model assumes that on each trial the S either learns (moves into State L) or does not, it will be referred to as an all-or-none model. Focusing momentarily on the two unlearned states, State E represents the temporary error state and State S represents a state in which the S makes the correct, or successful, response but is assumed not yet to have learned the discrimination. The letters associated with the arrows in the figure designate the probabilities of moving among the states after each trial. It can be seen that there are four parameters of the model, c, d, s, and q, and that there are two general classes of these four parameters. Parameters c and d represent the probabilities of learning, i.e., moving into the learned state, after a correct response and after an error, respectively. The second class of parameters includes the two parameters s and q which specify the probabilities of alternating the response given nonlearning. To aid conceptualizing the model, consider a rat which makes an error on trial n. According to the model, the rat was in State E on that trial, and after the trial the rat will move in one of three directions. He may learn the correct response, which occurs with probability d, or he may fail to learn, with probability $(1-d)$. If the rat fails to learn on trial n, he may either alter-

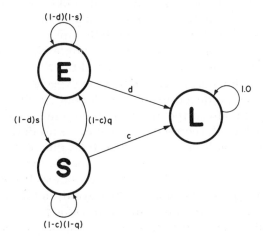

FIG. 1.   Diagram of the three states (Error, E; temporary Success, S; and Learned, L) of the model. The arrows represent transitions among the states, and the small letters refer to the probabilities of the transitions.

nate his choice (move into State S) with probability $(1-d)s$ or repeat his choice (stay in State E) with probability $(1-d)(1-s)$. Transitions from the temporary success state (S) can be similarly described, except that it should be noted that the probability of learning after a correct choice (probability c) may be different from the probability of learning after an error (probability d). A final assumption of the model is that the transition probabilities are independent of trial number, i.e., that the probabilities are constant throughout the training period. Stated another way, whether the S learns after an error is assumed to be independent of how many previous errors the S has made. This assumption is a most critical one, and will receive close inspection for the experimental data.

B. The Parameters of the Model

So far the model has been incompletely assembled, for in order to use it to describe spatial discrimination, it is desirable to relate the parameters of the model to the traditional variables of the learning situation. It is at this point that the distinction which was drawn between reinforcement and reward proves fruitful. Within the context of the model, durable changes in behavior occur when the S moves into the terminal learned state. As indicated, learning occurs after a correct response and after an error with probabilities c and d, respectively. Thus, the parameters c and d specify the probabilities that reinforcement will occur. The effect of rewards, when it is observed, therefore, must be to affect the learning process by an influence on the values of the parameters c and d. More explicitly, it will be assumed that the probabilities associated with learning following an error, d, and following a correct response, c, are dependent upon the observable consequences of these choices. For example, if the S is punished (given electric shock) following an error, d may be expected to be of a value different from that produced by no punishment. Similarly, if the subject is not permitted to correct his error, then d may be different from procedures in which the correction procedure is used. If the S makes a *correct* response, it will be assumed that the value of the parameter c (probability of learning after a correct response) will depend upon such traditional consequences as the magnitude of the reward given for the correct response, the delay of the reward, and the percentage of trials upon which the correct response is rewarded.

When the other parameters of the model, namely s and q, are considered, it is assumed that these two parameters are affected at least by the duration of the intertrial interval. The reasoning behind this assumption is as follows. When rats receive highly massed training, a dominant response tendency is to "spontaneously alternate," that is, choose on one trial the alternative not chosen on the preceding trial. It is also well established that spontaneous alternation tendencies decrease with increased intertrial interval (Dember & Fowler, 1958). Since s and q specify the probability of alternating given nonlearning, it, therefore, seems reasonable to assume that s and q are large when training is massed and relatively small when training is spaced, and further, that s and q decrease monotonically as intertrial interval increases (Clayton, 1966). There is a most important consequence of these assumptions. Since the model assumes that the parameter values are independent of trial number, this means that an unencumbered test of the model must come from an experiment in which the intertrial interval is constant throughout the training period.

C. Boundary Conditions of the Model

In addition to the assumption which restricts the application of the model to experiments involving a constant intertrial interval, it will also be assumed that the model applies to simple two-choice spatial discrimination learning. It is doubtful, for example, that the model is correct for a discrimination problem involving brightness as the relevant dimension and position as irrelevant. There are two reasons for this doubt. First, Mackintosh (1965) and others have argued that nonspatial discrimination involves two processes, one associational and the other (perhaps) attentional (cf. Kendler & Kendler, 1966). These arguments are considered persuasive. The present model is essentially a uniprocess model.[4] Second, a marked feature of the presolution performance of rats on a nonspatial task is to lapse into position-habits, and there is no clear way such tendencies could be handled by the all-or-none model without some revisions.

III. EXPERIMENTAL DATA

The major purpose of Exp. I was to provide an initial test of the

[4]On the other hand, the model may be extended by attaching another (perhaps attentional) process in front of the learning process assumed here. It could be assumed that this stage, too, is acquired all-or-none. Thus, the extended model would have two unlearned error states and two unlearned success states. Such a model would resemble House and Zeaman's (1963) One-look Model.

model within the boundary conditions specified above. For this reason a large number of rats were run under virtually identical treatment conditions, i.e., no independent variable was manipulated. The primary question was whether the model is at all feasible as a candidate for a description of T-maze learning. Thus, the critical assumption of all-or-none learning was examined in Exp. I with "normative" data based on many observations. Experiments II and III were designed to examine the relationships between the parameters of the model and observable events.

A. General Procedures

Several experimental conditions were similar throughout all three of the experiments to be reported below. For example, all Ss were trained on the same T-maze to a rigid criterion of learning. The common procedural details will be given in this section, and the specific ways that the experiments deviated from one another will be presented as each experiment is discussed separately.

All rats arrived 2–3 days prior to prehandling, and they were placed on ad lib food and water. The Ss for all experiments were experimentally naive male albino rats, 90–150 days of age. They were of the Sprague-Dawley strain, supplied by the Holtzman Rat Company (Exps. I and III) and the Dublin Laboratories (Exp. II).

Twenty-four hours prior to the beginning of prehandling the food was removed from their home cages. Prehandling lasted 10–16 days, and had as its general intent the adjustment of the animals to the daily feeding schedule, to the E, and to the food pellets which were later to be used as reward. On each day of prehandling each rat was given an individual session in which he was permitted to explore a large wooden box, given access to the reward pellets, and picked up and replaced at least five times by the E. These daily sessions lasted two minutes, and the rats were given their daily food ration 30–60 minutes after the session. The same daily feeding time prevailed throughout the experiment. A daily ration of powdered food was given in the amount required to maintain a constant body weight throughout prehandling and training. No preliminary exposure to the maze was given prior to the beginning of acquisition. The apparatus, which is more fully described elsewhere (Clayton, 1964), was an enclosed single-unit T-maze, painted flat black throughout.

On each trial the S was placed in the start box, and access to the stem of the maze was permitted when the S oriented toward the start box door. The treatment of the S depended upon which choice was made. After a correct choice, all rats were always rewarded and confined in the goal box for a fixed period of time; the amount of reward differed from experiment to experiment. After an incorrect choice, the treatment depended upon whether the correction or the noncorrection procedure was used. When the noncorrection procedure was used (Exps. I and III, and one-half the Ss in Exp. II), the goal box door was closed and the rats confined in the unbaited goal box for a fixed period of time. When the correction procedure was used (one-half the Ss in Exp. II), the goal box door was not closed, and the animal was permitted to stay in the maze until the correct response was made. Other procedural details (such as the duration of food deprivation, the intertrial interval, and the number of trials given per day) varied from experiment to experiment and will be described more fully below.

B. Experiment I – Initial Test of Model

1. Introduction

It is convenient to consider experimental tests of mathematical models as falling into three classes. First, there are tests which can be made without regard to the particular values of the parameters of the model; that is, no estimates of the parameters of the model are required before these tests can be applied. For example, a test of the assumption of all-or-none learning can be made, and the test would be the same regardless of the values of the parameters. One such test, which involves determining whether the lengths of the error runs are constant prior to the last error, formed the primary purpose of Exp. I and will be more fully explained below. Second, there are predictions which require that the parameters be estimated initially. For example, the model predicts that the error run lengths are distributed in a certain way as a function of the values of the parameters. Finally, tests can be made of additional assumptions concerning relationships between the model's parameters and traditional experimental variables. One example here is the assumption that the duration of the intertrial interval affects the values of the parameters s and q of the proposed model. As indicated above, Exps. II and III were designed to test specific additional assumptions about the effects of experimental conditions on certain parameters of the model.

2. Specific Procedures

After three days of ad lib food and water and 10 days of prehandling, 82 Ss were trained on the T-maze until 15 consecutive correct responses were made. For each S training was given in a single training session with 45 seconds intervening between the trials. The amount of reward given for a correct response was four 45-mg Noyes food tablets, and training was given under approximately 23 hours of food deprivation. Half the rats were rewarded with food for turning left, half for turning right.

3. Results and Discussion

The 82 rats required an average of 4.32 errors to reach criterion ($\sigma =$ 2.37). The test for all-or-none learning proceeded as follows. First, the error runs were identified in each S's protocol. An "error run" is defined as a series of one or more consecutive errors. If the model is correct, then the lengths of these error runs should be independent of amount of training. Stated negatively, according to the model, at any time a S begins an error run, the S has not learned; thus the length of the run should be independent of when the run begins. An alternative prediction, such as would be expected from a linear model (Bush & Mosteller, 1955), for example, is that the error run length should decrease with training. To test the all-or-none model, therefore, each protocol was examined and the first and last half of the error runs determined for each rat. For example, suppose a rat began training by making two consecutive errors followed by a correct response, then an error followed by a criterion run of 15 consecutive correct responses. In this example, the first run of two errors constitutes the first half and the final run of one error constitutes the second half of the error runs. (If an odd number of error runs were made, the intermediate run was discarded for this analysis. These intermediate runs accounted for approximately 15% of the total errors.) According to the model, the total length of the error runs in the first half should not differ except by chance from the total length of the error runs in the second half. As can be seen in the top half of Table I, 19 Ss showed an increase in error run length and 21 showed a decrease. The same number of errors in both halves of the error run sequences was made by 29 rats, and 13 had one or zero error runs. The hypothesis of no difference cannot be rejected ($X^2 < 1$, 1 df). Of the 69 rats which had two or more error runs, the mean number of errors in the first half of the runs was 2.20 as compared to an average of 2.14 errors in the last half of the error run sequences. To supplement the above X^2 with a potentially more powerful test, a t test was performed on the average difference between the first and second halves of the error runs. For each S a score was obtained by subtracting the total number of errors made in the second half from the number of errors made in the first half of the error run

TABLE I
Error Runs and Correct Response Runs Prior to Last Error

	Experiment			
	I	II	III	Combined
Error runs[a]				
Increased	19	11	13	43
Decreased	21	11	18	50
No change	29	5	4	38
One or no run	13	10	47	70
	82	37	82	201
Correct response runs[b]				
Increased	24	8	10	42
Decreased	17	10	10	37
No change	18	4	9	31
One or no run	23	15	53	91
	82	37	82	201

[a]For each S the number of errors in the first half of the error run sequence was compared with the number in the second half. The entries show the number of Ss whose error runs increased (had more errors in the second half), decreased (had fewer errors in the second), had the same number in both halves, or had less than 2 runs.
[b]The entries show the number of Ss whose correct response runs increased, etc., prior to criterion. (See text for details.)

sequences. Again, the null hypothesis that the average difference is equal to zero could not be rejected ($t = 0.40, 68\ df, p > .30$).

A similar analysis of the correct response runs was also performed. Consider the last error (or error run). If the model is correct, all correct responses which were made prior to the last error were made because the S was in State S, the temporary unlearned success state. Since the probability of leaving this state is assumed to be independent of trial number, then the average length of these correct response runs before the last error should be constant. Therefore, the first and second half of these runs were determined for each S and submitted to the same tests as were provided for the error runs. As seen in the bottom half of Table I, 24 rats showed an increase in correct response runs and 17 showed a decrease. This is not a significant departure from a 50-50 split ($X^2 = 1.20, 1\ df$). On the average 2.54 correct responses were made in the first half of these correct response runs and 3.14 were made in the second half. The t test on the mean of the difference scores revealed no significant departure from the predicted mean of zero ($t = -1.33, 58\ df, p > .10$).

In summary, therefore, several reasonably direct tests of the assumption that T-maze position discrimination is all-or-none have been made, and none led to a rejection of the assumption. There are several other predictions or derivations that can be made for the model, and a full test of the model could involve a comparison of each of these predictions with the experimental results. This is not the strategy adopted for the present report. Rather, attention will first turn to the investigation of the manner in which the error runs and the correct response runs were distributed. The importance of this question will become clear after the predictions are considered.

The model assumes that the probability of staying in State E is $(1-d)$ $(1-s)$. Thus, given that an error is made (that an error run has commenced) the predicted length of the error run (L_E) can be derived. In order for there to be exactly k errors in an error run, the S must stay in State E for $k-1$ trials and then move out of State E. The probability that the S will stay in State E for $k-1$ trials is $[(1-d)(1-s)]^{k-1}$ and the probability that the S will move out of State E is $[1-(1-d)(1-s)]$. Therefore, the probability that there will be exactly k errors in an error run, $\Pr(L_E = k)$, is

$$\Pr(L_E = k) = [1-(1-d)(1-s)][(1-d)(1-s)]^{k-1} \qquad (1)$$

The length of the correct response runs (L_c) prior to the last error is

$$\Pr(L_c = k) = [1-(1-c)(1-q)][(1-c)(1-q)]^{k-1} \qquad (2)$$

Two important points emerge from a comparison of Eqs. (1) and (2). First, both run-length variables are distributed geometrically (see Atkinson, Bower, & Crothers, 1965), and, second, the two distributions are affected by different parameters. With regard to the second point, specific hypotheses about the relationship between traditional experimental variables and the parameters of the model may be investigated by examination of these two distributions. For example, if a variable is assumed to affect the parameter d and no others, then the error runs should be affected and the correct response runs should not. There was no independent variable manipulated in Exp. I; nevertheless, the data do provide a large number of observations which permit a test of predictions that the run lengths are geometrically distributed.

In Exp. I there were 213 correct response runs and 261 error runs. As a test of the predicted distribution of the runs, parameters were estimated and the predictions compared with the observed values. There were a total of 354 errors made, 93 of which were followed by an error. As has been shown (Greeno & Steiner, 1964) the ratio of 93/354 provides a maximum likelihood estimate of $(1-d)(1-s)$. The obtained estimate (.263) produces the prediction shown on the right side of Fig. 2, which also reveals the obtained values. As can be seen, the obtained and predicted distributions are in close agreement. For the error run data, a X^2 test of goodness-of-fit produced a X^2 of 3.18, which with 3 df should occur by chance with $p > .10$.

The first indication of difficulty for the model comes from the distribution of the correct response runs. Parameter estimates obtained in a manner analogous to the estimates made for the error runs produced the predictions shown on the left side of Fig. 2. While the obtained data appear to be geometrically distributed, i.e., they are characterized as having a modal value equal to 1 and as decreasing monotonically with increased values of k, the X^2 test of goodness-of-fit reveals a significant departure from the predicted values ($X^2 = 18.14$, 5 df, $p < .01$). Thus, while the correct response run lengths appear to be geometrically distributed, as expected by the model, the precise values of the distribution were predicted poorly when parameters of the model were estimated. It should be noted that approximately one-half of the value of the goodness-of-fit X^2 comes from departures occurring for run lengths equal to 7 or greater. That is, too few lengthy correct response runs were predicted.

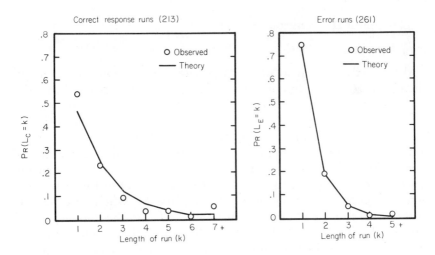

FIG. 2. Lengths of runs in Exp. I. The left side shows the obtained proportions of the correct response runs prior to the last error which were exactly k trials in length ($k = 1$, 2, . . .). The right side shows the obtained proportions of the error runs which were k trials in length. The obtained data, in circles, is compared with the theoretical values, which are connected by the lines in the figure. The numbers in parentheses at the top of the figure show the total number of runs made by the Ss.

Overall, the model has cleared two mild hurdles. First, since the run sequences appear to have remained stable, the assumption of all-or-none learning has received support. To the extent that this conclusion requires acceptance of the null hypothesis, it should be remembered that the experiment incorporated a large number of Ss to help prevent the acceptance of an untrue null hypothesis for lack of power. Confidence in this conclusion, of course, can be increased only by continued experimental support from subsequent research. Thus, tests of the all-or-none assumption will be repeated on the experimental data to be reported below. In addition, a brief comparison will be made at the end of this chapter between the predictions of this model and those of an alternative model.

The second hurdle, regarding the distributions of the run variables, was only partially cleared. While the error run lengths are most adequately predicted, the correct response run lengths were not. Whether the latter difficulty stems from the fact that the model is incorrect, or whether the parameter estimation is faulty cannot be fully assessed at this time. In any case, accepting the model for the moment as a reasonable candidate for the description of simple T-maze learning, attention now turns to the question of the relationships between some experimental variables and the parameters of the model.

C. Experiment II – Correction Procedure

1. Introduction

As argued above, in an attempt to relate the parameters of the models to standard experimental procedures, it will be assumed that the probability of learning following a correct response and following an error will be determined by the experimental consequences of these two choices. Experiment II represents an attempt to assess the assumption that the events following an error affect the probability of learning following an error. More specifically, two groups of rats were trained on the T-maze, differing only with respect to the correction procedure utilized for the error. For half the Ss, when an error was made, access to the choice area was blocked, and the animal was removed from the unbaited goal box (Noncorrection Group). For the other half of the subjects, when an error was made, access to the rest of the maze was not blocked, and the trial was not terminated until the correct response was made and rewarded (Correction Group).

The lengths of the correct response runs should be distributed identically for both groups and should conform to Eq. (2) above. The reasoning behind this is as follows. Since the two groups of rats were treated alike following a correct response, it seems reasonable to assume that the probability of learning following a correct response, probability c, is unaffected by the correction procedure. Since probability q, the probability of alternating from State S given nonlearning, is assumed to be dependent on intertrial interval, and since the intertrial interval was the same for both groups, it is further assumed that q is the same for both groups. Thus, the two parameters affecting correct response runs, c and q, are assumed to be unaffected by the correction procedure, and the correct response runs should be distributed identically for both groups.

In contrast, the lengths of the error runs may very well depend upon the correction procedure utilized. However, whether the error runs are expected to be related to the correction procedure depends upon additional assumptions. For example, since an error by a Correction Group is always corrected, it might be assumed that the probability of learning following a corrected error is the same as the probability of learning following a correct response made initially, i.e., that d for the Correction Group equals the c for both groups. (This is analogous to the equal-alpha assumption made for the linear model; Bush & Mosteller, 1955.) With regard to alternating given nonlearning, it might be assumed that the rat alternates his last response (the act of correcting). As a consequence of this assumption it would be expected that in the case of the Correction Group, the probability of making an error on trial $n + 1$ would be independent of which response was made on trial n. From these assumptions the distribution of the error run lengths, L_E, can be obtained in the same manner as found above for Eq. (1). This predicted distribution is

$$\Pr(L_E = k) = [1-(1-c)q] \, [(1-c)(q)]^{k-1} \tag{3}$$

Thus, Eq. (1) may be expected to hold for the Noncorrection Group and Eq. (3) for the Correction Group. Notice that whether and how the predictions differ depends on the precise values of the parameters. For example, if $c = d$ and $s = q = \frac{1}{2}$, then the two distributions are identical, i.e., the prediction from Eq. (1) is the same as from Eq. (3).

2. Specific Procedures

After three days of ad lib food and water and 16 days of prehandling, 58 Dublin rats were trained on the T-maze. The additional prehandling (16 days vs. the 10 in Exp. I) was necessary because these rats seemed to be much less docile than those provided by Holtzman. For each S one trial was given at the same hour of each day; thus, the intertrial interval was 24 hours. Since the food was given approximately one hour after the day's trials, training was given under approximately 23 hours of food deprivation. The amount of reward given for a correct response was four 94-mg Noyes food tablets. Rats were discarded if they failed to respond (make a choice) within three minutes after the onset of the trial for four consecutive trials, or for three consecutive failures to eat the reward pellets within 60 seconds following a correct choice. This criterion for discarding is essentially the same as used in the other two experiments; however, with the Dublin rats it resulted in a substantial loss of experimental subjects. Half of the Ss were trained with the correction procedure and the other half with the non-correction procedure, and within each group approximately half of the animals were trained with the left response rewarded, etc. The criterion of learning was 12 consecutive correct responses.

3. Results and Discussion

Of the original 58 rats, 21 were discarded because they failed to respond or failed to eat, leaving a total of 19 rats in the Correction Group and 18 in the Noncorrection Group.

The Correction Group required an average of 8.00 errors[5] to reach criterion as compared with 6.11 errors for the Noncorrection Group. For the Correction Group, the average trial number of the last error was 12.84 vs. 11.22 for the Noncorrection Group. While the Noncorrection Group is superior on both measures, neither difference is significant (for both $t < 1$, 35 df). Thus, the primary purpose of the experiment is somewhat vitiated since it was expected that the correction procedure manipulation would have an effect on learning rate.[6]

The tests of the assumption of all-or-none learning proceeded as described for the data of Exp. I. Turning first to the error run data, Table I shows the number of Ss whose error runs increased, decreased, etc., prior to criterion. On the average 3.70 errors were made in the first half of the error run sequences and 4.41 in the second half. Neither the X^2 test on the frequencies nor the t test on the means yielded a significant departure from the expectation of the model ($X^2 < 1$, 1 df; $t = -.79$, 26 df). Similar results were obtained from examination of the correct response run sequences. On the average 3.91 correct responses were made in the first half of the correct response runs,

[5]Comparing correction procedures requires an explicit definition of a correct response and an error. In this experiment a "choice" was defined as the initial choice of the S during the trial. Thus, while a Correction S *could* enter the unbaited goal box several times during a trial (this rarely happened), only the initial error is considered a choice in the present discussion.

[6]For a review of the literature on the effect of correction procedure on discrimination learning see Towart and Boe (1965).

and 3.50 were made in the second half. Again, neither the X^2 test on the frequencies (see Table I) nor the t test revealed a significant departure from the model's predictions ($X^2 < 1$, 1 df; $t = .49$, 21 df).

The distributions of the run variables are shown in Fig. 3. The expectation that the correction procedure would not affect the lengths of the correct response runs seems to have been supported as seen in the comparison given in the left side of Fig. 3. The two observed distributions do not differ significantly ($X^2 < 1$, 5 df). Since the observed distributions of correct response runs for the two groups did not differ, and since no difference was expected, their data were combined and tested against the predicted geometric distribution in the same manner as was followed in Exp. I. It will be recalled that the correct response run distribution in Exp. I differed significantly from that predicted since too few lengthy runs were predicted for these data. In contrast, for Exp. II the predictions (see Fig. 3) did not differ from the observed pooled data ($X^2 = 3.37$, 4 df).

The distributions of the error runs are shown on the right side of Fig. 3. No significant difference was detected between the observed error run distributions ($X^2 = 7.46$, 5 df, $p > .10$) or, as in Exp. I, between the observed and the predicted geometric distributions, which are also shown in Fig. 3. (For the Noncorrection Group, $X^2 = 5.53$, 4 df, $p > .10$; for the Correction Group, $X^2 = 7.90$, 4 df, $.05 < p < .10$.)

In summary, no significant differences were observed between the performance of rats which were permitted to correct an error and the

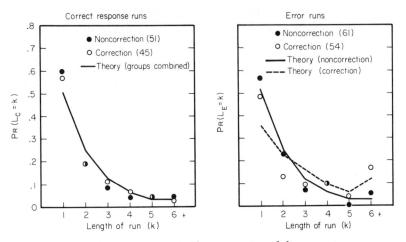

FIG. 3. Lengths of runs in Exp. II. The proportion of the correct response runs which were exactly k trials in length is given for both groups on the left side of the figure. The error run lengths are given for both groups on the right side. The numbers in parentheses are the total number of runs involved.

performance of rats which were not permitted to correct. As was illustrated above, in conjunction with the derivation of Eq. (3), there exist
reasonable combinations of error-state parameters (d and s) which
produce essentially equivalent behavior by corrected and noncor-
rected animals. No exhaustive study of various parameter combinations nor any attempt to choose among the alternatives will be considered here, however. Finally, while the model was ambiguous
concerning whether the error runs would differ from one another, it
was unambiguous concerning the correct response runs and the shape
of the run distributions. The data were compatible with these predictions and with the all-or-none assumption of no learning prior to the
last error. Attention now turns to a variable expected to affect the probability of learning following a correct response.

D. Experiment III – Magnitude of Reward

1. Introduction

It is well established that simple position discrimination learning
performance is directly related to the magnitude of reward given for
the correct response (Clayton, 1964; Waller, 1968). Experiment III
was performed to test the hypothesis that the effect of reward magnitude is to facilitate learning following a correct response. More explicitly, it is assumed that the parameter c, the probability of learning following a correct response, depends upon the reward magnitude given
for the correct response in such a manner that c is larger for a large
reward magnitude than for a small amount. Since the correct response
runs, prior to the last error, depend on the parameter c, it was anticipated that the correct response run lengths would be a function of
reward magnitude, being shorter under the condition of larger reward
magnitude.[7] Two groups of rats were run in the T-maze, one receiving
one 45-mg pellet for the correct response and the other receiving nine

---

[7]The reason that the correct-response run lengths should be shorter on the average for
the larger reward magnitude than for the smaller magnitude is explained as follows. In
general, if a variable X is distributed geometrically as

$$\Pr(X = k) = g(1 - g)^{k-1}$$

it has been established (see Atkinson et al., 1965, p. 57) that the expected value $E(X)$
of the variable is $E(X) = 1/g$.

For the particular random variable considered here distributed as given in Eq. (2),
the average, or expected value, becomes by substitution

$$E(L_c) = 1/[1 - (1 - c)(1 - q)]$$

Since c is expected to increase with increased reward magnitude, the denominator of
the ratio should increase with increased reward magnitude, and therefore the average
correct response run length should be smaller for the larger reward amount.

pellets for the correct response. Since the two groups were treated alike following an error, it was assumed that the parameters associated with transitions from the error state would be unaffected. Therefore, the expectation was that the error run lengths would be independent of reward magnitude. The experimental data also provide a third test of the all-or-none assumption of the model.

2. Specific Procedures

After three days of ad lib feeding and 10 days of prehandling, during each of which all Ss were exposed to five 45-mg pellets, the rats were given two trials daily on the T-maze separated by 12 hours. One-half the daily ration was given approximately an hour after each trial; therefore, the rats were under approximately 11 hours of food deprivation at the time of each trial. There were two separate replications of the experiment, and this variable, as well as the correct position variable, was manipulated factorially to the reward magnitude variable. A total of 82 rats was run, 41 in each reward magnitude group, until an individual criterion of 15 consecutive correct responses was attained.

3. Results and Discussion

The error curves for the two groups of rats are shown in Fig. 4, in

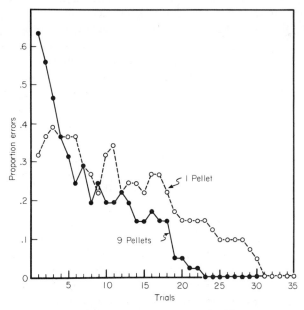

FIG. 4.   The error curves of the two groups in Exp. III. The proportion of Ss making an error is given for each of the first 35 trials of the experiment.

which it is seen that the nine-pellet rats, despite having started with a slightly higher probability of making an error, learned the correct response more rapidly than did the one-pellet rats. The average trial number of the last error was 6.02 for the nine-pellet group, as compared with 12.62 for the one-pellet group. This is a significant difference by analysis of variance ($F = 11.76$, $df = 1/72$, $p < .001$). On the average the nine-pellet group required 5.02 errors to reach criterion vs. 6.68 for the one-pellet group. In contrast to the previous research cited above, these two means, while in the expected direction, did not differ significantly ($F = 1.78$, $df = 1/72$). The last finding is apparently due to the fact that the one-pellet animals had a higher probability of making the correct response on the first trial than did the nine-pellet animals. On the first trial of training 68% of the one-pellet animals chose the correct responses vs. 37% for the nine-pellet rats ($X^2 = 8.26$, 1 df, $p < .005$). The cause of this discrepancy, which is rarely observed, is not fully understood. In any case, the observation is incidental to the primary purpose of the study. In terms of the model, it merely means that a significantly lower percent of the one-pellet animals began in the temporary error state than did the animals in the nine-pellet condition.

Tests of the assumption of all-or-none learning based on the number of Ss which showed an increase or decrease in their error run and correct response run lengths (see Table I) again provided no evidence of a significant tendency for the run lengths to change prior to criterion (in both cases $X^2 < 1$, 1 df). Similarly, all supplemental t tests showed no significant departure from the expectation that the run lengths were constant during presolution. For the one-pellet group 4.42 errors were made in the first half of the error run sequences and 4.29 in the second half ($t = .13$, 23 df), and 4.00 correct responses were made in the first half of the correct response sequences vs. 3.43 in the second half ($t = .70$, 22 df). For the nine-pellet animals 4.00 errors were made in the first half of the error run sequences vs. 4.45 in the second ($t = -.28$, 10 df), and 1.17 correct responses were made in the first half of the correct response run sequence vs. 2.00 in the second half ($t = -.80$, 5 df).

The distributions of the correct response run lengths are plotted in Fig. 5. As expected, the correct response runs were generally shorter for the nine-pellet group than for the one-pellet group, and the two distributions are significantly different ($X^2 = 8.49$, 2 df, $p < .025$).

In contrast to expectations, there is some support for the notion that the error run lengths were affected by the magnitude of reward (see

Fig. 5). The test on the error run distributions produced a X^2 value of 8.16, which with 4 df is significant at the .09 level.[8]

IV. GENERAL DISCUSSION AND CONCLUSIONS

The answers to two major questions have been sought in the present chapter: (1) Is the assumption of all-or-none learning applicable to simple spatial discrimination by the rat? (2) Has the distinction between reward and reinforcement made in the present chapter aided in an attempt to relate the parameters of an all-or-none model to traditional experimental variables? To the first of these questions, the tests provided by the data of three separate experiments have failed to reject the assumption of all-or-none learning. The principal flaw of this experimental strategy, as has been discussed by Grant (1962) and

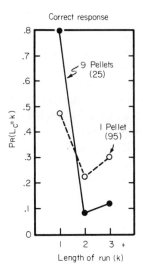
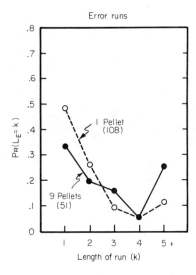

FIG. 5.   Length of runs in Exp. III. The proportion of correct response runs that were k trials in length is given on the left side for both groups. The proportions of error runs of length k is presented on the right. The numbers in parentheses are the total number of runs made.

[8]Each of the four observed run distributions was also tested separately against the predicted geometric distribution in the same manner as in Exp. I. For the correct response runs the X^2 values were 1.54 and 2.83 for the one- and nine-pellet groups, respectively (1 df, $p > .05$). For the error runs the X^2 values were 6.02 and 3.38, respectively (3 df, $p > .10$).

Binder (1963; 1964), is that the null hypothesis may be false, but the experimental tests lack power or the number of Ss providing the test may be too small. To further aid in the assessment of the model, therefore, two additional pieces of information will be considered. First, the data concerning the stability of the run lengths were combined across all three experiments. These data, from a total of 201 rats, are presented in the last column of Table I. The conclusion is the same. Of the 130 rats which had two or more error runs, 50 had fewer errors in the second half of their error run sequences than in the first half, as compared to 43 rats which showed an increase in the number of errors ($X^2 = .53$, 1 df). Similarly, the assumption that the correct response runs were constant prior to the last error cannot be rejected from the data combined across all three experiments ($X^2 = .32$, 1 df).

A. The Two-Operator Linear Model

The second set of supplementary data comes from an attempt to determine the prediction of an alternative model. In general, the strategy of comparing two models is superior to testing a single model in isolation (Sternberg, 1963). Also, support for a model should perhaps more properly come from a demonstration that its predictions are superior to that of an alternative model. However, a complete comparison of the models which may be considered as candidates for the description of T-maze learning would require more space than is available in this paper. Such a comparison will be a subject of a separate report. Nevertheless, one brief comparison of the prediction of the present all-or-none model with that of the two-operator linear model (Bush & Mosteller, 1955) will be considered. One purpose of the comparison is to determine whether the statistical analyses utilized in the present chapter are sufficiently powerful to reject the assumption of all-or-none learning when they are applied to data generated from a model that does not assume all-or-none learning.

Briefly, the version of the linear model considered here assumes that the probability of an error on trial n, q_n, is a linear function of the error probability on the preceding trial. It is also assumed that the change in error probability depends on the response made on the trial. More precisely, the model assumes

$$q_{n+1} = \begin{cases} \alpha_1 q_n & \text{if correct response on trial } n \\ \alpha_2 q_n & \text{if error on trial } n \end{cases} \tag{4}$$

where the values of α_1 and α_2 are independent of trial number and are in the unit interval (i.e., $0 \leq \alpha_i \leq 1, i = 1,2$). Unfortunately, most quantitative predictions of the model are difficult, if not impossible to determine precisely. For example, the expression for the error run lengths is not known for the linear model although one might expect that the runs should decrease with training because, according to the linear model in contrast to the all-or-none model, substantial learning can occur between adjacent errors. Nevertheless, predictions for the model can be generated by simulating it. This is done by running artificial Ss which abide by the rules (assumptions) of the model (Atkinson et al., 1965; Bush & Mosteller, 1955). For example, suppose the first trial error probability were ½ and α_1 equaled 0.9. A choice would be determined randomly for an artificial S ("stat-rat"), and if the S made a correct response on trial one, the new probability of an error would be calculated as ½ (.9) = .45; the second trial choice would again be determined with the new probability, etc., until the criterion of learning was attained for that S.

It will be recalled that the primary purpose for considering this model is to assess the adequacy of the statistical analyses performed on the data of the experiments reported here. For this purpose the following steps were taken. The data from the 41 rats in the nine-pellet group of Exp. III were used to estimate the three parameters of the two-operator linear model.[9] Then, 41 "stat-rats" were run. The individual protocols of these artificial Ss were then subjected to the same analyses as were performed on the data from the real rats of the present chapter. Of the 41 "stat-rats" only 5 had fewer errors in the first half of their error run sequences than in the second half. A decrease in the error run lengths was seen in 18 rats, 14 showed no change, and 4 rats had less than two error runs. The X^2 test on these frequencies permitted rejection of the null hypothesis of no difference between the two halves ($X^2 = 7.35$, 1 df, $p < .01$). On the average, 3.43 errors were made in the first half of the error run sequences vs. 1.84 in the second half. The t test permitted rejection of the null hypothesis that the mean difference between the two halves was equal to zero ($t = 13.25$, 36 df, $p < .0005$). It is concluded, therefore, that since the statistical analyses led to the rejection of all-or-none learning when it

---

[9]The procedures used to estimate the three parameters followed those recommended by Bush and Mosteller (1955, pp. 241-249). This involves using the mean error-to-criterion data and the mean number of errors before the first success. The latter average was equal to 2.51 for the 41 rats in the nine-pellet group. The parameter estimates obtained for the "stat-rat" run were 0.80 for α_1, 1.00 for α_2, and the observed value of .63 for the probability of an error on trial 1.

was applied to data conforming to a model which assumed incremental learning, the argument that the present support for all-or-none learning stems from the utilization of statistical analysis lacking power is severely countered.

B. Reward, Reinforcement, and Parameters of the All-or-None Model

This chapter began with a distinction between reward and reinforcement. As defined here, rewards are observable and synonymous with numerous traditional experimental variables, e.g., amount of food in the positive goal box. Reinforcement is inferred from durable changes in behavior and was therefore assumed to be synonymous with a model's parameters which represent the probabilities that the learner will move to the learned state from the unlearned states. In addition to yielding support for the assumption that spatial discrimination learning occurs in an all-or-none fashion, the results of the present experiments give support for certain assumptions about how rewards affect reinforcement. More specifically, the following results were obtained. First of all, the correct response runs were found to be unaffected by events following an error (Exp. II) and clearly affected by events following a correct response (Exp. III). These results are interpreted to mean that the events following (rewards given for) a correct response and only these events affect the probability of learning (reinforcement) following a correct response.[10]

While several additional predictions can be derived for the all-or-none model (e.g., the distribution of the errors-to-criterion), the only one considered in this paper is that the run lengths are geometrically distributed. None of the five observed error-run-length distributions differed significantly from this expectation. The single difficulty observed from an examination of the correct response run lengths is that the model predicted too few lengthy correct response runs. This deviation is observed in Exp. I but not in Exps. II and III.

It is difficult to find a general conclusion superior to the following quote from Atkinson *et al.* (1965, p. 73): "Establishing the validity and

---

[10]There is a slight ambiguity in this interpretation of the correct response run data. Since the correct response run lengths depend on q as well as c, it is possible that the effect of reward is on q, the probability of alternating given nonlearning, rather than on c, the probability of learning following a correct response. The latter interpretation, i.e., that reward magnitude is affecting c, is preferred because, as noted above, it is clearly established that alternation tendencies depend upon intertrial interval, which was independent of the reward magnitude in this experiment. Nevertheless, further research may have to be performed to disentangle completely these alternative explanations.

scope of a theoretical model is a continuing scientific task that goes through many stages before the model is thoroughly discredited or replaced by a new one." In this context, this chapter should be considered a progress report on the attempt to apply the all-or-none model to simple spatial discrimination learning. Thus far, this appealingly simple model has proved to be serviceable.

REFERENCES

Atkinson, R. E., Bower, G. H., & Crothers, E. J. *An introduction to mathematical learning theory*. New York: Wiley, 1965.

Binder, A. Further considerations on testing the null hypothesis and the strategy and tactics of investigating theoretical models. *Psychol. Rev.*, 1963, 70, 107-115.

Binder, A. Statistical theory. *Annu. Rev. Psychol.*, 1964, 15, 277-310.

Bush, R. R., & Mosteller, F. *Stochastic models for learning*. New York: Wiley, 1955.

Clayton, K. N. T-maze choice learning as a joint function of the reward magnitude for the alternatives. *J. comp. physiol. Psychol.*, 1964, 58, 333-338.

Clayton, K. N. T-maze acquisition and reversal as a function of intertrial interval. *J. comp. physiol. Psychol.*, 1966, 62, 409-414.

Dember, W. M., & Fowler, H. Spontaneous alternation behavior. *Psychol. Bull.*, 1958, 55, 412-428.

Estes, W. K., & Suppes, P. Foundation of linear models. In R. R. Bush and W. K. Estes (Eds.), *Studies in mathematical learning theory*. Stanford, Calif.: Stanford Univer. Press, 1959. Pp. 137-179.

Grant, D. A. Testing the null hypothesis and the strategy and tactics of investigating theoretical models. *Psychol. Rev.*, 1962, 69, 54-61.

Greeno, J. G., & Steiner, T. E. Markovian processes with identifiable states: General considerations and applications to all-or-none learning. *Psychometrika*, 1964, 29, 309-333.

House, Betty J., & Zeaman, D. Miniature experiments in the discrimination learning of retardates. In L. P. Lipsitt and C. C. Spiker (Eds.), *Advances in child development and behavior*. Vol. 1. New York: Academic Press, 1963. Pp. 313-374.

Kendler, H. H., & Kendler, T. S. Selective attention *vs.* mediation: Some comments on Mackintosh's analysis of two stage models of discrimination learning. *Psychol. Bull.*, 1966, 66, 282-288.

Mackintosh, N. J. Selective attention in animal discrimination learning. *Psychol. Bull.*, 1965, 64, 124-150.

Sheffield, F. D. Relation between classical conditioning and instrumental learning. In W. F. Prokasy (Ed.), *Classical conditioning: A symposium*. New York: Appleton, 1965. Pp. 302-322.

Spence, K. W. *Behavior theory and conditioning*. New Haven: Yale Univer. Press, 1956.

Sternberg, S. Stochastic learning theory. In R. D. Luce, R. R. Bush, & E. Galanter (Eds.), *Handbook of mathematical psychology*. Vol. II. New York: Wiley, 1963. Pp. 1-120.

Towart, Eileen M., & Boe, E. E. Comparison of the correction and rerun noncorrection methods in maze learning. *Psychol. Rep.*, 1965, 16, 407-415.

Waller, T. G. Effects of magnitude of reward in spatial and brightness discrimination tasks. *J. comp. physiol. Psychol.*, 1968, 66, 122-127.

CHAPTER 5

On Some Boundary Conditions of Contrast[1]

DAVID PREMACK

Of the four main classes of events which modulate the effectiveness of an occurrence as a reinforcer, one is more indirect than the others and would benefit from a clarification of its boundary conditions. Contrast (Skinner, 1938) is the name given to this case in the operant literature, although there are abundant synonyms in the other dialects of psychology (e.g., "elation," Crespi, 1942), beginning with "positive induction," the term Pavlov (1927) used in introducing the phenomenon. The standard contrast procedure is straightforward: a subject is alternately presented two stimuli S_1 and S_2, each of which is associated with a rate of reinforcement. The rate of reinforcement is lowered in S_1; an increase in responding is observed in S_2, but no increase in reinforcement accompanies this increased responding. Since no

[1] This paper was presented as an invited research address at the WPA meetings, San Diego, 1968. Portions of the research reported here were supported by NIH Grant MH-05798. I am indebted to Mary Morgan for her careful collection of the data, and to my colleagues D. Messick and E. Lovejoy for many lively discussions on topics to which this paper relates.

objective change is made in S_2, the effect is indirect, attributable to the direct change made in S_1.

The indirection of this case can be appreciated by comparing it with the three other principal determinants of reinforcement. First, the efficacy of a stimulus as a reinforcer varies with the probability the subject will respond to the stimulus (Premack, 1959). Second, it varies with the probability that the world will provide the stimulus. Third, since reinforcement involves a relation, the effectiveness can be made to vary, not by changing the reinforcing event, but by the choice of base events – the events that are to be reinforced (Premack, 1963; Schaeffer, 1965). This relationship is shown in Fig. 1. On the abscissa are ranked the responses of a subject according to their probability of occurrence in any interval of time; the ordinate shows the probability of occurrence which these responses attain as the result of reinforcement; and the parameter is the probability of the event that is to act as the reinforcer. If the probability of occurrence of, say, drinking is raised from .2 to .8, as shown in the graph, two consequences will be observable. First, there will be an increase in the magnitude of the increment which drinking will be capable of producing in any one response (shown by an increase along the vertical). Second, there will

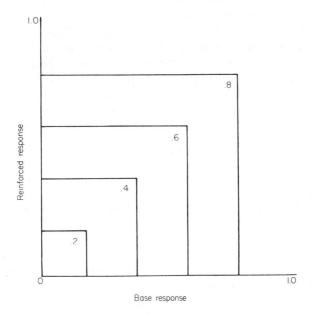

FIG. 1. Hypothetical curves showing the joint effects of the probability of the base response and contingent response on the reinforcement outcome.

be an increase in the number of responses which drinking will be capable of reinforcing (shown by an increase along the horizontal).

There are three things we should like to understand about contrast. First, the boundary conditions: Will any two cases of reinforcement interact, or are there limits in kind or time beyond which two experiences will not affect one another? Serious methodological problems would seem to ensue if there were no limitations, and yet, as we will see, the limits appear to be surprisingly broad. Second, two hypotheses as to the necessary and sufficient conditions for contrast have been proposed by Reynolds (1961a; 1961b) and Terrace (1966a), respectively; we will evaluate these hypotheses and propose an alternative. Third, there are three mechanisms which individually or in concert could be the basis of contrast; presently we cannot provide the evidence that would make a judgment among them possible, but we can show how this judgment can be made in principle.

I. BOUNDARY CONDITIONS

We might borrow Lewin's life space—the usual large, irregular, childlike circle—to represent the total experience of a subject. Insert two dots to represent two cases of reinforcement, and then inquire what the two dots must have in common in order that direct changes in one produce indirect changes in the other. The number of dimensions on which the dots could be related is exceedingly large, and very few of them have been tested. Of reinforcement's many parameters, only rate has been systematically used to produce contrast. A number of implications of isohedonic contours could be profitably tested in this context. But rather than succumb to an interminable list, we will bypass the molecular possibilities and move to a level where the chunks are larger. We are dealing with reinforcement, i.e., with a base or instrumental event, on the one hand, and a contingent event, on the other.

Will contrast occur when the instrumental events associated with S_1 and S_2 are *not* identical? More interesting, will it occur when the reinforcing events associated with S_1 and S_2 are *not* identical? In the existing data on contrast, both pairs of events are identical. Are these restrictions necessary, or will contrast occur under conditions weaker than that of identity? A third factor is time; we are concerned with successive experiences and can therefore ask within what limits in time one experience will affect another. In the existing data, the two experiences—the S_1 and S_2 components of the schedule—are contiguous. But this may be an unnecessary restriction, and contrast may occur under weaker conditions.

II. DIFFERENT INSTRUMENTAL EVENTS

In the afternoon, three thirsty rats (23 hours of water deprivation; free food) were trained to bar-press for the opportunity to drink milk. Approximately 16 hours later in a different test box the same rats were trained to run in an activity wheel for the opportunity to drink milk. The schedule in the morning sessions was a simple fixed ratio (FR). The rat was required to maintain a predetermined minimum running speed for at least 10 seconds (FR 10) for each reinforcement, and this schedule was not changed at any time. In the afternoon the schedule was the multiple schedule used to produce contrast, and it was changed several times as the paradigm requires. First, a base rate was established for multiple VI-20 VI-90, next the schedule was changed to multiple VI-90 VI-90, and finally the original conditions were reinstated.

In looking at the total procedure, two contrast designs emerge. One can be seen by considering the afternoon sessions alone, but the other, which is of greater interest, requires that we look at the afternoon and morning sessions together. By doing this, we notice that the two kinds of sessions may be seen as the two components in a larger or exterior contrast design: the morning sessions represent S_2, the component which is never changed, and the afternoon sessions S_1, the component in which reinforcement is reduced at step two. What is of special interest about the exterior contrast design is that it differs from the standard design in exactly the two particulars which concern us here. First, the instrumental events are not identical (bar-press vs. running), and second, the components are not temporally adjacent but were separated by about 16 hours.

Consider first the results obtained in the interior contrast design, the design embedded in the afternoon sessions. Despite the routine character of the afternoon procedures, the results obtained in those sessions were atypical. The results are shown in the upper portion of each of the graphs in Fig. 2. The three panels show the outcome for the three steps of the procedure in terms of the rate of responding in each of the two components. At step two, shown in the middle panel, contrast would require an increase in responding in S_2 concurrent with a decrease in S_1. But it may be seen that this result was not ob-

124 David Premack

tained in any of the three subjects. Instead, in one subject the change in reinforcement at step two produced a decrement in both components of the schedule. Conversely, in the other two subjects the change in reinforcement at step two produced an increased responding in both components of the schedule, which persisted after the original schedule was restored at step three. These inconsistent changes, incremental in two subjects and decremental in the third, suggest a failure in discrimination. The animals did not respond differentially to the bright steady light of S_1 and the dim blinking light of S_2.

The results for the morning sessions are shown in the lower portion

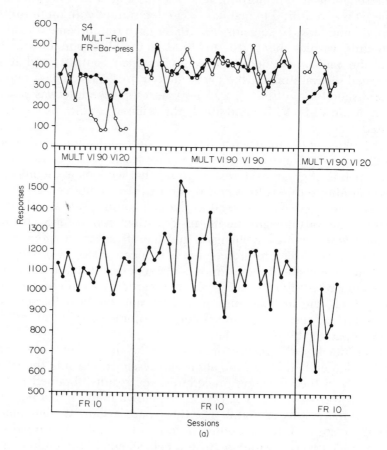

FIG. 2. The upper half of each graph shows the results for the multiple schedule of the afternoon sessions, the lower half the results for the FR schedule of the morning sessions. The three panels correspond to the three steps of the afternoon procedure; the morning procedure was constant. Each graph (a–c) is for an individual subject.

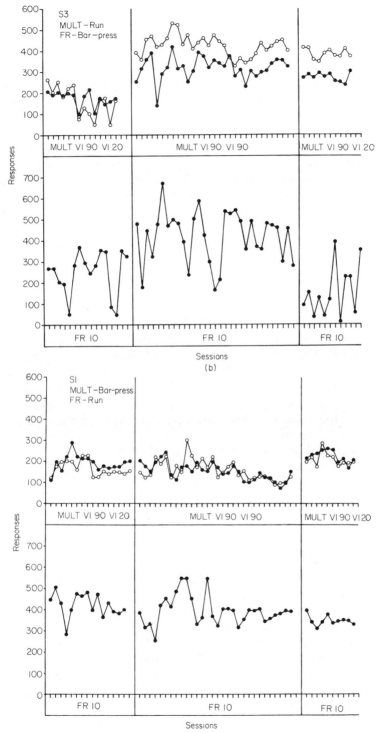

Responses

S3
MULT – Run
FR – Bar – press

MULT VI 90 VI 20   MULT VI 90 VI 90   MULT VI 90 VI 20

FR 10   FR 10   FR 10

Sessions

(b)

Responses

SI
MULT – Bar-press
FR – Run

MULT VI 90 VI 20   MULT VI 90 VI 90   MULT VI 90 VI 20

FR 10   FR 10   FR 10

Sessions

(c)

of the graphs in Fig. 2. There, too, the results are divided into three panels, corresponding to the three steps of the afternoon procedure, since the morning procedure was constant. Marked contrast effects were shown by two of the subjects. That is, two subjects showed an increased responding in the morning sessions (shown in the middle panel) at a time when reinforcement was reduced in the afternoon sessions. Subsequently, when reinforcement was restored in the afternoon sessions, they showed a decrease in responding in the morning sessions. The subjects which showed these effects were the same two that showed incremental changes at step two in the afternoon sessions. For both of them, the instrumental assignment was the same — running in the afternoon and bar-pressing in the morning. The rat that showed decremental effects in the afternoon sessions showed no (or only suggestive) morning contrast effects; for this animal the instrumental assignment was the reverse of that for the other two rats.

What events mediated the morning contrast effects? Mediation could have taken place at the level of the discriminative stimuli, since the dim blinking light that identified the S_2 component in the afternoon sessions was present at all times in the morning sessions. But this is unlikely since the atypical afternoon results suggest nothing so much as weak stimulus control, a failure by the rat to have discriminated S_1 from S_2. A more likely mediator is the common reinforcer milk which was used in both afternoon and morning sessions. Milk was used rather than water to cover the possibility that any contrast effects with water might be attenuated by the use of water in home cage drinking (though whether "attenuation" of this kind actually takes place is unknown).

III. DIFFERENT REINFORCERS

In any interval of time, a normal subject confronted with a set of alternatives will be more likely to engage in some than in others. A common measure viz., duration, can be applied to the set despite the diversity of the members, and this measure can be used to estimate response probability. We assume that any more probable alternative will reinforce any less probable one, and that the reinforcement prediction can be made with no knowledge other than that of the numbers that identify the position of the alternatives on the probability scale. Since this general view assumes that stimulus and response properties are irrelevant to the mechanism of reinforcement, it is not unreasonable to anticipate that contrast will not require an identity in the contingent events of the two components.

The two reinforcers we used are running and drinking. Although we cannot assign a number to their similarity (but see the bar-press case in the next section for a similarity assessment procedure), they would seem to overlap little, certainly far less than, for example, drinking and eating. Thirsty rats were trained on a standard multiple VI schedule. The test apparatus was an activity wheel equipped with two retractable bars and a retractable drinkometer. In one component of the schedule the rat bar-pressed for the opportunity to run in an activity wheel, and in the other component, for the opportunity to drink water. Every three minutes a different bar was presented along with a different stimulus condition. On a VI-30 schedule, operation of the left bar produced the opportunity to run for three seconds, while operation of the right bar produced the opportunity to drink for three seconds. The same schedule was used in both components as a convenience and not for theoretical reasons.

The classic three-step contrast paradigm was used along with several variations. First, the animals were stabilized on the multiple schedule. Second, bar-press to run was subjected to an extinction procedure in two rats and to time out in two other rats. That is, either bar-pressing no longer released the brake on the wheel, or the bar was simply not introduced. Running was thus equally precluded in both cases, though in one case the rat could bar-press while in the other it could not. No changes were made in the bar-press to drink component. Third and last, the original conditions were reinstated.

The main results are shown in the four panels of Fig. 3. Three of four rats showed clear contrast effects, two of them immediately. That is, coincident with the restriction on the opportunity to run at step two there was a notable increase in the frequency of bar-pressing to drink. The increase was substantial in both rats in the extinction condition, but was weaker when the restriction on running was produced by removing the bar. Some within session information is shown in Fig. 4. Response rates are shown for each of the five drink components which occurred in each session averaged over the last three sessions of step one (before the change was made) and over the last three sessions of step two, when the contrast effect was stable. The contrast effect was not confined to the early components of the session but was seen throughout the session.

At step three, when the original conditions are restored, we expect the increment in S_2 to subside, which is the typical outcome. But in

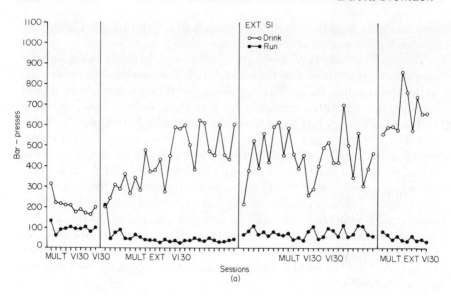

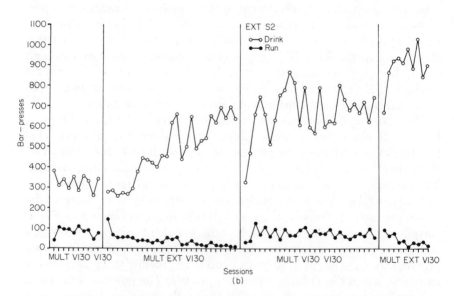

FIG. 3. Bar-presses per session for the opportunity to drink in one component of the multiple schedule and for the opportunity to run in the other component are shown as a function of sessions. The four panels show two cycles of a standard contrast design. Each graph (a–d) is for an individual subject. For Ext S_1 and S_2 the bar-press to run component was extinguished; for To S_1 and S_2 the bar was removed from the test box.

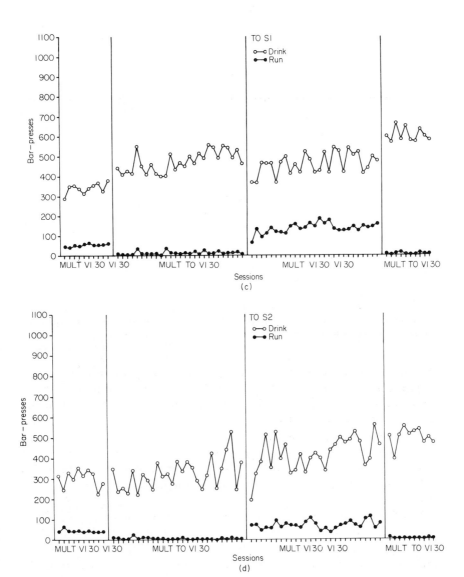

Sessions
(c)

Sessions
(d)

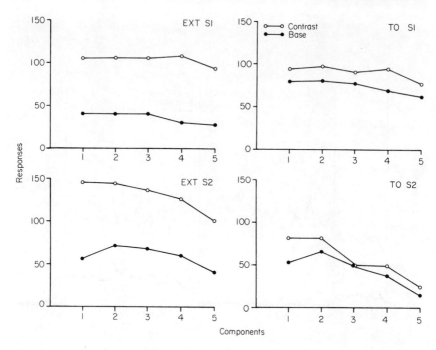

FIG. 4.   The two curves show the rate of bar-pressing to drink in each of the five-drink components of the multiple schedule before and during contrast. Each quadrant represents an individual subject.

the present data there was no decrement at step three, not even a suggestion of a return to the base value. Despite restoration of the opportunity to run, all animals continued to bar-press to drink at the augmented level originally associated with a restriction on running. It is reasonable to anticipate some residual in the present data, since in the conventional contrast design responding in S_2 generally does not return fully to the base value of step one. But we know of no previous data which prepare the way for the complete hysteresis of the present data.

The fourth panel in Fig. 3 shows the results of a second cycle of the contrast design. The same three animals which showed increased bar-pressing to drink on the first cycle moved to a still higher level of bar-pressing to drink when running was restricted for a second time. In addition, the animal that failed to show a contrast effect on the first cycle also failed to show a contrast effect on the second cycle. Whether the increment of the second cycle will be totally preserved like that of the first cycle, or whether the restoration of running will lead to some decrement in S_2 cannot be determined at this time. Further testing is needed to determine the number of cycles that can be run before the effect is asymptotic.[2]

If, as appears to be the case, reinforcers do not bound the contrast effect, it becomes important to determine what does. It is methodologically intolerable that every reinforcement experience should affect every other one. But is this conclusion actually supported by the present experiment? It would seem possible to argue that the present results are a special case, dependent upon the use of essentially identical instrumental events — right and left bar — in the two components, and that the results would not be obtained otherwise. That is, if not only the reinforcers but also the instrumental events were different from one component to the other, contrast would not occur.

IV. RESPONSE SIMILARITY

What is the overlap between right and left bar-presses? Certainly the apparent similarity is very great. But this is so, it should be observed, only on the assumption that topography (or perhaps environmental effect) is a sufficient basis for judging similarity between response classes. It is not clear that this criterion has ever been considered on the basis of other than the most casual reasoning. It may come as no surprise, therefore, that although the assumption may hold for many cases, it apparently does not hold for all, and those for which it does not hold do not seem to be marked by any conspicuous sign.

A test was made by E. Jacobson of the similarity between operating a right bar and a left bar. Because operant level bar-pressing has a low frequency in the rat, making changes in frequency difficult to detect, it was arranged that both bar-presses turn on the same central overhead light for an equal period of time. Each session consisted of three components: left bar alone, right bar alone, both bars. Components lasted 40 seconds, and the order of their occurrence was counterbalanced over the session.

What shall be taken as an operational definition of similarity? If two response classes are identical, the occurrence of either one should be a complete substitute for the other one, whereas if they are independent, the occurrence of one should affect only negligibly the occur-

---

[2]A control is being run to determine whether the (complete) failure to return to base, not reported when the reinforcers are identical, is a characteristic of mixed reinforcers or of other features of the present procedure, such as the use of two bars.

rence of the other. The unsuspected independence of the present bar-press responses was then shown by the fact that the frequency with which either response occurred when the left or right bar was offered alone approximated the frequency with which the same response occurred when both bars were offered together. Moreover, this kind of independence is by no means general. It was not seen, for example, in Jacobson's data for operant level wheel running; in keeping with standard expectations, clockwise turns substantially reduced the likelihood of counterclockwise turns, and vice versa.

If pressing right and left bars should prove to be as independent in the operant level case as they appear to be when the responses turn on a light, the contrast observed to take place across different reinforcers could not be attributed to a common instrumental event. We should have to say instead: right and left bar-presses appear to be independent; running and drinking are evidently not the same; nevertheless, contrast was observed.

This finding, taken in the light of the above assumptions, would seem to raise a broad experiential interactionism from a merely philosophical possibility to an experimental question. Two lines of investigation then suggest themselves.

First, we might consider that what shields one experience from the effect of another is simply time. On this view, we need only introduce a sufficient buffer of time between the two components to isolate one from the influence of the other. This will be an attractive view if one is persuaded that the basis of the effect is emotional. This seems easy enough to test, though of course the problem that arises is the old one of time versus the content of time; the design must somehow assure that time and content are not utterly confounded.

A second consideration is the near certainty, despite the anecdotal status of the evidence, that categories *can* be established which functionally isolate experiences. Our preference among toothpastes is presumably not influenced by our previous experience with automobiles; I say presumably because I have no evidence. But if this is so, we must wonder about the origin of these categories, and about the role of learning in establishing them. Can we teach the rat that running and drinking are not the same and thus should not influence one another, or that, for example, drinking alcoholic substances is different from drinking nonalcoholic substances — different in the operational sense that contrast will no longer occur across the boundaries of such categories? Can we compartmentalize the rat's experience so that there is a selectivity as to what influences what? It may turn out that the problem of interest is not how broad the boundaries of the rat are, but given that they are broad, can they be made narrow, and, if so, how?

V. TWO HYPOTHESES AND A COUNTERHYPOTHESIS

Two hypotheses have been suggested as to the necessary and sufficient conditions for contrast, one by Reynolds (1961a) and the other by Terrace (1966a); we will review them briefly and propose a third possibility.

Inevitably, both hypotheses have to do with rate, relative rate of reinforcement in one case and rate of responding in the other case, since these are the factors that are either changed or change in the course of the standard contrast procedures. Deciding between them has boiled down to a search for procedures that would permit varying one factor without varying the other.

Reynolds has *not* maintained that a change in the relative rate of reinforcement is a necessary condition, for he himself has shown that contrast can be produced without any change in reinforcement by adding electric shock to one of the components in the multiple schedule (Brethower & Reynolds, 1962). Terrace (1966b) has added to this conclusion by showing that changing an interval to a DRL schedule will produce contrast even though the change in schedules does not entail a change in the rate of reinforcement. Terrace noted that both when electric shock was added and when the schedule was changed to DRL, the response rate was lowered in one of the components. On the basis of this and other evidence he has argued that a change in rate of responding is a sufficient condition for contrast. Both authors, it should be noted, have proposed their conditions merely as sufficient; neither argues that his condition is a necessary one. We may ask, however, whether a change in rate of responding is even a sufficient condition.

That a change in the rate of responding is not a necessary condition is established without an explicit experiment; we find some percentage of both rats and pigeons which do not reduce their responding in S_1 despite a reduction in reinforcement for S_1, and nevertheless do show contrast, that is, an increase in S_2. This figure may be no higher than about 5-10%, but it is sufficient to establish that contrast can occur without a change in rate of responding.

But we may even wonder as to the sufficiency (let alone necessity) of a change in the rate of responding. The sufficiency of this condition would seem to be called to question by the probable outcome of the following three experiments, all of which are hypothetical at the present.

First, suppose the response rate in S_1 were reduced, not by a reduction in the probability of reinforcement, but by a reduction in the probability the subject will respond to the contingent stimulus. Although this study could not be done when the reinforcers were the same in both components – the decrement would affect S_2 no less than S_1 – it could be accommodated nicely by the mixed reinforcer paradigm, in which one can satiate the subject for one reinforcer with little (or measurable) side effect for the other reinforcer. The point is this: If the decrement in S_1 were produced not by a decline in the world's payoff, but by a decline in the utility the subject assigns to the contingent event, it seems rather unlikely that contrast would result. And this suggests that not all but only certain kinds of response decrements will produce contrast.

Second, not only DRL but also DRH may produce contrast. Terrace has shown that changing an interval schedule to DRL with reinforcement equated produces contrast; but any schedule which, like DRL, requires the animal to meet a rate criterion may produce contrast – whether the requirement is that the animal "slow down" relative to the VI, as in DRL, or "speed up," as in DRH. In a word, DRL and DRH schedules that are equated for relative aversiveness may be equally effective in producing contrast (cf. Fantino, 1968).

Third, suppose that S_1 is changed from VI to FVI, that is, an instrumental response is no longer required of the subject. Instead, access to the reinforcer is determined entirely by the experimenter's program. Suppose also that the change from VI to FVI were accompanied by varying reductions in the rate of reinforcement. The reduction in response rate would then be a constant, equal for all the reinforcement conditions; it seems reasonable to suppose, however, that the magnitude of the contrast effect would not be a constant but would be proportional to the change in the rate of reinforcement.

These considerations suggest that while a change in rate of reinforcement is apparently a sufficient condition for contrast, a change in the rate of responding may be neither a necessary nor a sufficient condition. Not all changes in rate of responding produce contrast – the change must be produced in a specific way – and contrast does occur on occasion when there is no change in the rate of responding.

VI. PREFERENCE

The first alternative hypothesis that comes to mind is preference. That is, contrast will result if, by whatever means, the subject is made to prefer (choose) one component of the multiple schedule over the other (cf. Bloomfield, 1967). Although a choice procedure is not included in the standard contrast design, if it were, we could be confident that (a) a VI schedule of a higher rate of reinforcement would be chosen over another VI schedule of a lower rate of reinforcement, (b) a component without electric shock would be chosen over a comparable component with shock, and (c) in some cases, an interval schedule would be chosen over a DRL schedule that is equated for number of reinforcements. All these conditions produce contrast; they have in common a predictable effect upon preference; and the hypothesis which they suggest is the more attractive because of the diverse ways in which the preference structure can be changed.

(Actually the hypothesis must deal with increasing preference rather than establishing it, for although most contrast designs do start out with the same schedule in both components, some do not, and contrast does not require that there be an initial lack of difference between the components.)

Unfortunately, however, this attractive hypothesis appears to fail in at least two cases. Contrast does not occur if the nonpreferred stimulus is either (a) an errorless S^Δ (Terrace, 1966a), or (b) a standard negative stimulus which as a result of many extinction sessions is, however, no longer negative. Terrace (1966b) reported that when the condition in S_1 was extinction, contrast disappeared over a long series of tests (though would it disappear if the conditions in S_1 were other than extinction?). The somewhat counterintuitive hypothesis which this suggests is that at least for those conative factors which determine the preference structure complete extinction is possible. That is, an errorless and a completely extinguished S^Δ may be functionally equivalent. In any case, Terrace reports that neither case produces contrast, and if this is so, the preference hypothesis cannot be correct.

As a means of clarifying the implications of this failure, consider the following experiment. In the same subject, three different stimuli, a, b, and c, are established as: a, an errorless S^Δ; b, a completely extinguished S^Δ; and c, a standard S^Δ. The context in which these stimuli are given their respective functions is, say, one in which the subject turns an activity wheel for the opportunity to drink. In a second context the subject is taught, for example, to bar-press to eat. Into this second context, a block of time which hitherto has consisted exclusively of the opportunity to bar-press to eat, each of the three stimuli are interpolated in turn. What will be the effect upon the subsequent frequency of bar-pressing to eat of an interpolated interval of stimuli a, b, and c?

According to the present hypothesis the interpolation of c (standard S^Δ) will produce contrast, i.e., following an interval of c, the frequency of bar-pressing will be increased. But the interpolation of a and b will have no effect. This failure is predicted despite the fact that both a and b were nonpreferred relative to the stimulus associated with the opportunity to bar-press to eat. Presumably the opportunity to choose between the respective stimuli would establish this directly. What then is unique to stimuli which, though nonpreferred relative to a set of alternatives, do not nonetheless produce contrast if interpolated as an obligatory member of a sequence of such alternatives?

The answer suggested by Terrace's data seems clearcut: such stimuli are incapable of generating inhibition or aversiveness, i.e., the dimension to which they belong would not give rise to an inhibitory gradient (cf. Jenkins, 1965). *Contrast results if and only if there is a change in the aversiveness associated with one of the components in the schedule.* This is the final hypothesis to which we are led. In adopting this hypothesis, inhibition itself is not clarified (except to suggest, as in the above experiment, that inhibition is not specific to the responses in whose context it is generated but is instead a state variable). The hypothesis says only that inhibition and contrast are two sides of the same coin. Specifically, the necessary and sufficient conditions for the two phenomena are the same.[3]

VII. THREE MECHANISMS OF CONTRAST

What is the explanation of contrast? Emotion is the most commonly heard answer (cf. Amsel, 1958; Bloomfield, 1967; Terrace, 1966a). Emotion is a mystery to which we all accede because it is temporary, but it is an unsatisfactory answer. Although there is no doubt that it occurs, the precise manner in which it affects behavior is hardly clearer today than it was in the beginning. More important, the preoccupation with emotion has diverted attention from two other equally compelling possibilities (Premack, in preparation). There is, moreover, no logical incompatibility between emotion and the other alternatives; emotion may be a catalytic concomitant or even a necessary condition for the other kinds of changes. What are these possible changes?

---

[3]An interesting implication of this conclusion is that inhibition can be produced without extinction, even as contrast can be produced without extinction, merely by a reduction in rate of reinforcement in S_1. A confirmation of the prediction that a gradient of inhibition can be produced merely by a reduction in rate of reinforcement can be found in Weisman and Premack (1966), and still more clearly in Weisman and Palmer (submitted).

A return to the beginning of the article will recall that two of the principal determinants of the efficacy of an event as a reinforcer are, first, the probability that the subject will respond to the stimulus (P_1), and second, the probability that the world will provide the stimulus (P_2). Either or both of these probabilities may be affected by the procedures which give rise to contrast. When the rate of reinforcement is lowered in S_1, the subject may upgrade the utility of the reinforcer. Operationally, the subject may increase in the duration for which it would respond to the contingent stimulus, were that stimulus unconditionally available. Alternatively, the subject may change its subjective estimate of P_2, the probability of reinforcement in the invariant component S_2. This estimate may rise and the subject may respond in the actually unchanged component as though the rate of reinforcement there had been increased. Either or both of these factors could account for the data of contrast. Moreover, their plausibility as possible mechanisms of contrast is increased by the suggestion that contrast is not restricted to typical instrumental events. For example, when rats were shifted from one sucrose concentration to another, the amount they drank—thus the duration for which they drank—was affected by the previously experienced concentration (Premack & Hillix, 1962).

VIII. CHANGES IN THE PREFERENCE STRUCTURE

Since contrast may involve a change in preference structure, we should begin with a measure of some part of that structure, introduce the operations that give rise to contrast, and then conclude by remeasuring the preference structure. A comparison of the preference structure before and during contrast should reveal quite directly whether contrast has involved any change in P_1, the utility the subject assigns to the reinforcer.

The preference structure can be assessed by including in the standard contrast design a measure either of unconditional response duration or of choice. Suppose one or more foods were to be used as reinforcer(s). If the individual foods were made unconditionally available, either on a continuous or discontinuous basis, a measure could be made of the duration of the subect's response to the food. A measure of this kind was made on the manipulation of *Cebus* monkeys (Premack, 1963) and on the drinking of rats (Premack, 1965). Alternatively, the food or foods can be paired, either the same food in two different hoppers, or different foods in each hopper, and a measure made of the choice of the two hoppers. (Since the former is a more primitive measure than the latter, e.g., A vs. context, as opposed to A plus context vs. B plus context, it is of interest to attempt to predict the latter from the former; cf. Greeno, 1968, for such an attempt.)

Pigeons were offered two different foods, milo and wheat. One key and two hoppers were used; each hopper contained a different food and was associated with the color on the key. Preference was measured by presenting the bird both hoppers and allowing it to eat from whichever one it chose. Choice trials were always given in a block of eight consecutive presentations of the two hoppers; each presentation lasted 3 seconds with 15 seconds between presentations.

The choice procedure was only part of a session the rest of which consisted of a standard multiple schedule. In one component of the schedule, pecks on the red key produced, according to a VI-1 schedule, three seconds' access to the milo hopper. In the other component of the schedule, pecks on the green key produced, according to a VI-1 schedule, three seconds' access to the wheat hopper. Each component lasted three minutes. A cycle consisted of two replications of the milo component followed by the wheat component; these were followed by a block of eight choice trials. Every session contained two cycles. Thus, each session included a period in which the opportunity to eat required that the bird peck the illuminated key, as well as a period in which the opportunity to eat required only that the bird choose between the two hoppers. The key was darkened during choice.

The familiar three-step contrast design was imposed on the above procedure. At step one both the rate of key-pecking and the choice data were stabilized. All five of the pigeons which M. Shanab and I have so far tested with this procedure preferred wheat to milo. In keeping with the preference data, the rate of key-pecking was higher in the wheat than in the milo conponent of the schedule.

At step two the milo component was placed on extinction, i.e., the multiple schedule was changed from VI-1 (milo) VI-1 (wheat) to Ext (milo) VI-1 (wheat). The change to extinction was made in all four of the milo components for some of the birds, i.e., in both cycles of the session, whereas for other birds, the change was confined to the first cycle of the session, and the milo components in the second cycle remained on the original VI schedule (birds for which milo was extinguished in the first cycle and in both cycles were called semi and full, respectively). The choice procedure was not changed at any time for any of the subjects.

The preference data for four of the five birds are shown in Table I, the data for the fifth bird being omitted since it shows no changes in preference. The data are divided into three sets of five sessions; the right column shows the number of times wheat was chosen and the left column the number of times milo was chosen. Although a total of 16 choices was possible per session, individual birds occasionally failed to choose either hopper in the three-second interval for which the hoppers were available, in which case their total choices per session was less than 16. A photoelectric device in the hoppers served to detect choices; no bird responded to both hoppers on a choice trial, probably because of the short presentation interval.

The first set of sessions show base line data, the second set data immediately after milo was extinguished (and contrast was beginning to develop), and the last set steady state data, stability having been reached in both the contrast effect and in the preference data. The contrast data, an increased responding in the wheat component, were largely typical for the four birds represented in Table I, and are not shown here.

A summary of the main outcome is provided by the milo/wheat (M/W) ratios; these show a definite increase in the preference for milo from the base line sessions at step one to the steady state sessions at step two. For the four birds which showed the effect these figures were: .28 vs. 1.05, .20 vs. 1.24, .09 vs. .49, and .25 vs. .40. The effect was greater in the birds for which the extinction of milo was confined to only one cycle of the session, shown in the upper half of the table, than for the birds in which milo was extinguished in both cycles. The basis of this difference is not understood at the present time, but the direction of the difference can be used to rule out a satiation-type interpretation of the data. If milo gained in preference because of relative satiation for wheat, resulting from the fact that milo could not undergo satiation because of the extinction condition, the effect should be greater when milo was extinguished in both cycles of the session. In fact, the effect was greater when milo was extinguished in only one cycle of the session.

Nevertheless, the preference data do not afford any simple explanation of the contrast data. The contrast effect consisted of an increased rate of key-pecking in the wheat components of the schedule, whereas the choice data showed an increase in the preference for milo. This result is particularly unfortunate in that it would appear not to permit eliminating any of the possible mechanisms with which we began. An

TABLE I
Preference Data

Subject 54 (Semi)

Base line (VI 1' VI 1')

Milo	Wheat	M/W
3	12	
3	11	
1	13	
3	12	
6	10	
16	58	.28

VI 1' Ext. (first 5 sessions)

Milo	Wheat	M/W
4	12	
9	5	
12	4	
6	9	
3	13	
34	43	.79

VI 1' Ext. (last 5 sessions)

Milo	Wheat	M/W
8	8	
11	5	
9	7	
6	10	
7	9	
41	39	1.05

Subject 25 (Semi)

Base line (VI 1' VI 1')

Milo	Wheat	M/W
4	12	
1	15	
4	12	
4	11	
0	15	
13	65	.20

VI 1' Ext. (first 5 sessions)

Milo	Wheat	M/W
1	14	
3	12	
3	12	
3	13	
0	16	
10	67	.15

VI 1' Ext. (last 5 sessions)

Milo	Wheat	M/W
9	7	
9	7	
6	8	
8	7	
10	5	
42	34	1.24

Subject 55 (Full)

Base line (VI 1' VI 1')		
Milo	Wheat	M/W
1	13	
1	14	
2	13	
1	15	
1	13	
6	68	.09

VI 1' Ext. (first 5 sessions)		
1	15	
1	15	
0	14	
0	15	
2	12	
4	71	.06

VI 1' Ext. (last 5 sessions)		
7	8	
7	9	
4	12	
4	12	
4	12	
26	53	.49

Subject 31 (Full)

Base line (VI 1' VI 1')		
Milo	Wheat	M/W
2	9	
2	9	
2	12	
4	11	
3	11	
13	52	.25

VI 1' Ext. (first 5 sessions)		
2	13	
2	10	
4	9	
2	11	
0	13	
10	56	.18

VI 1' Ext. (last 5 sessions)		
4	6	
7	9	
3	10	
3	11	
2	12	
19	48	.40

increase in the bird's estimate of the likelihood of wheat during the wheat components cannot be ruled out, nor can emotionality which may be a concomitant of changes in the preference structure in any case. Moreover, since the preference measure is a relative one, we cannot even eliminate an increase in the utility for wheat, although the rate of increase would have to be less than that for milo. Other experiments involving different measures of preference may prove to be more revealing.

IX. IS CHOICE SUBJECT TO CONTRAST?

We have used choice between the two grains as a presumably uncomplicated measure of the bird's preference for the grains, but to do so may overlook a major complication. Can we be certain that choice is not itself subject to contrast?[4] Is the increased choice of milo necessarily indicative of an increase in the reinforcement value of milo, or is it simply another form of contrast (and thus as much in need of interpretation as are the key-peck data)? If the latter, then the change in both choice and key-pecking would reflect the same process. They would be at the same causal level, and neither could be regarded as an explanation of the other.

In an ideally simple world choice would be impervious to the influence of contrast and would remain an uncomplicated index of preference. Or contrast might affect choice but only in influencing the rate at which the organism chooses, and not the frequency with which one alternative is chosen over another. In this case choice would retain its uncomplicated status, for preference is measured by relative frequency and not by the rate at which choices occur.

Suppose a bird were trained on one key and two hoppers. However, the two hoppers not only contain the same food but also occur equally often in association with the two components of the multiple schedule. In addition to the single key and its multiple schedule, there are two other keys, and these are associated with a concurrent schedule. Having produced contrast by extinguishing S_1 of the multiple schedule, we look for changes in responding on the concurrent schedule. The proportionality of choices could not reasonably change, for the hoppers were equally associated with the two components. However, the rate of responding in the concurrent schedule may increase, though equally in both alternatives.

---

[4] I am indebted to A. Erlebacher for calling this point to my attention.

It is only when one of the hoppers is associated with a particular component of the multiple schedule, as in the present experiment, that contrast could take the form of a change in the choice proportionalities. But for which hopper or food should choice increase? In either case the increase could not be viewed strictly as a contrast phenomenon for the simple reason that the paradigm does not seem to supply an unequivocal answer. An increase might be anticipated in choices of the food or hopper associated with the S_2 component of the multiple schedule since it is in that component that instrumental responding increases. But it is all too easy to defend the opposite view.

In summary, although the present results afford no simple explanation of contrast, they suggest rather strongly that the preference structure may undergo changes in the course of a contrast procedure. Changes of this kind can be detected only if contrast designs include measures of preference.

X. SELECTIVE RECAPITULATION

A basic question in contrast is whether there is a logical need for a mechanism additional to those already available for dealing with changes in the value an organism assigns to an event. Value can in many cases be measured directly by the relative duration for which an organism responds to unconditionally available events. A difference in value between two events gives to one of them the ability to reinforce or punish the other, a fact which more than any other gives value its importance. Presently we recognize two main ways in which value undergoes change. The duration for which an organism responds to an event declines with successive responding and recovers in varying degree with rest (Premack & Collier, 1962). (Given the assumption that organisms are under a constraint to respond, habituation emerges as a mechanism for assuring diversity of contact; without habituation organisms would respond only to the first stimulus they contacted.) This set of procedures, involving time and composition of maintenance environment relative to that of test, represents the intrinsic parameters of value: the effect does not rely upon a contingency, upon a relationship with events other than the response in question. The great extrinsic mechanism of value change is reinforcement (or punishment) itself. In a successful contingency, some or all of the value of the contingent event transfers to the instrumental event. Do the phenomena of contrast require still another mechanism for value change?

   The mechanism suggested by some contrast data is that of adaptation theory (Helson, 1959): the value of an event depends not only upon the event but also upon previously experienced events. But is this true for rates of reinforcement as it may be for judgments of brightness or shock intensity? Do organisms estimate reinforcement rates, are the estimates conditioned by other than the current rates, and if so, is it sufficient to assume a simple proportionality between the estimate and the response rate? Furthermore, if this were the mechanism of contrast, then why does contrast appear to be uniquely linked to rate of reinforcement? Changes in duration of reinforcement are reported not to produce contrast (e.g., Shettleworth & Nevin, 1965), and there are no reports of positive contrast produced by a change in value (e.g., sucrose concentration) of reinforcement. Yet nothing in adaptation theory suggests that rate of reinforcement should be more susceptible to relativity of judgment than either duration or value of reinforcement.

   A question off to the side of the main one is: What must be the similarity among the reinforcing events whose rates of occurrence are manipulated? In all previous data the possible events were identical; moreover, the time between them was slight. But the present data suggest that these constraints may be overly strict. Contrast was produced when the instrumental events were not identical, when the time between the two components instancing the different reinforcement rates was extended, and when the contingent events in the two components were neither identical nor even particularly similar. With running as the reinforcer in one component and drinking in the other, reducing the opportunity to run resulted in an increase in bar-pressing for the opportunity to drink. Notice, however, that even here the parameter remained rate of reinforcement. That is, the shift was from one reinforcement schedule for running to extinction, and was not a shift from one reinforcer to another of a lower value (e.g., substituting the opportunity to run for the opportunity to drink). Thus, the data do not show that the reinforcing events can be changed, but only that the events whose rates are changed need not be identical.

   A choice between two foods was introduced into an otherwise standard contrast design. Relative preference for the two foods was obtained both before and during contrast, so as to determine once and for all whether the change in rate of reinforcement which gives rise to contrast does so by changing the preference structure. Preference was changed but not in a direction that could account for contrast. This topsy-turvy outcome epitomized the present inquiry: more questions than answers.

REFERENCES

Amsel, A. The role of frustrative nonreward in noncontinuous reward situations. *Psychol. Bull.*, 1958, **55**, 102-119.

Bloomfield, T. M. Frustration, preference and behavioral contrast. *Quart. J. exp. Psychol.*, 1967, **19**, 166-169.

Brethower, D. M., & Reynolds, G. S. A facilitative effect of punishment on unpunished behavior. *J. exp. Anal. Behav.*, 1962, **5**, 191-199.

Crespi, L. P. Quantitative variation of incentive and performance in the white rat. *Amer. J. Psychol.*, 1942, **55**, 467-517.

Fantino, F. Effects of required rates of responding upon choice. *J. exp. Anal. Behav.*, 1968, **11**, 15-22.

Greeno, J. G. *Elementary theoretical psychology*. Reading, Mass.: Addison-Wesley, 1968, in press.

Helson, H. Adaptation level theory. In S. Koch (Ed.), *Psychology: A study of a science.* Vol. 1. New York: McGraw-Hill, 1959. Pp. 565-621.

Jenkins, H. M. Generalization gradients and the concept of inhibition. In D. I. Mostofsky (Ed.), *Stimulus generalization.* Stanford, Calif.: Stanford Univer. Press, 1965. Pp. 55-61.

Pavlov, I. P. *Conditioned reflexes.* (Trans. by G. V. Anrep) London and New York: Oxford Univer. Press, 1927.

Premack, D. Toward empirical behavioral laws: I. Positive reinforcement. *Psychol. Rev.*, 1959, **66**, 219-233.

Premack, D. Rate differential reinforcement in monkey manipulation. *J. exp. Anal. Behav.*, 1963, **6**, 81-89.

Premack, D. Reinforcement theory. In D. Levine (Ed.), *Nebraska symposium on motivation.* Lincoln, Nebr.: Univer. of Nebraska Press, 1965. Pp. 123-180.

Premack, D., & Collier, G. Analysis of nonreinforcement variables affecting response probability. *Psychol. Monogr.*, 1962, **76**, 5 (Whole No. 524).

Premack, D. & Hillix, W. A. Evidence for shift effects in the consummatory response. *J. exp. Psychol.*, 1962, **63**, 284-288.

Reynolds, G. S. Behavioral contrast. *J. exp. Anal. Behav.*, 1961, **4**, 57-71. (a)

Reynolds, G. S. An analysis of interactions in a multiple schedule. *J. exp. Anal. Behav.*, 1961, **4**, 107-117. (b)

Schaeffer, R. W. The reinforcement relation as a function of the instrumental response rate. *J. exp. Psychol.*, 1965, **69**, 419-425.

Shettleworth, S., & Nevin, J. A. Relative rate of response and relative magnitude of reinforcement in multiple schedules. *J. exp. Anal. Behav.*, 1965, **8**, 199-202.

Skinner, B. F. *The behavior of organisms.* New York: Appleton, 1938.

Terrace, H. S. Stimulus control. In W. K. Honig (Ed.), *Operant behavior: Areas of research and application.* New York: Appleton, 1966. Pp. 271-344.

Terrace, H. S. Behavioral contrast and the peak shift: Effects of extended discrimination training. *J. exp. Anal. Behav.*, 1966, **9**, 613-617. (b)

Weisman, R. G., & Premack, D. Positive and negative generalization gradients depending on the relative rates of reinforcement in two components of a schedule. Paper read at Psychono. Soc. meeting, St. Louis, 1966.

CHAPTER 6

Activity, Reactivity, and the Behavior-Directing Properties of Stimuli[1]

JACK T. TAPP

Animal #8, 24 hours food-deprived, placed in apparatus at 1:30. Moved immediately to corner and began sniffing at walls. Movements in apparatus confined to walls. Occasionally animal rears on hind legs and sniffs at the ceiling. Contacted food cup at 1:35. Sniffed at hole in cup, then moved along adjacent wall. Returned to food cup. Moved to lever and sniffed at lever. Came down on lever and activated food delivery apparatus. Rat stopped moving following noise of food dispenser. Began grooming, then returned to lever and sniffed more. Moved to food cup. Ate pellet . . . .

   Hit lever again at 1:57. Stopped moving after click. Returned to food cup and ate pellet. Moved slowly toward bar, sniffing at wall. Hit bar and continued to

[1]The author would like to express his appreciation to the students who did the work on these experiments and whose discussions contributed substantially to the ideas developed in this chapter. The efforts of Paul S. D'Encarnacao, Roger S. Zimmerman, Charles J. Long, Donna M. Mathewson, Lance L. Simpson, and Paula Jarrett are most gratefully acknowledged. The research was supported by training grants MH 8107, MH 08528, NSF-URP GY 3054, and research grants MH 13452 and MH 07265, and by the Department of Psychology of Vanderbilt University.

sniff at wall. Returned to food cup and ate pellet. Returned to bar area, sniffed at bar. Chewed corner of lever and operated dispenser. Went to food cup and ate pellet. Returned to bar and sniffed around lever. Pushed bar with forepaw. Went to food cup when click sounded. Ate pellet and returned to bar. Pressed lever, then ate pellet.

Consistently pressing lever at 2:15.

This set of notes is a description of a rat's behavior in a Skinner box. It could have been abstracted from any of a thousand similar protocols made by students of experimental psychology. Though the animal described here was a rat, it could have been almost any mammal, and the apparatus could have been any of a variety of pieces of equipment used in the study of instrumental learning. The purpose of this description is to point up some of the questions that have been the center of much speculation and research in the behavioral sciences for the past 70 years.

Four aspects of the animal's behavior are apparent from this description, and they represent the foundations upon which an analysis of behavior must proceed. First, when placed in the test environment, the animal emits a variety of random behaviors which constitute the basis for the elaboration of subsequent "learned" behaviors. That is, the rat is active, and this activity is composed of many different movement patterns such as sniffing, walking, grooming, rearing, chewing, and bar-pressing. Second, these behaviors appear to be influenced by stimuli within the environment in that some of these acts take on specific direction. He sniffs at the walls of the box and the food cup; he chews the bar; he eats the food pellet, etc. Third, some of the movements that the animal makes alter the stimuli present in the environment. When the lever is moved, a click and a food pellet become a part of the total stimulus array. Fourth, some of the stimuli exert a profound effect on the particular movements the animal makes and markedly change the animal's behavior within the situation. The presentation of the food following a lever-press increases the frequency of lever-presses until the animal engages in little behavior other than lever-pressing.

Each of these phenomena point to several interrelated questions that are fundamental to the understanding of behavior in general and instrumental learning in particular. What movements do animals make when they are confronted with a test environment? How do the consequences of behaviors affect the behavior of the animal? How do variations in the internal state of the animal alter the behavior of the animal?

Over the past few years, we have conducted a number of experiments to examine certain aspects of some of these questions. The goal of this work has been to investigate in some detail the nature of the behaviors that occur as antecedants to instrumentally learned behaviors and the factors which control them. Specifically, the experiments reviewed in this chapter investigate the role of environmental stimuli in the regulation of the spontaneous activity emitted by the laboratory rat and the manner in which these behavior patterns are altered by depriving the animal of some substance essential to its survival.

I. THE NATURE OF ACTIVITY

A. Observational Experiments

As a first approximation we felt it necessary to remind ourselves of the nature of spontaneous activity. What specific behaviors do rats engage in within a relatively simple test environment? To examine these behaviors we followed the suggestion made by Bindra (1961), and subsequent research by Bolles (1967), and made a number of systematic, quantified observations of the behavior of adult, male, albino rats within a standardized test environment. In these experiments the animals were observed in a double Wahman cage, and their behavior was sampled every three seconds during the first and third 15-minute periods of a one-hour session. In addition, the animal's activity was recorded automatically by means of a photocell arranged such that when the rat interrupted a red light beam projecting on a photocell, a count was automatically recorded on an electric counter (P). A summary of the observations of six animals is shown in Fig. 1.

During the first 15-minute period, the animals engaged in a considerable amount of movement characterized by large locomotor responses which moved them through a distance of two body lengths (M), rearing on their hind legs (R), and a movement pattern which we have called typical activity (Ta). This last behavior is represented by short movements less than a body length in distance, which are accompanied by rapid movements of the vibrissae. As can be seen from Fig. 1, this behavior pattern was observed most frequently. Grooming (G), e.g., washing and scratching, also occurs frequently, though it typically does not appear until after the first five minutes or so in the apparatus. Very few of the observations made during this initial period indicated that the rats were not moving (N).

These behavior patterns shifted in a very consistent manner during the third 15-minute period of the session. During this period, the ani-

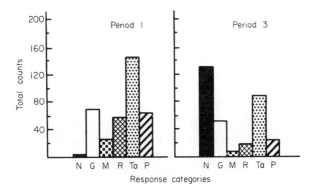

FIG. 1. Frequency count of responses observed during the first and third 15-minute periods of a one-hour session (see text for details).

mals' movements were considerably reduced, and the majority of the observations indicate that they were sitting quietly or lying still. Grooming persisted in approximately the same amounts during the third period, but all other movement patterns were reduced, though their relative proportions remained approximately the same. The decrease in responding was also reflected in the photocell counts (P). Thus, the summary statistics of Fig. 1 accurately reflect the well-documented decrease in response output that occurs over an extended test session.

Our observations revealed one aspect of the rats' behavior that is not reflected in the summary statistics. Though the animals engaged in a considerable amount of activity in the test environment, the particulars of the response patterns that make up this activity are finite in number, quite easily discriminated and classified, and very similar for all rats. For example, typical activity takes the same stereotypic form in all of the animals, differing from animal to animal only in its temporal distribution and direction. These observations indicated to us that rat activity is composed of sets of response patterns that are quite similar for all the rats in this experiment. As a result of this investigation, we began a search of the literature related to rat activity with the hope of finding measures that were differentially sensitive to the particular behaviors we had observed.

B. Interrelations between Activity Measures

The results of our literature survey revealed that the many different methods used to measure activity in the rat range in complexity from simple observational procedures to rather complex electronic devices. Yet, in spite of this plethora of measures, it is implicitly assumed in some of this literature that all of these measures are assessing the same behavior — spontaneous activity.

Observations of rat behavior certainly question the validity of this assumption. Spontaneous activity does not appear to be a single entity, characterized by any particular behavior. Rather, the rat engages in sets of responses which are composed of a variety of acts. Recognizing this fact, several authors have attempted to classify activity into its component behaviors suggesting that different activity measurement devices were differentially sensitive to different components of the rat's total behavior (cf. Behrendt, Deninger, & Hillers, 1962; Kreeger, 1942; Reed, 1947; Strong, 1957). For the most part, these classification schemes are based on observation and intuition, and the usefulness of these schemes has not been demonstrated empirically. We thought that by examining the relationships between various measures of activity we could define subsets of these measures that were interrelated and thus derive an empirical classification scheme for the activity of the rat.

Five different pieces of apparatus were selected from the literature as representative of the equipment most frequently used for the assessment of spontaneous activity. Forty Holtzman rats, maintained on ad libitum food and water, were then run in all pieces of the equipment for five two-hour sessions on alternate days. The order of running in each apparatus was systematically counterbalanced within the experiment, and all testing was conducted within a darkened environment. In brief, the five different testing devices were:

Williamson activity cage. This is a small, $6 \times 6 \times 6$ inch cage, balanced on a fulcrum. When the cage moves very slightly, a response is counted. An integrating unit accumulates these "jiggles" and records approximately every twentieth jiggle on a revolving paper disc. Because the cage is small, the apparatus is very sensitive to every movement the animal makes.

Photocell cage. Activity is measured in this device by means of a photocell mounted in the back of a double Wahman cage. When the animal breaks a light beam which projects on the photocell through an infrared filter, a count is recorded. Eight such cages were housed in a light-tight compartment. This device has been used extensively in research on activity and probably is maximally sensitive to larger locomotor responses though it also assesses other movements.[2]

_____
[2]Atrons, D. Personal communication, 1967.

Activity wheel. A standard Wahman activity wheel was included in the test battery since it is used so extensively in research on rat activity.

Circular field. This device is analogous to the open field described by numerous investigators. It consists of a 36-inch diameter circular field with three 2-inch wide treadles mounted on switches placed at equal distances around the field. A smaller circle, set in the middle of the apparatus, forms a 7-inch wide track around the perimeter. When the animal moves around the track, it walks across the treadles and a count is recorded. Large locomotor movements can be assessed by counting the number of times a response on one treadle is followed by a response on an adjacent treadle (alternations). Smaller repetitive movements may be reflected in the total counts made on all the treadles.

Light-contingent bar-pressing. The selection of the fifth measure was based on a concern for evaluating the behavior-directing properties of a particular stimulus–response contingency. Our observations of the behavior of the rat would suggest that many of the rats' movements were occuring in response to the stimuli within the environment. For most activity measures we were not able to specify what those stimuli were. To evaluate this aspect of behavior, we included a double-bar, lever-pressing apparatus made of Plexiglas and housed in a gutted refrigerator cabinet. When one of the bars was pressed, it produced the onset of an adjacent .5-foot-lambert light mounted outside the apparatus on the inside wall of the refrigerator cabinet. The light remained on for the duration of the response. The other lever served as a control, and when it was depressed nothing happened. Both total responses and the difference between the lighted and nonlighted bars (preference) were determined, since they potentially reflect different aspects of behavior within this situation.

The total response output over the two-hour period was determined for each device for all of the rats in the experiment, and these numbers were intercorrelated with one another over rats. This experiment afforded a limited test of the hypothesis that activity is a unitary dimension of behavior since, if activity as measured by these pieces of equipment is a unitary phenomenon, the intercorrelations between all measures should be high. The extent to which these assessment devices are differentially sensitive to similar behaviors should be reflected in low intercorrelations.

The results of the experiment are partially summarized in the correlation matrix of Table I. Only two of the correlations were significantly different from zero: the correlation between alternations and total

TABLE I
Matrix of Intercorrelations between Activity Measures (N = 40)[a]

Test number	Test	1	2	3	4	5	6	7
1	Williamson cages		−.03	.11	.18	.19	.06	.06
2	Photocell cages			−.02	−.01	.11	.14	.32
3	Activity wheel				.15	.19	−.04	.38
4	Circular field (alternations)					.90	.00	.05
5	Circular field (total counts)						−.01	.10
6	Light-contingent bar-pressing (total counts)							.33
7	Light-contingent bar-pressing (preference)							

[a] From Tapp, Zimmerman, & D'Encarnaçao (1968).

counts in the circular field, and the correlation between the preference measure in the light-contingent bar-pressing situation and total counts in the activity wheel. The former result would be expected since the numbers are derived from one another. The latter result may be due to common aspects of the two measures. Both the wheel and the light-preference measure reflect situations in which a response produces a change in the stimuli within the environment. When the rat runs in the activity wheel, the wheel turns and affords sensory feedback for the response. Similarly, pressing the lever which produces light onset also has this property. Since the correlation is rather low and represents only 5% of all the correlations in the total matrix, this interpretation is, at best, tenuous.

The intercorrelations summarized in Table I reflect only one of the potential consistencies in behavior that occurred within the experiment, i.e., the consistencies in the animals' tendencies to emit similar relative levels of responding in each piece of apparatus. The low interrelationships observed between these measures suggest that, for the most part, the rat's behavior in one situation is independent of its behavior in the other tasks. Comparable low intercorrelations between rat activity measures have been observed in similar experiments by other investigators (Anderson, 1938; Bolles, 1959). Such results imply that these devices are not measuring a common component of behavior and, therefore, that the activity of the rat is not a unitary dimension of its behavior. In the language of human measurement, this means that activity as assessed by these tests is not a general trait that characterizes the behavior of the rat.

These results are not surprising if one considers the nature of the equipment employed for measuring "activity." The assessment of behavior is limited by measurement capabilities of the apparatus in two important ways. First, by the nature of the physical arrangements of the apparatus and its sensing units, the equipment will be differentially sensitive to different components of the animal's total behavior. The Williamson cages, for example, confine the animal to a small space and therefore cannot assess locomotor movements other than small "jiggles." In contrast, the circular field will best reflect locomotor movements that take the animal around the track. Second, there is a high degree of interaction between the equipment and the rat's behavior in the apparatus that potentially contributes to the manifestations of behavior within the test situation. When an animal runs in a wheel, the wheel turns and creates a force that the animal must overcome if it is to stop or change its behavior. Sparks and Lockhard (1966) have recently reported high intercorrelations between three measures of activity taken in a moving tilt cage. As they point out, the tilting action of the cages probably contributed much to these interrelations by forcing the animal to readjust its posture every time the cage moved, thus increasing the activity of the animals.

In contrast to the intercorrelational data, one result of this experiment did reflect consistencies in behavior in all pieces of equipment. The total response output decreased consistently over the two-hour session for every measure except preference for the lever which produced light onset. In each apparatus, 50% of the total responding occurred in the first 30-minute period and subsequently decreased to 25, 15, and 10% of the total levels for the remaining three successive periods. Preferences for the lever which produced light onset were not observed for any of the 30-minute periods. This result indicates that each measure (except light preference) is sensitive to a common process that has a similar manifestation for all animals, i.e., a decrease in responding. Though each piece of equipment may be differentially sensitive to different components of the rat's total behavior, they all assess the change in behavior in a similar manner.

In general, the results of these experiments are testimony to the relatively complex nature of activity. Considerations such as those discussed above have undoubtedly contributed to the "wild and wooly" nature of contemporary research on rat activity (cf. Bolles, 1967). However, unity in the research on activity does exist insofar as measures of activity change in consistent ways to reflect a common process. In these experiments, all measures did decrease consistently within each session. This change reflected the decreases in exploratory tendencies that occurred within each piece of apparatus.

The methodological implication of the results of these experiments is more explicit than their theoretical interpretations. In order to determine the effects of a particular independent variable on "activity" we must examine the behavior of the animal in a variety of test situations to accurately assess the nature of the behavioral change. In particular, to the extent that independent variables similarly affect these measures of behavior, we can conclude that the effect is on "general activity." To the extent that the experimental manipulations differentially affect these behaviors, they are altering a process which contributes, in part, to the animal's activity, but which affects only a subset of the animal's total behavior.

II. THE EFFECTS OF HUNGER ON ACTIVITY

The implications of the above results warrant some further test. Particularly, what are the similarities and differences between independent variables which affect the "activity" of rats? There are a great number of variables which alter rat "activity." From the arguments presented above, it would seem desirable to investigate the effects of these manipulations on all of the activity measures used in the previous experiments in order to more definitively analyze their effects. D'Encarnacao (1968) has performed such an analysis on several different pharmacological agents which affect activity. For the purpose of the present report, the following discussion will concentrate on the examination of a somewhat different aspect of the problem and ask how alterations of an animal's need state alter the patterns of responding that are emitted by the animal.

This is an important problem in the context of an examination of the behaviors antecedent to the acquisition of an instrumental behavior. Instrumental learning is usually "motivated" by the need for some material that will restore homeostatic balance. When the need for such a material exists, it is reasonable to assume that some orientational neural systems are activated which allow the animal to respond differentially and appropriately to environmental stimuli (O'Kelly, 1963). If such systems uniformly increased responding, they would offer the animal biological advantages by allowing it to come into contact with the materials that satisfied the need.

It is commonly assumed that increases in need that are produced by increases in deprivation result in increased activity levels in the rat. However, this assumption is inconsistent with a very extensive literature on this problem (cf. Baumeister, Hawkins, & Cromwell, 1964; Bolles, 1967). With the exception of the fact that both hunger and thirst increase activity in the wheel and in stabilimeter cages, there are few definitive conclusions that can be made about the effects of these deprivation conditions on rat activity. In light of such research, it may be more reasonable to assume that deprivation differentially alters the specific response patterns that animals engage in. Bolles (1967) has reported some observations made in the home cages of deprived rats that suggest that this assumption has some validity. The deprived rats in his experiments exhibited increases in some behaviors, i.e., sniffing and standing (typical activity?), with relatively little change in others, i.e., grooming and rearing. Since our experiments suggested that the activity measures we had employed were assessing different components of activity, we were interested in determining if these measures would differentially reflect the effects of deprivation.

Four experiments were conducted to examine the behaviors of food-deprived and ad libitum animals in each of four different activity devices. Different groups of Holtzman rats were run for one hour in the Williamson cages ($N = 18$), the photocell cages ($N = 16$), the circular field ($N = 16$), and the double-bar Skinner box ($N = 16$) described above. Half of the animals in each experimental group were adapted to a maintenance diet of 13 gm   of powdered Purina chow per day for 12 days. These animals were fed at times which corresponded to the end of their test session. The remaining animals were maintained on ad libitum food.

The activity profiles for the food-deprived and ad libitum animals are shown in Fig. 2. For all tests there was again a consistent decay in responding over the one-hour session, but these behaviors were dif-

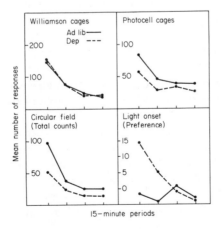

FIG. 2.   Activity counts for food-deprived and ad libitum rats in four different measurement devices plotted over each 15-minute period of a one-hour session.

ferentially altered by food deprivation. In the Williamson cages, both groups responded at virtually the same levels throughout the session. In both the photocell cages and the circular field the deprived animals were less active than the ad libitum animals ($p < .05$). In the double-bar Skinner box, the deprived and ad libitum animals did not differ in their total levels of responding, and response levels decayed in a similar manner for both groups. However, in this apparatus there was a difference in preference for the lever which produced the light onset. The deprived animals reliably preferred the lever which produced the onset of the light during the first 15 minutes of the two-hour session ($p < .05$). The ad libitum animals did not show a preference for the onset of the light at any time during the test session.

This profile indicates that food deprivation manipulated in this manner (a) does not alter activity as reflected in the Williamson cages, (b) decreases locomotor behavior as measured by the photocell cages and the circular field, and (c) increases the animal's preference for a lever which produces light onset. The last result offers an interpretation of the findings of all four of the experiments. The transitory preference for light onset that was observed in the double-bar Skinner box suggests that the deprivation condition enhances the rats' tendency to respond to whatever stimuli exist within the environment. In the circular field and the photocell cages, this tendency to respond to stimuli produces behaviors that are incompatible with the particular responses that are measured in these tests. By directing their behavior toward the variety of stimuli in these apparatus, the deprived animals do not move about as freely as the satiated animals, and consequently lower counts are accumulated on the sensing devices within the equipment. Since Williamson cages assess all of the movements the animals make, they are not differentially sensitive to the animals' tendencies to react to the stimuli within the test environment.

This interpretation is consistent with the hypothesis suggested by Campbell and Sheffield (1953). These authors describe an experiment in which they discovered that the activity of food-deprived rats in stabilimeter cages was enhanced to a greater extent than that of ad libitum animals following offset of noise (an electric fan) and the onset of light (the room lights). On the basis of this result, the authors suggest that hunger does not increase total response output or activity in and of itself, but rather results in heightened states of activity by lowering the threshold for responding to the external stimuli which normally control activity. In other words, the normal manifestations of activity are due to the rats' tendency to respond to environmental stimuli.

Deprivation enhances this tendency to react and consequently produces apparent increases in activity. Though such an interpretation is consistent with the results of our experiments, the lack of experimental control over the stimuli in all our equipment but the light preference apparatus did not allow us to identify what particular stimulus events were producing the behaviors we observed in the photocell cages or in the circular field.

This last series of experiments, as well as other research that has examined the Campbell and Sheffield hypothesis in more detail, points to the fact that the stimuli within the test environment play a critical role in the regulation of those behaviors described as "spontaneous" activity. In addition, they raise a methodological point that is extremely critical in the assessment of "activity." In the previous experiments, we assumed that the experimental conditions that were imposed on the test situation had at least reduced, and at best eliminated the extraneous stimuli from the test environment. Obviously, these manipulations had eliminated only those stimuli over which we had some experimental control, e.g., the illumination and sounds in the apparatus. All of the remaining stimuli which we were not able to control were allowed to vary in a haphazard manner. The slightest lapse into anthropomorphism makes it very apparent that any test situation represents a complex array of sights, sounds, and odors for the rat. In our previous studies where we thought we had imposed control on the test situation, we had, perhaps, enhanced the variation of stimuli in the environment. To control the stimuli within the test environment, it would be necessary to manipulate the stimuli and assess the effects of these manipulations on behavior.

The manipulation of environmental stimuli could be done in all of the tasks which purport to measure "spontaneous" activity. Such investigations would go a long way toward illucidating the nature of those behaviors. In the material that follows, however, we will limit the discussion to only one of the measures we have discussed thus far, the double-bar lever-pressing apparatus.

III. THE EFFECTS OF NEEDS ON REACTIONS TO STIMULI

A. The Effects of Hunger

Several factors contributed to the decision to limit our investigations to light-contingent bar-pressing, not the least of which was the similarity between this task and others in which instrumental learning is traditionally investigated. Instrumental learning is characterized by the fact that subjects engage in behaviors that bring them into proximity with, or remove them from, particular stimulus events. These stimuli have been termed rewards or punishments, depending on their effects on the organism's behavior. In general, rewards are approached and punishments are avoided. From our previous experiments light onset is a "reward" by this classification only when the animals are deprived of food. The 48 ad libitum animals we had run in this task thus far had not shown a reliable preference for the lever which produced light onset. This finding contributes to an apparent contradiction that exists in the literature on the effects of deprivation on rats' tendencies to press levers to produce the onset of dim lights. Numerous investigations have shown that rats will work when the only apparent reward for their effort is light onset (Kish, 1966), and several studies have reported that food or water deprivation enhances this tendency (Davis, 1958; Premack & Collier, 1962; Segal, 1959). On the other hand, several investigators have failed to find that deprivation enhances this behavior (Clayton, 1958; Forgays & Levin, 1958; Kiernan, 1965; Smith & Donahoe, 1966; Wilson, 1962). In this latter group of studies, the failure to demonstrate the enhancement of lever-pressing by deprivation results from the finding that both deprived and satiated animals pressed the lever to produce light onset at similar rates. This is in sharp contrast to our results.

Another factor led us to further investigations of the behavior of deprived and satiated tasks in this situation. The double-bar lever-pressing apparatus, unlike the other tests of activity, provides a measure of "spontaneous" activity in which there is some degree of control over the presentations of the stimuli and the responses which produce them. Such control potentially allows more definitive statements to be made about the role of environmental stimuli in the regulation of "spontaneous" behavior, at least as it is reflected in lever-pressing. This is of particular importance for the determination of how deprivation alters the rat's reactions to environmental stimuli, and it allows further tests of the Campbell and Sheffield hypothesis.

The intercorrelational study had revealed a significant correlation between the preference for the lever which produced light onset and the total number of revolutions in the activity wheel. This result was interpreted as indicating that perhaps these two tasks share a common component of behavior since they both produce a change in the stimuli within the test environment when the animal makes a response. The fact that food deprivation appears to enhance both of these behaviors further indicates that both of these measures are assessing a common process which contributes differentially to the behavior of deprived and satiated animals. This process would appear to be related to the fact that both environments provide a source of feedback to the animal when it engages in the appropriate behavior, i.e., running or lever-pressing. However, in both situations there are at least two kinds of feedback which contribute to the animal's behavior: (a) the intrinsic proprioceptive feedback that occurs from the movement associated with the responses, and (b) the extrinsic feedback that occurs as a consequence of the response. The light-contingent bar-pressing situation allows us to investigate the relative importance of these two sources of stimulation in controlling the behavior of deprived and satiated animals.

The next experiment was conducted to examine the relative roles of proprioceptive and visual cues as determinants of the differences in the behavior of deprived and ad libitum animals. Twenty-four food-deprived animals which had been adapted to a diet of 15 gm of food per day and 24 ad libitum rats were tested in the lever-pressing apparatus for a single four-hour test session (Tapp & Simpson, 1966). The apparatus was modified slightly in order to manipulate proprioceptive feedback necessary to produce light onset. Specifically, one of the two levers was made stationary, i.e., it did not move when pressed, while the other moved through a distance of 12 mm with a force of 25 gm when it was depressed. A response was recorded when the animals touched either lever.

The animals were tested in one of three conditions. In Condition I, neither touching nor pressing either lever produced the onset of the light, i.e., the apparatus remained dark. In Condition II, when the animal touched the stationary lever, the adjacent light was turned on for the duration of the response. In Condition III, the light was turned on when the animal pressed the movable lever through the total distance of its throw. Half of the animals from each condition were from the deprived group, and half were from the ad lib group.

The results of the experiment are depicted in Fig. 3. In Condition I, the total response output tended to be higher for the ad libitum animals than for the deprived animals, and for the first hour of the session this difference was statistically reliable ($p < .05$). In this condition, neither group consistently preferred either lever. In Condition II, both the deprived and ad libitum animals showed a preference for the lever which produced the onset of the light. Though the deprived animals tended to produce more total responses than the sated subjects, the relative preference for the lever which produced light onset was not different for the two groups. In Condition III, only the de-

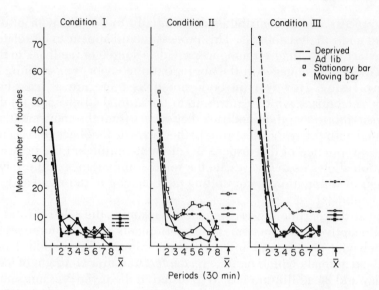

FIG. 3. Mean numbers of touches on the moving and stationary bars for each 30-minute period. The mean level of responding, $\overline{X}$, for each condition is shown at the right of each graph. Open figures indicate the bar which produced light onset. (From Tapp & Simpson, 1966.)

prived animals exhibited a durable preference for the lever which produced light onset. The sated animals contacted both levers at approximately equal rates throughout most of the session, though they did show slight preference for light onset for the first 30-minute period ($p < .05$). Deprivation thus enhanced the tendency to produce a change in environmental stimuli if the response necessary to produce stimulus onset was of sufficient magnitude.

The results of this experiment suggest that neither the proprioceptive cue nor the onset of the light was sufficient in and of itself to discriminate between the preferential responding of the deprived and of ad libitum groups. Rather, it appeared that the combination of both cues contributed substantially to the differences between these groups. Furthermore, these data indicated that light onset can influence the lever-pressing response for both ad libitum and deprived groups if the magnitude of the effort necessary to produce the stimulus onset is sufficiently low. The onset of the light does enhance total responding on both levers for the deprived animals (Condition I vs. Condition II). When both the proprioceptive and visual cues are combined, the deprived animals also exhibit increased responding, but this behavior becomes directed toward that lever which produces the greatest feedback from both cues. These results provide strong support for the hypothesis that stimuli control the response patterns of both deprived and satiated animals and that deprivation enhances this tendency to respond or react to these stimuli.

To further examine the effects of deprivation on the differential preference behavior of the deprived and ad libitum animals, we were interested in determining if the behavior observed in Condition III of the previous experiment was a function of the degree of hunger. There are, of course, many ways to manipulate hunger by manipulating deprivation, and all of these seem to produce losses in body weight. After reviewing a considerable amount of literature on the relationships between deprivation and degree of need, Bolles concluded that ". . . we seem to be left with no prospects in the immediate future for any conception better than anchoring hunger to the animal's need for calories and measuring this by weight loss" (Bolles, 1967, p. 160). Body weight loss also seems to be a critical factor that influences activity, at least in the activity wheel (Duda & Bolles, 1963; Moskowitz, 1959; Treichler & Collins, 1965).

To determine if body weight is related to the animal's behavior in the lever-pressing apparatus, three groups of 16 adult Holtzman rats each were adapted to either 15 gm, 20 gm, or ad libitum daily maintenance regimens for 15 days. This manipulation produced markedly different mean body weights in these groups by the end of this period (340, 379, and 424 gm, respectively). For testing purposes, the 15- and 20-gm maintenance groups were further subdivided, and half the animals were fed two hours before (prefed) and half immediately after (postfed) their scheduled testing time. After the initial adaptation period, the animals were run in the light-contingent bar-pressing situation every fourth day for three two-hour testing sessions. Both levers were adjusted to move through distances of 12 mm with a force of 25 gm. The number of responses was recorded for each 15-minute period.

Our results indicated that increasing the severity of the maintenance condition both increased the initial level of responding on the lever which produced light onset and prolonged the total response output on both levers throughout the two-hour test session ($p < .01$). This result is shown in Fig. 4, which depicts the response decay on each lever that occurred over the test sessions for each of the three maintenance groups. The ad libitum animals showed a slight preference for the lever which produced light onset during the first 15-minute period ($p < .05$). The 20-gm maintenance group showed a similar pattern of responding on the two levers, i.e., a significant initial pref-

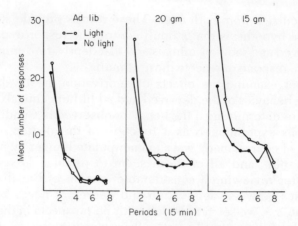

FIG. 4.   Mean levels of responding on the lighted and nonlighted bars for three maintenance regimens. Averages for each 15-minute period were computed over three test sessions.

erence, and then responding decayed to low asymptotic levels that were slightly higher than those exhibited by the ad libitum animals. The 15-gm animals maintained their preference for the lever which produced light onset for the first four periods, and the rate of response decay was much less rapid than that exhibited by the ad libitum and 20-gm groups.

The preferential responding that was exhibited by the 15- and 20-gm maintenance groups was primarily due to the behavior of the postfed animals. The 15- and 20-gm prefed animals and the ad libitum group showed no preference for the lever which produced light onset. The groups differed from one another only in the rate at which responding decayed. They did not differ in the total number of responses emitted. Only the postfed animals preferred the lever which produced light onset, and the magnitude of their preference was not related to the severity of the maintenance regimen. This result is summarized in Fig. 5 which shows the average daily response levels on both levers for all three maintenance groups.

The results of this study confirm the results of the previous experiments and further indicate that food deprivation enhances the rat's tendency to respond to produce the onset of environmental stimuli. The manipulations in body weight which increase hunger contribute to the animal's behavior only by reducing the rate of response decay.

B. The Effects of Thirst

Though it is generally assumed that a variety of needs produce simi-

lar effects on behavior, there are a number of experiments in the literature on various measures of activity that suggest that thirst operates
differently from hunger and does not produce changes in activity of
the same order of magnitude as hunger (Campbell, 1960; Campbell &
Cicala, 1962; Hall, 1955). To examine the assumption that different
needs produce similar behavioral changes, we next investigated the
effect of water deprivation on the rat's reaction to the onset of light.

The experiment was essentially a replication of the previous study.
Sixteen rats were adapted to a 23.5-hour water deprivation schedule
for 13 days. Half of the animals received their daily ration prior to the
scheduled test session (prewatered), and the remaining animals were
given access to water immediately following the testing time (postwatered). The animals were placed in the apparatus for a two-hour test
session on alternate days for a total of four sessions.

The results of the experiment are summarized in Fig. 6, which
shows the average daily levels of responding for both groups. The total levels of responding on both levers were not different for the two
groups, but the postwatered animals preferred the lever which produced the onset of the light ($p < .05$). The prewatered animals did not
exhibit such a preference.

This experiment adds generality to the previous results and suggests that two needs, hunger and thirst, operate similarly to increase
the rat's tendency to react to environmental stimuli. However, the
magnitude of total response output (compare the ordinates of Figs. 5
and 6) is quite different for these two deprivation manipulations even
though they were tested under virtually identical conditions. The
water-deprived animals appear to be responding at lower levels than
even the food-deprived animals on the 20-gm maintenance regimens.

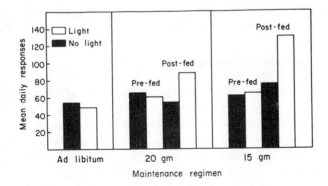

FIG. 5.   Mean daily levels of responding averaged over three test days for each experimental condition.

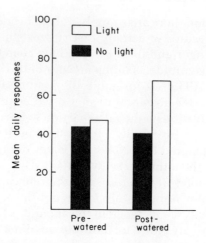

FIG. 6. Mean daily levels of responding averaged over four test sessions on the lighted and nonlighted levers.

It is difficult to evaluate these differences in total responding because direct statistical comparisons between the experiments are limited by such factors as slight differences in the age of the animals and their being shipped from the supplier at different times. Furthermore, a 23.5-hour water-deprivation schedule produced a different pattern of body weight change than any of the maintenance diets employed. Finally, in both experiments the behavior of those animals fed or watered after their scheduled running times could have resulted from the conditioned expectation of being fed or watered that developed over the course of the experiment. For these reasons, we conducted an experiment to examine the similarities and differences in this behavior in food- and water-deprived animals employing a still different manipulation of hunger and thirst.

C. Hunger and Thirst Compared

Campbell (1964) has shown that terminal deprivation of either food or water produces similar patterns of weight loss in rats, and these manipulations have apparently different effects on activity in stabilimeter cages. Such manipulations would not require feeding or watering the animals and would perhaps eliminate some of the cues that might accompany adaptation to a deprivation schedule.

In the next experiment (Tapp, Mathewson, & Jarrett, 1968), three groups of eight rats each were tested in the lever-pressing apparatus for a series of ten two-hour test sessions. On day 1 all animals were placed in the apparatus, and the food or water was removed from the home cages of two of the three groups. The third group was maintained on ad libitum food and water in their home cages. For ten consecutive days, the animals were tested daily at the same time, and responses were counted for each 15-minute period of the session. Neither of the deprived groups received its respective nutrients at any time during this series of tests.

The results of the experiment are partially summarized in Fig. 7, which shows the preferential behavior of the deprived and ad libitum groups for all ten days of the experiment. Both the food- and the water-deprived animals exhibited a similar tendency to respond more on the lever which produced light onset than ad libitum controls. On days 5, 7, 8, 9, and 10 the deprived groups reliably preferred the lever which turned on the light ($p < .05$), and on days 7, 9, and 10 the magnitude of this preference was greater for the food-deprived animals than for the water-deprived animals ($p < .05$). In contrast, the ad libitum group reliably preferred the lever which produced light onset only on the eighth and tenth days of the experiment.

Though there is a similarity between the behavior of the food- and the water-deprived animals, a striking difference in their behaviors is apparent in Fig. 7. Beginning on the sixth day of deprivation, the food-deprived animals reliably increased their total levels of responding above those exhibited by the ad libitum and water-deprived groups. It is of particular interest that this effect was primarily due to the tendency of food-deprived animals to continue to respond at high rates throughout the two-hour session, i.e., their levels of responding did not decay to the same low asymptotic rates within the session that

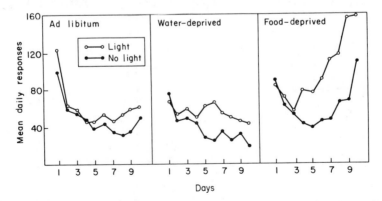

FIG. 7. Mean daily levels of responding computed over the two-hour daily test sessions. Deprivation was continuous for the ten days of the experiment. (From Tapp, Mathewson, & Jarrett, 1968).

166 *Jack T. Tapp*

were exhibited by the ad libitum and water-deprived animals. This result is shown graphically in Fig. 8.

The results of this study confirm our previous findings. Both food and water deprivation enhance the rat's reaction to environmental stimuli since deprived animals showed a reliable preference for the lighted bar much earlier in the testing sequence than the ad libitum controls. Terminal food deprivation, unlike terminal water deprivation, also appears to increase the total levels of responding that occur within the test situation.

There are at least two other major problems that limit the generality of these conclusions, both of which involve the evaluation of the effects of stimuli on responding as they affect the behavior of hungry and thirsty rats. First, the enhancement of total response output that was observed for the food-deprived rats could have been due to an increase in "activity" that was independent of the stimuli within the test situation. Second, the enhancement of the preferential behavior in both the food- and water-deprived animals may have been peculiar to the light onset. Were the deprived animals responding to produce a change in sensory stimulation (Lockhard, 1966; McCall, 1965; Mc-Call, 1966) or was there something about the onset of the light that differentially affected the rats' behavior in this task?

To examine these possibilities we replicated the previous experiment with terminal food and water deprivation and ad libitum controls using three different stimulus conditions (Tapp, Mathewson, & Simpson, 1968). In the first condition there was no light contingency. The animals were placed in the darkened lever-pressing apparatus, and responses on both levers were counted. In the second condition, a response produced the offset of a dim light (.5 foot-lamberts) above the adjacent lever. In a third condition, a response produced light onset

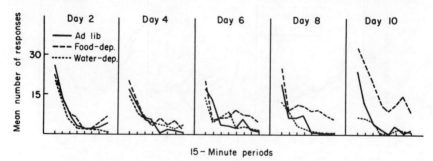

FIG. 8. Response decay curves plotted for each 15-minute period of the two-hour session for the days indicated. The ordinate is based on the mean number of responses on both levers combined. (From Tapp, Mathewson, & Jarrett, 1968.)

(.5 foot-lamberts). In both of these latter conditions, the light adjacent to the opposite bar was off and did not change when the animal pressed the lever. All animals were tested for ten days in their respective deprivation conditions for one hour each day.

The results of the experiment are summarized in Fig. 9. In the no-light condition, all three maintenance groups showed similar levels of responding on both levers throughout the experiment. In the offset condition, the ad libitum animals respond at consistently lower levels on the bar which produced light offset than on the control bar. Similarly, the water- and food-deprived animals preferred the control lever on the first two days of the experiment. As deprivation increased, there was a shift in this preference, and on days 9 and 10 of the experiment the deprived animals preferred the lever which produced light offset ($p < .05$). Total levels of responding were not altered by deprivation or by the stimulus condition and were the same as those observed for the no-light condition.

The light onset condition did produce an enhancement of the total levels of responding above the levels exhibited in the other test conditions, and total response levels tended to be higher for the food-deprived animals. Most importantly, however, the lever which produced light onset was preferred by the food- and water-deprived animals to a greater extent than for the ad libitum animals. The ad libitum rats reliably preferred the light onset lever on days 5, 6, and 10. The food- and water-deprived animals exhibited this preference on all but two of the test days, and for both of these groups one of those days was day 1, when they were tested under ad libitum conditions. The magnitude of this preference was not significantly greater for the food-deprived animals than for the water-deprived animals, perhaps because the test session was only one hour in length.

The results of this series of experiments quite clearly indicate that food and water deprivation produce a similar effect on the rat's behavior by enhancing the animal's reaction to changes in extrinsic stimuli within the environment that are produced as a consequence of its behavior. This interpretation is supported both by the observation that in extreme deprivation (terminal deprivation) the hungry and thirsty animals responded to produce light offset and by the fact that when no stimulus change occurred, responding was not increased above the levels exhibited by ad libitum controls.

This view is consistent with data reported by Campbell (1964). He observed that both hunger and thirst produced increased responding over satiated controls in two activity measures in which a response produced a movement-induced change within the test apparatus. One

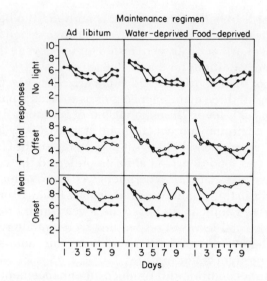

FIG. 9.   Mean daily levels of responding for the ad libitum and continuously food-
and water-deprived animals for each of the three test conditions. Closed circles represent the nonlighted bars. Open circles depict response rates on the levers which produced an illumination change. (From Tapp, Mathewson, & Simpson, 1968.)

of these measures was the activity wheel. The other was a stabilimeter
cage, modified in such a way as to make it unstable. Because exteroceptive stimuli were not manipulated, Campbell concluded that his
results were due to either the movement-produced feedback or some
other stimulus component common to both the activity wheel and the
unstable stabilimeters. Our results would suggest that the response-
produced changes in exteroceptive stimuli comprise the stimulus
component common to all three measures of activity.

   The results of our studies are similar to those reported by Campbell
(1964) in another important respect, specifically that terminal food and
water deprivation differ in their effects on the levels of total response
output. In Campbell's experiments, as in ours, the food-deprived animals responded at higher total levels than the water-deprived groups.
In our studies, this result would appear to be due to the tendency for
the food-deprived animals to continue to respond throughout the test
session. This effect was apparent only under the conditions in which a
response produced light onset; it was not observed in the offset
condition. The suggestion from these data is that food deprivation pro-
longs the habituation of responding that is manifest in the ad libitum
and water-deprived animals. The fact that this result was observed

only in the light onset condition suggests that the maintenance of responding in the food-deprived animals is also influenced by the stimuli within the environment.

The similarities in the effects of hunger and thirst are easier to discuss than their differences, for they suggest a common underlying process of considerable biological significance. Specifically, food and water deprivation appear to enhance the rat's tendency to react to the consequences of its behavior on environmental stimuli. In other words, the stimuli within the environment elicit behaviors in the rat. These behaviors produce other stimuli which, in turn, give direction to the animal's behavior. Increasing the need state of the animal results in increased tendencies for the animal to react to the stimulus events produced by his behavior.

Hunger, unlike thirst, also appears to prolong the animal's reaction to the response-produced changes in environmental stimuli, resulting in greater rates of responding over an extended period and increases in total response output. These differences between hunger and thirst are difficult to explain. Since the terminally water-deprived rats do not lose water, it is probable that there is a buildup of endogenous poisons which suppress behavior. It is also possible that these differential behaviors are mediated by alterations in neurohumoral mechanisms which appear to be important in the control of hunger and thirst (Grossman, 1967; Miller, 1965) and habituation (Carlton, Chapter 10, this volume).

D. Comparisons between Stimuli

The differences that were observed between the effects of light offset and light onset on the behavior of the animals in the previous experiments suggest that stimuli differ in their capacity to direct behavior. Specifically, the onset of the light had an apparently greater potential for directing responding than offset. Similarly, numerous experiments have demonstrated that the onset of a variety of qualitatively different stimuli, including a mild electric shock (Harrington & Linder, 1962), a tone (Andronico & Forgays, 1962), the taste of nonnutritive sweet substances (Young, 1966), and certain odors (Long & Tapp, 1967) can direct the lever-pressing behavior of the rat. In the final experiment of this series, we were interested in evaluating the relative capacity of the onset of several qualitatively different stimuli to direct the behavior of sated and food-deprived rats (Tapp & Long, 1968).

In this experiment, the double-bar lever-pressing apparatus was modified to allow the presentation of qualitatively different stimuli to the animals (for details of the apparatus, see Long & Tapp, 1968). We then compared the relative preferences of different groups of rats for the onset of a light (.5 foot-lamberts), a tone (680 cps, 65 dB against a background noise of 58 dB, re: .0002 dyne/cm^2), a puff of air (50 ml), and an odor (amyl acetate) to no stimulus change. When the animal made a response on one lever, the appropriate stimulus was turned on for one second. All stimuli were compared with one another in 15 groups of eight food-deprived and eight sated rats each. Deprivation was manipulated by pre- and postfeeding the animals 15 gm of food per day, one hour before or immediately after their test session. After 10 days of adaptation to the maintenance regimen, the animals were placed in the apparatus for one hour per day on alternate days for a total of three days.

Since all pairs of the five stimuli were compared with one another, the results of the experiment were summarized by determining the paired comparison scale values for each of the five stimuli for the deprived and satiated groups. These results are summarized in Table II. For both groups, the odor was the most highly preferred stimulus. Light onset was also preferred, but to a lesser extent. The other three stimuli had approximately the same scale values and were generally not preferred to one another. These results should be interpreted with some caution since the stimuli were not equated in any meaningful way prior to the experiment with regard to intensity or quality. The results do suggest that olfactory stimuli are an important class of stimuli for directing the rat's behavior.

Deprivation had an effect on total responding in the way that would be predicted from the results of the previous studies, i.e., the food-deprived animals responded more than the satiated animals ($p <$ .001). The levels of responding for these groups were not differentially affected by the particular stimulus conditions, suggesting some degree of independence between total response levels and the depri-

TABLE II
Paired Comparison Scale Values[a]

Stimuli	Scale values	
	Deprived	Satiated
Odor	1.55	1.39
Light	.86	1.09
Air	.15	.48
No stimulus	.00	.00
Tone	.07	−.01

[a]From Tapp & Long (1968).

vation conditions. However, the particular analysis which would allow us to determine if deprivation differentially enhanced the rat's reaction to the stimuli is to be found in those four stimulus conditions in which a response on only one lever produced stimulus onset. The summary data for these four conditions are presented in Table III, which gives the mean levels of responding averaged over the three test days. The deprived animals tended to respond more on the lever which produced stimulus onset than the sated animals, but this effect attained only marginal levels of significance ($p < .10$). The results are consistent with the hypothesis developed above, i.e., deprivation enhances the rat's tendency to react to the stimuli within the environment.

TABLE III

Mean Daily Responses on Control (No Stimulus) and Stimulus Onset Levers for Satiated and Deprived Groups[a]

Stimulus condition	Satiated		Deprived	
	Control lever	Stimulus lever	Control lever	Stimulus lever
Odor	50.6	54.3	61.0	97.0
Light	51.3	54.9	51.6	69.5
Air	49.2	64.6	60.4	92.4
Tone	42.8	51.4	40.3	64.7
Group means	48.5	56.3	53.3	80.9

[a]From Tapp and Long (1968).

IV. SUMMARY AND CONCLUSIONS

These experiments were conducted to examine the nature of those behaviors exhibited by the rat which occur antecedent to instrumental learning. We were hopeful that we could derive some knowledge of factors that affect these behaviors and in so doing gain some understanding of the general principles that underlie these behaviors. By way of summary, it is appropriate to restate the principles that have been suggested by these experiments.

From our observations of the rats' behavior it appears that the animals engage in stereotype patterns of responding that are consistent from animal to animal, both in the particulars of their manifestations and in the fact that they decay over the test session. These behavior patterns constitute the "spontaneous" activity of the rat. It is clear, both from our observations and from our attempts to quantify spontaneous activity, that these behaviors are composed of different acts that are influenced to a great extent by the environments within which they are measured. The particular appearance of these behavior patterns and their consistency from animal to animal suggest that these behaviors represent species-specific response patterns that seem to occur as reactions to the stimuli within the environment.

The importance of environmental stimuli in the regulation of these behavior patterns is substantiated by those experiments conducted in the lever-pressing apparatus. In particular, these studies indicate that the changes in external stimulation that occur as a consequence of the animal's behavior give direction to the particular response sequences in which the animals engage. The change in stimulation produced by the animal's responses is not sufficient in and of itself to give direction to the animal's behavior. Rather, it appears the stimuli differ in their behavior-directing properties. The onset of odors and lights seems to have a greater potential for directing the rat's behavior than the onset of a tone or a puff of air, or the offset of light.

The differences between stimuli in their behavior-directing attributes may also be related to characteristics of the species. In general, rodents are regarded as macrosmotic animals. This implies that rats are relatively dependent on odors to provide them with information about their environment. To the extent that this is true, it would be expected that rats would engage in behaviors which maximize the information they can acquire from olfactory stimulation. Our observations would tend to substantiate the validity of this hypothesis. The most frequently occurring behavior that we observed was the short, jerky body movement of the rat that was accompanied by a rapid movement of the vibrissae (sniffing). This behavior pattern suggests that the animal is sampling the odors within the test environment. Evidence from experiments described elsewhere (Long & Tapp, 1967) corroborates this hypothesis by indicating that rats will react to odors in ways that are similar to their reactions to light onset. Furthermore, odors appear to be much more potent than other exteroceptive stimuli in their capacity to direct the rat's behavior. This hypothesis suggests that animals enter test situations with predispositions to respond to certain classes of stimulus events that exist within that situation. For the rat, odor appears to be a very important source of stimulation. For other species, such as the primates, perhaps visual stimuli would be more relevant in that they would provide more information about the environment (Glickman & Sroges, 1966). This does not preclude the fact that animals react to the stimuli which affect other sense modalities, but it points to the primacy of one modality over others for any given species. Our preliminary research suggests ways that comparisons between modalities could be made and their relative hierarchies assessed.

These considerations suggest the generality that different species of animals are preprogrammed to react to their environments in ways which maximize the acquisition of information about that environment. Thus, the response patterns that are emitted are organized around a dominant sensory system to facilitate this process. The stimuli within the environment direct the particular sequence of responses that occur. In this capacity the stimuli elicit particular behavior patterns, and in this capacity stimuli can serve as potential rewards for these responses.

The use of rewards in this context is somewhat misleading, for it is only a reward in the sense used by K. N. Clayton (Chapter 4, this volume) as something given for some act that the animal has performed. The extent to which the stimulus event will elicit approach behaviors is perhaps the better indicant of its potential to "reinforce" a particular response. However, to speak of the reinforcing properties of a stimulus is also misleading, for there are currently a variety of measures that are applied to determine the extent to which a stimulus will "reinforce" behavior. At the simplest level, reinforcers have the capacity to direct an organism's behavior. Those stimuli that are approached are regarded as positively reinforcing, while those that are avoided are negatively reinforcing. Reinforcers are also discriminated in terms of their capacity to regulate behavior over varying periods of time, either within or between test sessions. They are discriminated on the basis of the control they exert over behavior in the absence of the particular stimulus event (see Berlyne, Chapter 7, this volume). They are also discriminated in terms of the amounts of work that the animal will engage in to achieve the stimulus, where work is defined in terms of rate or effort per unit of time. Finally, they are discriminated in terms of their capacity to control behavior in a variety of test situations. By these criteria virtually all stimuli are potential reinforcers to some extent, for under the appropriate test conditions it is likely that any discriminable stimulus could be demonstrated to be a reinforcer for some response.

These reflections on the operations which delineate the nature of reinforcers together with the results of our experiments have forced us to re-evaluate the utility of the concept of reinforcement and consider instead those factors which give a stimulus the capacity to elicit approach or withdrawal behaviors, i.e., direct the animal's behavior toward or away from the source of stimulation. There are, of course, a

variety of factors which contribute to the behavior-directing properties of a stimulus. Some of the physical dimensions of the stimuli, such
as intensity, contribute to the tendency of the animal to approach or
avoid the stimulus (Schneirla, 1959). Weak stimuli are generally approached while intense stimuli are avoided. There are other classes of
stimuli that are approached over the total ranges of their detectable
intensities, such as sugars (see Pfaffman, Chapter 8, this volume). The
behavior-directing properties of these attributes of stimuli are probably the result of a long evolutionary history, in which the approach or
avoidance of stimuli with these attributes has promoted survival of the
organism's ancestry more often than not.

The contingency between the stimulus and the response also contributes to the behavior-directing properties of the stimulus. In this
capacity, the stimulus serves as a source of feedback to the animal
about the relevance of one response over the many others that are
occurring within the situation. To the extent that a stimulus will elicit
behaviors that are compatible with the response that produced the
stimulus (approach), the occurrence of that behavior is further facilitated.

Increases in need appear to enhance the rat's reaction to the response-produced changes in environmental stimuli. Though the ad
libitum, or sated, animals occasionally showed reactions to these stimuli, their behaviors were, at best, transitory in nature. On the other
hand, both food and water deprivation, manipulated in several ways
in these experiments, shared the common property of increasing the
animals' reaction to the changes in exteroceptive stimuli that were
produced as a consequence of their behavior. Under these conditions
the stimuli gave the behavior of deprived animals definitive direction
that was manifest in their preference for the lever that produced the
change of stimulation. In this regard these results offer strong support
for the hypothesis that increases in need lower the animal's threshold
to respond in ways that produce changes in external environmental
stimuli. Though hunger and thirst share this property, hunger results
in an increase in the total levels of responding. In hungry animals this
increased tendency to respond to exteroceptive stimuli appears to be
dependent also on the presence of changing stimuli in the test environment, and may reflect the prolongation of the animal's reaction to
the stimuli.

There are numerous questions that arise from this work that are yet
to be answered. What other properties of stimuli and/or the animal's
experiences with them give them the capacity to direct the animal's
behavior? How important is the change of stimulation as a behavior-

directing property? Must the stimuli be produced by the behavior of the animal in order to direct behavior? How do stimuli differ in their behavior-directing properties for different sense modalities and for different species? Do stimuli work together and contribute to one another in terms of their behavior-directing attributes? Do all stimuli similarly affect the behavior of hungry and thirsty animals? How do hunger and thirst differ from one another in their effects on other measures of activity? What mechanisms underlie the differences that we have observed in these studies on the effects of hunger and thirst? These and the numerous other questions generated by this work await further research.

REFERENCES

Anderson, E. E. The interrelationship of drive in the male albino rat: II. Intercorrelations between 47 measures of drives and learning. *Comp. Psychol. Monogr.*, 1938, **14** (Whole No. 6).

Andronico, M. P., & Forgays, D. G. Sensory stimulation and secondary reinforcement. *J. Psychol.*, 1962, **54**, 209-219.

Baumeister, A., Hawkins, W. F., & Cromwell, R. L. Need states and anxiety level. *Psychol. Bull.*, 1964, **61**, 438-453.

Behrendt, W. A., Deninger, R., & Hillers, H. O. Methods for simultaneous numerical computation of different types of spontaneous motility. *Int. J. Neuropharmacol.*, 1962, **1**, 125-128.

Bindra, D. Components of general activity and the analysis of behavior. *Psychol. Rev.*, 1961, **68**, 205-215.

Bolles, R. C. Group and individual performance as a function of intensity and kind of deprivation. *J. comp. physiol. Psychol.*, 1959, **52**, 579-585.

Bolles, R. C. *Theory of motivation.* New York: Harper, 1967.

Campbell, B. A. Effects of water deprivation on random activity. *J. comp. physiol. Psychol.*, 1960, **53**, 240-251.

Campbell, B. A. Theory and research on the effects of water deprivation on random activity in the rat. In M. J. Wayner (Ed.), *Thirst.* New York: Macmillan, 1964. Pp. 317-334.

Campbell, B. A., & Cicala, G. Studies of water deprivation in rats as a function of age. *J. comp. physiol. Psychol.*, 1962, **55**, 763-768.

Campbell, B. A., & Sheffield, F. D. Relation of random activity to food deprivation. *J. comp. physiol. Psychol.*, 1953, **46**, 320-322.

Clayton, F. L. Light reinforcement as a function of water deprivation. *Psychol. Rep.*, 1958, **4**, 63-66.

Davis, J. D. The reinforcement effect of weak light onset as a function of the amount of food deprivation. *J. comp. physiol. Psychol.*, 1958, **51**, 496-498.

D'Encarnacao, P. S. The differential behavioral effects of drugs affecting catecholamines. Unpublished doctoral dissertation, Vanderbilt Univer., 1968.

Duda, J. J., & Bolles, R. C. Effects of prior deprivation, current deprivation, and weight loss on the activity of the hungry rat. *J. comp. physiol. Psychol.*, 1963, **56**, 569-571.

Forgays, D. G., & Levin, H. Learning as a function of change in sensory stimulation: I. Food-deprived versus satiated animals. *J. comp. physiol. Psychol.*, 1958, **51**, 50-54.

Glickman, S. E., & Sroges, R. W. Curiosity in zoo animals. *Behaviour*, 1966, **26**, 151-188.

Grossman, S. P. *A textbook of physiological psychology.* New York: Wiley, 1967.

Hall, J. F. Activity as a function of restricted drinking schedule. *J. comp. physiol. Psychol.*, 1955, **48**, 265-266.

Harrington, G. M., & Linder, W. K. A positive reinforcing effect of electrical stimulation. *J. comp. physiol. Psychol.*, 1962, **55**, 1014-1015.

Kiernan, C. C. Effect of food deprivation and unconditioned operant pretests on bar pressing for light in the albino rat. *J. comp. physiol. Psychol.*, 1965, **60**, 268-271.

Kish, G. B. Studies of sensory reinforcement. In W. K. Honig (Ed.), *Operant behavior: Areas of research and application.* New York: Appleton, 1966. Pp. 109-159.

Kreeger, G. L. Techniques for the investigation of psychological phenomena in the rat. In J. Q. Griffith & E. J. Farris (Eds.), *The rat in laboratory investigation.* Philadelphia: Lippincott, 1942. Pp. 192-273.

Lockhard, R. B. Several tests of stimulus change and preference theory in relation to light-controlled behavior of rats. *J. comp. physiol. Psychol.*, 1966, **62**, 413-426.

Long, C. J., & Tapp, J. T. Reinforcing properties of odors for the albino rat. *Psychon. Sci.*, 1967, **7**, 17-18.

Long, C. J., & Tapp, J. T. An apparatus for the assessment of the reinforcing properties of odors in small animals. *J. exp. Anal. Behav.*, 1968, **11**, 49-51.

McCall, R. B. Stimulus changes in light contingent bar pressing. *J. comp. physiol. Psychol.*, 1965, **59**, 258-262.

McCall, R. B. Initial-consequent-change-surface in light-contingent bar pressing. *J. comp. physiol. Psychol.*, 1966, **62**, 35-42.

Miller, N. E. Chemical coding of behavior in the brain. *Science*, 1965, **148**, 328-338.

Moskowitz, M. J. Running wheel activity in the white rat as a function of combined food and water deprivation. *J. comp. physiol. Psychol.*, 1959, **52**, 621-625.

O'Kelly, L. I. The psychophysiology of motivation. *Annu. Rev. Psychol.*, 1963, **14**, 57-92.

Premack, D., & Collier, G. Analysis of non-reinforcement variables affecting response probability. *Psychol. Monogr.*, 1962, **76** (Whole No. 524).

Reed, J. D. Spontaneous activity of animals. A review of the literature since 1929. *Psychol. Bull.*, 1947, **44**, 393-412.

Schneirla, T. C. An evolutionary and developmental theory of biphasic processes underlying approach and withdrawal. In M. Jones (Ed.), *Nebraska symposium on motivation.* Lincoln, Nebr.: Univer. of Nebraska Press, 1959. Pp. 1-42.

Segal, E. F. Confirmation of a positive relation between deprivation and the number of responses emitted for light reinforcement. *J. exp. Anal. Behav.*, 1959, **2**, 165-169.

Smith, R. C., & Donahoe, J. W. The effects of food deprivation on unreinforced and light-reinforced bar pressing. *J. genet. Psychol.*, 1966, **108**, 213-219.

Sparks, L. M., & Lockhard, R. B. Relationships among three measures of home cage activity. *Psychol. Rep.*, 1966, **19**, 740.

Strong, P. N., Jr. Activity in the white rat as a function of apparatus and hunger. *J. comp. physiol. Psychol.*, 1957, **50**, 596-600.

Tapp, J. T., & Long, C. J. A comparison of the reinforcing properties of stimulus onset for several sense modalities. *Canad. J. Psychol.*, 1968, **22**, 449-455.

Tapp, J. T., & Simpson, L. L. Motivational and response factors as determinants of the reinforcing value of light onset. *J. comp. physiol. Psychol.*, 1966, **62**, 143-146.

Tapp, J. T., Mathewson, D. M., & Jarrett, P. Effects of terminal food and water deprivation on the reinforcing properties of light onset. *Psychon. Sci.*, 1968, **13**, 9-10.

Tapp, J. T., Mathewson, D. M., & Simpson, L. L. Effects of hunger and thirst on reinforcing properties of light onset and light offset. *J. comp. physiol. Psychol.*, 1968,
66, 784-787.

Tapp, J. T., Zimmerman, R. S., and D'Encarnacao, P. S. Intercorrelational analysis of
some common measures of rat activity. *Psych. Rep.*, 1968, **23**, 1047-1050.

Treichler, F. R., & Collins, R. W. Comparison of cyclic and continuous deprivation on
wheel running. *J. comp. physiol. Psychol.*, 1965, **60**, 447-448.

Wilson, J. J. Photic reinforcement as a function of optimal level of stimulation. *Psychol.
Rec.*, 1962, **12**, 17-23.

Young, P. T. Hedonic organization and regulation of behavior. *Psychol. Rev.*, 1966, **73**,
59-86.

CHAPTER 7

The Reward-Value of Indifferent Stimulation[1]

D. E. BERLYNE

[1]The preparation of this chapter and the research reported in it were supported by Research Grants MH-06324 and MH-12528 from the National Institute of Mental Health, U. S. Public Health Service, No. 70 from the Ontario Mental Health Foundation, and APT-73 and APB-73 from the National Research Council of Canada.

I. INTRODUCTION

A. The Nature of Reinforcement

The word "reinforcement" has had a rather checkered history since it was first used by Pavlov (1927). For Pavlov, it meant something whose application causes a conditioned reflex to become established and whose removal brings on extinction. In classical conditioning, it could be identified with the unconditioned stimulus, the stimulus that evoked the response originally. This was usually, but not invariably, a stimulus of overriding biological importance, such as the appearance of food or an electric shock administered to the leg.

In English-speaking countries, the word "reinforcement" has come in many circles to be identified exclusively with "reward," the kind of reinforcement that affects instrumental or operant conditioning. This means that some event coming immediately after a response increases the probability or vigor with which that response will subsequently be performed in comparable stimulus situations. The intense interest in instrumental conditioning among American psychologists and the influence of a powerful school, led by Hull (1943), that held all learning to be instrumental conditioning encouraged the use of the words "reinforcement" and "reward" as synonyms.

This seems a regrettable historical accident. There is now evidence (see Solomon & Brush, 1965) that classical and instrumental conditioning are different in some respects, particularly with regard to the ways in which they are reinforced. And as for the various forms of verbal learning and acquisition of motor skills that are found in human beings, there is so far little agreement on how they are related to classical and instrumental conditioning or how far they represent additional types of learning with their own kinds of reinforcement. So it would seem best to use the word "reinforcement" in the widest and most noncommittal sense, recognizing that different kinds of events may fulfill the reinforcing function for different kinds of learning.

From this point of view, the best definition of reinforcement, I suggest, is that "reinforcement is whatever has to be added to contiguity to obtain learning" (Berlyne, 1968, p. 3). It seems to be clear enough that, for any kind of learning to occur, something must be contiguous with something. Unfortunately, there has not been unanimous agreement on what has to be contiguous with what. The most common view has been that a response must accompany or closely follow a stimulus.

But some have believed that, in addition to or instead of this, learning can result when two stimuli or two responses occur together or in close succession. Sometimes, learning can be said to take place as a result of the contiguity of two internal events, such as thoughts (Berlyne, 1965).

But whichever of these cases may be realized, it is clear in all of them that contiguity alone does not guarantee learning. In some circumstances, a stimulus and response (or two stimuli or two responses) can be paired many times without leading to any detectable learning whatever. At other times, learning will be dramatic and indelible after one pairing. Whether learning will take place and how strong the learned response will be depend on other conditions, which are the ones that the term "reinforcement" properly designates. In classical conditioning, the reinforcing event is the unconditioned stimulus. In instrumental conditioning, the reinforcing event is a "reward" or the event consequent on the response. Though there has been little investigation of how intellectual and other forms of verbal learning are reinforced, it is perhaps even clearer in these kinds of learning that contiguity alone is not enough. The additional factors that are necessary to ensure retention may well turn out to be ones that, in everyday parlance, we should class as factors governing "attention" (Berlyne, 1967).

B. Need to Distinguish Reinforcement from Performance Effects

In what follows, I am going to concentrate on reward, but, as a preliminary, it is necessary to make some observations that apply to reinforcement in general. According to the definition I have just suggested, reinforcement is something that promotes learning. And, according to most (but possibly not all) current conceptions, learning means a relatively permanent change in behavior—a change that lasts a matter of days or longer and not merely a matter of minutes or hours (Kimble, 1961). A conclusive test of reinforcement value or of any other learning effect, therefore, requires an experimental design in which (a) an interval of at least 24 hours intervenes between training and testing and (b) different groups of subjects (or different responses within the same subject) have been trained under different conditions but are tested under identical conditions. If we then find differences in response strength on test days, we are obliged to conclude that different degrees of learning have resulted from the differences between training conditions.

"Reinforcement" has sometimes been carelessly defined as anything that raises response rate. A small boy will sometimes tie a tin can to a cat's tail, knowing that this will cause the cat to run around frantically. The sounds resulting from collisions of the can with the ground will certainly raise the rate of locomotion sharply, but can we conclude from this that they are reinforcing or indeed that any learning has occurred? The answer is clearly no, because at least two other possible effects of the sounds, which nobody in his right mind would surely want to class as reinforcing effects, could be producing the rise in response rate. First, the sounds could be affecting the cat's motivational or emotional condition, making the animal more "agitated," "excited," or "aroused" and thus more mobile. Second, the sound consequent on one movement could act as a cue evoking another movement, whether through an unlearned reflex or a learned association. If, on the other hand, we were to observe the cat on the following day with the can no longer present and if we then found some difference in its behavior (e.g., fleeing from small boys) as compared with cats that had not undergone the ordeal, we could then conclude that learning had taken place and that the sounds made by the can had had some kind of reinforcing effect.

The same difficulties beset any attempt to demonstrate that some event, x, has a greater reward-value than some other event, y. A demonstration that bar-pressing in a Skinner box occurs more rapidly when this response is followed by x than when it is followed by y is not enough. We cannot tell whether this difference appears because x is more effective as a reinforcer than y, because x is more conducive than y to a motivational condition characterized by greater motor activity, or because x is more likely than y to evoke a repetition of the bar-pressing response. When, however, animals (or responses) trained with x and y are compared the next day under identical conditions (e.g., extinction conditions), the existence of differential effects on learning can be established.[2] The interval of 24 hours may seem rather arbitrary, but it is generally long enough to ensure that transient ef-

---

[2]It must, of course, be ascertained empirically whether the two techniques mentioned, namely the application of different consequences to different groups of subjects and to different responses within the same subjects, yield the same conclusions about relative reward-value. Some of our recent experiments suggest that they might not. Similarly, there are experiments in the literature indicating that measures of relative "preference" derived from between-subject comparisons and from within-subject choices do not always tally (see Berlyne, 1967). The experiments discussed in this chapter all used between-subject comparisons, so that one must be cautious about generalizing the conclusions to situations in which relative strengths of different responses performed by the same subjects are measured.

fects on response strength, classifiable as "performance effects," have had time to die down.

C. Use of Indifferent Stimuli as Rewards

By far the greater part of the experimental work on reward that has been done so far has concentrated on food, water, opportunities for sexual activity, and termination or avoidance of pain. It would be absurd to belittle the valuable contributions to knowledge that have been made in this way. But in some respects, it might be a mistake to build theories of reward solely on the study of these familiar kinds of reward.

They are not by any means the only agents that can act as rewards. In many ways, they are atypical. Their rewarding effect is exceptionally powerful. They have immense and unmistakable biological significance. They correspond to biological activities associated with identifiable centers in the brain, particularly in the hypothalamus.

Evidence is, however, accumulating that virtually anything can act as a reward in suitable circumstances (Berlyne, 1960; Berlyne, 1963; Berlyne, 1966; Berlyne, 1967). It has been shown, by Asratian (1961) with reference to classical conditioning and by Premack (1962) with reference to instrumental conditioning, that the reinforcer-reinforced relation may be reversible; if S_1 strengthens the association of some response to S_2 in one set of conditions, the opposite may hold in other conditions. The practice of pairing a biologically neutral event with an event of overriding biological significance or intensity masks this symmetry.

Some essential aspects of the reinforcement process may be brought into view most readily by examining the reward-value, not of the most familiar and frequently studied forms of reward, but of arbitrarily chosen "indifferent" stimuli. Strictly speaking, anything that is rewarding cannot properly be called "indifferent." But the term has acquired a usage originating with Pavlov, according to which it refers to stimuli that are not associated with recognizable effects of biological importance on tissues other than the sense organs and nervous system. For example, Russian writers speak of the "formation of connections between indifferent stimuli," by which they mean what English-speaking psychologists would call "latent learning" or "sensory preconditioning." The reward-value of indifferent stimuli is less marked than that of, say, food or the relief of pain and is harder to interpret, which may make its investigation particularly enlightening. To paraphrase Samuel Johnson's famous comparison of a woman preaching with a dog standing on his hind legs, they do not reinforce very well, but it is surprising that they reinforce at all.

D. Specificity versus Generality

One salient fact about reinforcers, and rewards in particular, is that their efficacy depends on the motivational condition of the subject. DeBold, Miller, and Jensen (1965) have contrived an elegant demonstration that water will not provide reinforcement for classical conditioning unless a rat is thirsty. As for instrumental conditioning, several experiments (see Kimble, 1961) have indicated learning to be influenced by the degree of hunger or thirst during training, with amount of food or water used as reward held constant.

Something of a debate has grown up between those who believe that various rewarding agents have little in common apart from their power to reinforce instrumental responses and those who suspect that all rewards must work through some common mechanism so that one could in principle estimate how rewarding a particular event will be before trying it out. The close tie between reward and motivational condition links this controversy with the parallel controversy between partisans of a "general drive" (or, in its most recent variants, "arousal") and those who favor lists of specific drives.

There are grounds for holding that states of high drive generated by different drive conditions have both shared properties and distinguishing properties (Berlyne, 1967). Nevertheless, two currents of research have tended to encourage recognition of specific drives, and correspondingly of specific rewards, only. The first of these is the work of the ethologists on the behavior of invertebrates and submammalian vertebrates. These lower animals have limited repertoires of behavior, and their activities generally fall neatly into a small number of distinguishable classes. V. Dethier (in a lecture at the University of Toronto, 1967) has stated that the blowfly's time is taken up with feeding, copulation, and activities preparatory to these two behaviors. Von Holst and von St. Paul (1960; 1962) have discovered points in the brain stem of the domestic hen at which stimulation evokes "almost all the forms of activity and vocalization familiar to those acquainted with chickens." These seem to belong to some half-dozen or so systems. Second, the study of alimentary, defensive, aggressive, and reproductive functions in higher mammals has proceeded hand in hand with neurophysiological research, which has revealed distinct centers corresponding to such categories of behavior in the central nervous system, especially in the hypothalamus.

Nevertheless, these lines of research, invaluable as they have been, may have introduced some distortion of perspective. In human beings, the range of possible activities and the range of possible sources of reward, especially among indifferent stimuli, are so vast that we can hardly suppose each of them to have its own center in the brain stem. They must surely make use of some "final common paths."

One can well imagine that, if learning theorists had confined their attention to specialized responses like feeding, copulation, or sneezing, they might well have been impressed with the peculiarities of each of them and done little to seek laws governing behavior in general. But anyone who considers instead the learning of an arbitrarily chosen response, like bar-pressing or alley-running in the rat and panel-pecking in the pigeon, is bound to be convinced before long that similarities must underlie the differences. The study of the reward-value of indifferent stimuli may perform a comparable function.

E. Photic Reinforcement

The phenomenon with which the experiments I am going to discuss were concerned has been given various names. It has been called "response-contingent light change" and "light-contingent bar-pressing." Perhaps the best name, if only because it is the shortest, is "photic reinforcement."

In the early 1950's, several investigators discovered independently that rats and mice will press a lever at a higher rate when the response is followed by a brief increase in illumination than when it is not. Some of them (Henderson, 1953; Hurwitz, 1956; Kish, 1955), like most of those who have since pursued this line of research, used light *onset*, i.e., a change from darkness to light. Girdner (1953), however, used light *increment*, i.e., a change from less intense to more intense light. We ourselves, in the experiments to be reported, have used light increment for two reasons. First, the reward-value of light onset is perhaps understandable, since complete darkness can be biologically dangerous even for a nocturnal animal such as the rat that habitually shuns brightly lit places. The reward-value of a light increment that does not noticeably add to what is visible is, on the other hand, harder to account for and thus more instructive. Second, in one of our experiments, we planned to separate degree of change from consequent level of illumination, which is not possible with light onset. Shortly after the early reports, similar effects were found in other species and with auditory stimuli (see Berlyne, 1960, Chap. 6), and recently, Long and Tapp (1967) performed similar experiments with olfactory stimuli.

The phenomenon was somewhat startling when it was first demonstrated. Prevalent theories of motivation held that rewarding events correspond to biological needs and are associated either inherently (primary reward) or indirectly through learning (secondary reward) with events that conduce to relief of these needs. There seemed to be no clear way in which light change, at least in the form of light increment, had anything to do with removal of a threat to survival. One influential view, sponsored by Miller and Dollard (1941), maintained that rewards always entail drive reduction, which was taken to mean reduction in overall stimulation. This echoed a suggestion once made by Freud (1915) to the effect that behavior is ultimately aimed at keeping "excitation" (which should presumably increase with stimulation) down to a minimum. But in the experiments in question, animals seemed to be going out of their way to seek increased stimulation. Several experimenters (Flynn & Jerome, 1952; Hefferline, 1950; Keller, 1941) had shown shortly before that a drop in illumination from a relatively intense level could reinforce an instrumental response in the rat, and there are plenty of hints in the literature that rats are photophobic.

Nevertheless, the findings were not so surprising as they might have been. At about the same time, experimenters using other techniques (Berlyne, 1950; Berlyne, 1955; Butler, 1953; Harlow, 1950; Montgomery, 1953) were beginning to point out the propensity of animals like the rat for exploratory behavior, which involves seeking exposure to indifferent stimulation. The photic-reinforcement effect seemed to be related to what they had observed. Bar-pressing for light change is, in fact, an example of the kind of behavior for which the term "diversive exploration" has been proposed (Berlyne, 1960). Its affinities with a wide variety of animal and human activities, commonly subsumed under labels like "play," "entertainment," and "aesthetics," suggested themselves.

II. IS LIGHT INCREMENT REALLY REWARDING?

When we first set out to do experiments on photic reinforcement, we were surprised to find how little solid evidence there was that increases in illumination actually possess the reward-value that had been under discussion for some ten years. Most experimenters had contented themselves with ascertaining that bar-presses occur more frequently when they are followed by light change. But as I have already pointed out, this in itself does not imply any more than a transient performance effect. For example, it seems not unlikely that intermittent changes in illumination will raise an animal's general activity level through some motivational effect, perhaps by raising arousal level. Even when an experimental group (trained with light change) performs more responses than a control group (trained without light change) in an extinction test held immediately after training (Barnes & Baron, 1961), the difficulty still remains. A motivational condition brought on by light changes might well last for a fair number of minutes after the light changes have ceased and may decline slowly.

Two techniques, however, have come into use to test the possibility that light changes merely heighten general activity for a short time after they have occurred. Kling, Horowitz, and Delhagen (1956) introduced the yoked-control design. Whenever an experimental animal presses a bar, he not only receives a light change himself but also causes a light change to occur simultaneously in an adjacent Skinner box containing a control subject. The control subjects thus experience light changes in the same number and with the same temporal distribution as their experimental partners, but for them the contiguity between response and light change is removed. Barnes and Kisch (1958) used two bars, only one of which switched on the light change. The facts that experimental animals press the bar more often than yoked-control animals and that an active bar is pressed more often than an inactive bar exclude the hypothesis that light changes make a rat more active in general rather than selectively strengthening those responses on which they are consequent.

Yet, there remains the possibility of the other kind of performance effect that we have considered, namely the cue effect. It might seem farfetched to suppose that a light change following one bar-press will evoke a further bar-press through some inherited reflex or through previous learning. But one form of cue effect, what we have called "positive feedback facilitation," is not so easily excluded. This takes the form of a temporarily increased tendency to repeat whatever the animal has just done. Since an animal is generally facing and looking at the bar when the light change occurs, it is surely conceivable that, if the principal effect of the light change is to make an animal more reactive, a repetition of the bar-pressing response that he has just performed may be more likely at that moment than any alternative act.

So we come back to the conclusion mentioned earlier, namely that the only conclusive way to demonstrate reward-value is to make sure that an effect on learning of some durability has taken place. This means giving experimental and control animals, which have been trained under different conditions, a test under identical conditions at least 24 hours after the last training trial.

Two groups of experimenters have done this with light onset. Forgays and Levin (1958) gave their rats seven daily extinction trials after 14 daily training trials and verified that there was more bar-pressing during extinction in the experimental group that had had light changes during training than in the control group that had not. A delayed test in extinction conditions was also given by Crowder, Morris, Dyer, and Robinson (1961), who obtained differences of only border-line significance.

In the case of light onset, we can regard the experiment by Forgays and Levin as a satisfactory enough demonstration of reward-value. But nobody had provided a comparable demonstration for the reputed reward-value of light increment, and, for the reasons mentioned above, this seemed worth attempting. The first experiment in the series (Berlyne, Salapatek, Gelman, & Zener, 1964) set out to ascertain, with all necessary controls, whether light increment can reinforce an instrumental response in the rat.

A. Experiment 1: No Light Change during Test Trials

Three groups of 22 rats went through 15-minute sessions in a Skinner box on each of 14 consecutive days. Days 2, 6, and 14 were Test days, and the remaining days were Training days.

The test chamber was illuminated by light coming through frosted glass from a port in the ceiling. For most of the time, the luminance of the port was 1 mL, but a *light change* consisted of a rise from 1 mL to 2 mL with a return to 1 mL after 1 second.

On Test days, no light changes occurred for any of the animals when the bar was pressed. On Training days, however, the treatment varied from group to group. The experimental (E) group received a light change every time the bar was pressed. Each member of the yoked-control (YC) group received a light change whenever its E partner in the adjacent box pressed the bar. No light changes were experienced by the control (NLC) group.

By having test sessions during which animals of all groups were treated alike and separating each test session from the last training session by one day, we were able to ascertain whether the occurrence of a light change as a consequence of bar-pressing would produce a learned strengthening of the bar-pressing response. Differences in reward-value could be distinguished from performance effects, including motivational effects, positive-feedback facilitation, and other cue effects. If, however, we had had only the E and NLC groups, greater responding by the E group on Test days could conceivably have been due to another factor that we needed to exclude. If light changes increase arousal or activity level, this increase could become conditioned to the stimuli constituting the interior of the test chamber, and these stimuli could raise response rate on Test days through this activation conditioned on training days. Inclusion of the YC group controlled for this possibility.

The mean numbers of responses on Test days are shown in Fig. 1. The means for the YC and NLC groups are close together. Analysis of variance of logarithmic transforms revealed that the E group pressed the bar a significantly greater number of times over all three Test days ($p < .05$) and on Day 6 ($p < .01$).

A remaining possibility is that the difference between E and control groups on Test Days was due to a difference in novelty. Since the NLC rats had exactly the same conditions on a Test day as they had had on previous Training days, the situation was not novel for them. But since the E group had had light changes following each bar-press on Training days, the failure of a light change to accompany a bar-press on Test days introduced an element of novelty. The obvious way

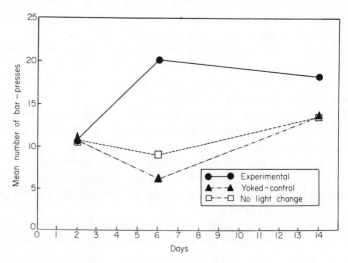

FIG. 1. Experiment 1 (Section II). Test day means. (Data from Berlyne, Salapatek, Gelman, & Zener, 1964.)

to control for this possibility is to conduct an experiment in which, on Test days, both experimental and control groups undergo the treatment that experimental groups received on Training Days. In such an experiment, the Test-day situation would be novel for the control group but not for the experimental groups, and if novelty were the operative factor, the effect found in Experiment 1 should be reversed.

B. Experiment 2: Light Change during Test Trials

The second experiment lasted for six days, with Days 2 and 6 as Test days. Since the YC group had served its purpose in Experiment 1, only an E group and an NLC group, each of 22 rats, were used for this experiment. On Training days they received light changes and no light changes, respectively, when the bar was pressed. On Test days, every bar-press resulted in a light change for both groups.

The Test day means are shown in Fig. 2. Logarithmically transformed scores were higher in the E group than in the NLC group over both Test days ($p < .005$) and on Day 2 alone ($p < .001$).

Over both experiments, the E groups pressed the bar significantly more often than the NLC groups on Test days 2 and 6 taken together ($p < .005$). The means are, however, significantly greater in Experiment 1 than Experiment 2 ($p < .005$), which indicates that performance was depressed by the presence of light on Test days.

It is possible to see whether there was an effect of novelty by seeing whether the Groups × Experiments interaction was significant on Test days. This comparison is, of course, now orthogonal to the E/NLC comparison. Over both Test days, novelty did not have a significant effect, but the Novelty × Days interaction was significant ($p < .025$). There were significantly ($p < .025$) fewer responses on Day 2, but not on Day 6, with a novel Test day condition. We can therefore conclude that the novel Test day condition depressed performance when it was first encountered but not later.

III. EFFECTS OF DEGREE OF CHANGE AND CONSEQUENT LEVEL

Having arrived at a satisfactory demonstration that light increment has reward-value for the rat, we set out in search of factors on which this reward-value depends.

According to one interpretation of photic reinforcement and cognate

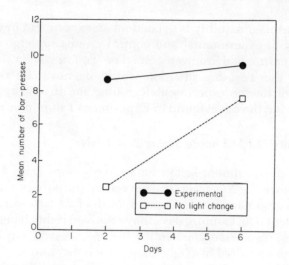

FIG. 2. Experiment 2 (Section II). Test day means. (Data from Berlyne, Salapatek, Gelman, & Zener, 1964.)

forms of behavior (e.g., Fox, 1962; Glanzer, 1958; McClelland, Atkinson, Clark, & Lowell, 1953; Robinson, 1961), animals seek to approximate an optimal influx of information or rate of stimulus change. With this interpretation in mind, one might expect the reward-value of light increment to depend on the degree of change or difference between the initial level of illumination and the consequent level or level resulting from the bar-press.

According to another view, whose foremost spokesman has been Lockard (1962), animals seek to approximate a preferred, usually intermediate, level of illumination. This view points to the consequent level as the principal determinant of reward-value.

It is not possible to separate degree of change from consequent level using light onset, since, when the initial level is zero, there must be a perfect correlation between these two variables. But the use of light increment permits one to seek evidence for either or both of these hypotheses through appropriate manipulation of initial levels.

A. Experiment 1: Light Increment

An experiment (Berlyne & Koenig, 1965) was performed with an experimental (E) group and a control (NLC) group, each of 54 rats.

Each group was divided into nine subgroups, corresponding to the cells in Table I. The number in each cell indicates the initial level of illumination (luminance of the ceiling port). The rows correspond to three degrees of change—doubling, quadrupling, and octupling—yielding the consequent levels shown at the heads of the columns.

The experiment lasted for 12 days, with odd-numbered days as Training days and even-numbered days as Test days. On Training days, each bar-press produced a change from the initial level to the consequent level for E animals but no light change for NLC animals. On Test days, the initial level remained unchanged, despite the bar-pressing, for both groups.

As Fig. 3 shows, there were significantly more responses in the E group on Test day ($p < .001$). We, therefore, had extended our demonstration of the reward-value of light increment to a wider range of initial and consequent levels.

The means for the different consequent levels and degrees of change are shown in Table II. There is a hint that the 4-mL consequent level may be more effective than the others, but the effects of both consequent level and degree of change are actually nonsignificant on both Training and Test days.

B. Experiment 2: Light Decrement

A second experiment (Berlyne & Koenig, 1965) studied effects of light decrement. The design used in Experiment 1 was essentially inverted, as shown in Table III. Three consequent levels, 0.25, 0.5, and 1 mL, were combined factorially with three decremental degrees of change—dividing by two, four, and eight—by using as initial levels the values shown in the cells of the table. There was an E group and an NLC group of 18 rats each.

TABLE I

Experiment 1 (Sect. III): Initial Levels, Consequent Levels, and Degrees of Change

Degree of change	Consequent level	2 mL	4 mL	8 mL
× 8		0.25 mL	0.5 mL	1 mL
× 4		0.5 mL	1 mL	2 mL
× 2		1 mL	2 mL	4 mL

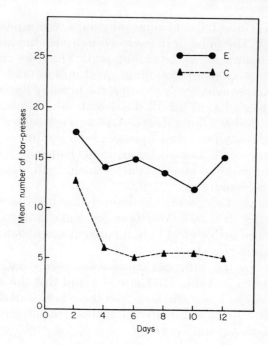

Fig. 3. Experiment 1 (Section III). Test day means. (From Berlyne and Koenig, 1965.)

TABLE II
Experiment 1 (Sect. III): Mean Number of Responses per Day

	Group	Consequent level	2 mL	4 mL	8 mL
Test days	E		15.2	17.0	11.5
	NLC		6.6	6.2	7.3
Training days	E		16.4	17.9	11.7
	NLC		8.3	7.8	8.9

	Group	Degree of change	× 2	× 4	× 8
Test days	E		14.2	16.1	13.3
	NLC		5.7	7.5	6.9
Training days	E		14.2	16.7	15.2
	NLC		6.6	8.9	9.5

The purpose of this experiment was dual. First, the effects of degree of change and consequent level on reward-value were probed further by extending the range of values. Second, it was of interest to find out whether light decrement as well as light increment can reinforce instrumental responses. If so, reward-value can be attributed to change in illumination, whether upward or downward.

As Table IV shows, neither independent variable produced a significant effect once again. There was, however, a significant ($p < .001$) superiority of the E group on both Training and Test days.

C. Conclusions

It seems that light increment or light decrement can act as a reward. But within the range of values sampled in these two experiments, it appears that degree of change and consequent level make little, if any, difference to reward-value. If the range were extended, one would expect some differences to appear, if only because absolute or differential thresholds, on the one hand, or a painful intensity of illumination, on the other hand, would be approached.

Since these two experiments were completed, rather similar experiments have been reported by McCall (1965) and by Lockard (1966).

TABLE III

Experiment 2 (Sect. III): Initial Levels, Consequent Levels, and Degrees of Change

Degree of change	Consequent level	0.25 mL	0.5 mL	1 mL
× ⅛		2 mL	4 mL	8 mL
× ¼		1 mL	2 mL	4 mL
× ½		0.5 mL	1 mL	2 mL

TABLE IV

Experiment 2 (Sect. III): Mean Number of Responses per Day

	Group	Consequent level	0.25 mL	0.5 mL	1 mL
Test days	E		15.1	15.0	14.3
	NLC		4.2	6.1	4.8
Training days	E		16.3	18.7	18.1
	NLC		3.8	6.5	5.6

Both of these experimenters took a number of levels of illumination and used them as initial levels and consequent levels in every possible combination, so that their experimental designs can be represented by matrices. They also had two days of extinction following a series of Training days, so that the requirements for detection of differences in reward-value were met.

On Training days, the two experiments yielded findings that diverge from each other as well as from our own experiments. McCall obtained evidence that bar-pressing rate increases with degree of change, whether increasing or decreasing. Lockard deduces from his data that response rate is governed predominantly by consequent level, with moderate levels more effective than the most intense levels (10 and 100 foot-candles). The findings on extinction days are, however, of most concern to us here, since they alone reveal effects on learning. It is interesting to note that both McCall's and Lockard's data are congruent with our own. McCall found no effect of intensities of illumination or of degree of change on response rate during extinction. Lockard found a significant effect of initial level, which can be regarded as a performance effect, since the same initial level was present during training and during extinction. Apart from this, he found a difference only between groups corresponding to the principal diagonal of the matrix (i.e., groups with no light change during training) and groups corresponding to other cells (i.e., animals that had been trained with light increment or decrement pressed a bar that had produced light changes on Training days more often than a bar that had not). Consequently, we must class the effects of degree of change and consequent level that occurred on Training days as performance effects. As far as reward-value is concerned, the findings of McCall and of Lockard, like ours, indicate that light changes have reward-value but that neither degree of change nor consequent level has an appreciable influence.

IV. DEPRIVATION OF STIMULUS-CHANGE, NOVELTY, AND AROUSAL

Pursuing further our quest for factors governing the reward-value of light changes and other indifferent stimuli, we took up two additional possibilities suggested in the literature. The two hypotheses to be tested were (a) that the reward-value of an indifferent stimulus is enhanced after a subject has spent some time in an impoverished environment, and (b) that the reward-value of an indifferent stimulus increases with its novelty.

An experiment by Premack, Collier, and Roberts (1957) seemed at one time to have shown the rate of bar-pressing for light onset to be greater the longer rats have been in darkness before the response becomes available. This turned out, however, in the light of later experiments (Premack & Collier, 1962) to be simply an effect of intertrial interval regardless of whether the interval was spent in darkness or in conditions of abundant visual stimulation. That incidence of diversive exploratory responses tends to increase with the duration of a period of prior deprivation of visual change has, however, been demonstrated both in monkeys (Butler, 1957; Fox, 1962) and in human subjects (Jones, Wilkinson, & Braden, 1961). There have been some indications that novelty influences the reward-value of indifferent stimulation in the rat, but findings have not been consistent on this point (see Berlyne, 1960, pp. 145–146).

The stimulus-deprivation and novelty hypotheses sound rather similar, but they can be distinguished by the presence or absence of cross-modality transfer. The stimulus-deprivation hypothesis implies that the reward-value of, say, light change will depend on how much stimulus-change of any modality the subject has recently had. Novelty, on the other hand, is a matter of whether or not the subject has recently had stimulation resembling that whose reward-value is to be investigated.

A. Experiment 1: Novelty and Stimulus Deprivation

The two hypotheses were examined in an experiment by Berlyne, Koenig, and Hirota (1966). The experiment lasted for eight days, during which the odd-numbered days were Training days and even-numbered days were Test days. On Training days, groups of equal size received eight different treatments, indicated in Table V. Every animal was first placed in the Skinner box for a 30-minute pretraining period with the bars retracted. During the pretraining period, equal numbers of animals received every 60 seconds (1) a 1-second light change from 2 mL to 4mL, (2) a 1-second buzzer sound, (3) both the light change and the buzzer sound simultaneously, and (4) neither light change nor buzzer sound.

At the end of the pretraining period, the bars were introduced, and the 15-minute training session began. Half of the animals that had had each pretraining period treatment then received a light change and the other half a buzzer sound whenever the bar was pressed. On Test days, there was simply a 15-minute test session with no pretraining period, and bar-pressing produced neither stimulus.

As the notation in Table V shows, the design presented three ortho-gonal factors for analysis of variance: (1) presence (S) or absence (NS) during the pretraining period of stimulation identical with what re-sulted from the bar-press during the training period, (2) presence (D) or absence (ND) during the pretraining period of a stimulus differing in modality from the one that was to be used during the training peri-od, and (3) occurrence of light change or buzzer when the bar was pressed during a training session.

By chance, an additional independent variable, which turned out to be of some importance, was introduced. Four rats in each of the eight groups had to be housed in a room adjacent to one in which some ex-tremely noisy printout counters were active during working hours. The remaining six rats in each group were housed in a quiet room.

The results, showed, first, that the D/ND variable produced no sig-nificant effects or interactions. There was thus no evidence for an ef-fect of stimulus deprivation and, in what follows, we shall be discuss-ing only novelty effects. Similarly, whether light change or buzzer was used made no significant difference, except that animals housed in the quiet room performed more responses for the light change than for the buzzer on Training days ($p < .005$).

With regard to the S/NS variable or, in other words, the difference between a novel and a familiar reinforcing stimulus, an unexpected but dramatic interaction appeared, as Fig. 4 reveals. Novel reinforcing stimuli (i.e., those that had not been experienced during the pretrain-ing period) induced more responses than familiar reinforcing stimuli (which had been experienced 30 times during each pretraining

TABLE V
Experiment 1 (Sect. IV): Training Day Conditions

Pretraining period treatment	Reinforcing stimulus	
	Light change	Buzzer
Light change only	S + ND	NS + D
Buzzer only	NS + D	S + ND
Light change + buzzer	S + D	S + D
No stimulus change	NS + ND	NS + ND

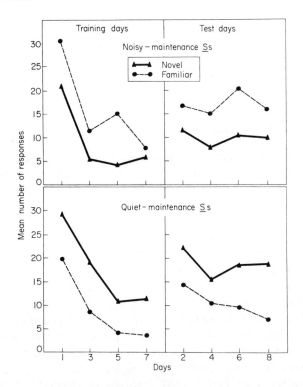

FIG. 4.   Experiment 1 (Section IV). Training day and Test day means for rats housed in noisy and in quiet conditions. (From Berlyne, Koenig, & Hirota, 1966.)

period) on both Training days ($p < .005$) and Test days ($p < .001$) in animals housed in the quiet room. But the opposite occurred with animals housed in the noisy room ($p < .025$ on Training days, $p < .005$ on Test days).

When we asked ourselves what could have accounted for this difference between rats kept in noisy and quiet environments, it seemed plausible that they differed in arousal level. Since rats are nocturnal animals, to rouse a rat housed in a quiet room at 3 PM for an experiment is like pulling somebody out of his peaceful bed at 3 AM. If we were to compare his condition at 3 AM with that of another person whose bedroom lies next to a pressroom in which the next morning's newspapers are printed all night long, we might well expect a sharp difference between their arousal levels. We could therefore account for the unanticipated interaction found in the present experiment by assuming that the reward-value of an indifferent stimulus is an inverted U-shaped function of its novelty and that the most rewarding degree of novelty is lower where arousal is supranormal than when it is normal.

B. Experiment 2: Novelty and Methamphetamine

The assumption that noisy maintenance gives rise to a higher prevailing arousal level than quiet maintenance is central to the explanation that has just been suggested. In order to check this explanation further, one could have attempted to measure effects of our noisy environment on arousal in rats. But, apart from practical difficulties of doing this, effects of arousal are of wider significance than effects of noise. It was decided to test our assumptions by using some agent that could be relied on to generate supranormal arousal. An injection of methamphetamine at 2.5 mg/kg seemed suitable for this purpose.

An additional experiment was done with 37 rats. Seventeen of them received an intraperitoneal injection of methamphetamine 15-17 minutes before the start of each pretraining period on Training days. The remaining 20 received control injections of isotonic saline solution instead. Nine rats in the methamphetamine group and ten in the placebo group received 2-4 mL light increments during pretraining periods on Training days, while the others did not. Bar-pressing was followed by a light change during each training session for all animals. On Test days, no injections and no light changes were given. Once again, the experiment lasted for eight days, and Test days alternated with Training days. The Test-day means appear in Table VI. Familiar light changes were more effective as reinforcers under methamphetamine, but novel light changes were more effective under saline injections ($p < .025$).

We have, therefore, obtained some confirmation for the hypothesis arising out of Experiment 1, namely that reward-value depends on novelty, with the most rewarding degree of novelty going down as arousal rises above a normal waking level.

V. THE REWARD-VALUE OF LIGHT CHANGE AT SUPRANORMAL AND SUBNORMAL AROUSAL LEVELS

The last two experiments demonstrated that the reward-value of a stimulus can be influenced jointly by the degree of novelty of the stimulus and the arousal level of the subject. Novelty is one of several stimulus properties that have been found to intensify indices of increased arousal (components of the orientation reaction). It, therefore, constitutes one ingredient of what I have called "arousal potential" (Berlyne, 1960).

One would suspect that these findings might be representative of a relation linking reward-value, arousal level, and arousal potential, in general. If so, one would anticipate analogous effects when interactions between arousal level and other determinants of arousal increment are studied. For example, one would expect the consequences (visual, tactual, and kinaesthetic) of a bar-press followed by a short increase in illumination to be more arousing than the consequences (tactual and kinaesthetic alone) of a bar-press not followed by a light change. Consequently, the reward-value of light increment as compared with absence of light increment should interact with arousal level in much the same way as the reward-value of a novel light increment as compared with a familiar light increment.

A. Experiment 1: Effects of Methamphetamine on the Reward-Value of Light Increment

Eighty rats took part in an experiment (Berlyne, in press) in which six Training days alternated with six Test days. There was a break of one day between the third Test day and fourth Training day.

Four groups of eight rats each were injected, respectively, with 0, 1, 2, and 3 mg/kg of methamphetamine in saline solution 20 minutes before every training session. No injections were administered on Test days. On Training days, half of the animals in each dosage group received a 1-2 mL light increment whenever the bar was pressed, while the remainder had no light increment. No animals received

TABLE VI
Experiment 2 (Sect. IV): Test Day Responses

Reinforcing stimulus	Methamphetamine	Placebo	Mean
Familiar	13.9	4.8	9.4
Novel	6.5	10.7	8.6
Mean	10.2	7.8	

light changes or injections on Test days. There were no pretraining periods before the training sessions.

The mean Test day scores are shown in Fig. 5. Logarithmic transforms were analyzed. Since the linear component of the dose × light change/no light change interaction differed significantly ($p < .025$) from Week 1 to Week 2, the data for the two weeks are presented separately and were subjected to separate analyses of variance.

Logarithmically transformed numbers of responses increased linearly with dosage both in Week 1 ($p < .001$) and Week 2 ($p > .005$), even though on Training days, when the animals were drugged, the mean transformed scores decreased linearly ($p < .01$ for Week 1 and $p < .001$ for Week 2) as the dose rose. It is evident that, the greater the dose of methamphetamine on Training days, the greater the learned strengthening of the bar-pressing response. It is, however, not possible to tell from these data whether this is because the drug heightened the reinforcing effect of the consequences of the response or whether different doses produced differing amounts of conditioned arousal, resulting from exposure to the interior of the box while under the influence of the drug.

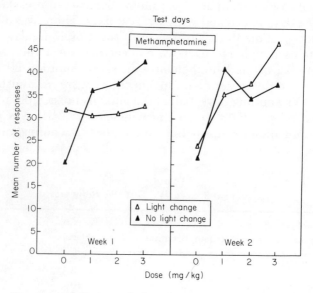

FIG. 5.   Experiment 1 (Section V). Test day means. (From Berlyne, in press.)

Turning to the results of chief interest, namely those depending on the presence or absence of light increments on Training days, and considering first the results for Week 1, we find, as expected, that light change produces more responding than no light change in the 0 mg/kg group. But in animals that had been injected with methamphetamine on Training days, no-light-change subgroups press the bar more often, and the superiority of absence of light change over light change increases with dosage. In fact, the linear trends differ significantly ($p < .05$).

Figure 5 shows how by Week 2 light change had become relatively less rewarding in the two lower dosage groups and relatively more rewarding in the two higher dosage groups. This fits the finding of the last experiment reported, in which a novel light increment was more rewarding than a familiar light increment at the control level of arousal but less rewarding at the level of arousal induced by 2.5 mg/kg of methamphetamine, except that here it is a matter of long-term novelty (whether or not the light change has been experienced during the last few days), whereas, in that experiment, it was a matter of short-term novelty (whether or not the light change had been experienced during the last few minutes). A congruent finding has been reported by Kiernan (1965): after experiencing light onsets during the two previous days, rats injected with amphetamine sulfate pressed the bar more often than saline-injected rats to obtain light onset, but the difference was in the opposite direction with rats that had never experienced light onset in the box before.

We thus have some confirmation that the long-term novelty or familiarity of an indifferent stimulus and the presence or absence of light increment interact with arousal level in determining reward-value in much the same way as short-term novelty or familiarity was found to do in the previous experiments. This strengthens the grounds for supposing that these phenomena exemplify the interaction of reward-value, arousal level, and arousal potential, in general.

B. Experiment 2: Effects of Pentobarbital on the Reward-Value of Light Increment

So far, our discussion has been restricted to comparisons between a normal waking level of arousal and supranormal levels. To complete the picture, we obviously need some investigation of what happens when arousal is subnormal. At this point in our research, several possibilities offered themselves:

1. It may be that the crossover is a phenomenon peculiar to high levels of arousal, in which case the difference between the reward-values of a more and a less arousing stimulus might be the same at low levels of arousal as at an intermediate level.

2. It may be that the tendency for more arousing stimuli to lose reward-value and less arousing stimuli to gain reward-value, as arousal level rises, covers the whole spectrum of arousal levels, in which case the superiority of arousing stimuli would be even greater at low arousal levels than at an intermediate arousal level.

3. It may be that the superior reward-value of more arousing stimuli is confined to an intermediate range of arousal levels where the efficiency of the nervous system is at its peak and the organism is most able to cope with challenges, in which case at subnormal arousal levels, as at supranormal arousal levels, less arousing stimuli would be more rewarding than more arousing stimuli.

One rather widespread view (e.g., Fiske & Maddi, 1961; Hebb, 1955) holds low levels of arousal to be aversive or productive of "negative affect," so that acts whose consequences tend to push arousal up from a low level toward a normal, intermediate level will tend to be repeated. According to this view, the reward-value of an arousing stimulus such as light increment will surely be greater at subnormal arousal levels than at a normal arousal level. It is worth emphasizing that this hypothesis of *optimal arousal level* is different from the hypothesis that I have offered here and in previous writings (Berlyne, 1960; Berlyne, 1963b; Berlyne, 1967). I suggest that there is a maximally rewarding or *optimal arousal increment*, which is to be obtained from an *optimal degree of arousal potential* (or influx of arousing stimulation).

To test these possibilities, an experiment (Berlyne, in press) was carried out that resembled the experiment just reported in all particulars except for the following. On Training days, five groups of 16 rats were injected, respectively, with 0, 5, 10, 15, and 20 mg/kg of pentobarbital. Half of the animals in each dosage group received light increments on training days and the other half did not.

There was no sign of any significant differences between Week 1 and Week 2, except that the logarithmically transformed scores were significantly lower over all groups in Week 2 ($p < .05$). The mean numbers of responses for both weeks are presented in Fig. 6 and were analyzed together.

It is seen that, once again, the presence of light change on Training days leads to a greater response rate on Test days in animals injected with pure saline solution. But this superiority of light change is not in evidence in animals injected with pentobarbital. Both the linear ($p <$ .005) and the quadratic ($p <$ .025) components of the trends (of logarithmic transforms) across doses differ significantly between light-change and no-light-change subgroups. The difference between the light-change and no-light-change subgroups is significant ($p <$ .001) in the saline group but not in any of the other dosage groups examined separately.

The suggestion is that, at the subnormal arousal level investigated in this experiment, the difference in reward-value between light change and absence of light change tends to disappear.

There is, however, another possibility that has to be considered. All animals in this experiment were tested without injections, and a difference in reward-value appeared among animals that had been trained with inactive injections but not among animals that had been trained under pentobarbital. This is precisely the result that would be expected if the state-dependent-learning effect reported by Overton (1964) were at work. He found that rats trained to escape from electric shock under pentobarbital failed to show evidence of learning when

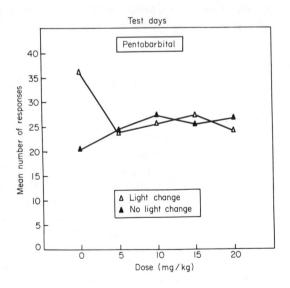

FIG. 6.   Experiment 2 (Section V). Test day means. (From Berlyne, in press.)

tested without the drug. Evidence of learning appeared, however, when the animals were once again drugged as they had been during training. Overton's findings thus raise the question of whether a difference in reward-value between light change and absence of light change might manifest itself if rats were tested, as well as trained, under pentobarbital.

In order to test for this possibility, two groups of 14 rats each were injected with 15 mg/kg of pentobarbital on both training and test days. An experimental group received light increment whenever the bar was pressed on Training days but not on Test days. A control group received no light increments either on Training or on Test days. Other conditions were exactly as in the experiment just discussed.

Mean numbers of Test day responses were 21.6 for the experimental group and 16.2 for the control group. This difference was far from significant: $t(26) = .55$. A combined analysis of the scores of these two groups and those of the two 15 mg/kg groups of the last experiment showed that rats tested under pentobarbital performed fewer responses on Test days than rats tested without injections ($p < .01$). But the main effect of light change vs. no light change was not significant. Most important of all, the interaction between light change/no light change and presence or absence of drug during testing did not approach significance. There seems to be no support for the view that the results of the last experiment represented state-dependent learning.

VI. REWARD AND AROUSAL

Elsewhere (Berlyne, 1967) I have reviewed all the evidence that I could find on the conditions that govern reinforcement value and particularly reward-value. Relevant evidence was gathered together from an astonishing variety of sources – from research on brain physiology, psychopharmacology, animal learning, human verbal learning, and verbal expressions of preference, among others. These are admittedly very different phenomena, and it is dangerous to suppose that principles that apply to one phenomenon must apply to the rest. Be that as it may, higher animals seem to possess one central nervous system each. They have to make do with the same brain for all the multifarious activities in which they engage, and it is hard to resist altogether the suspicion that at least some common principles must pervade the operations of this brain, however heterogeneous. This review of literature led to a number of tentative conclusions. These conclusions, to which the reported experiments on photic reinforcement made substantial contributions, are as follows.

1. *Reward-value depends on increases or decreases in arousal.* The main basis for this conclusion is the consideration that, of the large number of stimulus properties that evidently contribute to reward-value, all have been shown at one time or another to influence indices of arousal or components of the orientation reaction. Apart from this, there is evidence of close connections and interactions between the brain structures subserving arousal and those subserving reward. Finally, additional evidence for intimate relations between the neural processes underlying arousal and reward come from the interactions between properties of the reinforcing stimulus and the organism's arousal level in the determination of reward-value.

2. *In some conditions, rewarding agents act to reduce arousal, but in other conditions an increase in arousal can be rewarding independently of any drop in arousal that might follow.* Several writers have identified the newer concept of "arousal" with the older concept of "drive" (see Berlyne, 1960; Berlyne, 1963). This is a little rash in some respects. The two concepts seem to fit together quite well when one concentrates on the diffuse "energizing" or "activating" role that has often been ascribed to "drive" (in the singular). Relations between arousal and the specific "directive" or "selective" functions of "drives" (in the plural) remain obscure, although relevant evidence is beginning to accumulate.

Translated into terms of "drive," the present conclusion implies that reward sometimes results from drive reduction and sometimes from drive induction. Stalwart drive-reductionists have often explained behavior through which animals appear to seek increases in drive by asserting that such increases are invariably soon followed by decreases, which are really responsible for the reinforcing effect. There seems now to be enough evidence of several different kinds to cast doubt on this view.

3. *Moderate increases in arousal are rewarding, while larger increases are aversive.* According to this usage, something is said to be "aversive" if its termination or reduction is rewarding. Something that is aversive in this sense need not be "punishing" (i.e., conducive to a learned weakening of a response that follows) or avoided. But it will usually be punishing.

4. *There is a reward system and an aversion system in the brain,*

*whose degrees of activation depend on the arousal value of a stimu-
lus. The aversion system has a higher threshold than the reward system.* The existence of two such systems (which are, of course, likely to
interact with other systems that are indirectly concerned with
reinforcement) is indicated by data collected by Olds (1963; 1965), by
Schneirla (1959; 1965), and by Grastyán (Grastyán, Karmos, Vereczkey, Martin, & Kellényi, 1965; Grastyán, Karmos, Vereczkey, &
Kellényi, 1966).

Either system will be activated whenever its input excitation exceeds a threshold value. We assume that the input excitation varies
directly with the *arousal increment* induced by incoming stimulation.
The arousal increment will vary directly in its turn with *arousal potential.* This is a term that may be used, for convenience, to denote
collectively the various stimulus properties with which arousal seems,
on the whole, to increase. That is to say, arousal varies directly with
these properties over most of their range, but the relation is unlikely
to be monotonic throughout. There is reason to believe (Berlyne,
1960; Berlyne, 1963b) that arousal may climb when arousal potential
becomes extremely low (boredom) and drop when arousal potential
becomes inordinately high (supramaximal inhibition). Arousal potential includes the psychophysical (e.g., intensity, color), ecological
(e.g., association with biologically beneficial and noxious events), and
collative (e.g., novelty, complexity, ambiguity, variability) determinants of arousal. It corresponds to what has sometimes been called
"amount of stimulation" in a loose sense that covers more than simply
intensity and rate of change.

As arousal potential increases, the degree of activation of either system will rise concomitantly until it reaches an asymptote or plateau. It
seems reasonable therefore to conjecture that the degree of activation
of either system will be a sigmoid function of arousal increment. Further, if we assume that the aversion system has a higher threshold than
the reward system and also that its asymptote is more distant from the
base line than that of the reward system, the two curves in Fig. 7 will
depict the activity of the two systems.

If we sum the ordinates of these two curves algebraically, we obtain
a resultant curve of the shape shown in Fig. 8. This curve has an interesting history. It was first put forward by Wundt (1874), who apparently did not base it on experimental data but on his interpretation of
common human experience. It related "pleasantness"-"unpleasantness," conceived as an attribute of conscious experiences, to intensity
of stimulation. As stimulus intensity rose from a threshold value, there

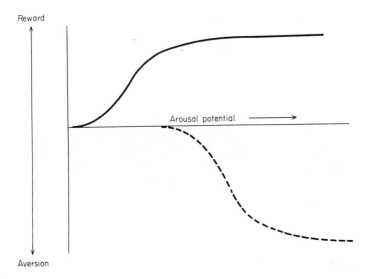

FIG. 7. Curves representing activity of reward and aversion systems as functions of arousal potential. (From Berlyne, 1967.)

would be a rise from indifference to a peak of pleasantness, then a decline in pleasantness to indifference, and finally increasing unpleasantness. In the decades after the original publication of this curve, it received some support from human introspective experiments and later from experiments on animal behavior.

Let us broaden the interpretation of Wundt's curve by identifying the abscissa with *arousal potential* (which includes stimulus intensity as well as other stimulus properties such as novelty, surprisingness, complexity, variability, and ecological significance). The ordinate can be equated with *reward value and aversion value,* which can, strictly speaking, be derived only from behavioral data supplied by learning experiments, but which are likely to be highly correlated with verbal judgments of "pleasantness" and "unpleasantness" (or equivalent attributes). Then the curve can serve tolerably well to summarize presently available knowledge.

In keeping with this reinterpretation of Wundt's curve, maximum reward-value seems generally to coincide with an intermediate amount of arousal potential. But the experiments reported in this chapter, as well as other experiments that could be cited (Berlyne, 1967), show the location of this maximum to vary with the organism's arousal level.

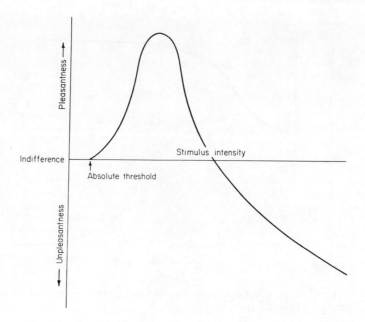

FIG. 8. Wundt's curve. (From Berlyne, 1960.)

This variation in the observed reward-value could come about in either of two ways. One possibility is that the function connecting reward-value with arousal increment remains invariant but that the arousal increment resulting from a given amount of arousal potential, and thus from a particular stimulus, goes up with arousal level. These hypotheses give rise to Model 1, which is represented in Fig. 9.

A second possibility is that the arousal increment resulting from a given amount of arousal potential, and thus from a given stimulus, remains constant, but that the function connecting reward-value with arousal potential varies with arousal level, so that the location of the maximum is variable. One plausible hypothesis for which a few fragments of support can be mustered (Berlyne, 1967) is that the most rewarding degree of arousal potential is higher at intermediate levels of arousal than at supranormal and subnormal levels. In other words, an animal will be most inclined to welcome arousing stimuli when its capacities for dealing with them are at their peak but will prefer less challenging and troublesome stimulation when arousal level is too high or too low for full efficiency. These assumptions suggest Model 2, which is represented in Fig. 10.

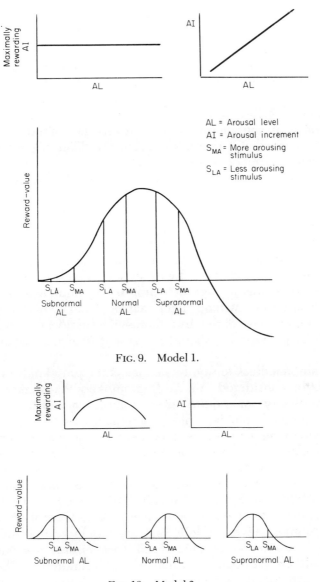

FIG. 9.   Model 1.

FIG. 10.   Model 2.

Several considerations can be cited in favor of Model 1. First, there are a few hints in the literature that the arousal value of a particular stimulus may increase with arousal level. GSR amplitude seems to be greater in human subjects with higher prevailing skin conductance

(Maltzman, 1967) and in human subjects who are subjected to conditioned fear (Meryman, 1953, cited by Brown, 1961). There are also indications that thresholds for activation of the brain stem reticular formation and for EEG desynchronization are lowered by injections of amphetamine (see Killam, 1962). As can be seen from Fig. 9, several of our findings tally with Model 1 rather impressively. Stimuli with higher arousal value were less rewarding than stimuli with lower arousal value at supranormal arousal levels, the difference was reversed at intermediate arousal levels, and the difference more or less disappeared at subnormal arousal levels.

Nevertheless, these findings of ours can also be reconciled with Model 2, as Fig. 10 shows. There is one crucial prediction by which Model 1 could be tested. This is that the reward-value of all stimuli, whether of higher or lower arousal value, should decrease as arousal level drops below the normal, intermediate range. However, in the last experiment reported above (Section V, Experiment 2), while pentobarbital made rats trained with light change less responsive on Test days, there was no sign of a drop in the number of responses made by rats trained without light change. Their scores actually increased with the dose of the drug, though not significantly, so, of these two models, perhaps we should at present lean somewhat toward Model 2.

These are, needless to say, by no means the only kinds of models that might be considered. It is far from unlikely that some combination of the two or some quite different approach will turn out most tenable as research into these phenomena advances.

However, in the light of these considerations, it may be worth offering a speculation regarding one of the most troublesome problems that have obscured the relations between arousal, on the one hand, and reward and hedonic processes, on the other. Several writers, notably Hebb (1955) and Fiske and Maddi (1961), have hypothesized that higher organisms tend to keep arousal as close as possible to an intermediate, optimal level. It follows from this view that subnormal arousal will be aversive and that, when it occurs, arousal-raising stimulation will be particularly welcome and reinforcing. There are, however, facts that do not accord very well with this hypothesis (see Berlyne 1960; Berlyne, 1963b). A state of drowsiness or somnolence is often judged to be extremely agreeable. The results of Experiment 2, Section V, reported above also failed to show that a lowering of arousal level enhances the reward-value of stimuli that tend to raise arousal.

On the other hand, some conditions of markedly low arousal, e.g., some induced by depressant drugs and states of psychotic depression, can be singularly unpleasant. Sensory deprivation, which can so easily be found intolerable, seems (although more research on these points would not be amiss) to produce a split between cortical and behavioral arousal: slow waves appear in EEG recordings, while muscular tension and autonomic activity rise (see Schultz, 1965). There has been some evidence (apparently of particular relevance to cortical arousal) that high arousal, whether induced by amphetamine (Barmack, 1938), by caffeine (Barmack, 1940), or by posthypnotic suggestion (Geiwitz, 1966), reduces boredom.

Perhaps a clue to the resolution of this problem can be sought in the hypothesis (following from Model 2) that a drop in arousal makes it easier for stimuli to generate an arousal increment that falls within the aversive range. We should then expect low arousal to be hard to endure when a subject is unable to escape from stimulation. The stimulation in question may be external. In depressed patients, in people who feel sleepy when they have work to do, and in bored people (especially if highly intelligent or given to fantasy, which makes them more susceptible to boredom; see Geiwitz, 1966), it will be preponderantly internal. But for somebody spending a hot summer's day in a hammock, where stimulation is lacking or can be easily avoided, there may be no inducement at all to put an end to low arousal.

REFERENCES

Asratian, E. A. Some aspects of the elaboration of conditioned connections and formation of their properties. In J. F. Delafresnaye (Ed.), *Brain mechanisms and learning.* Oxford: Blackwell, 1961.

Barmack, J. E. The effect of benzedrine sulfate (benzyl methyl carbinamine) upon the report of boredom and other factors. *J. Psychol.,* 1938, **5,** 125-133.

Barmack, J. E. The time of administration, and some effects of 2 gr. of alkaloid caffeine. *J. exp. Psychol.,* 1940, **27,** 690-698.

Barnes, G. W., & Baron, A. The effects of sensory reinforcement on extinction behavior. *J. comp. physiol. Psychol.,* 1961, **54,** 461-465.

Barnes, G. W., & Kish, C. B. On some properties of visual reinforcement. *Amer. Psychologist,* 1958, **13,** 417.

Berlyne, D. E. Novelty and curiosity as determinants of exploratory behavior. *Brit. J. Psychol.,* 1950, **41,** 68-80.

Berlyne, D. E. The arousal and satiation of perceptual curiosity in the rat. *J. comp. physiol. Psychol.,* 1955, **48,** 238-246.

Berlyne, D. E. *Conflict, arousal and curiosity.* New York: McGraw-Hill, 1960.

Berlyne, D. E. Motivational problems raised by exploratory and epistemic behavior. In S. Koch (Ed.), *Psychology—a study of a science.* Vol. 5. New York: McGraw-Hill, 1963. Pp. 284-364.

Berlyne, D. E. *Structure and direction in thinking.* New York: Wiley, 1965.

Berlyne, D. E. Curiosity and exploration. *Science,* 1966, **153,** 25-33.

Berlyne, D. E. Arousal and reinforcement. In D. Levine (Ed.), *Nebraska symposium on motivation.* Lincoln: Univ. of Nebraska Press, 1967.

Berlyne, D. E. The reward value of light increment under supranormal and subnormal arousal. *Canad. J. Psychol.,* (in press).

Berlyne, D. E., & Koenig, I. D. V. Some possible parameters of photic reinforcement. *J. comp. physiol. Psychol.,* 1965, **60,** 276-280.

Berlyne, D. E., Koenig, I. D. V., & Hirota, T. Novelty, arousal, and the reinforcement of diversive exploration in the rat. *J. comp. physiol. Psychol.,* 1966, **62,** 222-226.

Berlyne, D. E., Salapatek, P. H., Gelman, R. S., & Zener, S. L. Is light increment really rewarding to the rat? *J. comp. physiol. Psychol.,* 1964, **58,** 148-151.

Brown, J. S. *The psychology of motivation.* New York: McGraw-Hill, 1961.

Butler, R. A. Discrimination by Rhesus monkeys to visual-exploration motivation. *J. comp. physiol. Psychol.,* 1953, **46,** 95-98.

Butler, R. A. The effect of deprivation of visual incentives on visual exploration motivation in monkeys. *J. comp. physiol. Psychol.,* 1957, **50,** 177-179.

Crowder, W. F., Morris, J. B., Dyer, W. R., & Robinson, J. V. Resistance to extinction and number of weak-light reinforcements. *J. Psychol.,* 1961, **51,** 361-364.

DeBold, P. C., Miller, N. E., & Jensen, D. D. Effect of strength of drive determined by a new technique for appetitive classical conditioning of rats. *J. comp. physiol. Psychol.,* 1965, **59,** 102-108.

Fiske, D. W., & Maddi, S. R. A conceptual framework. In D. W. Fiske & S. R. Maddi (Eds.), *Functions of varied experience.* Homewood, Ill.: Dorsey, 1961. Pp. 11-56.

Flynn, J. P., & Jerome, E. A. Learning in an automatic multiple-choice box with light as incentive. *J. comp. physiol. Psychol.,* 1952, **45,** 336-340.

Forgays, D. G., & Levin, H. Learning as a function of change of sensory stimulation: I. Food-deprived vs. food-satiated animals. *J. comp. physiol. Psychol.,* 1958, **51,** 50-54.

Fox, S. S. Self-maintained sensory input and sensory deprivation in monkeys. *J. comp. physiol. Psychol.,* 1962, **55,** 438-444.

Freud, S. Triebe und Triebsschicksale. *Int. Z. ärtztl. Psychoanal.,* 1915, **3,** 84-100. (Instincts and their vicissitudes. Freud, S., *Collected Papers.* Vol. 4. London: Hogarth, 1925)

Geiwitz, P. J. Structure of boredom. *J. Pers. soc. Psychol.,* 1966, **3,** 592-600.

Girdner, J. B. An experimental analysis of the behavioral effects of a perceptual consequence unrelated to organic drive states. *Amer. Psychologist,* 1953, **8,** 354-355.

Glanzer, M. Curiosity, exploratory drive, and stimulus satiation. *Psychol. Bull.,* 1958, **55,** 302-315.

Grastyán, E., Karmos, G., Vereczkey, L., Martin, J., & Kellényi, L. Hypothalamic motivational processes as reflected by their hippocampal electrical correlates. *Science,* 1965, **149,** 91-93.

Grastyán, E., Karmos, G., Vereczkey, L., & Kellényi, L. The hippocampal electrical correlates of the homeostatic regulation of motivation. *Electroencephalog. clin. Neurophysiol.,* 1966, **21,** 34-53.

Harlow, H. F. Learning and satiation of response in intrinsically motivated complex puzzle performance by monkeys. *J. comp. physiol. Psychol.,* 1950, **43,** 289-294.

Hebb, D. O. Drives and the C. N. S. (conceptual nervous system). *Psychol. Rev.,* 1955, **62,** 243-254.

Hefferline, R. F. An experimental study of avoidance. *Genet. Psychol. Monogr.,* 1950, **42,** 231-234.

Henderson, R. L. Stimulus intensity dynamism and secondary reinforcement. Unpublished doctoral thesis, Univer. of Missouri, 1953.

Hull, C. L. *Principles of Behavior*. New York: Appleton, 1943.

Hurwitz, H. M. B. Conditioned responses in rats reinforced by light. *Brit. J. anim. Behav.*, 1956, 4, 31–33.

Jones, A., Wilkinson, H. J., & Braden, I. Information deprivation as a motivational variable. *J. exp. Psychol.*, 1961, 62, 126–137.

Keller, J. S. Light aversion in the white rat. *Psychol. Rec.*, 1941, 4, 235–250.

Kiernan, C. C. Modification of the effects of amphetamine sulphate by past experience in the hooded rat. *Psychopharmacologia*, 1965, 8, 23–31.

Killam, E. K. Drug action on the brain-stem reticular formation. *Pharmacol. Rev.*, 1962, 14, 175–223.

Kimble, G. A. *Hilgard and Marquis' Conditioning and Learning*. (2nd ed.) New York: Appleton, 1961.

Kish, G. B. Learning when the onset of illumination is used as a reinforcing stimulus. *J. comp. physiol. Psychol.*, 1955, 48, 261–264.

Kling, J. W., Horowitz, L., & Delhagen, J. E. Light as a positive reinforcer for rat responding. *Psychol. Rep.*, 1956, 2, 337–340.

Lockard, R. B. Some effects of maintenance luminance and strain differences upon the self-exposure to light by rats. *J. comp. physiol. Psychol.*, 1962, 55, 1118–1123.

Lockard, R. B. Several tests of stimulus-change and preference theory in relation to light-controlled behavior of rats. *J. comp. physiol. Psychol.*, 1966, 62, 415–426.

Long, C. J., & Tapp, J. T. Reinforcing properties of odors for the albino rat. *Psychon. Sci.*, 1967, 7, 17–18.

Maltzman, I. Individual differences in "attention": The orienting reflex. In R. M. Gagné (Ed.), *Learning and individual differences*. Columbus, Ohio: Merrill, 1967.

McCall, R. B. Stimulus change in light-contingent bar pressing. *J. comp. physiol. Psychol.*, 1965, 59, 258–262.

McClelland, D. C., Atkinson, J. W., Clark, R. A., & Lowell, E. L. *The achievement motive*. New York: Appleton, 1953.

Meryman, J. J. The magnitude of an unconditioned GSR as a function of fear conditioned at a long CS-UCS interval. Unpublished doctoral thesis, State Univer. of Iowa, 1953.

Miller, N. E., & Dollard, J. *Social learning and imitation*. New Haven: Yale Univer. Press, 1941.

Montgomery, K. C. Exploratory behavior as a function of "similarity" of stimulus situations. *J. comp. physiol. Psychol.* 1953, 46, 129–133.

Olds, J. Brain centers and positive reinforcement. Paper read to XVI Int. Congr. Psychol., Washington, 1963.

Olds, J. Drives, rewards, and the brain. In F. Barron, W. C. Dement, W. Edwards, H. Lindman, L. D. Phillips, J. Olds, & M. Olds (Eds.), *New directions in psychology II*. New York: Holt, 1965.

Overton, D. A. State-dependent or "dissociated" learning produced with pentobarbital. *J. comp. physiol. Psychol.*, 1964, 57, 3–12.

Pavlov, I. P. *Conditioned reflexes*. London and New York: Oxford Univer. Press, 1927.

Premack, D. Reversibility of the reinforcement relation *Science*, 1962, 136, 255–257.

Premack, D. & Collier, G. Analysis of non-reinforcement variables affecting response probability. *Psychol. Monogr.*, 1962, 76, No. 5 (Whole No. 524).

Premack, D., Collier, G., & Roberts, C. L. Frequency of light-contingent bar pressing as a function of the amount of deprivation of light. *Amer. Psychologist*, 1957, 12, 411.

Robinson, J. S. The reinforcing effects of response-contingent light increment and decrement in hooded rats. *J. comp. physiol. Psychol.*, 1961, 54, 470–473.

Schneirla, T. C. An evolutionary and developmental theory of biphasic processes underlying approach and withdrawal. In M. R. Jones (Ed.), *Nebraska symposium on motivation.* Lincoln, Nebr.: Univer. of Nebraska Press, 1959. Pp. 1-42.

Schneirla, T. C. Aspects of stimulation and organization in approach-withdrawal processes underlying vertebrate behavioral development. In D. L. Lehrman, R. Hinde, & E. Shaw (Eds.), *Advances in the study of behavior.* New York: Academic Press, 1965. Pp. 1-74.

Schultz, D. P. *Sensory restriction.* New York: Academic Press, 1965.

Solomon, R. L., & Brush, E. S. Experimentally derived conceptiond of anxiety and aversion. In M. R. Jones (Ed.), *Nebraska symposium on motivation.* Lincoln, Nebr.: Univer. of Nebraska Press, 1956.

von Holst, E., & von St. Paul, U. Electrically controlled behavior. *Sci. Amer.*, 1962, 3, 50-59.

von Holst, E., & von St. Paul, U. Vom Wirkungsgefüge der Triebe. *Naturwissenschaften*, 1960, 47, 409-422.

Wundt, W. *Grundzüge der physiologischen Psychologie.* Leipzig: Engelmann, 1874.

CHAPTER 8

Taste Preference and Reinforcement[1]

CARL PFAFFMANN

I. INTRODUCTION

The sense of taste is of particular interest because it is a modality in which stimuli, specifiable in chemical terms, give rise to afferent neural processes that can be analyzed electrophysiologically, and these in turn elicit clear-cut behavioral responses of acceptance or rejection depending upon the species of molecule or ion and its concentration. The well-known taste preference-aversion function embodies features basic to all responses, i.e., a polarity from positive to negative, acceptance to rejection, from pleasantness to unpleasantness. Wundt (1874), in his general theory of hedonic value, noted that many forms of stimulation were pleasant at medium intensities, but unpleasant at higher values. He diagrammed this relation in a classic figure (Fig. 1), which is very much with us even today.

[1]Preparation of this chapter was carried out under support by The Rockefeller University and under a project of the National Science Foundation.

Troland (1928) attempted to substitute recepto-physiological cate-gories and biological utility for the subjective terms of pleasure and pain by speaking of nociception, neutroception, and beneception. Holt (1931) couched this same polarity in response terms when he spoke of adience, signified by movement toward, and abience, by movement away from a stimulus. Schneirla (1939; 1959; 1965) over the years has developed a theory of biphasic response processes on an approach-withdrawal scale, defining approach by the objective sign of an organism's movement closer to a stimulus source, and withdrawal when it increases its distance from the source, attributing A (approach) or W (withdrawal) to intensity without regard to quality. "Intensity of stimulation basically determines a direction of reaction with respect to source, and thereby exerts selective effect on what conditions generally affect the organism. For all organisms in an early ontogenetic stage, low intensity of stimulation tends to evoke ap-proach reactions, high intensities, withdrawal reactions with refer-ence to the source (Schneirla, 1959, p. 3)." The A type of mechanism favors adjustments such as food getting, shelter getting, and mating. The W type of mechanism underlies such adjustments as defense, huddling, flight, and other protective reactions.

On an earlier occasion I noted that qualitative differences within certain taste modalities seemed not to follow the simple rule of ap-proach for all low levels or aversion for high levels of stimulation. "Certain taste stimuli in weak concentrations, for example, are avoid-ed, and increasing concentrations lead only to increasing aversion — still other stimuli lead to increased preferences even when extremely high concentrations are employed (Pfaffmann, 1961)." Since the bi-phasic formulation was developed primarily for organisms early in their ontogenesis, Schneirla rejects this objection derived largely from taste preferences studied experimentally on adult organisms. But so far only one study, Warren (1963), shows that one substance, sucrose octoacetate (SOA), normally avoided by adult mice can be attractive in proper concentration to neonates. In our earlier studies of the re-sponse of newborn guinea pigs to SOA, no evidence of a positive pref-erence was encountered (Warren & Pfaffman, 1958). Guinea pigs, however, are quite mature at birth compared with the mouse.

Berlyne also (1960, pp. 200-202) emphasizes the intensive aspect of stimulation and reiterates Wundt's generalization (as in Fig. 1) that many forms of stimulation are pleasant at medium but unpleasant at higher intensities. But Berlyne relates the hedonic dimension to ar-ousal; that is, stimulus intensity is said to increase arousal level di-rectly. The biphasic character of response, then, comes from the fact

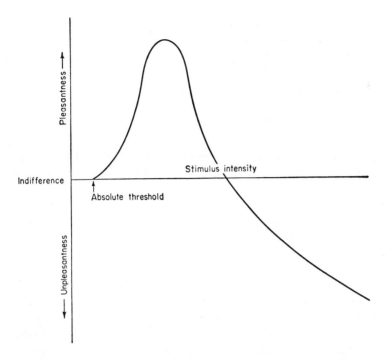

FIG. 1. Wundt's schema of the relation between sensory intensity and hedonic value.

that moderate arousal potential is maximally preferred, whereas high arousal is aversive. Thus, organisms will normally strive to maintain an intermediate amount of arousal potential. In a more recent formulation of the arousal concept (Chapter 7, this volume), Berlyne essentially follows Schneirla's scheme of two systems; the A system instigates increasing acceptance of a stimulus, rises to a plateau, and remains there. The second and somewhat higher threshold system, W, also increases with stimulus intensity, but since it is of opponent sign, counteracts the effect of the A system. The algebraic summation of these two systems yields a typical biphasic reaction curve.

Against the mainstream of objectivity, Young (1949, 1955, 1966) has espoused a hedonic view of behavior. He called attention to the fact that sensory stimulation per se is unidimensional, sensation magnitude increasing as stimulus intensity increases, whereas increasing sensory effect may have either an increasing positive (attractive) or negative (aversive) value. The biphasic response is taken as evidence of the distinction between stimulus and hedonic scales. Stimuli toward which the organism moves or which it maintains are said to be hedonically positive or pleasant. Those from which the organism retreats are hedonically negative or unpleasant. Young believes that the hedonic processes which organize and control behavior have an objective physiological existence. What that may be is still unknown despite certain clues from recent brain stimulation experiments.

II. HEDONIC SCALES

The classic experimental study relevant to the Wundtian formula is that of Engel (1928a), whose subjects rated the pleasantness of sour, salty, bitter, and sweet solutions. The curve of hedonic values versus intensity for the first three taste qualities was typically biphasic. That for sucrose rose to a maximum and was judged mostly pleasant even at the highest concentrations (see Fig. 2).

Replication of the hedonic rating study in our laboratory using college students as subjects and a single stimulus rating scale revealed the same trends for sucrose and sodium chloride. Notable individual differences, however, were also found. Four of 18 subjects showed an increasing dislike of stronger sugar, whereas the remaining 14 found increasing concentration to be increasingly pleasant. In his original report, Engel also remarked on individual differences; some of his subjects showed little preference for sugar. In a more recent study, Eckman and Akesson (1965) studied both sensory magnitude and preferences for saltiness and sweetness using a ratio estimate with

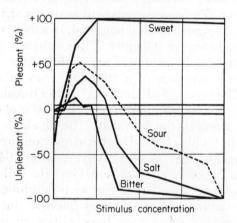

FIG. 2.   Hedonic ratings for increasing concentration of the four basic tastes. The ratings are expressed as percent "pleasant," and minus percent "unpleasant." The abscissa is proportional to the concentration, the full length of the base line representing 40% cane sugar, 1.12% tartaric acid, 10% salt, and .004% quinine sulfate (all by weight). (Based on data of Engel, 1928b.)

pairs of stimuli. Sensation magnitudes for both salt and sweet increase as power functions of the stimulus. In the case of preference five of the seven subjects perceived an optimum at a midvalue, on both sides of which preference decreased. Two of the subjects appeared to show decreasing preference as concentrations increased.[2] Individual differences again were notable.

On the other hand, Fisher (1967), using a slightly different method, found that hedonic ratings were typically biphasic for NaCl but monotonic for sucrose. Increasing concentrations of sugar were rated as increasing pleasantness. It is clear that further work is needed to clarify the relation of hedonic rating to stimulus intensity.

III. ANIMAL STUDIES OF TASTE

A. Electrophysiology and Behavior

Animal studies currently provide a stronger basis for the analysis of the mechanisms underlying acceptance and rejection processes of the biphasic response to taste stimuli. A wide variety of creatures, from insects to man, except for a few like the cat or certain birds, find sugar attractive. The squirrel monkey avidly licks and works for sugar. When the animal is hungry or deprived, the strength response is considerably enhanced, but need-free animals will, in fact, work for and be rewarded by the sweet taste per se (e.g., Dufour & Arnold, 1966; Fisher, Pfaffmann, & Brown, 1965; Pfaffmann, 1960, 1965; Sheffield & Roby, 1950; Young, 1955). The character of the sensory input which guides and directs such behavior can be determined electrophysiologically in the chorda tympani nerve of an acute and anesthetized preparation (Snell, 1965). Figure 3 shows summator records of activity in the nerve of one side for a series of fructose solutions of increasing concentration. Ammonium chloride solution was used as the standardizing stimulus before and after each sugar series. Neural activity starts with an initial high burst, but soon drops to a steady state level. The weakest sugar concentrations produce a slight increment in neural activity, which at higher concentrations becomes quite obvious.

Neural activity and the behavioral reactions as a function of stimulus concentration of the four basic stimuli — quinine, sodium chloride, hydrochloric acid, and sucrose — are shown in Fig. 4. The upper preference–aversion curves were obtained in a 24-hour two-bottle choice situation on a different group of animals. There is a reasonable correspondence between the electrophysiological and behavioral

[2]Stimuli ranged from .5% (grams/100 ml H_2O) (.015 M, approximately) to 7.4% (.2 M, approximately).

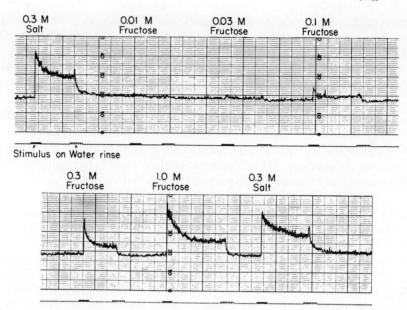

FIG. 3. Electrophysiological responses of the squirrel monkey chorda tympani as recorded with a summator and inkwriter. Heavy vertical lines on record chart indicate one-minute intervals. (From Pfaffmann, 1965.)

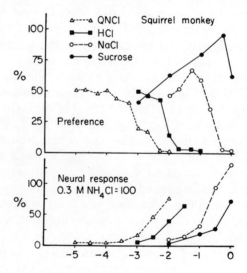

FIG. 4. Comparison of neural responses of squirrel monkey chorda tympani with two-bottle preference behavior to four standard test solutions. (From Pfaffmann, 1965.)

measures. Note that the most effective stimulus is quinine in terms of stimulus concentration. For very weak solutions, the animal accepts quinine equally with water and gives no evidence of discrimination. As the neural discharge increases above base line level, the animal begins to display an increasing aversion. The behavior is also an aversion for the acid series. The next stimuli, sodium chloride and sucrose, elicit both preferences and aversions. Sodium chloride is more effective electrophysiologically at suprathreshold concentrations than is the sucrose; however, in the behavioral responses, the preference for the sucrose is greater than that for saline. The salt preference never equals that for sucrose. The responses to both show a turndown, an aversion, at high concentrations.

These four behavioral response curves indicate that mere magnitude of total neural discharge in the chorda tympani cannot be directly correlated with behavioral effect. Further, one cannot predict from the total nerve response alone whether the animal will accept or reject the stimulus. This implies that qualitative differences among taste stimuli must lead to differences in the neural input which are not apparent in this type of recording. Single unit analysis is required to show how receptor-neural units selectively respond to stimuli.

One basic question is how the intensity of neural input for any one stimulus relates to magnitude of behavioral response. In the case of the two-bottle preference–aversion curve for sucrose, as we have seen, there is a nonmonotonic response. The intake turndown occurs around 1 M sucrose. Guttman (1953) was one of the first to show that in the rat this turndown can be influenced by intake or reinforcement schedule during a test series. He studied the rate of bar-pressing reinforced by a drop of sugar solution as a function of concentration. On a continuous reinforcement schedule, the response rate showed a turndown at higher values. However, on an aperiodic schedule such that many bar-presses led to a small amount of sugar ingestion, there was no turndown, and the curve shows a tendency to level off: the relationship was monotonic. Collier and his students (Collier & Myers, 1961; Collier & Siskel, 1959) have mapped the relations between volume, intensity, and schedule quite systematically.

We have also found the similar lack of turndown in the response functions in squirrel monkeys in both lick rate and bar-press rate. The responses of the squirrel monkey on a fixed interval schedule of 30 seconds when reinforced by different concentrations of sucrose solution are monotonically increasing functions of concentration on both lick rate and bar-pressing. Of particular interest is whether sugars of different sweetening capacity have different reinforcement functions.

In man, the different sugars have different sweetness and different magnitudes of chorda tympani response (Diamant, Funakoshi, Ström, & Zotterman, 1963). These sugars also have different effectiveness in stimulating the chorda tympani nerve of the squirrel monkey. Fructose is the most effective, sucrose next, then dextrose, lactose, and maltose, which are about equal, as shown in Fig. 5. Do such curves imply differences in reinforcing effectiveness? In the simplest interpretation, we might expect fructose to be the most effective. Actually, as illustrated by response curves in Fig. 6 for one animal, sucrose is the most effective reinforcer, fructose is next, and glucose and the other sugars least. There, thus, is a discrepancy between the sensory electrophysiology and the behavioral indications if we make the assumption that within each modality, there is a simple correspondence between magnitude of sensory-neural effect and behavioral significance.

Several possibilities might account for this discrepancy. One is that a mild satiating effect might operate even during the ingestion of small amounts of sugar, and it is conceivable that the schedule did not reduce the postingestive effect sufficiently. In that case, response measures early in the session compared with late in the session might show less postingestive effect, and a reversal from the first to the last sessions in test trials might be apparent. However, the relative efficiency of sucrose over fructose in the first five minutes compared with the last few trials was the same.

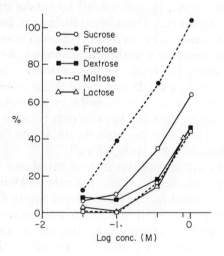

FIG. 5.   Relative magnitudes of chorda tympani nerve response of squirrel monkey to different sugars. (From Snell, 1965.)

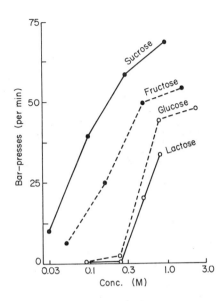

FIG. 6. Bar-pressing rates of one squirrel monkey to different concentrations of different sugars. (From Jay, 1965.)

Another possibility is that the animal had been pretrained on one sugar, sucrose, prior to the test trials with different sugars. It is conceivable that the test trials suffered from generalization decrement. One animal was pretrained on fructose on a fixed interval 30-second schedule (FI 30). Figures 7 and 8 compare the response measures, both bar-press and lick rate, for the three sugars, fructose, glucose, and sucrose. It can be seen that the sucrose held its superiority on both measures. The lick rate difference for fructose and sucrose is seen at .1 M; the two higher concentrations show no difference, presumably because the maximum response rate had been reached. In bar-pressing there is a clear difference at the .3 M concentration for all three sugars. At .1 and 1.0 M the response functions come together, and there is no discernible significant difference.

It is of interest to compare the consummatory response measures, licking, with the instrumental response measures, bar-press. The licking rate was the same for .3 M fructose and sucrose probably because of a ceiling effect, yet the bar-press rates were quite different. In other words, the similarity of consummatory response measures did not obscure differences in the instrumental effectiveness of the sugars. Here is another instance where the consummatory response and instrumental behavior can be dissociated as shown by other workers (e.g., Davis & Keehn, 1959). Figure 9 shows the cumulative records which illus-

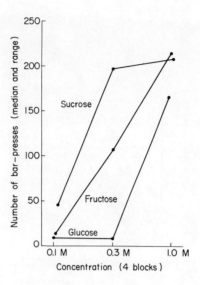

FIG. 7. Bar-pressing rates of squirrel monkey originally trained on fructose. (From Pfaffmann & McCutcheon, unpublished data.)

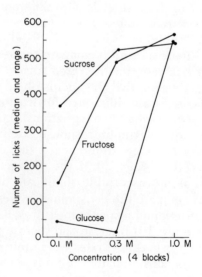

FIG. 8. Lick rates of squirrel monkey originally trained on fructose. (From Pfaffmann & McCutcheon, unpublished data.)

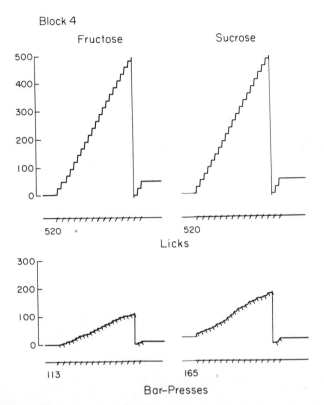

FIG. 9.   Cumulative records of licking and bar-pressing in the same animal for two different sugars showing equal consummatory response rates with unequal instrumental response rates.

trate the same licking rates, but sucrose gives higher bar-press rates than does fructose.

There still remains the fact that although fructose, sucrose, and glucose elicit sweetness, they are by no means identical in quality. Human observers (Cameron, 1947) can discriminate various sugars by virtue of temporal or other qualitative features. It is conceivable that the quality of the taste sensation is an important factor, and not merely its intensity. This certainly applies to substances as diverse as sucrose and quinine, but it may hold even within one submodality.

Dr. Linda Bartoshuk has examined the single-unit response patterns of the squirrel monkey chorda tympani. Do all single fibers in the chorda tympani nerve of this animal show fructose to be the most effective stimulant? Figure 10 shows a single-unit preparation in which fructose is more stimulating than the other three sugars. But further study has shown that this relationship does not always hold. Figure 11 is an oscillogram from another unit where fructose is less effective than the sucrose, lactose, or dextrose. In short, it is quite clear that although the predominant response pattern favors fructose, this is not true for all individual fibers studied. We are now plotting out in more detail the distribution of sensitivities to different sugars in a number of single-fiber preparations.

A population of receptors with slightly different multiple response characteristics could provide a basis for discrimination among different sugars. The sensory code from a group of five or six fibers, some of which were more reactive to fructose, some to sucrose, some to glucose, etc., would provide the cue as to which sugar had been placed on the tongue. For example, if Fiber A were relatively a fructose-sensitive element and Fiber B a sucrose-sensitive element, activity in A greater than activity in B would signify fructose, activity in B greater than activity in A would indicate sucrose. Such ratios of stimulation would presumably hold in a population of heterogeneous receptors in spite of different intensities or concentrations. This is a mechanism of discrimination not unlike that proposed by Pfaffmann (1959) to account for the discrimination among stimuli of different character, such as sugar and salt.

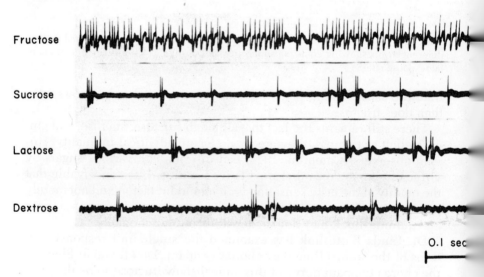

FIG. 10. Electrophysiological responses of the same single unit to different sugars. The chorda tympani nerve fiber was dissected. (From Bartoshuk, unpublished data.)

The validity of this concept is suggested by experiments on an invertebrate, the blowfly, which possesses a sugar receptor of a single type. All sugars will stimulate that receptor to varying degrees, but no qualitative differences appear. Behavioral tests by Dethier, Evans, and Rhoades (1956) indicate that, indeed, the blowfly is unable to distinguish one sugar from another. All sugars are alike to the receptors of this organism, except in amount.

B. Behavioral Studies of Sugar Response

Although in our bar-pressing and lick rate data the intensity-response functions for different sugars are pushed along the base line depending upon reinforcing value, each shows the same trend, namely that response is an increasing monotonic function of concentration.

The turndown in intake measures of varying concentrations of sugar compared with water in the typical 24-hour preference test probably reflects the intrusion of postingestive factors, such as osmotic load or caloric value. Most of the analysis leading to this conclusion has been carried out in the rat. McCleary (1953) was one of the first to show inhibition of drinking of sugar solutions by stomach-tubing the animal

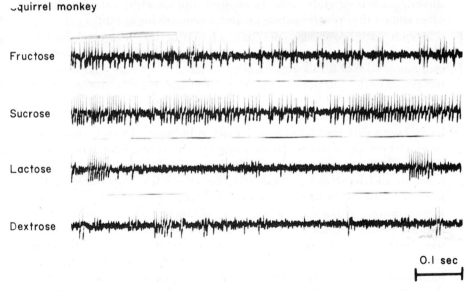

FIG. 11. Same as Fig. 10 for another unit. The chorda tympani nerve fiber was dissected.

with osmotically active solutions. He found a direct proportionality between osmotic pressure of substances introduced into the gut or even blood streams and inhibition of drinking. It is assumed that the ingestion of hypertonic solution dehydrates the organism as water is drawn into the stomach. Such dehydration makes the animal thirsty, which provides a negative feedback to protect the animal from maximizing taste alone and responding only with an increasing preference. The postingestive mechanism strikes the balance between taste and dehydration.

A similar line of reasoning was applied by Shuford (1959) to the relative palatability of glucose and sucrose solutions. He equated three pairs of each of the sugars, glucose and sucrose, at concentrations which produce the same degree of fluid intake during a 12-minute single-bottle test. When the test was continued for a longer interval (20 minutes), at least two of the original equations in intake, 35% glucose-27.6% sucrose, and 15% glucose-9.6% sucrose, no longer held. The 2% sucrose-5% glucose pair did not diverge in the course of the test. But these matches were based on intakes in single-bottle tests, and there were no direct choices between stimuli. Jacobs (1961) commented that such evidence, though indirect, was quite in keeping with the hypothesis of osmotic effect as a limiting factor controlling intake. But in further studies he noted that the osmotic factor per se did not seem to operate in the *nonthirsty* animal. Here caloric value or even some other postingestive property seemed important.

Mook's esophogastomy preparation in the rat permitted him to dissociate the mouth and gut factors in intake (1963). He divided the esophagus so that fluids entering the mouth did not enter the stomach, but passed out through the exteriorized esophagus. A stomach tube introduced into the lower esophagus was supplied from a reservoir and controlled by a solenoid valve, so that the stomach could be loaded with different solutions. Drinking behavior was monitored by an electronic drinkometer, which opened the solenoid valve controlling the fluid entering the stomach. The animal thus could drink one solution and have introduced into the stomach either nothing, the same solution as in normal intake, or a different solution. When the same solution was tasted and ingested, drinking patterns were similar to those in the normal animal. When water alone was introduced into the stomach, then drinking sugar solutions no longer showed the typical preference-aversion biphasic response, but rather the licking rate increased as sugar concentration rose. Furthermore, there is a correspondence between the amount of licking and the efficacy of two different sugars, sucrose and glucose, as determined electrophysiologically by Hagstrom and Pfaffmann (1959) from the rat's chorda tympani nerve. The implication here is that under these circumstances drinking is determined entirely by sensory input; the biphasic response normally could be attributed to an interaction of taste and postingestinal factors. As previously noted, the appropriate choice of intermittent schedule in the operant bar-pressing task tends to approximate the results when oral stimulus factors dominate. It would be of interest to add studies of fructose and other sweetening agents in the rat to those already carried out. The electrophysiological responses to fructose, as well as sucrose and glucose, have recently been determined by Tateda and Hidaka (1966).

Stellar and McCleary early (1952) noted that different behavioral procedures yielded different measures of preference. Young and Greene (1953) also have shown that either in a one-hour or brief test, the relative preference between two sucrose concentrations, 9% and 36%, favors the higher concentration, whereas 9% intake is greater when each is tested separately.

Carpenter (1958) used a multiple array, that is, from .01 to 1.0 M sucrose. Figure 12, which compares the multiple choice with two-bottle

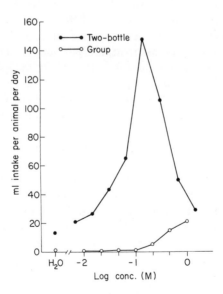

FIG. 12. Comparison of volume intake per animal in two-bottle ascending procedure and in group multiple-bottle methods. (Redrawn from Carpenter, 1958.)

(sugar and water) ascending method, shows dramatically the complication due to volume of intake, especially in the midranges. The turndown in behavioral response to sugar solutions which is associated with much larger volumes of intake is consistent with the hypothesis that postingestive influences could provide negative feedback upon ingestive behavior. Interestingly, the group method with saccharin yielded typically the biphasic relation. Concentrations between .001 and .03% were preferred; the stronger saccharin solutions were avoided. The turndown in the preference–aversion curve for saccharin often cited as an example of the biphasic response is probably not like the sugar response but may be due to the intrusion of a bitter or aversive taste quality which in man is readily apparent in the stronger solutions. The biphasic responses may be the resultant of a variety of individual mechanisms which, of themselves, are quite different.

Wagner, Green, and Manley (1965) have studied the preference values over a wide range for glucose for the squirrel monkey in a paired comparison test. Solutions ranged from 5 to 10, 20, 30, and 40% (.275, .55, 1.11, 1.65, and 2.22 M). The preference scale value for glucose continued to rise with concentration over this entire range, even though the amount of the higher concentrations consumed fell off somewhat. Wagner (1965) reexamined the possible role of postingestive factors on *relative* preference for two different concentrations, 25 and 12.5% glucose, by measuring relative intakes at the beginning of a test series and at the end of an hour. He found no shift in relative preference over the hour, so that preference per se is not influenced by postingestive effects. A two-stimulus comparison rather than simple ingestion measure seems to reveal the monotonic response function more adequately.

It appears then that sugars primarily elicit approach behavior, and the strength of such behavior seems determined directly by concentration. In short "the sweeter it is, the better it is." All such evidence supports the view that the sugar stimulus activates primarily an acceptance system and that the divergencies in behavioral tests from a simple monotonic relation between stimulus and response results from the intrusion of a secondary system, presumably postingestive in locus (see Fig. 13).

Although preference behavior can be taken to indicate the operation of a positive system, as we shall see later, the exact form of the preference function does not in itself correspond to parameters of the positive system. At any one stimulus level the behavioral preference may be the algebraic resultant of one or more positive and negative systems.

C. The Definition of Preference

The term taste preference has been used in a variety of conflicting ways in animal studies:

1. In the simplest case we speak of preference when the organism takes a large quantity or accepts one particular stimulus in amounts greater than water following the paradigm of a single-bottle ingestion measure.

2. In the classic Richter two-bottle type, the intake of taste solution is compared with that of water, but since only one taste substance is used, this situation often resembles the case of the one-bottle test, especially with highly preferred solutions and relatively small water intake. The typical biphasic preference–aversion functions occurring here, as in the one-bottle intake methods, reflect the interaction of postingestive and stimulus determinants.

3. Operant procedures using one stimulus, but measuring rate of response, not volume intake, under schedules where volume of intake is small as on a variable interval or fixed interval schedule, generally yield a response measure presumably less contaminated by postingestive factors. Such measures often yield monotonic sugar functions and appear to reflect primarily taste determinants of behavior.

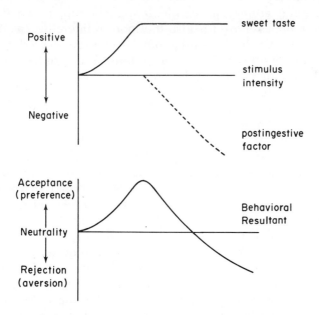

FIG. 13. Hypothetical mechanisms underlying preference-aversion behavior (see text).

4. In comparative measures of preference, "true preferences" among two or more stimuli are compared in the actual test. Here the measure is not simply intake but relative intake or approaches to the bottle or relative number of bar-presses if stimulus presentation is controlled in this manner. The comparative method has not been used as widely as it should be. It may involve more variable behavior when preferences are balanced, such as much switching from one stimulus to another, except when one is clearly preferred. It is possible to use both long-term and short-term comparative tests in operant two-bar comparative tests as well.

Contradictory results in preference studies may be the outcome of confusion of terminology and failure to clearly distinguish one method from another. Often, the simplest test to administer as the two-bottle Richter test may be more difficult to interpret than the apparently more complex operant procedure utilizing different schedules, etc. The term preference should be used more cautiously and if not restricted to "true preferences" should be clearly defined operationally.

D. Preference and Reinforcement

The relation between preference and reinforcement likewise may be intimate but not direct and simple. It might be supposed that of two stimuli, the more preferred is also the more reinforcing, that is, approaches to lick at a drinking tube may be more reinforced by sugar than by water. The expression of a preference depends upon such differential reinforcement, but the preferred stimulus is not always a reinforcer in all situations.

In the two-bottle and single-bottle test, non-needy normal animals display the well-known NaCl preference–aversion behavior. Evidence is now accumulating that a major part of both, the rising and falling, phases of NaCl intake can be attributed to a gastric factor. If in Mook's preparation an animal is drinking saline solution but water is being introduced in the stomach, there is no preference–aversion function. The curve of response is entirely flat except at the higher concentrations where the taste of salt is aversive and drinking is inhibited. When nothing is introduced into the stomach, there is slight intake of hypotonic solutions, but the full response requires gastric loading with saline. In a T-maze, the arms of which are baited with water on the one side and optimally preferred .9% saline on the other, a mildly thirsty rat learns to run to the side containing water, not salt. Although the T-maze test can show learning to go to the salt side under certain conditions, this is not the common finding. The "preferred" solution in a two-bottle test does not reinforce maze behavior. Prior experience, interactions with thirst, and other learning factors may influence outcome (Brookshire, 1967; Deutsch & Jones, 1960; Stearns, 1965).

Likewise, the maximally "preferred" saline solution will not reinforce bar-pressing in a normal animal in a one-hour test, except in the animal that has been made salt-needy by adrenalectory or by a protracted salt-free diet (Lewis, 1960; Wagman, 1963). These observations have led to the question of whether the normal animal's apparent preference for salt may be entirely an artifact of gastric factors. The role of taste per se becomes dominant only in a deprived or needy state, yet the fact that more approaches are made to the salt bottle when these are measured in the two-bottle test situation shows that the saline must have reinforced responses to the position of that tube. Correspondingly, when salt and water are both presented in a two-bottle test in choice experiments ("true preference test") with the Mook preparation, the rat clearly drinks preferentially at the salt tube when only water enters the stomach (Mook, 1967).

Thus, although the saline taste initiates a preference toward the solution, the gastric factor may control volume intake. The normal animal may be trapped in a type of positive feedback loop. It takes saline in preference to water; the saline gastric effect increases volume intake. Yet this whole sequence is reinforcing because the number of approaches to the salt tube is greater than to the water (Chiang & Wilson, 1963). Whether such preferences can be mediated entirely by gastric factors without the intermediary of taste needs further study. Borer and Epstein (1965) found no taste preference or aversions for the basic taste modalities when the chronic gastric tube delivered solutions directly into the stomach in response to bar-pressing. When the same animals were able to taste and ingest the same solutions, the usual two-bottle preference functions were readily observed in the relative rates of bar-pressing. Actually, the Borer-Epstein study did show the NaCl preference to be reinforcing for bar-pressing. Here the animals were on an ad lib 24-hour two-bar test in which one delivered water, the other salt of various concentrations. Perhaps the low thirst level and ad lib conditions or prior "shaping" to bar-press for sucrose facilitated reinforcement by NaCl.

The reinforcing effect of saline for the normal animal can be easily demonstrated by using a response that is easier for the animal than the typical bar-press. Fisher developed a contingent lick procedure (Fisher, 1965) in which licking itself is treated as an instrumental response in a manner similar to Hulse, Snyder, and Bacon (1960). Two tubes were employed, one fixed, the other retractable, after the animal licked a criterion number of times at the fixed tube; the second was presented for a fixed period and then withdrawn. In order to "call for" the second tube, the animal had to make a specified number of licks at the fixed tube. The presentation of the second tube, therefore, was contingent upon behavior at the first. The fixed tube was always present so that the animal could stay on it or shift to the second tube when it appeared. The presence of both tubes provided a choice, but the required number of licks at the first tube insured that the animal always sampled the first tube. Licking at each tube was monitored by a drinkometer, appropriate counters, and recorders.

Eight animals were exposed to three 15-minute sessions at four levels of water deprivation (23 hours, 6 hours, 3 hours, and 1 hour). The fixed tube contained water and the second, saline (W → S series). This order was then reversed, the fixed tube contained saline and the retractable tube water (S → W). In the third session a W → S sequence was followed by the control and final session, water in both tubes (W → W).

Lick rates were computed by dividing the total number of licks at a tube by the time each tube was available. The median lick rates of all animals on both tubes for the last session are presented graphically in Fig. 14. It can be seen that in the first (W → S) sequence, the animal licked primarily at the first (H_2O) tube during high water deprivation, but took less water with lower deprivation and further training. In the second (S → W) stage, rates of licking at the fixed tube (saline) were higher at all levels of H_2O deprivation. Licking at the fixed tube (water) was less than at the same tube (NaCl) in the first (W → S) sequence.

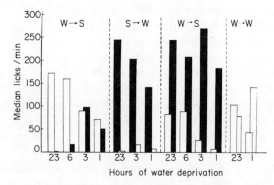

FIG. 14.   Median rates of licking for all animals on the third day of each level of water deprivation. The filled bars indicate saline licking; the unfilled bars indicate water licking. W → S indicates that licking at the water tube resulted in presentation of saline, S → W indicates that licking at saline presented water, W → W indicates that licking at the water tube resulted in presentation of another water tube. (From Fisher, 1965.)

After training, the animal stayed at the saline tube and did not shift to water when it became available, but when the water tube brought saline, there was an immediate shift to saline. The animal prefers saline even in the presence of water and at different levels of thirst.

The same effect is reflected in the pattern of drinking. When the animal is required to make ten licks to produce the retractable tube containing salt, there is a clear stepwise progression in the cumulative record of licking on the fixed tube (H_2O). The animal makes only the required number of licks to bring the preferred saline in the second tube. On the other hand, in the S → W period there is steady licking on the fixed tube (saline) and no shift to water, except for a few sampling trials. Thus, the animal is exposed to both stimuli but clearly demonstrates a saline preference.

When a strong reinforcer like sucrose is tested each day in both the W → S and S → W sequences, a clear preference is displayed for the tube containing sucrose. Animals drink at the water tube just sufficiently to produce the sugar tube or, if the first tube contains sugar, they stay on it with only an occasional sampling of the second H_2O tube. If a concentration series is presented on successive days, a reinforcement threshold is indicated by the shift from indiscriminant response to the sugar-containing tube, as at $10^{-3}\,M$ in Fig. 15, to the consistent selection of the tube containing sugar.

The observations on NaCl raise the question of whether there is a response hierarchy of measures of reinforcement. For different stimuli different responses may be more appropriate than others. Thus, the normal non-needy preference for saline may be insufficient to motivate an arbitrary response like in the bar-press, at least in a restricted

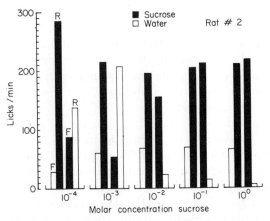

FIG. 15. Contingent lick measures of sucrose solutions of increasing concentration. (From Fisher, 1967.)

one-hour test period. On the other hand instrumental licking, which requires little effort and brings the stimulus close to the relevant receptors on the tongue, can be readily reinforced.

E. Origin of Preference-Aversion Functions

To review the genesis of the biphasic taste intake preference curve for saline, it would appear that in a single-bottle, or one solution, versus water two-bottle test, the normal animal is attracted to the salt bottle, but the volume ingested here depends on postingestinal factors. Thus, the biphasic character of the salt preference reflects a combination of both taste and gastric effects different from that seen for sugars or saccharin. We might diagram the processes which underline the several different biphasic responses as in Fig. 16. Taste and postingestive factors may each be biphasic and summate to give the form of the response in normal animals in some instances. In the figure the lesser positive value attributed to salt taste compared with the postingestive factor is inferred from the fact that when nothing, rather than water, is introduced into the stomach of a fistulated animal, there is still a small preference. The greater postingestive aversive effect of strong NaCl solutions is assumed, because to the severe dehydration deleterious to life is added the gastric irritation. Taste alone would probably not be deleterious, only aversive. Sucrose, as already noted, activates a purely acceptance taste system and negative postingestive factors. In the case of saccharin, the positive and negative effects reside almost entirely in taste, probably the summation of one positive (sweet) and one aversive (bitter) modality. All these solutions are so dilute that postingestive osmotic factors probably would not operate.

The aversive stimuli have not been examined in sufficient detail to know whether primarily aversive responses consist of one or more components. As mentioned above, there is little evidence except in some of Engel's hedonic ratings for a positive effect in man of bitter and acid stimuli. In animals, the one instance of a positive response to the predominantly aversive stimulus (SOA) was transitory and dropped out on repeated tests (Warren, 1963).

This raises an additional interesting question of how certain stimuli develop primarily aversive or positive features. Schneirla has hypothesized that a neonatal biphasic A/W response through "behavioral development as a progression of patterned changes due to maturation and experience variables depending upon individual conditions" might diverge in the adult toward the dominance of either A processes or W processes over behavior (1965). How and why certain stimuli over a wide range of organisms come to show similar relations, that is, a large aversion for "bitter" and an attraction for "sugar" or "sweet," is an intriguing question the answer to which is not immediately obvious from the A/W formulation. In most studies that have been attempted so far, taste preferences have been resistant to a major shift from aversion to attractiveness by early infantile experience (Siqueland, 1965; Warren & Pfaffmann, 1958). Perhaps such experimental tests so far have not been carried out under appropriate conditions. Other evidence does show that changes in diet at various ages lead to reduced food intake (if not complete aversion) until habituation to the new food has occurred. The value of taste and flavor stimuli can certainly be modified or developed, but it may require training

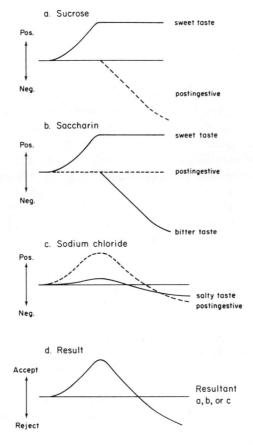

FIG. 16. Composite array of different hypothetical taste and postingestive factors underlying the typical preference–aversion functions.

and experience perhaps over a period longer than that used so far in most experiments. The cultural basis of dietary preferences and food habits in man is, of course, so well known that we take it for granted. It would be especially valuable to study their genesis in greater detail.

The physiological study of the basis for the preference and aversion responses is a most challenging one. We are entirely in the dark as to where and how physiologically the afferent input acquires the potency to turn behavior on or off, to change response from preference to aversion, from approach to withdrawal, from positive to negative hedonic effect. Uncovering the physiological processes, states, or loci that give to sensory input its value, and the resulting polarity that typifies taste preference and its related reinforcing properties will have general significance for the physiological understanding of a wide range of behaviors.

IV. SUMMARY

In this account we have taken the subject of taste preferences to illustrate the basic positive to negative polarity of behavioral responses, and have attempted to analyze some of the physiological factors which instigate preference, on the one hand, or aversion, on the other. Evidence was presented and reviewed indicating that in one instance, at least, it was appropriate to think of a stimulus such as sugar as a purely positive or acceptance stimulus and as a positive reinforcer. The rejection of sugar under some conditions could be attributed to the arousal of a secondary aversive component residing in postingestive factors. The typical biphasic preference-aversion curve, although of similar form for most preferred solutions, does not have a common explanation. In the case of saccharin, postingestive factors probably play a minimal role, and the preference may arise from the summation of a positive taste and a negative taste component. In the case of salt, the biphasic preference-aversion function may reflect the interaction between a slight positive salt response and postingestive effects that increase volume intake. Beyond the isosmotic point, both taste and the postingestive factor lead to an aversion and reduced intake. Whether both taste and osmotic postingestive effects shift from positive to negative at the same concentration value has not been determined. Thus, although taste preference-aversion relations seem to have a common source, some stimuli elicit primarily acceptance or positive effects, some apparently purely negative or aversive components, and some a combination of these. Taste or postingestive factors may not necessarily correspond to either the positive or negative components.

Further discussion of the nature of behavioral tests and the relation of response measures of reinforcement indicated that not all responses seem equally appropriate as response criteria. Some responses may be more appropriate for certain modalities, and some responses may be more easily reinforced than others. Instrumental licking, for example, seems more readily related to taste stimulation than such responses as bar-pressing or maze-running. The sensitivity of behavior tests or the type of function revealed may reflect a contribution of different response as well as stimulus factors to the behavior elicited.

Some comments on the ontogeny of the positive and negative reactions are made primarily to point to the need for further research. Finally, the basic question of how and at what point in the nervous system afferent neural inputs acquire their affective value or reinforcement significance still remains one of the important areas of research to bridge the gap between physiology and motivated behavior.

REFERENCES

Berlyne, D. E. *Conflict, arousal and curiosity.* New York: McGraw-Hill, 1960.

Borer, K. T., & Epstein, A. N. Disappearance of salt and sweet preferences in rats drinking without taste and smell. *Physiologist*, 1965, **8**, 118.

Brookshire, K. H. Inversion of discrete trial water-saline preference as a function of prior drinking experience. *J. comp. physiol. Psychol.*, 1967, **63**, 24-27.

Cameron, A. T. *The taste sense and the relative sweetness of sugars and other substances.* New York: Sugar Res. Found., 1947. (*Sci. Rep. Ser.*, No. 9)

Carpenter, J. A. A comparison of stimulus-presentation procedures in taste-preference experiments. *J. comp. physiol. Psychol.*, 1958, **51**, 561-564.

Chiang, H., & Wilson, W. A., Jr. Some tests of the diluted-water hypothesis of saline consumption in rats. *J. comp. physiol. Psychol.*, 1963, **56**, 660-665.

Collier, G., & Myers, L. The loci of reinforcement. *J. exp. Psychol.*, 1961, **61**, 57-66.

Collier, G., & Siskel, M., Jr. Performance as a joint function of amount of reinforcement and interreinforcement interval. *J. exp. Psychol.*, 1959, **57**, 115-120.

Davis, J. D., & Keehn, J. D. Magnitude of reinforcement and consummatory behavior. *Science*, 1959, **130**, 269-271.

Dethier, V. G., Evans, D. R., & Rhoades, M. V. Some factors controlling the ingestion of carbohydrates by the blow fly. *Biol. Bull.*, 1956, **111**, 204-222.

Deutsch, J. A., & Jones, A. D. Diluted water: An explanation of the rat's preference for saline. *J. comp. physiol. Psychol.*, 1960, **53**, 122-127.

Diamant, H., Funakoshi, M., Ström, L., & Zotterman, Y. Electrophysiological studies on human taste nerves. In Y. Zotterman (Ed.), *Olfaction and taste.* Oxford: Pergamon Press, 1963. Pp. 193-203.

Dufour, V. L., & Arnold, M. B. Taste of saccharin as sufficient reward for performance. *Psychol. Rep.*, 1966, **19**, 1293-1294.

Ekman, G., & Akesson, C. Saltiness, sweetness and preference. *Scand. J. Psychol.*, 1965, **6**, 241-253.

Engel, R. Experimentelle Untersuchungen über die Abhängigkeit der Lust und Unlust von der Reizstärke beim Geschmackssinn. *Arch. ges. Psychol.*, 1928, **64**, 1-36. (a)

Engel, R. In R. S. Woodworth (Ed.), *Experimental psychology*. New York: Holt, 1928. (b)

Fisher, G. L. Saline preference in rats determined by contingent licking. *J. exp. Anal. Behav.*, 1965, **8**, 295-303.

Fisher, G. L. Personal communication, 1967.

Fisher, G. L., Pfaffmann, C., & Brown, E. Dulcin and saccharin taste in squirrel monkeys, rats and men. *Science*, 1965, **150**, 500-507.

Guttman, N. Operant conditioning, extinction and periodic reinforcement in relation to concentration of sucrose used as reinforcing agent. *J. exp. Psychol.*, 1953, **46**, 213-224.

Hagstrom, E. C., & Pfaffmann, C. The relative taste effectiveness of different sugars for the rat. *J. comp. physiol. Psychol.*, 1959, **52**, 259-262.

Holt, E. B. *Animal drive and the learning process*. New York: Holt, 1931.

Hulse, S. H., Snyder, H. L., & Bacon, W. E. Instrumental licking behavior as a function of schedule, volume, and concentration of a saccharine reinforcer. *J. exp. Psychol.*, 1960, **60**, 359-364.

Jacobs, H. L. The osmotic postingestion factor in the regulation of glucose appetite. In M. R. Kare and B. P. Halpern (Eds.), *The physiological and behavioral aspects of taste*. Chicago: Univ. of Chicago Press, 1961. Pp. 16-38.

Jay, J. R. Reinforcing effects of five sugars in different concentrations on rates of bar pressing and licking in the squirrel monkey (Saimura Sciurea). Unpublished master's thesis, Brown Univer., 1965.

Lewis, M. Behavior resulting from sodium chloride deprivation in adrenalectomized rats. *J. comp. physiol. Psychol.*, 1960, **53**, 464-467.

McCleary, R. A. Taste and postingestion factors in specific hunger behavior. *J. comp. physiol. Psychol.*, 1953, **46**, 411-421.

Mook, D. G. Oral and postingestinal determinants of the intake of various solutions in rats with esophageal fistulas. *J. comp. physiol. Psychol.*, 1963, **56**, 654-659.

Mook, D. G. Some determinants of preference and aversions in the rat. Conference on Neural Regulation of Food and Water Intake. New York: New York Acad. Sci., 1967.

Pfaffmann, C. The afferent code for sensory quality. *Amer. Psychologist*, 1959, **14**, 226-232.

Pfaffmann, C. The pleasure of sensation. *Psychol. Rev.*, 1960, **67**, 253-268.

Pfaffmann, C. The sensory and motivating properties of the sense of taste. In M. R. Jones (Ed.), *Nebraska symposium on motivation*. Lincoln, Nebr.: Univer. of Nebraska Press, 1961. Pp. 71-108.

Pfaffmann, C. De Gustibus. *Amer. Psychologist*, 1965, **20**, 21-33.

Schneirla, T. C. A theoretical consideration of the basis for approach-withdrawal adjustments in behavior. *Psychol. Bull.*, 1939, **37**, 501-502.

Schneirla, T. C. An evolutionary and developmental theory of biphasic processes underlying approach and withdrawal. In M. R. Jones (Ed.), *Nebraska symposium on motivation*. Lincoln, Nebr.: Univer. of Nebraska Press, 1959. Pp. 1-42.

Schneirla, T. C. Aspects of stimulation and organization in approach/withdrawal processes underlying vertebrate behavioral development. *Advanc. Study Behav.*, 1965, **1**, 1-74.

Sheffield, F. D., & Roby, T. B. Reward value of a nonnutrituve sweet taste. *J. comp. physiol. Psychol.*, 1950, **43**, 471-481.

Shuford, E. H., Jr. Palatability and osmotic pressure of glucose and sucrose solutions as determinants of intake. *J. comp. physiol. Psychol.*, 1959, **52**, 150–153.

Siqueland, E. R. Experimental modification of taste preference. *J. comp. physiol. Psychol.*, 1965, **59**, 166–170.

Snell, T. C. The response of the squirrel monkey chorda tympani to a variety of taste stimuli. Unpublished master's thesis, Brown Univer., 1965.

Stearns, E. M. Reward value of saline and water for the rat. *Psychon. Sci.*, 1965, **2**, 193–194.

Stellar, E., & McCleary, R. A. Food preference as a function of the method of measurement. *Amer. Psychologist*, 1952, **7**, 256.

Tateda, H., & Hidaka, I. Taste response to sweet substances in rat. *Mem. Fac. Sci., Kyushu Univer. Ser. E*, 1966, **4**, No. 3, 137–149.

Troland, L. T. *The fundamentals of human motivation*. Princeton, N.J.: Van Nostrand, 1928.

Wagman, W. Sodium chloride deprivation: Development of sodium chloride as a reinforcer. *Science*, 1963, **140**, 1403–1404.

Wagner, M. W. The effects of age, weight and experience on relative sugar preference in the albino rat. *Psychon. Sci.*, 1965, **2**, 243–244.

Wagner, M. W., Green, K. F., & Manley, M. B. Paired comparison method for measurement of sugar preference in squirrel monkeys. *Science*, 1965, **148**, 1473–1474.

Warren, R. P. Preference-aversion in mice to bitter substances. *Science*, 1963, **140**, 808–809.

Warren, R. P., & Pfaffmann, C. Early experience and taste aversion. *J. comp. physiol. Psychol.*, 1958, **52**, 263–266.

Wundt, W. *Grundzüge der physiologischen Psychologie*. Leipzig: Englemann, 1874.

Young, P. T. Food seeking, drive, affective process, and learning. *Psychol. Rev.*, 1949, **56**, 98–121.

Young, P. T. The role of hedonic processes in motivation. In M. R. Jones (Ed.), *Nebraska symposium on motivation*. Lincoln, Nebr., Univer. of Nebraska Press, 1955.

Young, P. T. Hedonic organization and regulation of behavior. *Psychol. Rev.*, 1966, **73**, 59–86.

Young, P. T., & Green, J. T. Quantity of food ingested as a measure of relative acceptability. *J. comp. physiol. Psychol.*, 1953, **46**, 288–294.

CHAPTER 9

The Hypothalamus and Motivated Behavior[1]

ELLIOT S. VALENSTEIN, VERNE C. COX, AND JAN
W. KAKOLEWSKI

I. INTRODUCTION AND HISTORICAL PERSPECTIVE

Prior to the turn of the century, the hypothalamus was a relatively neglected part of the brain. If the few clinical reports from pathologists are excluded, the descriptions of the function of the hypothalamus consisted mainly of brief accounts of its role as an olfactory integrative center. A new view of this area of the brain started to develop shortly after the beginning of the century with the pioneering series of papers by Karplus and Kreidl (1909-1914) demonstrating that sympathetic responses could be elicited by electrical stimulation of the hypothalamus. This work provided experimental support for Sherrington's characterization of the hypothalamus as the "head ganglion of the autonomic nervous system." Later, the classic studies of Hess (1954) and Ranson (1937) and their respective collaborators supplied much more information about the hypothalamic control of both auto-

[1]Supported by NIMH grants M-4529, Career Scientist Award MH-4947, and Research grant NsG-437 from NASA.

nomic "reflexes" and more integrated or organismic responses such as those involved in eating, sleeping, defecation, and aggressive behavior. Gradually the impression was formed that these integrated responses involved more than a complex of somatomotor responses such as snarling, hissing, and teeth baring, and reflected affective states as well. For example, Hess (1954) rejected Sherrington's term "sham rage" which was applied to decorticate cats, and indicated that he regarded Bard's label "angry behavior" as more appropriate to the states produced by hypothalamic stimulation.

Supplementing the work directly involving the hypothalamus were the studies and theories about the function of the medial wall of the cerebral hemisphere, called by Broca (1879) "la grande lobe limbique" and now referred to as the limbic system. Klüver and Bucy (1937) had described emotional changes following lesions in the limbic system, and in the same year Papez (1937) speculated that a circuit involving the limbic system and hypothalamus comprised the anatomical substrate for emotion. Earlier, Herrick (1933) and numerous other anatomists before him (e.g., Edinger & Wallenberg, 1902; Gudden, 1881; E. G. Smith, 1896) had described the many anatomical connections between the medial wall of the cerebral hemisphere and the hypothalamus. More recently, investigators have suggested that many of the changes in emotionality produced by limbic system lesions were dependent on the connections between limbic structures and the hypothalamus.

This new orientation provided the impetus for a great number of experiments over the past 15 years which have provided examples of specific motivated behavior elicited by electrical stimulation of the hypothalamus. The behavior described has included eating (Coons, 1963; Coons, Levak, & Miller, 1965; Delgado & Anand, 1953; Fantl & Schuckman, 1967; Hutchinson & Renfrew, 1966; S. Larsson, 1954; Morgane, 1961; Roberts, Steinberg, & Means, 1967; Steinbaum & Miller, 1965; Tenen & Miller, 1964), drinking (Anderson & McCann, 1955; Greer, 1955; Mendelson, 1967; Mogenson & Stevenson, 1967), gnawing (Roberts & Carey, 1965), hoarding (Herberg & Blundell, 1967), stalking-attack (Flynn, 1967; Hutchinson & Renfrew, 1966; Roberts & Kiess, 1964; Roberts, et al., 1967), copraphagia (Mendelson, 1966), and male copulatory behavior (Caggiula & Hoebel, 1966; Roberts et al., 1967; Vaughan & Fisher, 1962). As nondeprived animals exhibit the behavior only during the period of stimulation, the term "stimulus-bound" behavior has been applied. Stimulus-bound behavior has generally been considered a motivated act rather than a stereotyped motor act because it is not exhibited unless appropriate goal objects are present and because during stimulation animals will perform some learned task in order to obtain access to the relevant goal object (Coons et al., 1965). There exists a widespread acceptance of the idea that stimulus-bound eating is elicited by activation of specific neural circuits underlying "hunger," drinking from activation of specific "thirst" circuits, and similar conclusions have been drawn with regard to the other elicited behavior that has been studied. Somewhat separate from the issue of specific neural circuits is the implication that relatively discrete hypothalamic regions are responsible for the control of behavior related to specific biological needs.

During the past year the authors have been studying the possibility of modifying the behavior elicited from hypothalamic stimulation. Our experience has led us to conclude that there has been an overemphasis of the role of the hypothalamus in controlling specific motivated behavior and that a number of the commonly held views of hypothalamic function need revision. We would like to review our initial findings and to present the results of a number of additional experiments, some unreported previously, which helped to clarify these findings. The data suggest alternative interpretations of the role of hypothalamic control of motivated behavior, and we will offer some preliminary comments on the direction these interpretations may take in the future.

The experiment that initiated our series of studies of hypothalamic stimulation and motivated behavior emphasized stimulus-bound eating, drinking, and gnawing. We found that in every case in which hypothalamic stimulation elicited any one of these three behaviors, it was possible to change the elicited behavior to one of the other two (Valenstein, Cox, & Kakolewski, 1968a). The second elicited behavior was exhibited with as much reliability and vigor as the first. As the stimulus parameters were not changed in any way, we concluded that the activation of the same neural substrate could elicit a variety of behaviors, and therefore it might be appropriate to reexamine the question of whether hypothalamic stimulation produces an excitation of specific motivational states. The methodology of the first experiment is described at length, since the same basic procedures were utilized in many of the subsequent experiments to be reported here in less detail.

II. EXPERIMENTS ON STIMULUS-BOUND BEHAVIOR

A. General Experimental Methodology

Mature Holtzman albino rats (250–350 gm) of both sexes were implanted with electrodes in the lateral hypothalamus. The bipolar electrodes were made from .25 mm wire which was insulated except for the cross section at the tip. Other details of the electrode assembly have been described elsewhere (Valenstein, Hodos, & Stein, 1961). In most instances bipolar electrodes were implanted in the lateral hypothalamus on the left and right sides of the midline. Following surgery, but prior to any stimulation, animals were placed individually in Plexiglas cages which served as living quarters and testing chambers. Light in the room was on from 7:00 AM to 7:00 PM each day. The cages contained three goal objects: Purina Lab Chow pellets, a water bottle with a metal drinking tube, and a pine wedge mounted on either the floor or one of the walls.

Animals were stimulated with either a 30-second train of 60-cycle sine wave or biphasic rectangular pulses (frequency, 100 pulse-pairs per second; pulse duration, .2 millisecond). Stimulus intensities used for the animals in the first experiment are provided in Table I. During preliminary screening designed to determine an appropriate stimulus intensity, animals were stimulated for a 30-second period followed by a 60-second interstimulus interval. All stimulation was programmed by automatic equipment, and the time and duration of delivery were never under the experimenters' control. The intensity was adjusted until the stimulus elicited a forward moving "searching" behavior. If after a period of time the animal did not exhibit either eating, drinking, or gnawing in response to stimulation, the intensity was raised or lowered to what appeared to be a more promising level. If no specific behavior pattern emerged, the animal was stimulated for a 12-hour period throughout the night with stimulation delivered for 30 seconds every five minutes, and this sequence constituted a *night schedule*. If the animal still did not exhibit any eating, drinking, or gnawing in response to stimulation, the night schedule was repeated at least one additional time. No electrode was classified as negative unless there was stimulation on at least two night schedules in addition to the observations necessary to select the appropriate stimulus intensity and to evaluate the effects of the night schedules. The classification of negative implies only the absence of one of the three investigated

TABLE I
Eating (E), Drinking (D), and Gnawing (G) Behavior
Elicited during Hypothalamic Stimulation[a]

Animal	Behavior	First series 1	First series 2	First series 3	Second series 1	Second series 2	Competition	Stimulus parameters[b] (μA)
60S	E	0	0	0	15	17	11	
	D	20	20	20	—	—	14	R, 80
	G	0	0	0	0	0	0	
61S	E	0	0	0	20	20	15	
	D	20	20	20	—	—	12	R, 120
	G	0	0	0	0	0	0	
63S	E	0	0	0	0	0	0	
	D	0	0	0	20	20	12	R, 500
	G	20	20	20	—	—	8	
74S	E	0	0	0	20	20	12	
	D	20	20	20	—	—	13	S, 20
	G	0	0	0	0	0	0	
80SR	E	19	16	12	—	—	10	
	D	1	5	8	19	16	10	R, 120
	G	0	0	0	2	2	6	
91S	E	0	0	0	20	20	11	
	D	20	20	20	—	—	9	R, 120
	G	0	0	0	0	0	0	
93SR	E	0	0	0	15	16	10	
	D	17	17	19	—	—	9	R, 100
	G	3	2	2	0	0	0	
89S	E	0	0	0	18	20	16	
	D	19	19	20	—	—	4	S, 24
	G	0	0	0	0	0	0	
5T	E	0	0	0	20	14	13	
	D	15	18	19	—	—	9	R, 80
	G	0	0	0	0	0	0	
84SL	E	14	10	10	—	—	5	
	D	14	12	11	—	—	10	R, 80
	G	0	0	0	10	5	1	
33TL	E	20	20	17	—	—	16	
	D	2	2	0	20	20	10	R, 120
	G	0	0	0	0	0	0	

[a] Each test had 20 stimulation periods. Maximum score for any one behavior is 20, but animals could exhibit different behaviors during each period.

[b] S = sine wave; R = rectangular pulses.

behaviors and does not suggest any aversive effects. With this procedure, stimulation of approximately 25–30% of the electrode sites resulted in either eating, drinking, or gnawing by the animals.

Although a considerable amount of time was expended testing negative sites, we were still concerned that additional testing or simply allowing a period of time to elapse might result in a display of some stimulus-bound behavior. To explore this possibility, an additional group of animals with 36 electrode placements that had been classified previously as negative were left in their home cages for three weeks and then placed on the night schedule and observed the following day. A smaller group was retested after three months in their home cages. The fact that there was only one instance in which any stimulus-bound behavior was displayed during the retests testified to the adequacy of our criterion for classifying electrodes as negative.

The animals that exhibited stimulus-bound behavior were then given a series of three standard tests (30 minutes' duration). A *standard test* consisted of twenty 30-second stimulation periods separated by a 60-second interstimulus interval. During these tests all three of the goal objects were present. There was a minimum of 30 minutes between each standard test.

The behavior was scored by an observer located only a few feet from the animal. Eating and drinking were recorded only when there was clear evidence of consuming the food or water. The food pellets were generally held with the front paws and pieces were bitten off, chewed, and swallowed; the drinking tube was lapped, and the animal could be observed ingesting the water; gnawing consisted of biting off pieces of wood from the wedge. In most cases the animal began the elicited behavior within 1–2 seconds after the onset of the stimulus and stopped abruptly after its termination. In a few instances the response latency was as long as 15 seconds. The duration of the elicited behavior was variable. A number of animals ate, drank, or gnawed for almost the entire 30-second stimulation period, but in a few cases the behavior was observed for only about a 5-second period. Scoreable behavior was seldom observed during the interstimulus period. We will discuss this dearth of interstimulus behavior in more detail in another context of this chapter.

Following the standard tests confirming the presence of stimulus-bound behavior, the goal object to which the rat oriented was removed, and the animal was placed on the night schedule with the other two goal objects present. If, for example, the rat exhibited drinking during stimulation in the first series of tests, the water bottle was removed during the night, and only the food pellets and wood were left in the cage. *The stimulus parameters remained unchanged.* If the animal did not exhibit a new elicited behavior, it was placed a second, third, or even more times on the night schedule. In most cases, however, one night was sufficient time for a new behavior to emerge. After a new behavior emerged, the animals were given two standard tests with the initial goal object absent and a third standard test (*competition test*) with all three goal objects present. When the animal was not being stimulated, the three goal objects were always available; therefore, the animals had an opportunity to become satiated on food, water, and wood prior to testing. Eleven animals completed this sequence of testing, and these results constitute the first experiment.

B. Initial Results, Subsequent Experiments, and Discussion

1. Initial Results

Table I presents the results with the 11 animals studied in the first experiment. Seven of the 11 animals exhibited only one behavior during the first three standard tests. During this series of tests the elicited behavior was exhibited with almost every stimulus presentation. The second series of tests was administered after a variable amount of experience receiving stimulation in the absence of the goal object to which the animal first oriented. It can be seen that in most cases the second elicited behavior was exhibited as consistently as the first (Table I). During the competition test, when all three goal objects were present, approximately equal amounts of the two elicited behaviors were displayed in most instances. Generally, one of the behaviors was elicited for three or four consecutive stimulus presentations and then the other behavior for an approximately equally long series. In most competition tests, the animals displayed more than one elicited behavior during several of the 20 stimulus presentations.

We were interested in determining whether the first behavior would reestablish its dominance if we gave a series of competition tests. Although a variety of patterns have emerged from this testing, we feel secure in concluding that once a second stimulus-bound behavior has been established, the initial behavior that was elicited by the stimulation is no longer the dominant response. In fact, several animals displayed a clear predominance of the second behavior during a series of competition tests. This lack of dominance of the first stimulus-bound behavior was evident also from other observations. We have noted consistently that among animals exhibiting only one behavior initially, those displaying the most vigorous pattern (judged by the brief latency, long duration during stimulation, and great consistency) required the least amount of training for a second pattern to emerge. However, even in these cases the new behavior took several hours to emerge, indicating that it was a response not previously associated with the stimulation.

Four animals displayed more than one behavior during the first series of tests. In three of the animals the dominant goal object was removed during the experience on the night schedule and during the second series of tests. The results took two forms. In two cases (80SR and 33TL) the other behavior initially displayed was exhibited with increased frequency. Animal 80SR also exhibited a third behavior pattern, gnawing, during the second series of tests and the competition test. Animal 93SR, which had initially displayed drinking, and gnawing to a lesser extent, switched to eating during the second series of tests and competition test. Animal 84SL, which displayed approximately equal amounts of eating and drinking initially, was given experience on the night schedule with only the wood present. During the second series of tests this animal displayed gnawing during stimulation, although not with a very high frequency. In general, the results of the competition tests with these four animals confirmed the results with the first seven in the respect that the dominant behavior displayed initially did not necessarily remain dominant after additional selective experience.

2. Other Behaviors

We have had no clear failures in changing the behavior with our technique and now have had experience with many more animals than have been reported here. In some instances it has been necessary to place the animal on the night schedule for as many as six or seven nights before the new behavior emerged, but with the exception of those few animals in which we suspected the electrode had moved or damaged tissue (judged by increases in threshold), we have had uniform success. It might also be important to note that in some cases in which the second behavior took a long time to emerge we noted some stimulus-bound behavior that did not fit into our arbitrary tripartite categories of eating, drinking, and gnawing. Among these behaviors we observed face washing, tail chasing, and a foot shuffling of the food pellets. Dr. Edward Deaux of Antioch College tested animals displaying the stimulus-bound shuffling of food in a chamber with the floor covered with a bedding material (Sanicel). These animals exhibited a stimulus-bound digging response and were later switched to displaying stimulus-bound drinking and eating. Subsequently, we have determined that the digging meets the usual criterion of a motivated response in that these animals will leave the bare floor on one side of a shuttle box to dig on the other side when stimulated. Although we have only a minimum number of observations with these other behaviors, *it would appear that the switching of stimulus-bound behavior is not restricted to oral responses.* Dr. Charles Gallistel has indicated to us[2] that he has tested an animal which initially displayed stimulus-bound male copulatory behavior only from a caudally placed hypothalamic electrode, while only a rostral electrode elicited stimulus-bound drinking. Following restricted training, the rostral electrode elicited copulation as well as drinking, and in the absence of a female, the caudal electrode elicited both eating and drinking. Moreover, the copulatory behavior elicited by the rostral electrode was more vigorous than that observed following stimulation with the caudal electrode. We have also noted stimulus-bound eating and drinking from this caudal area, lateral to the fornix at the level of the premamillary nucleus, the region considered by Caggiula and Hoebel (1966) to be a possible male copulatory site. More recently, Caggiula reported[3] that he has observed a number of cases of stimulus-bound eating and drinking elicited from electrodes also capable of eliciting male copulatory behavior. It seems obvious to us that much more work is needed to establish the limits of the plasticity we have described.

3. *Positive and Negative Electrodes and Self-Stimulation*

As the majority of our electrodes did not elicit stimulus-bound behavior in spite of the fact that the placements could not be distinguished from our positive sites (cf. Section II, B, 5), we felt it necessary to provide evidence that the negative electrodes were functional. Although we were convinced that they were functional because stimulation clearly produced an increase in locomotion which we have referred to as "searching" behavior, we have provided more quantitative data in the case of animals 92SR and 10TL. These animals were trained to self-stimulate at the same intensity with which they had been tested. Using a .5-second train duration in three successive 10-minute tests, 92SR averaged 84, 77, and 75 responses per minute, while 10TL averaged 23, 25, and 37 responses. Animal 10T was also tested with its negative electrode on the right side (10TR) and averaged 35, 28, and 22 responses per minute. Clearly, stimulation at these

[2] Personal communication, 1968.
[3] Personal communication, 1968.

negative sites was not only effective, but also positively reinforcing. These results are supported by the recent findings of Christopher and Butter (1968), who noted that locomotor exploration was much more commonly associated with sites yielding self-stimulation than any of the consummatory behaviors observed. As it was possible that the 30-second duration stimulation used in the tests for elicited behavior may have had some aversive consequences, we determined if these same animals would self-stimulate for a longer train with the identical stimulus parameters employed to elicit stimulus-bound behavior. Judging by the number of times the animal turned the stimulus on during successive 10-minute periods, the 30-second train duration stimulus was also positive. The maximum number of times possible for an animal to turn on the 30-second duration stimulus was 19 in each 10-minute period. The scores for 92SR were 18, 17, and 17; for 10TR they were 11, 12 and 8; and for 10TL the results were 14, 12, and 11. Animal 10TL was tested for a full hour and exhibited no tendency to stop self-stimulating for the 30-second duration stimulus. It was also established that animals with electrodes which elicited stimulus-bound behavior would self-stimulate for the long stimulation trains. In spite of these results we do not feel completely confident that there may not be some aversive component to an otherwise rewarding long train stimulus. Animals may be willing to experience some unpleasantness in order to receive the positive stimulation. In another context one of the authors has pointed out some of the difficulties involved in establishing criteria for aversiveness with long duration rewarding stimulation (Valenstein & Valenstein, 1964).

4. Argument of Simultaneous Activation of Discrete Systems

The fact that we have been successful in changing the specific behavior pattern elicited by hypothalamic stimulation raises a number of questions about our own results and interpretations of previous results. It might be argued that all the animals used in the present experiment were special cases in which stimulation simultaneously activated neural circuits mediating two motivational systems. Furthermore, because of the particular distribution of neurons activated, one system might be dominant, and only the behavior relevant to that system would be displayed. We do not feel that this hypothesis can readily account for our results. First, animals were not selected, and all that exhibited any stimulus-bound behavior were studied. The majority of the animals did not exhibit more than one behavior pattern prior to our effort to modify their responses.[4] Second, we might have expected that removal of the preferred goal object would result in the immediate display of a second behavior if our stimulation was simultaneously activating distinct neural systems. We have already commented that this is not the case. Also, we would not have anticipated that animals displaying the most vigorous and consistent stimulus-bound behavior would require the least amount of training for the second pattern to emerge. It should be recalled that even in these cases the new behavior did not appear immediately. Similarly, if this hypothesis were correct, we would expect that replacement of the initially preferred goal object would reinstate the dominance of the initial behavior. However, as noted, the new behavior is displayed during subsequent competition tests at least as frequently (if not more so) than the first behavior.

Another related criticism concerns the size of our electrodes. Our bipolar electrodes are relatively large when contrasted with the area of the rat's hypothalamus even though they are bare of enamel only at the cross section of the tip. If functionally distinct neural systems existed within this area of the hypothalamus, then these large electrodes might activate more than one of these systems. This is undeniably a relevant point; however, we would like to make several comments in this connection. Our electrodes, as large as they may be, are the type and size most commonly used for these studies. The plasticity we have observed, therefore, should apply as well to the experimental animals of others if similar opportunity to display alternate behavior were provided. It is difficult to make comparisons between different stimulation techniques. Some investigators employ monopolar stimulation, where one can only make an educated guess about the effective current spread. In many instances where smaller diameter electrodes have been used to obtain stimulus-bound behavior, the insulating enamel has been scraped back from the tip, often creating a stimulating surface larger than that of a wire of greater diameter with only the tip bare.

As a partial answer to the problem of the relevance of the size of the

---

[4]More recently, we have administered long series of competition tests with all goal objects available and have noted several instances of animals adopting a second and third stimulus-bound behavior pattern. It is possible that the procedure of removing the initially preferred goal object may only facilitate this process. The fact that these additional stimulus-bound behavior patterns continue to compete effectively with the first behavior is viewed as an argument for the plasticity of the system.

electrode and activated neural field, we have undertaken some similar studies with smaller diameter electrodes. For this purpose we have used comparable bipolar electrodes except that the diameter (.125 mm) was one-half of that used previously. Consequently the exposed area of the electrode was approximately one-fourth the area of our original electrodes. The percentage of the cases displaying stimulus-bound behavior was appreciably reduced, but we have established that an animal displaying only stimulus-bound drinking in response to stimulation through these smaller electrodes could be switched to displaying equally vigorous stimulus-bound eating. The possibility of simultaneous activation of functionally distinct systems cannot be ruled out by this approach, as the minimal size electrode capable of eliciting behavior is almost certain to activate a number of neurons. But we have offered a partial answer to those criticisms of our initial work that were based on electrode size.

Another approach to the problem of the simultaneous activation of functionally distinct systems has been explored. In preliminary experiments, we determined the threshold for eliciting stimulus-bound eating and drinking in animals displaying both of these behaviors. Employing the biphasic, rectangular-pulse stimulus parameters (cf. Section II, A), we reduced the current in 2 μA steps until the behavior disappeared. Usually this occurred at intensities between 30 and 35 μ-A. With this technique we observed threshold differences between eating and drinking in the range of 2–10 μA.

While the results of the threshold tests suggested that it might be possible to independently activate these systems, additional experimentation cautioned us against assuming that this refinement of our technique was revealing a fixed relationship between hypothalamic fields and specific behavior. In the first place, the differences obtained in separate tests for eating and drinking were not confirmed by the results of competition tests with both food and water available simultaneously. The thresholds obtained from competition tests were often very different from those obtained with separate food and water tests. Perhaps more critical to the issue are the results obtained from animals provided with additional restricted experience at those lower intensities where only one behavior was elicited. This experience consisted of placing animals on our night schedule, at the lower intensities, with only the goal object previously ignored at these intensities available. In subsequent threshold tests we have found that the results became quite variable, and in several instances the relative thresholds of the two behaviors were reversed. It appears, therefore, that the behavior elicited at near threshold intensities is also subject to change. At this junction, in spite of the logical appeal of the argument of simultaneous activation of independent motivational systems, much of the available evidence argues against this hypothesis. Perhaps the most critical evidence is derived from the data on the length of time required before the second behavior appears after the removal of the first goal object and the lack of dominance of the first behavior in subsequent competition tests.

An alternative hypothesis to explain our basic findings has recently been advanced by Wise (1968), who reported that all of the electrodes used in his study were capable of eliciting more than one behavior if a sufficient range of stimulus intensities were explored. Furthermore, since Wise found that the threshold for eliciting a particular behavior tended to decline over time, he has concluded that the second or third behavior which emerged in our studies with one stimulus intensity resulted from the gradual decline in threshold of the neural circuits responsible for the behavior. Wise maintains that there are separate "fixed neural circuits" functionally isolated from one another, and it is the threshold changes in these circuits that create the impression of plasticity. As this will be an appealing argument to those who find it more convenient to think of the hypothalamus as containing discrete neural circuits related to each motivational system, we feel it is particularly important that we indicate why we cannot accept this alternative hypothesis as an explanation of our results.

Wise has assumed that the first behavior we observed in response to stimulation was elicited at threshold current levels obtained by gradually raising the current. The implication is clear that if we used suprathreshold currents the second behavior would have been observed from the very beginning of the experiment. Our procedure did not involve threshold values in the initial experimental report, and we did not state that it did. Actually, in the course of the controversy stirred by our report, we have been accused of obtaining several behaviors from stimulation at the same site because our current levels have been too high. In the initial report our current levels were two to three and one-half times the threshold for eliciting the behavioral response. Only in subsequent studies have we used threshold values where we obtained similar results. Thus, our initial results have been criticized because we used currents too high and too low.

In a number of experiments that could not be included in our abbreviated report in *Science*, we have either raised the current level as high as possible without damage to the animal or have stimulated the animal over several weeks of testing at the initial current level. In the majority of these cases, as long as the first goal object to which the animal responded was still available, a second stimulus-bound behavior pattern was not displayed. In the case of those animals stimulated over a several-week period, the threshold changes reported by Wise should have occurred. It was only after we removed the first goal object that the second behavior *gradually* emerged. In the experiment reported by Wise, the first goal object was removed simultaneously with the exploration at higher current levels. Stimulation in the absence of the initially preferred goal object is the procedure we employed, minus the current manipulation, to obtain a second behavior. Wise's procedure confounds current manipulation with the effect of removing the initially preferred goal object. No quantitative or qualitative information is provided on the time course of emergence of this second behavior. In our experience the emergence of the second behavior may take several hours of intermittent stimulation or in a few instances a much longer period. Once this new behavior is associated with the stimulus, it is then possible to elicit it at lower current levels. *The relevant point is that it is not the stimulation which produced the lower threshold, but the acquisition of the behavior pattern.*

It is not a new observation that the threshold for eliciting behavior by electrical stimulation may decline over successive test sessions. There are probably multiple factors contributing to this decline; among these are variables related to an increased readiness to respond in a particular way and factors related to stimulus generalization gradients. We have noted this behavioral threshold decline in the context of self-stimulation experiments and have cautioned against assuming that the excitability of the neural elements directly activated by the electrical stimulus are responsible (Valenstein, 1964). Wise seems to imply that it is the repeated stimulation which lowers the threshold. Actually, a large body of data from the neurophysiological literature could be mustered in support of the position that repeated stimulation should raise, rather than lower, the threshold of the neural units directly activated by the electric current.

Although Wise has presented some data which will be useful to bear in mind in subsequent experimentation, we feel no need to revise our original conclusion that the relationship between the activation of neural circuits and stimulus-bound behavior is not fixed. Our conviction in this conclusion has been strengthened as a result of our experience and that of others with a greater variety of behavior patterns.

5. Anatomical Analysis[5]

The location of the electrode tips of the positive and negative electrode sites discussed in this chapter are presented in Fig. 1. We have made no attempt to distinguish between the positive sites on the basis of the behavior displayed because of the demonstrated plasticity in the elicited behavior and because no way of classifying the electrodes (for example, on the basis of first behavior displayed) resulted in any meaningful clustering of points. The positive sites are simply those that yielded any combination of the three elicited behaviors under study. The conclusion we have drawn from an examination of the figure is that the overlap between positive and negative sites in the lateral hypothalamus and zona incerta is sufficiently great to preclude predicting the presence or absence of elicited behavior from the anatomical location. It would be similarly impossible to have predicted the presence of either eating, drinking, or gnawing from among the positive sites. Subsequent work with many more animals and electrode sites has completely substantiated this conclusion. Figures 2 and 3 illustrate 50 positive and 72 negative sites obtained from 104 additional animals. The points charted on the figures are from animals in which both the behavioral and histological data were judged to be reliable in terms of specified criteria for acceptability. A greater number of additional points which were rejected because they did not meet these criteria appeared to be completely consistent with the results charted on Figs. 2 and 3. It should be noted that there was convincing evidence that stimulation at the negative sites was effective. In the first place, stimulation always produced signs of an active "searching" or "locomotor exploration" behavior. Also, we selected at random over 10 animals with negative electrodes and determined that stimulation with identical parameters supported self-stimulation in every case. It is possible that an analysis of a larger number of cases might reveal a slight tendency for a given behavior to be elicited more frequently from a general anatomical region, but from what we have observed to date this would offer at best only a small probability advantage in making predictions. In addition to our own work, a survey of the anatomical evidence from other laboratories reveals a great overlap in placements yielding either stimulus-bound eating, drinking, gnawing, or male copulatory behavior (Caggiula, in press; Coons,

[5]At the completion of the experiment animals were anesthetized, perfused with saline and formalin, and cresylechtviolett-stained; frozen brain sections were examined for localization of electrode tips. The authors are indebted to Barbara Case and Rosemarie Friz for their competent assistance in the histological work.

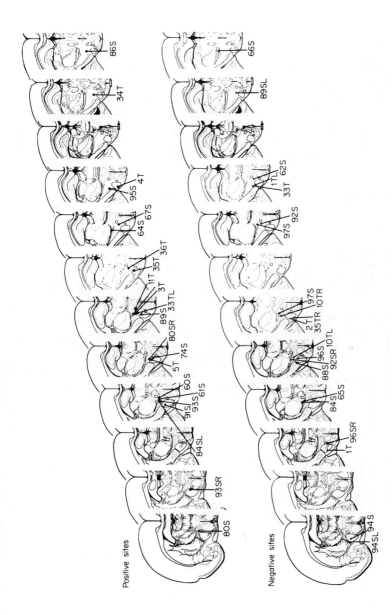

FIG. 1. Localization of positive sites (top) at which stimulation elicited at least two of the investigated behaviors (eating, drinking, and gnawing). Eating, drinking, or gnawing was not elicited by stimulation at negative sites (bottom). Negative transfer sites (▲) represent points from which the investigated behaviors could not be elicited, but the animal also had a positive electrode site (cf. text). After König and Klippel (1963).

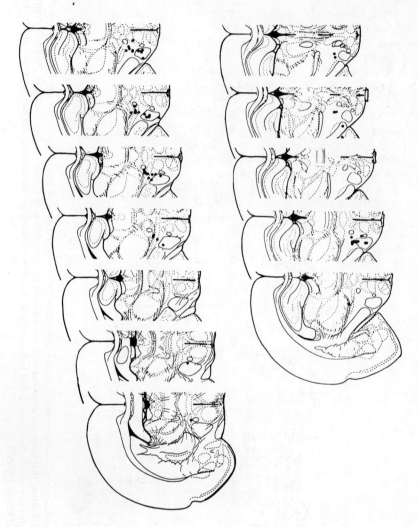

FIG. 2. Localization of additional positive sites at which stimulation elicited at least two of the investigated behaviors (eating, drinking, and gnawing).

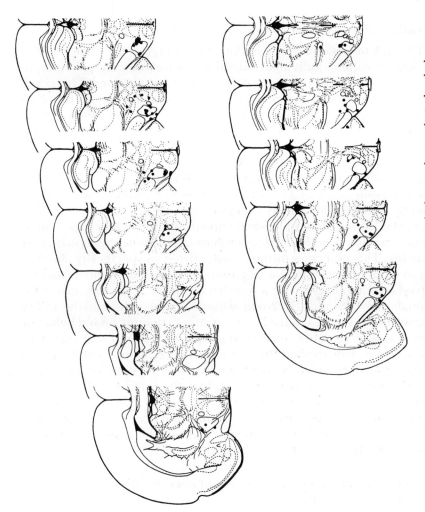

Fig. 3. Localization of additional negative sites at which stimulation elicited only locomotor exploration, but not stimulus-bound eating, drinking, or gnawing.

1963; Mogenson & Stevenson, 1967; Morgane, 1961; Roberts & Carey, 1965). It might also be mentioned in this context that there is no tendency of the points producing stimulus-bound eating or drinking to be concentrated in the far lateral region associated with aphagia and adipsia produced by experimental lesions.

6. Individual Animals and Stimulus-Bound Behavior

The lack of anatomical separation could suggest that some variable associated with an individual animal might be the principal determinant of whether positive or negative results were obtained. This possibility could be partially evaluated by examining those cases in which one electrode was positive and the other negative in a given animal. Animals 89S, 84S, 33T, and 35T met this criterion. In these cases, behavior could be elicited from one electrode but not the other, in spite of the fact that the negative electrodes were located at sites in which other animals displayed stimulus-bound behavior. This result has also been confirmed by a large number of animals tested subsequently. We have concluded, therefore, that it is unlikely that any factor in the history of an individual animal can be the sole explanation for the fact that stimulation does or does not elicit eating, drinking, or gnawing. This point was further substantiated by specifically attempting to elicit behavior from a negative electrode after animals had received a series of tests with a positive electrode. This was done with animals 89S, 84S, and 33T. None of these animals exhibited the ability to transfer the elicited behavior or any other stimulus-bound behavior from the positive to the negative site during a series of standard tests. It should be made explicit that these results do not rule out the possibility of transfer of behavior between two positive sites. We shall have occasion to refer to this possibility again in the context of other experimental evidence. The absence of an anatomical difference between positive and negative sites and any indication of an idiosyncratic factor related to the individual animal suggests the existence of some functional difference between electrodes.

7. A Functional Difference between Positive and Negative Electrodes (Poststimulus Effects)

The results of a recently completed study suggest the existence of a functional difference between positive and negative electrode sites that may provide a clue to the process underlying the elicitation of consummatory behavior by stimulation. During our standard tests we observed that animals rarely ate or drank during the one-minute periods between stimulations. Particularly striking were those animals which displayed stimulus-bound eating, often to the point of choking, but seldom drank during the interstimulus interval. We also noted that if animals displaying stimulus-bound behavior were deprived of food or water, they still did not eat or drink between the periods of stimulation. This phenomenon was investigated systematically in a study involving 22 animals. Interstimulus inhibition of eating or drinking was associated with a significantly larger number of positive animals than negative animals (Cox, Kakolewski, & Valenstein, in press). Rats with positive and negative electrodes were deprived of either food or water for 48 hours and observed during the standard tests. The rats with positive electrodes seldom ate or drank during the interstimulus periods, whereas rats with negative electrodes ate and drank freely during the entire test. The same results were obtained when the positive and negative animals were stimulated in the absence of food and water, which were moved into the chamber only during the interstimulus periods. Therefore, it is not the eating and drinking elicited by stimulation which inhibits further eating and drinking. Our preliminary findings with longer interstimulus intervals indicate that this poststimulus inhibition lasts approximately four minutes. It may be appropriate in this context to recall that in the report of stimulus-bound male sexual behavior (Caggiula & Hoebel, 1966) animals did not display copulatory activity during the three-minute interstimulus periods although the receptive female remained available. The sexual behavior appeared to cease abruptly with the offset of the stimulus, suggesting the presence of an inhibitory process. Indeed, in a later publication Caggiula (in press) has written: "Typically, when the stimulation period ended the males would reorient away from the females, even if in the process of mounting. Some males would lie down to one side of the chamber and remain relatively quiet, but this usually only happened later in the test when the S was approaching sexual exhaustion. More frequently stimulation offset was followed by some exploratory activity, much grooming, and occasional eating if food was available. Thus in many cases the male stopped copulating, but did not display evidence of a general inhibition of all behavior."

This functional difference between the positive and negative sites suggests that the neural events mediating the poststimulus inhibition may be an integral part of the neural process underlying stimulus-bound eating and drinking. It is possible only to speculate on the relevance these findings have to previous reports of eating or drinking in satiated animals following stimulation at various sites (Brügger, 1943; Delgado & Anand, 1953; Maire, 1956; Milgram, 1968; Miller,

1963; Robinson & Mishkin, 1968; O. A. Smith, 1956; O. A. Smith, McFarland, & Teitelbaum, 1961; Wirth, 1961). It may be that the persistence of some neural response after stimulation has been terminated is characteristic of all sites producing stimulus-bound behavior. However, its particular mode of expression, such as inhibition, initiation of behavior, or the continuation of behavior begun during the stimulation, may depend in part upon neural site and stimulus parameters.

8. *Further Experiments Involving Different Stimulus-Bound Behavior from the Same Animal*

In view of our demonstration of the plasticity of stimulus-bound behavior, we speculated about the possible reasons why previous investigators have emphasized the specificity of the relationship between the site stimulated and the particular behavior elicited. As far as we could determine most investigators, but not all, have focused on a specific behavior and have provided animals with special training and limited opportunity to display different patterns. The few instances in which animals were given brief tests with a second goal object present usually followed an extensive opportunity to display the initial behavior pattern and relatively limited experience with stimulation in the absence of the initial goal object.

We performed two experiments which bear on the question of the relevance of restricted experience for the subsequent display of stimulus-bound behavior. The first experiment utilized three animals that exhibited stimulus-bound eating and drinking from the same electrode with the identical stimulus parameters. Each animal received four daily training tests under conditions which provided an opportunity for the animal to associate a goal object with a distinctive test chamber, room, and time of day. Two tests were administered in the morning in a white chamber with only water available, and two tests were administered in the afternoon in another room in a black chamber with only food available. The animals received from 36 to 48 training tests, each consisting of 20 stimulus presentations. Following this training, the animals were given from 8 to 12 competition tests under the same conditions except that food and water were both available in each chamber, and only five stimulations were administered. It can be seen from Table II that the behavior in the competition tests only briefly reflected the restricted experience of the animals during the training tests. After the first few competition tests, one of the behaviors tended to dominate regardless of which chamber was used for that test. Apparently, when two behaviors are elicited by stimulation via a single electrode, previous experience of the type we employed has only a mild, transient influence. It appears that establishing an expectancy or anticipation of the availability of a particular reward in a given environment may not be a major factor in determining which of the two behaviors elicited by a particular electrode will be displayed.

The second test of the influence of previous experience utilized animals in which stimulation via different hypothalamic electrodes elicited different behaviors. The results from rat 24W are an example of this procedure. This animal displayed stimulus-bound drinking with the right electrode and stimulus-bound eating with the left electrode. Each of the behaviors was exhibited almost immediately during the first stimulus presentations on each of the respective electrodes. Thus, 24W seemingly provided a striking example of the correlation of neural site with a specific behavior. The animal was given three standard tests with both electrodes with food and water available and displayed only drinking with the right electrode and eating with the left electrode. At this point we provided the animal with restricted experience with each electrode to maximize the possibility of maintaining the difference in the behavior elicited by the two electrodes. For this purpose, 20 training tests were administered with each of the electrodes with only the appropriate goal object available. Thus, only water was available when the right electrode was used and only food was available with the left electrode. *Each test consisted of 20 stimulations, and in every instance (400 stimulations with each electrode) stimulus-bound drinking was displayed with the right and stimulus-bound eating with the left electrode.* Following these training tests, 10 competition tests with food and water simultaneously available were administered with each of the two electrodes. It is clear from inspection of Table III that the animal is able to maintain a considerable degree of independence in the behavior elicited by stimulation at the two electrode sites. With the exception of a few instances, the animal displayed only the behavior associated with the respective electrodes in the competition tests. Apparently, the animal is able to distinguish between stimulation at different positive sites, a result not completely surprising, since it had been previously suggested (Valenstein, 1964) that electrical stimulation of any brain site may provide a distinctive cue. Following the competition tests, the animal was given a series of *restricted tests* with the right and left electrodes with only the opposite goal object available. The behavior of the animal was most interesting and consistent. During the first two stimulations on each side, the animal spent all of its time appearing to be

TABLE II
Drinking (D) and Eating (E) during Training and
Competitive Tests in the White (W) and Black (B) Chamber[a]

Test	Chamber	23U		24U		30U	
		E	D	E	D	E	D
Training	W	–	20	–	19		
	W	–	20	–	20		
	B	20	–	17	–		
	B	20	–	18	–		
	W	–	20	–	20		
	W	–	20	–	20		
	B	20	–	20	–		
	B	20	–	19	–		
	W	–	20	–	17		
	W	–	20	–	19		
	B	6	–	17	–		
	B	17	–	20	–		
	W	–	20	–	20	–	18
	W	–	20	–	18	–	20
	B	18	–	20	–	20	–
	B	13	–	20	–	20	–
	W	–	20	–	15	–	20
	W	–	20	–	17	–	20
	B	4	–	20	–	20	–
	B	13	–	20	–	19	–
	W	–	20	–	20	–	16
	W	–	20	–	20	–	15
	B	20	–	20	–	14	–
	B	18	–	20	–	17	–
	W	–	20	–	20	–	16
	W	–	20	–	20	–	17
	B	20	–	20	–	4	–
	B	20	–	20	–	1	–
	W	–	20	–	20	–	16
	W	–	20	–	20	–	15
	B	18	–	20	–	6	–
	B	20	–	20	–	7	–
	W	–	20	–	20	–	18
	W	–	20	–	20	–	17

TABLE II —*Continued*

Test	Chamber	Animal 23U E	23U D	24U E	24U D	30U E	30U D
Training	B	20	—	20	—	15	—
	B	20	—	20	—	17	—
	W	—	20	—	20	—	20
	W	—	20	—	20	—	20
	B	20	—	20	—	13	—
	B	16	—	20	—	10	—
	W	—	20	—	20	—	16
	W	—	20	—	20	—	18
	B	20	—	20	—	11	—
	B	20	—	20	—	11	—
	W	—	20	—	20	—	20
	W	—	20	—	20	—	20
	B	5	—	18	—	14	—
	B	4	—	20	—	16	—
Competition	W	2	5	4	5	0	5
	W	3	5	2	5	0	5
	B	4	3	3	5	3	1
	B	2	5	3	5	1	5
	W	2	5	0	5	1	4
	W	3	4	0	5	0	5
	B	2	5	4	4	1	5
	B	2	5	4	2	0	5
	W	3	5	0	3		
	W	3	5	2	5		
	B	2	5	2	5		
	B	1	5	3	5		

[a]The dash (−) indicates whether the food or water had been removed during the test. The maximum score during the training tests was 20. During the competitive tests the maximum score for any one of the behaviors was 5, but both behaviors could be displayed during a single stimulus presentation. Four tests were administered each day. See text for additional experimental details.

"searching" for the customary goal object. Thus, when tested with the right electrode the animal concentrated its activity at the normal position of the water bottle, and when tested with the left electrode the animal displayed almost peckinglike movements at the floor of the test chamber where the food pellets were normally distributed. From the third stimulation on, the animal displayed vigorous stimulus-bound eating when tested with the right electrode and vigorous drinking when tested with the left electrode. The results of five restricted tests with each electrode are summarized in Table III. Finally, the animal was given a series of seven competition tests with both food and water available with the left electrode. It can be seen (Table III) that stimulus-bound eating was no longer the dominant response. Figure 4 illustrates the site of the left and right electrodes.

The results of tests with 24W have been described in detail because animals displaying different stimulus-bound behavior at different sites form the basis for one of the strongest arguments for specificity. Anyone who has observed an animal eat when stimulated at one site and drink when stimulated at another is likely to regard this as very compelling evidence. We have demonstrated, however, that it is possible for a second behavior to become associated with stimulation at each site, and with selective experience the second behavior may compete quite effectively with the first. Experience with animals such as 24W has suggested to us that although a considerable amount of behavioral independence may be observed under certain testing conditions, the ability to transfer the behavior associated with each site is enhanced. Normally, it takes at least several hours of stimulation for a second behavior to become associated with the stimulation. However, if the animal already has the second behavior associated with the stimulation at another site, this second behavior is adopted

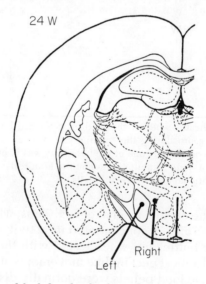

FIG. 4.   The location of the left and right electrodes in the hypothalamus of rat 24W.

TABLE III

Eating (E) and Drinking (D) by Rat 24W in
Competition and Restricted Tests[a]

Test	Left electrode		Right electrode	
	E	D	E	D
Competition tests				
1	20	0	0	20
2	20	0	1	18
3	20	0	1	20
4	20	0	0	20
5	20	0	0	20
6	17	3	2	18
7	20	0	0	20
8	20	0	1	20
9	20	0	1	20
10	20	0	0	20
Restricted tests				
11	—	18	18	—
12	—	20	17	—
13	—	20	19	—
14	—	20	20	—
15	—	20	20	—
Competition tests				
16	10	10		
17	7	12		
18	12	9		
19	15	5		
20	12	8		
21	14	6		
22	3	17		

[a]Each test consisted of 20 stimulations. Maximum score for any one behavior was 20, but during competition tests animal could exhibit both eating and drinking during a single stimulation. The goal object (food or water) which was removed during the restricted tests is indicated by a dash (−). See text for previous history of animal.

within one or two stimulus presentations. It appears as though stimulation at different sites that produce stimulus-bound behavior has some property in common which facilitates the transfer of behavior. In contrast, our experience suggests that when animals displaying only one behavior are given a long series of restricted tests with only the one goal object available, it is considerably more difficult to establish a second stimulus-bound behavior.

9. Natural Motivational States and Stimulus-Bound Behavior

The initial experiments described have shown that the behavior first elicited by lateral hypothalamic stimulation does not possess any immutable relationship to that stimulation, and indeed with selective training a very different behavior pattern emerges which may have equal or even a higher frequency of occurrence. Nevertheless, questions concerning the factors determining which behavior is elicited initially are of interest. It is conceivable that the behavior first seen with stimulation had a high probability of being expressed at that time even if no stimulation was provided. The combination of hypothalamic stimulation with a prepotent response may create, or at least contribute to, the conditions for establishing a relationship between hypothalamic stimulation and a particular behavior pattern. Similarly, it is conceivable that a negative site might become capable of eliciting a specific behavior if stimulation was provided in association with the execution of a consummatory response. Among the many reasons why a particular response might have a higher probability at a given moment, perhaps the most likely hypothesis is that a motivational or drive state imposes a specific response hierarchy which favors the occurrence of the response in question. Even though the animals tested were satiated, it is possible that positive results were dependent upon those fluctuations in drive states which presumably motivate the animal to periodically eat and drink. The coincidence of an elevated drive state and hypothalamic stimulation might create the conditions necessary for the regular elicitation of a particular behavior pattern by that stimulation. In order to test this hypothesis we deprived animals under several conditions.

In the first condition we used animals that had not exhibited any elicited behavior, but had shown the type of activity and searching pattern in response to stimulation that is observed prior to the emergence of a specific pattern. These animals had all received at least two nights of stimulation and had been classified as negative. Six animals were deprived of food or water for 48 or 72 hours and then three standard tests with both food and water present were administered. The first test was given simultaneously with the replacement of either the food or water. After the first test, food and water were removed for 30 minutes and then replaced during the second test. Finally, after the second test, food and water were left in the cage for four hours before the third test was administered.

The results of this experiment were unambiguous. None of the animals exhibited any stimulus-bound eating or drinking or any other specific pattern. Following the deprivation period, the animals satisfied their need state by eating or drinking, and this behavior was exhibited both during stimulation and during the interstimulus periods. After the animals had satiated themselves there was no tendency for any specific behavior to be elicited by hypothalamic stimulation. These results were obtained in spite of the fact that the deprived animals were stimulated when they were in a high drive state and while they were engaged in the consummatory behavior necessary to reduce the drive level.

The second test of the relevance of deprivation and natural drive states used three animals that had exhibited more than one behavior pattern in response to hypothalamic stimulation. The animals' (89S, 61S, and 74S) elicited behavior record is listed in Table I. We attempted to make the behavior pattern that was exhibited least frequently in the competition test the dominant pattern. For example, if in the competition test more eating than drinking was exhibited, the animal was deprived of water for the following 24 hours and then given a series of additional competition tests. The first of these tests was administered simultaneously with the replacement of the water (or food). Therefore, during this first test the animals received lateral hypothalamic stimulation while in a high thirst or hunger drive state. In spite of this, none of the animals exhibited any *permanent* shift in the relative frequency of the two behaviors elicited by the stimulation during competition tests. During the standard tests administered when the animal was in a high drive state, there were changes in the relative frequency of the two behaviors exhibited during stimulation. Animal 89S is a good example of the temporary, but not permanent, change observed during a test when the animal had been deprived of water for 24 hours. The first competition test was the routine test given to all animals in Experiment 1. The animal ate 16 times and drank on four stimulus presentations (Table I). The second competition test was given after 24 hours of water deprivation, and the animal ate nine times and drank 12 times. Following this test, water was made available to the animal ad libitum. The next standard test was administered two hours later, and the last test was given after a further lapse of 18 hours. During the last test the animal ate 20 times and drank only once in response to hypothalamic stimulation, clearly indicating that stimulus-bound drinking had not become the dominant behavior as a result of the manipulation of drive state by deprivation.

The last test of the relevance of natural motivational state to the elicitation of stimulus-bound behavior involved associating a particular environment with the satisfaction of a need state. Six rats were deprived of water for 23 hours in their home cages and then transported to the test cage and premitted to drink for one hour. Each animal had two hypothalamic electrodes, but had never received any stimulation. The animals were maintained on this schedule from 22 to 31 days. Three animals were then tested with hypothalamic stimulation when deprived of water, while three animals were tested when satiated. After determining an appropriate stimulus intensity, the animals were given a standard test and then left on the night schedule for two consecutive nights with each of their electrodes. A standard test was administered after each night. In no case (12 electrode sites) did any stimulus-bound drinking emerge. *Clearly, combining lateral hypothalamic stimulation with a natural drive state and the execution of the consummatory behavior necessary to satisfy the drive, even in an environment associated with the repeated satisfaction of that drive, did not produce conditions necessary for the emergence of stimulus-bound behavior.*

10. The Nature of the Motivation Underlying Stimulus-Bound Behavior

The fact that the manipulation of natural drive states had little influence on stimulus-bound behavior added to the doubts that were beginning to accumulate in our minds concerning the nature of the motivational state underlying stimulus-bound behavior. The observation that animals that were stimulus-bound drinkers appeared just as motivated to obtain food after a second stimulus-bound behavior (eating) was established raised the issue of whether thirst and hunger were involved at all. In some cases we observed that the location of the goal objects might determine which behavior was displayed during stimulation. When, for example, the food was piled up in a particular corner of the test cage, the animal displayed stimulus-bound eating; when the water bottle was placed in this same corner and the food placed elsewhere, stimulus-bound drinking was displayed. It is difficult to conceive of the stimulus eliciting hunger or thirst in such instances unless one postulates that stimulation elicits hunger or thirst only in the presence of a particular environmental configuration. A complementary observation has been reported by Hutchinson and Renfrew (1966) who noted that whether stimulated cats "displayed stalking attack toward a rat or stalked and consumed food depended entirely upon which object was contacted first."

A number of earlier experiments had demonstrated that animals exhibiting stimulus-bound eating, drinking, or gnawing have much in common with animals under the influence of natural drives such as those induced by deprivation. Animals will work to obtain appropriate goal objects (Coons *et al.*, 1965) and appear willing to tolerate aversive stimulation, such as shock (Morgane, 1961) or quinine additives (Tenen & Miller, 1964), in order to obtain the desired objects. There also exists another type of evidence to suggest that these different behaviors were controlled by independent motivational states. For example, Roberts and Carey (1965) have shown that if animals from which stimulus-bound gnawing could be elicited were made hungry, they would leave the food they were eating when stimulated to gnaw on a piece of wood. Similarly, Coons (1963) had observed that if animals exhibiting stimulus-bound eating were made thirsty, they would leave the water they were drinking to eat food when stimulated.

We have confirmed these observations in our own laboratory, but from the vantage point of our present knowledge, we would attach a different significance to these results. We believe these results indicate the strength of the bond, once established, between the state induced by the stimulation and the act of eating, drinking, or gnawing. There is little doubt that the animal is highly motivated to perform the particular act which has become associated with the stimulation. However, one should not conclude from any of this evidence that there is either an immutable relationship between the hypothalamic area stimulated and the particular stimulus-bound behavior observed or that the motivational state underlying the behavior is similar to such natural states as hunger or thirst. The thirsty animal that leaves water to display stimulus-bound eating is very likely (almost a certainty, judging from our experience) to display stimulus-bound drinking if given a series of stimulations with water present and food absent.

We undertook an investigation of the nature of the motivation underlying stimulus-bound behavior and have concluded that the eating and drinking elicited by electrical stimulation and that motivated by deprivation-induced hunger and thirst differ significantly. In the first study (Valenstein, Cox, & Kakolewski, 1968b) we selected five animals that displayed a predominance of stimulus-bound eating of a canned cat–dog food. These animals were given a series of three standard tests with Purina Lab Chow pellets, water, and the cat–dog food available. At the completion of these tests the cat–dog food was removed, and the animals were placed on the night schedule with only the water and the Purina Chow present to determine which goal object would be utilized when a new stimulus-bound behavior pattern was displayed. The results, which are summarized in Table IV, indicate that on the initial standard tests three of the animals displayed stimulus-bound eating of the cat-dog food exclusively, while the other two animals exhibited a clear dominance of this behavior. When the cat-dog food was removed, all of the animals switched to a predominance of stimulus-bound drinking. In spite of the fact that the Purina Lab Chow was very familiar to these animals, they did not readily switch to it when deprived of the food they had been eating during stimulation.

Another experiment illustrates a related point. An animal that was displaying stimulus-bound eating of the Purina Lab Chow pellets was tested with both a dish of the pellets, now ground to a powder, and water available. The animal walked over the food dish, sniffed at the food, and shook it off its paws while exhibiting the characteristic "searching" pattern elicited by stimulation; but the powdered food

TABLE IV

*Eating of a Cat-Dog Food (c/d), Food Pellets (FP), and
Drinking of Water (W) during Standard and Switch Tests[a]*

Animal	Behavior	Tests					
		Standard			Switch		
		1	2	3	1	2	3
94U	c/d	20	19	20	–	–	–
	FP	0	0	0	2	7	4
	W	0	0	0	16	14	16
95U	c/d	18	18	19	–	–	–
	FP	0	0	0	1	1	2
	W	0	0	0	15	19	18
97U	c/d	18	16	17	–	–	–
	FP	0	0	0	0	0	0
	W	0	0	0	15	12	11
39T	c/d	20	18	19	–	–	–
	FP	0	0	0	0	0	0
	W	0	0	4	19	20	19
7V	c/d	12	10	12	–	–	–
	FP	0	2	0	0	1	1
	W	0	0	0	13	12	18

[a]Each test had 20 stimulation periods. Maximum score for any one behavior is 20. The dash (−) in the switch tests indicates that the cat-dog food was omitted.

was not eaten during stimulation, and eventually the animal began to display consistent stimulus-bound drinking. Control tests indicated that this animal, as well as others, readily ate the powdered food when made hungry by food deprivation. It would appear that *animals displaying stimulus-bound eating do not generalize along a dimension appropriate to satisfying a hunger need.*

A similar experiment has been performed in our laboratory with animals displaying stimulus-bound drinking (Valenstein, Kakolewski & Cox, 1968c). The stimulus-bound drinking consisted of lapping the drinking tube connected to the water bottle. The animals ($N = 5$) were then familiarized with a dish of water from which they rapidly drank when thirsty. However, when stimulated with only the dish of water and food pellets present, animals switched first to stimulus-bound eating, a behavior not previously observed in the majority of the cases (Table V). One animal (45W) that displayed vigorous stimulus-bound drinking from the water bottle exhibited no stimulus-bound drinking from the dish. Most animals displayed stimulus-bound drinking from the dish only after eating was first established and after an extensive number of stimulations. Their behavior was characteristic of animals acquiring a new stimulus-bound behavior pattern.

The results of an additional study point to still another difference between the drinking of animals elicited by stimulation and that motivated by thirst induced by deprivation (Valenstein *et al.*, 1968c). Water-deprived, thirsty animals do not prefer a 30% glucose solution to water, although the same animals prefer the glucose solution when satiated. Animals displaying stimulus-bound drinking of water, exclusively or predominately, were tested with both water and the glucose solution available. During stimulation, the animals clearly preferred the glucose solution, and in this respect their preference was very different from that of thirsty animals (Table VI). Dr. Jay Trowill[6] has obtained similar results with drinking induced by the administration of cholinergic substances into the brain, suggesting that the behavior evoked by chemical stimulation may be subjected to a similar analysis.

In a further study of stimulus-bound drinking, we stimulated the animals in the presence of a drinking bottle filled with water and the 30% glucose solution in a dish. The animals had been used in the two previously described studies; they were familiar, therefore, with the dish and also had demonstrated their preference for the glucose solution. In this way we were able to contrast the effectiveness of the pre-

---

[6] Personal communication, 1968.

TABLE V

Stimulus-Bound Drinking from a Water Bottle (WB) and
Water Dish (WD), and Eating (E) during Standard,
Pseudo, and Switch Tests[a]

| Animal | Behavior | Stimulus-bound behavior | | | | | | | Current (μA) |
| | | Standard | | | Pseudo | Switch | | | |
		1	2	3		1	2	3	
31X	WB	15	18	17	–	–	–	–	60,R
	E	0	0	0	0	1	19	6	
	WD	–	–	–	9	0	2	12	
48X	WB	20	20	20	–	–	–	–	20,S
	E	0	0	0	2	15	14	6	
	WD	–	–	–	8	2	6	14	
24X	WB	18	20	19	–	–	–	–	9,S
	E	2	1	2	0	14	18	19	
	WD	–	–	–	11	5	0	0	
26X	WB	16	13	16	–	–	–	–	16,S
	E	3	2	0	6	11	15	6	
	WD	–	–	–	7	1	0	5	
45W	WB	20	18	19	–	–	–	–	150,R
	E	0	0	0	0	0	0	0	
	WD	–	–	–	8	0	0	0	

[a]The Standard and Switch Tests consisted of 20 stimulations. The maximum score for any one behavior on a single test was 20, but animals could exhibit more than one behavior during a single stimulation. The dash (–) indicates which goal object was removed. No stimulation was presented during the Pseudo Test, but animals, water-deprived for 24 hours, were scored for drinking during comparable periods. The Pseudo Test demonstrated the animals' familiarity with the water dish. The stimulating current was either a 60 cycle sine wave (S) or a biphasic, rectangular pulse (R) as produced by the Grass S6 Stimulator.

ferred glucose solution and the dominant response of licking the tube attached to the drinking bottle. The results were striking; the animals displayed very little stimulus-bound drinking of the preferred glucose solution. Clearly, the motor aspects of the stimulus-bound behavior were dominant over the sensory input. The importance of the performance of the motor component of stimulus-bound behavior was demonstrated in another way. Animals that displayed stimulus-bound drinking from a water tube were tested after water was removed from the bottle. The behavior of some of the animals demonstrated a remarkable resistance to extinction of the response pattern.

TABLE VI. *Preference for Water(W) and a Glucose Solution(G) during Drinking Induced by Hypothalamic Stimulation and by Water Deprivation.ᵃ Eating(E) and Drinking(D) during a Standard Stimulation Test Are Indicated*

Animal	Standard E	Standard D	Preference	Hypothalamic stimulation [no. drinks/consumption (ml)] 1	2	3	Water deprivation [30-minute consumption (ml)]
45W	0	19	W	15/3.0	14/3.0	10/4.0	29
			G	19/16.2	20/19.2	19/18.4	29
24X	11	20	W	13/4.0	9/2.0	8/5.0	20
			G	18/13.0	19/16.0	20/17.0	14
26X	2	17	W	9/6.0	7/4.0	2/3.0	19
			G	14/20.0	14/14.0	12/12.8	11
31X	14	6	W	8/1.8	4/3.0	3/2.0	38
			G	17/11.7	19/17.5	20/16.2	21
48X	2	18	W	9/3.6	2/3.0	b	15
			G	15/8.1	13/7.5	b	15
56X	15	10	W	7/6.0	12/4.0	4/4.0	14
			G	16/12.0	20/19.0	20/25.4	11
70X	0	20	W	8/5.0	3/4.0	6/3.0	19
			G	20/9.4	20/10.0	20/19.0	8
82X	0	20	W	2/2.0	9/3.0	4/3.0	14
			G	9/9.0	19/10.0	18/11.5	7
Average			W	8.8/3.9	7.5/3.3	5.2/3.4	21
			G	16.0/12.4	18.0/14.2	18.4/17.2	14.5

ᵃIf an animal drank from a particular bottle any time during a 30-second stimulation period, it received a score of 1. Animals could drink from both the glucose and water bottles during a single stimulation. The preference for the glucose during hypothalamic stimulation was further indicated by 121 times animals switched from the water to the glucose compared to the 41 times they switched from the glucose to the water.

ᵇThird test could not be administered.

One rat lapped the tube on every one of the 175 stimulations presented, while another lapped the tube during 172 of the stimulation periods. The persistence of this response pattern certainly exceeds that
which would be expected from animals in which the behavior was
maintained solely by the opportunity to ingest water (Valenstein *et
al.*, 1968c). We will return to this topic in Section III, but for the
present we need only comment that this demonstrated response ste-
reotypy is characteristic of stimulus-bound drinking, but not drinking
induced by thirst.

It is true that the animals displaying stimulus-bound eating may
work as hard and overcome as much adversity as a hungry animal in
order to obtain food. These demonstrations indicate the strength of
the bond between the stimulation and the behavior, rather than provide evidence that natural motivational states are involved. Animals
trained to eat or drink as instrumental responses for avoiding shock
may also display vigorous eating when the appropriate warning stimulus is presented, but few would suggest that the stimulus evokes hunger or thirst. It seems to us that we can muster more evidence for the
conclusion that the stimulation does not elicit hunger and thirst. Of
course, hunger and thirst must ultimately be described with reference
to some operational definition, but our current view is that the dissim-
ilarities are more convincing than the similarities.

There are a great number of implications that follow from our conclusion that hypothalamic stimulation does not elicit hunger, thirst,
and other motivational states. Most generally stated, any interpretation of the influence of a variable that modifies stimulus-bound behavior in terms of the action of that variable on natural motivational states
must be viewed with caution. An example may be helpful. Mendelson
(1967) studied the behavior of animals displaying both self-stimulation and drinking in response to lateral hypothalamic stimulation.
Mogenson and Stevenson (1967) have reported similar studies. Mendelson selected animals that would display stimulus-bound drinking
at current levels below those which would support self-stimulation. At
these low intensities the animals would not press the lever if water
were not available, and when satiated they would not press the lever
to receive water without the hypothalamic stimulation. Mendelson
concluded: "Thus if the rat is given the thirst it will press for water; if
given the water it will press for the thirst." These results may be most
important, but with respect to interpretation, the implication that the
stimulation induced thirst does not seem justified. We would have to
predict that these animals could be switched to displaying stimulus-
bound eating, and the same phenomenon could then be demonstrated

with food. It is now known from the recent work of Coons and Cruce (1968) that animals displaying stimulus-bound eating will self-stimulate at below "reward thresholds" if food is available. Rather than evoking hunger and thirst, it would be much more parsimonious to postulate that the reinforcement produced by the execution of an elicited behavior summates with the reinforcement produced directly by that stimulation. It would follow that the summation of the reinforcement from executing the behavior and the subthreshold reinforcement from the brain stimulation may be sufficient to maintain the instrumental behavior. Indeed, Mendelson (1966) had demonstrated earlier that satiated animals which display stimulus-bound eating prefer the combination of food and brain stimulation to brain stimulation alone.

III. GENERAL DISCUSSION

Our conclusion that hypothalamic stimulation probably does not evoke natural motivational states when eliciting stimulus-bound behavior has forced us to search elsewhere to understand the significance of this phenomenon. At present we can offer only a few additional comments which reflect our present thinking and are likely to direct our research in the immediate future. This appears to be a period for searching for alternative explanations rather than one for definitive statements.

It seems to us that electrodes capable of eliciting stimulus-bound behavior are creating a condition which increases the incidence of occurrence of well-established motor responses. The execution of these behavior patterns in conjunction with the stimulation may become reinforcing for one of two reasons. There is more than a small amount of circularity in the above statement, but in spite of this, it does suggest a bias in terms of its emphasis. First, we have emphasized the motor aspects of the stimulus-bound behavior, but not in the sense that the stimulus directly elicits motor responses. Although we have seen a number of instances of hypothalamic stimulation eliciting "eating" or "drinking" motor reactions in the absence of food or water,[7] the majority of the animals do not display such "vacuum respon-

---

[7]During periods of hypothalamic stimulation, some animals have been observed to display lapping responses in the absence of water, and in the absence of food other animals have been observed holding up their paws in front of their mouths (as they do when holding a pellet) and making chewing movements directed at the space between the paws.

ses." Most animals exhibit only an active "searching" pattern in the absence of the goal objects. It seems quite clear that as a general rule the stimulus does not directly trigger the motor response and, indeed, it has often been pointed out that animals may learn a number of very different instrumental responses in order to acquire the appropriate goal object. Our point is that in spite of the differences in instrumental behavior the final consummatory behavior may be quite stereotyped. We have seen the importance of the stereotyped response in the experiment that pitted the preferred glucose solution in a dish against the less preferred water in the drinking bottle (cf. pp. 273-274). In this situation, the stimulus-bound water drinking was displayed. Apparently the execution of the response was more significant to the animal than the sensory feedback. Our best guess at this time is that the motivation is somehow tied to the execution of this stereotypical behavior rather than the biological consequences for the animal. We should emphasize that this interpretation does not conflict with the important role that the sensory input may play in eliciting stimulus-bound behavior and in determining the animals' orientation in a choice situation. Miller (1960) has reported observing a rat which displayed stimulus-bound drinking of a 4% solution of sucrose, but not an 0.8% solution of NaCl, while another animal drank the sucrose and saline solutions, but not water. We have made similar observations, but in most cases we have been able to obtain vigorous drinking of the ignored solution by presenting this solution alone for a period of time and thereby minimizing the "contrast effect."

Perhaps the strongest justifications for emphasizing the motor aspects of stimulus-bound behavior are derived from experiments demonstrating the difficulty of transferring the behavior to similar or modified goal objects requiring a different consummatory behavior. We have observed this difficulty when we placed the water in open dishes rather than in the customary drinking bottles and when food pellets were ground to a powder. While hungry and thirsty animals immediately started to consume the powdered food or the water in the open dish, animals exhibiting stimulus-bound eating or drinking did not readily make this transfer. The few animals that transferred the stimulus-bound behavior to the modified goal object required as much time and seemed to go through the same process as animals learning a completely new response. Furthermore, we have presented evidence that stimulus-bound drinking may persist if only the opportunity to execute the response is provided without water being present. The stimulated animals seem motivated to display a very specific consummatory pattern, and they do not readily respond to modified goal ob-

jects that require a different motor pattern. In spite of this motor specificity, the animal is capable of associating a completely new consummatory response with the stimulation. We have shown that the
new response does not seem to be related to the initial response by a
shared, underlying motivational state such as hunger or thirst. Furthermore, the new response may be very dissimilar from the initial
response in terms of the motor elements involved. For this reason we
do not believe that there is any direct connection between the hypothalamic stimulation and the neural substrate underlying the motoric
reaction. The stimulus-bound behavior appears to be a more indirect
reaction to the state induced by the stimulation. The fact that animals
exhibiting the most vigorous stimulus-bound behavior are the fastest
to adopt a completely new stimulus-bound behavior seems to support
the position that the behavior is an indirect reaction to the stimulation.

Although there is a great diversity of responses elicited by electrical
stimulation, they do not appear to be arbitrary, "voluntary" responses.
The stimulus-bound behaviors we and others have observed are well-
established responses such as those referred to in the literature
as "fixed action patterns" and "species specific" behavior. The responses include eating, drinking, gnawing, grooming, copulation,
maternal behavior (retrieving), and scent marking, among others.[8] The
evidence that the motor patterns for these responses may be organized
in a "preformed" state has been discussed by Glickman and Schiff
(1967).

In some way not understood at present, the execution of these well-
established responses either (or both) adds to the reinforcement or
reduces some aversive component produced by the stimulation. We
have already noted the existence of evidence demonstrating that the
combination of reinforcing stimulation and the opportunity to execute
the associated response is more reinforcing than the brain stimulation
alone. It is also possible that these well-established responses may in
some cases help the animal to "cope" with some aversive sensations
induced by the stimulation. In this sense, the stimulus-bound behavior would be similar to the psychiatric conception of "compulsive
behavior," and in both cases behavioral (symptom) substitution is
possible. We have observed instances of animals which display stimulus-bound drinking facing directly at the drinking tube during the in-

[8]At the Eastern Psychological Association Meeting in April, 1968, J. Mendelson
showed a film of rats displaying stimulus-bound retrieving of pups, and S. Glickman
showed a film of gerbils exhibiting a stimulus-bound rubbing of a ventral scent gland on
objects.

terstimulus period. While we are aware of alternative explanations, this pattern seems reminiscent of those animals performing at an avoidance task, which face directly at the manipulandum between trials. This hypothesis will be explored in two ways. Animals will be trained to "cope" with aversive stimulation by using some well-established pattern such as drinking or eating as an instrumental avoidance response. Later, we will determine whether this response readily transfers to hypothalamic stimulation as a result of the initial training. We also plan to study the relationship between the latency of stimulus-bound behavior after the onset of the stimulus and the stimulus duration selected by the animal in a self-stimulation test, which permits the animal to control the duration. It has already been established in our threshold tests that the stimulus-bound behavior latency decreases as a function of increasing intensity and in this respect seems to parallel the preferred stimulus duration selected by animals in self-stimulation tests.

The main drawback to the idea that there may be instances of stimulus-bound behavior which represent a "coping" with some aversive aspect of the stimulus is that there is very little evidence of an aversive component to the stimulus. In all cases we have tested, stimulation at the sites that produce stimulus-bound behavior supports self-stimulation behavior. The animals press a lever repeatedly and thereby turn on the stimulus even when the stimulus is as long in duration (30 seconds) as that used for the elicitation of stimulus-bound behavior. It is true that when animals are given control over the duration of the stimulus, they normally select shorter durations, but we have indicated elsewhere that it cannot be concluded from this fact that the stimulus is aversive (Valenstein & Valenstein, 1964). The fact that the stimulus is reinforcing as judged by its ability to support self-stimulation behavior cannot be the explanation for the initiation of the behavior, as stimulation at negative sites will also support self-stimulation. It is possible that the maintenance, if not the initiation, of stimulus-bound behavior is dependent on the reinforcing properties of the stimulus. The behavior is not of an instrumental nature in that it does not produce the stimulation and is therefore not seen prior to the onset of the stimulation. However, the evidence that the execution of the behavior elicited by the stimulation results in an enhancement of the reinforcement suggests that the association with "positive brain stimulation" may help to maintain the behavior.

While it may be more elegant to have a single theory that explains all stimulus-bound behavior, it is possible that there are several heterogeneous phenomena that have been assumed mistakenly to have the same underlying mechanism. In some cases the execution of stimulus-bound behavior may increase the reinforcing properties produced by stimulation, but in other cases the stimulus-bound behavior may be a means of "coping" with some aversive properties of the stimulus. Among other possibilities, one that strikes us as deserving further consideration is that nonspecific "activation" may produce a type of stimulus-bound behavior in environments which contain stimulus objects with the capacity to elicit a high frequency of a particular behavior pattern. In this context Barfield and Sachs (1968) have administered a mildly painful electric shock delivered to the skin of male rats (through common safety pins) at regular intervals. The shock was administered during tests with receptive females, and over repeated tests the sexual behavior displayed by the males became increasingly concentrated around the time of shock delivery. When males were resting during the sexual refractory period following an ejaculation, the delivery of a shock would arouse the males' sexual interest in the females. Earlier, K. Larsson (1963) had demonstrated the effectiveness of nonspecific stimulation on the sexual behavior of older male rats. Larsson reported that merely handling the older rats for a few seconds, twice a minute, resulted in an increase in copulatory behavior to the level of younger males. We feel that in some instances of stimulus-bound behavior the role of nonspecific stimulation in an environment that provides a great amount of direction to the behavior has not been adequately considered.

In considering the possibility that stimulus-bound behavior may be a multidetermined phenomenon, it should also be understood that hypothalamic sites which we have investigated are generally considered to be positive in the sense that they are capable of supporting at least some level of self-stimulation. "Attack" and "killing" behavior, which can be elicited from other hypothalamic sites, may be governed by a completely different set of mechanisms. Generally, such behavior has been elicited from hypothalamic sites more medial than those we have explored, and the motivational consequence of stimulation at these sites has been described as aversive or "ambivalent."

The major puzzle confronting us is why only some positively reinforcing stimulation becomes associated with consummatory responses. Our future work will include electrical recording studies aimed at determining whether the indications of poststimulus persistence of neural activity we have described provide a clue to the distinctiveness of our positive electrode sites. The neural state induced by the stimulation may trigger well-established response patterns. It seems to us that it is worth considering the possibility that the stimulation inhibits (disrupts) the physiological processes normally involved in the suppression of these well-established patterns and thereby results in their release. At some brain sites the behavior is released during the stimulation, and an inhibition follows the offset of the stimulus; at other sites a behavioral inhibition occurs during the stimulation, and a release follows the offset of the stimulus. Milgram (1968) has recently observed, for example, that hippocampal stimulation produced a brief period of immobility, and the cessation of the stimulus "was followed by a long period of hyperactivity during which there was frequent rearing, sniffing, grooming, and locomotion." These same animals exhibited a significant increase in eating during the period following stimulation. Earlier in this chapter we referred to the recent work by Caggiula (in press) which indicates an inhibition of sexual behavior following the offset of hypothalamic stimulation that elicits copulatory behavior. The inhibition or "rebound" behavior we have observed does not appear to be limited to the motor aspects of the behavior, but rather is suggestive of a motivational "rebound." During the interstimulus intervals we have noted instances of animals pushing the food away with their forepaws in a manner reflecting an opposite motivational state rather than a mirror image of a motor response.

It is clear from our data that the mere execution of a response in the presence of reinforcing brain stimulation even at a time of activation of an appropriate drive state does not produce stimulus-bound behavior. In another context (cf. p. 271), we have referred to the studies by Coons (1963) and Roberts and Carey (1965) which demonstrated that hungry and thirsty animals stimulated when either eating or drinking would switch to the stimulus-bound behavior typically displayed. Apparently, contiguity, that is, the coincidence of the response and stimulation, is not a very relevant factor. The problem we must face, then, is how the stimulus gains access to and facilitates particular motor elements, but any solution to this problem must contain sufficient freedom for other response patterns to be established.

Our work certainly does not imply that the hypothalamus is not involved in the expression of motivated behavior. However, the tendency during the last ten years has been to conceive of the hypothalamus as comprised of a number of centers located in discrete anatomical regions, each playing the major role in controlling a specific motivational state. This is a much too simplistic analysis based upon very limited experimental approaches. In this chapter we have attempted to show that the data obtained from a broader experimental base suggest that we need to revise our view of hypothalamic functioning. The accumulative evidence that the lateral hypothalamus is critically involved in motivation is not contested. We do believe that to a much greater extent than the recent literature has emphasized, this region may provide only the neurological matrix from which goal-directed behavior can emerge when activated in conjunction with other bodily cues which express specific organic conditions.

REFERENCES

Andersson, B., & McCann, S. M. Further study of polydipsia evoked by hypothalamic stimulation in the goat. *Acta Physiol. Scand.*, 1955, 33, 333-346.

Barfield, R. J., & Sachs, B. D. Sexual behavior: Stimulation by painful electrical shock to the skin in male rats. *Science*, 1968, 161, 392-393.

Broca, P. Localisations cérébrales: Recherches sur les centres olfactifs. *Rev. Anthropol.*, 1879, 2, 385.

Brügger, von M. Fresstrieb als hypothamisches Symptom. *Helv. Physiol. Pharmacol. Acta*, 1943, 1, 183-198.

Caggiula, A. R. Analysis of the copulation-reward properties of posterior hypothalamic stimulation in male rats. *J. comp. physiol. Psychol.* 1969, in press.

Caggiula, A. R., & Hoebel, B. G. "Copulation-reward site" in the posterior hypothalamus. *Science*, 1966, 153, 1284-1285.

Christopher, M., & Butter, C. M. Consummatory behavior and locomotion exploration evoked from self-stimulation sites in rats. *J. comp. physiol. Psychol.*, 1968, 66, 335-339.

Coons, E. E. Motivational correlates of eating elicited by electrical stimulation in the hypothalamic feeding area. Unpublished doctoral dissertation, Yale Univer., 1963.

Coons, E. E., & Cruce, J. A. F. Lateral hypothalamus: Food current intensity in maintaining self-stimulation of hunger. *Science*, 1968, 159, 1117-1119.

Coons, E. E., Levak, M., & Miller, N. E. Lateral hypothalamus: Learning of food-seeking response motivated by electrical stimulation. *Science*, 1965, 150, 1320-1321.

Cox, V. C., Kakolewski, J. W., & Valenstein, E. S. Inhibition of eating and drinking following hypothalamic stimulation. *J. comp. physiol. Psychol.* 1969, in press.

Delgado, J. M. R., & Anand, B. K. Increase of food intake induced by electrical stimulation. *Amer. J. Physiol.*, 1953, 172, 162-168.

Edinger, L., & Wallenberg, A. Untersuchungen über den Fornix und das Corpus mammillare. *Arch. Psychiat. Nervenkrankh.*, 1902, 35, 1-21.

Fantl, L., & Schuckman, H. Lateral hypothalamus and hunger: Responses to a secondary reinforcer with and without electrical stimulation. *Physiol. Behav.*, 1967, 2, 355-357.

Flynn, J. P. The neural basis of aggression in cats. In D. C. Glass (Ed.), *Neurophysiology and emotion.* New York: Rockefeller Univer. Press, 1967. Pp. 40-60.

Glickman, S. E., & Schiff, B. B. A biological theory of reinforcement. *Psychol. Rev.*, 1967, 74, 81-109.

Greer, M. A. Suggestive evidence of a primary "drinking center" in the hypothalamus of the rat. *Proc. Soc. exp. Biol. Med.*, 1955, 89, 59-62.

Gudden, B. V. Beitrag zur Kenntniss des Corpus mammillare und der sogenannten Schenkel der Fornix. *Arch Psychiat. Nervenkrankh.*, 1881, 11, 428-452.

Herberg, L. J., & Blundell, J. E. Lateral hypothalamus: Hoarding behavior elicited by electrical stimulation. *Science*, 1967, **155**, 349-350.

Herrick, C. J. Morphogenesis of the brain. *J. Morphol.*, 1933, **54**, 233-258.

Hess, W. R. *Diencephalon: Autonomic and extrapyramidal functions.* New York: Grune & Stratton, 1954. (Original publication in German: *Die funktionelle Organisation des vegetativen Nervensystems.* Basel: Benno Schwabe, 1948)

Hutchinson, R. R., & Renfrew, J. W. Stalking attack and eating behaviors elicited from the same sites in the hypothalamus. *J. comp. physiol. Psychol.*, 1966, **61**, 360-367.

Klüver, H., & Bucy, P. "Psychic blindness" and other symptoms following temporal lobectomy in the rhesus monkey. *Amer. J. Physiol.*, 1937, **119**, 352-353.

König, J. F. R., & Klippel, R. A. *The rat brain: A stereotaxic atlas of the forebrain and lower parts of the brain stem.* Baltimore: Williams & Wilkins, 1963.

Larsson, K. Nonspecific stimulation and sexual behavior in the male rat. *Behaviour*, 1963, **20**, 110-114.

Larsson, S. On the hypothalamic organization of the nervous mechanism regulating food intake. *Acta Physiol. Scand.*, 1954, **32**, Suppl. 115, 7-63.

Maire, F. W. Eating and drinking responses elicited by diencelpalic stimulation in unanaesthetized rats. *Fed. Proc.*, 1956, **15**, 124.

Mendelson, J. Role of hunger in T-maze learning for food by rats. *J. comp. physiol. Psychol.*, 1966, **62**, 341-349.

Mendelson, J. Lateral hypothalamic stimulation in satiated rats: The rewarding effects of self-induced drinking. *Science*, 1967, **157**, 1077-1079.

Milgram, N. W. Effect of hippocampal stimulation on feeding in the rat. Unpublished doctoral dissertation, McGill Univer., Montreal, 1968.

Miller, N. E. Motivational effects of brain stimulation and drugs. *Fed. Proc.*, 1960, **19**, 846-854.

Miller, N. E. Implications for theories of reinforcement. In D. E. Sheer (Ed.), *Electrical stimulation of the brain.* Austin: Univer. of Texas Press, 1963. Pp. 575-581.

Mogenson, G. J., & Stevenson, J. A. F. Drinking induced by electrical stimulation of the lateral hypothalamus. *Exptl. Neurol.*, 1967, **17**, 119-127.

Morgane, P. J. Distinct "feeding" and "hunger" motivating systems in the lateral hypothalamus of the rat. *Science*, 1961, **133**, 887-888.

Papez, J. W. A proposed mechanism of emotion. *A.M.A. Arch. Neurol. Psychiat.*, 1937, **38**, 725-734.

Ranson, S. W. Some functions of the hypothalamus. *Harvey Lectures*, 1936-37, Baltimore: Williams & Wilkins. Pp. 92-121.

Roberts W. W., & Carey, R. J. Rewarding effect of performance of gnawing aroused by hypothalamic stimulation in the rat. *J. comp. physiol. Psychol.*, 1965, **59**, 317-324.

Roberts, W. W., & Kiess, H. O. Motivational properties of hypothalamic aggression in cats. *J. comp. physiol. Psychol.*, 1964, **58**, 187-193.

Roberts, W. W., Steinberg, M. L., & Means, L. W. Hypothalamic mechanisms for sexual, aggressive and other motivational behaviors in the opossum (Didelphis virginiana). *J. comp. physiol. Psychol.*, 1967, **64**, 1-15.

Robinson, B. W., & Mishkin, M. Alimentary responses to forebrain stimulation in monkeys. *Exp. brain Res.*, 1968, **4**, 330-366.

Smith, E. G. The "fornix superior." *J. Anat. Physiol.*, 1896, **31**, 80-94.

Smith, O. A., Jr. Stimulation of lateral and medial hypothalamus and food intake in the rat. *Anat. Rec.*, 1956, **124**, 363-364.

Smith, O. A., Jr., McFarland, W. L., & Teitelbaum, H. Motivational concomitants of eating elicited by stimulation of the anterior thalamus. *J. comp. physiol. Psychol.*, 1961, **54**, 484-488.

Steinbaum, E., & Miller, N. E. Obesity from eating elicited by daily stimulation of hypothalamus. *Amer. J. Physiol.*, 1965, **208**, 1-5.

Tenen, S. S., & Miller, N. E. Strength of electrical stimulation of lateral hypothalamus, food deprivation, and tolerance for quinine in food. *J. comp. physiol. Psychol.*, 1964, **58**, 55-62.

Valenstein, E. S. Problems of measurement and interpretation with reinforcing brain stimulation. *Psychol. Rev.*, 1964, **71**, 415-437.

Valenstein, E. S., Cox, V. C., & Kakolewski, J. W. Modification of motivated behavior elicited by electrical stimulation of the hypothalamus. *Science*, 1968, **159**, 1119-1121. (a)

Valenstein, E. S., Cox, V. C., & Kakolewski, J. W. The motivation underlying eating elicited by lateral hypothalamic stimulation. *Physiol. Behav.*, 1968, 3969-3972. (b)

Valenstein, E. S., Hodos, W., & Stein, L. A simplified electrode-assembly for implanting chronic electrodes in the brains of small animals. *Amer. J. Psychol.*, 1961, **74**, 125-128.

Valenstein, E. S., Kakolewski, J. W., & Cox, V. C. A comparison of stimulus-bound drinking and drinking induced by water deprivation. *Commun. Behav. Biol.*, 1968, **2**, 227-233.

Valenstein, E. S., & Valenstein, T. Interaction of positive and negative neural systems. *Science*, 1964, **145**, 1456-1458.

Vaughan, E., & Fisher, A. E. Male sexual behavior induced by intracranial electrical stimulation. *Science*, 1962, **137**, 758-760.

Wirth, K. E. Nahrungsaufnahme der Ratte nach Ausschaltungen und elektrischer Reizung im Hypothalamus. *Arch. ges. Physiol.*, 1961, **272**, 602-611.

Wise, R. A. Hypothalamic motivational system: Fixed or plastic neural circuits? *Science*, 1968, **62**, 377-379.

CHAPTER 10

Brain-Acetylcholine and Inhibition[1]

PETER L. CARLTON

I have two purposes in writing this article. First, I hope to show that pharmacological manipulations can be used to make meaningful inferences about the events that control operant behavior. Second, I want to make a few public guesses about one small but important aspect of the physiological mechanisms that underlie the ways in which one kind of animal (the rat) interacts with the stimuli that make up its environment.

We can begin by elaborating the point of view advanced by Schneirla (1959) and group all of these stimuli into two categories. One of these contains stimuli that lead to approach, whereas the second contains those that lead to withdrawal. Stimuli in the first class are circularly defined as relatively weak stimuli, whereas those in the second are relatively strong.

At this point I want to introduce a new term: habituation. The definition of habituation is a simple one. If a relatively weak stimulus produces some initial behavioral effect, that initial effect can be lost as a consequence of simple exposure to the stimulus. A novel sound can produce characteristic "orienting" behavior in a dog, for example;

[1]The original research reported was supported by MH-08585.

repetition of the sound leads to a lack of the initial response pattern. Or, a rat placed in a novel environment may explore that environment, thus exposing itself to its multiple aspects. As a consequence of this exposure, exploratory activity declines. (This decline in exploratory activity is used as an index of habituation in several experiments to be discussed later.)

The class of weak stimuli contains those to which the animal habituates. But it is obvious that not all stimuli that control approach behavior habituate. Accordingly, we must define two classes of weak stimuli. Both of these classes lead to approach, but only one contains those stimuli that undergo habituation. The question then becomes one of developing a rule that will determine whether or not a particular weak stimulus will *fail* to habituate. The rule is a simple one: Those stimuli that fail to habituate are those that are themselves biologically significant or are contiguous with others having such significance.

The phrase "biologically significant stimuli" requires a definition. These stimuli are those that are demonstrably significant in determining either individual or species survival. It is obvious that there must have been natural selection, which accounts for a lack of habituation to such significant stimuli and those associated with them. For example, a species in which habituation to food and food-contiguous stimuli *did* take place could not survive to reproduce. Thus, the species would necessarily be driven to extinction. Such significant stimuli have another name; in discussions of those species that can learn, biologically significant stimuli are called rewards.

A direct demonstration of these relationships has been provided by Glickman and Feldman (1961). Direct stimulation of the brain produces EEG arousal and orienting; this reaction will wane, habituate, with repetition (Sharpless & Jasper, 1956). Glickman and Feldman found, however, that arousal produced by stimulation of certain sites did not habituate. These are those that were subsequently found to maintain self-stimulation behavior. Thus, "neutral" stimuli did habituate, but rewarding stimuli did not.

Thus far I have mentioned only the two classes of weak stimuli that lead to approach behavior. The third class (strong stimuli) do not, as a general rule, lead to approach nor do they habituate (see Maier & Schneirla, 1935). Rather, these stimuli control aversive behavior, withdrawal. These "dangerous" stimuli are biologically significant in that withdrawal from them can be rewarding.

At this point I want to introduce still another term: reinforcement. If a response by an animal leads to the presentation of a stimulus, that response will tend to be repeated if the stimulus is a significant one.

In this case we say that the animal is rewarded and that it may learn. But there are also response-produced stimuli (in the rat, a brief period of dim light, for example) that will produce levels of responding greater than those that would occur if the stimulus was not produced. But unlike the effects seen with rewards, these initially high levels of responding decline.

Many stimuli can inflate the tendency to respond. Some of these also *maintain* responding; i.e., they do not habituate. These we call rewards. Still other stimuli can increase responding, but only transiently because they do habituate. These we will call reinforcers. All rewards can increase responding; therefore, all rewards are reinforcers. However, there is a large class of stimulus events that can increase responding in a transient manner and thus can be called reinforcers, but not rewards. Thus, the distinction between a reward and a reinforcement is made on the basis of the presence or absence of habituation to the stimulus.

All this amounts to is the obvious fact that a rat will first explore its environment, "check it out," and may do so with substantial persistence. The animal is reinforced by the stimuli in what amounts to its phenomenological world. Although there can be initially high levels of responding, such responding eventually declines as habituation takes place. If, however, the stimuli turn out to be significant or correlated with others having significance, then responding is maintained, rewarded. Thus, biological significance, reward, effectively protects against that loss of stimulus effectiveness that we call habituation.

The remainder of my discussion will focus on the business of habituation, although, as is necessarily so, reward and reinforcement will be involved.

I. ANTICHOLINERGICS AND HABITUATION

The first question I want to raise about habituation is: What events in the brain may underlie it? There are two ways of answering such a question. The more traditional way is in terms of anatomy: a description of the brain areas involved. The second kind of answer is a chemical one: a description of the chemical events involved. It is this second kind of answer that I want to take up now. We will return to the first kind later.

How may we manipulate the chemistry of the brain so as to determine what is involved in habituation? One way is to administer drugs known to alter brain activity. Particularly pertinent to the question about habituation are the actions of one class of drugs, the anticholinergics (scopolamine and atropine), so called because they are known to attenuate the actions of acetylcholine (i.e., "cholinergic" activity) in both the peripheral and the central nervous system.

Just as one can destroy certain nervous tissue and hope to make guesses about what that tissue did on the basis of what happens when it is gone, one can also attenuate endogenous chemical activity with a drug and make guesses about what that chemical normally does on the basis of the drug's effect. Both approaches are patently gross, but the latter at least has the advantage of reversibility.

In 1963, I reviewed a number of experiments on the anticholinergics and, on the basis of these, suggested that a very wide range of results could be accounted for by making a rather simple assumption, based on the obvious fact that the characteristic behavior seen in a variety of operant situations develops because of the contingencies of both reward and nonreward. The data on the anticholinergics suggested, to me at least, that these drugs lead to an intrusion of unrewarded responses into the animals' repertoire. Under normal circumstances, these responses are inhibited. The anticholinergics appear to lead to a *disinhibition* of these responses so that normally inhibited behavior is emitted.

Anticholinergics evidently interfere with the inhibitory processes engendered by nonreward. However, nonreward is the condition that sets the occasion for habituation. What, then, might the effects of anticholinergics be on this process? Consider a rat in a T-maze: Turns to the right are rewarded; turns to the left are not. According to the rules about habituation, we would expect that during training, "left" stimuli would lose whatever initial control they exerted. Thus, part of learning to go right involves not going left. MacCorquodale and Meehl (1954) elaborated this view some time ago.

If anticholinergics interfere with habituation, they should interfere with maze performance. And indeed they do, as Macht (1923) and Miles (1929) showed many years ago. More recently, Whitehouse (1964; 1966) has shown that atropine interferes with both maze learning and performance, just as one would expect if anticholinergics interfere with habituation. [Whitehouse (1966) also reported that physostigmine, a drug that can *increase* cholinergic activity, facilitates the rate of acquisition, perhaps by augmenting the course of habituation, by speeding up the rate at which the rat "did not go left." Russell (1966) has recently described data, obtained with yet another drug, that are commensurate with this view.]

A particularly important aspect of one of Whitehouse's experiments is that he compared atropine with methyl atropine. These data are re-plotted in Fig. 1 as differences from undrugged controls. Atropine, but not methyl atropine, clearly interfered with maze learning. This dif-ference was evidently not due to motivational differences because the depression of directly measured food intake was the same for these two drugs (the right panel of the figure). The dose levels that were used in the experiment on food intake were the same as those used in the learning experiment.

What does this differential mean? It undoubtedly means that (1) rats do not eat much dry food when their mouths are dry, a peripheral ef-fect of both drugs, and (2) the difference seen in the maze is due to the fact that atropine passes freely from the bloodstream into the brain, whereas methyl atropine does so rather poorly. Thus, doses of two drugs that are matched in terms of peripheral effect (depression of food intake in this instance) produce very different effects on learning. Thus, we are almost certainly talking about an effect of atropine on the brain.

The Whitehouse data illustrate the well-documented theme about anticholinergics and nonreward. What we need, however, are direct tests of the hypothesis that anticholinergics can attenuate habituation. On this score, I will describe several experiments, all of which have

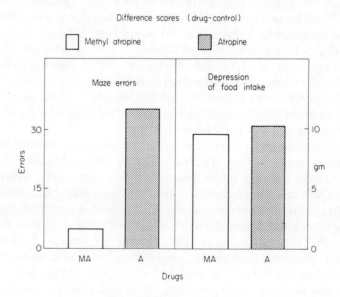

FIG. 1.   Maze errors (on the left) and food intake (on the right) following atropine and methyl atropine. (Data from Whitehouse, 1964.)

two things in common. First, all involve exploration of one kind or another as an index of habituation. The rationale behind this measure was outlined earlier. Second, all experiments suggest the same thing: Anticholinergics interfere with habituation.

The first of these experiments (Carlton & Vogel, 1965) capitalized on the fact that a thirsty animal will explore the novel aspects of its environment before it drinks. The experiment involves four groups of rats: two were given 15 minutes to explore a chamber; two were not. One of the groups that was exposed to the chamber was given scopolamine before exposure; the other was given saline. The corresponding injections were given to the unexposed animals. Following these treatments, the animals were returned to their living cages. One day later they were water deprived. When the rats had been deprived for one day, all of the groups were returned to the chamber to which only two had previously been exposed. One change had been made for this test: a water bottle was available in the chamber for the first time. An important feature of this experiment is that *no* animal was given an injection before test (i.e., the only injections were given before initial exposure).

The reasoning behind the experiment is simple. Consider an animal that has had a chance to explore the chamber. On the test day, this animal is exposed to an array of stimuli to which it has been exposed and to which habituation has presumably taken place. There is, however, a single, novel stimulus—the water bottle. In contrast to this animal, the rat that has never been exposed to the chamber finds all facets of its ambience novel—the water bottle as well as all other aspects of the chamber. It is reasonable to suppose that the thirsty animal that had an opportunity to habituate to "chamber-less-bottle" would get around to drinking much faster than the rat that had not had the opportunity. In order to measure this anticipated difference, we simply recorded the amount of time it took each rat to make its first contact with the drinking tube.

That is one expectation: Animals that had had prior exposure should drink sooner than animals that had not had prior exposure. But what about scopolamine? If anticholinergics do attenuate habituation, an animal given a prior opportunity to habituate following drug injection should show less effect of this prior exposure in the subsequent test. There are thus two expectations; both are borne out by the data in Fig. 2.

Each of the bars represents the drinking time for a single rat. The animals that had no prior exposure did not differ, whether they had had scopolamine or not; their data are pooled at the center of the fig-

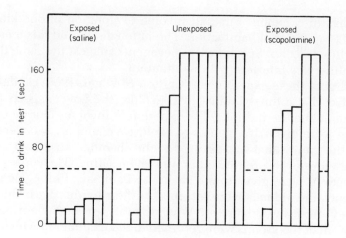

Fig. 2. Effects of prior habituation on time to drink for previously exposed, unexposed, and injected animals.

ure. The data for exposed saline animals are at the left. The horizontal dashed line indicates the longest time recorded from this group. Clearly, prior exposure reduced the time it took the animals to initiate drinking. But this proactive effect of habituation did not occur when prior exposure was given following an injection of scopolamine.

It is important to bear in mind that the animals that had been given scopolamine prior to the habituation session were, if anything, hyperactive, hyperexploratory, in that session. Despite this effect they subsequently behaved essentially as if they had not been exposed at all, as if habituation had not taken place.

We have obtained comparable data in a variety of similar studies. Furthermore, amphetamine in a dose (1.0 mg/kg, i.p.) that would have a profound effect on operant performance was, unlike scopolamine, ineffective in attenuating habituation (see Carlton, 1968).

A second kind of experiment involves a T-maze. In this case, no reward is involved. A rat is simply allowed to explore the maze; after it has turned into one arm, it is removed, returned to the starting point at the bottom of the T and allowed to choose an arm again. Normal animals tend to alternate arms under these circumstances. One interpretation of this tendency is that the initial control exerted by the stimuli of one arm is attenuated because of habituation. Therefore, the stimuli of the opposite arm come to control the animals' subsequent choice. If anticholinergics reduce habituation, they should substantially reduce the tendency to alternate. Papers by Meyers and Domino (1964) and by Douglas and Isaacson (1966) have reported just this result. The Meyers and Domino data have been replotted at the top of Fig. 3. (The tendency to alternate is expressed as its complement, i.e., percent repetition, so as to facilitate comparison with the data at the bottom of the figure.)

In the study by Leaton (1967) rats were given free access to a T-maze on some trials and were "forced" on others. (On these latter trials, one arm of the T was blocked off; the trial continued until the animal had entered the available arm.) Leaton gave his animals 8 trials per day; on trials 4 and 8 the animals were forced to the arm they had chosen less frequently during the 3 preceding free trials when both arms were available.

The end boxes of the arms of the T were not the same. One of them contained various objects (the "exploration" box containing "toys"); the other was empty (the "neutral" box). One group of animals was

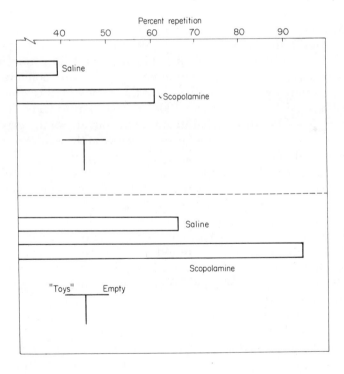

FIG. 3.   Effects of scopolamine on percent repetition in an empty T-maze (top, from Meyers & Domino, 1964) and a T-maze baited with novel objects ("toys") in one arm (bottom, from Leaton, 1967).

injected with scopolamine (0.5 mg/kg) before each session, whereas the others received saline.

As indicated at the bottom of Fig. 3, scopolamine clearly led to an increase in choice of the exploration box. The scopolamine animals came to choose the exploration end box almost 100% of the time. That is, they learned the response as they might have if they had been hungry and food were present in the exploration box. Saline animals consistently chose this box about 65% of the time.

That this preference was "directed" to this end box is indicated by the fact that the exploration box was placed in the arm that was opposite to that which had been preferred in preliminary tests in which both end boxes were neutral. The effect of the exploration box was thus working against an initial position preference. Furthermore, Leaton found that the drugged animals reversed their choice (to 100%) when the position of the "exploration" box was reversed in a later series of trials.

We can assume that the exploration box is relatively more reinforcing than the neutral one and that habituation can take place; the objects ("toys") in the end box are not rewards. But scopolamine antagonizes the development of habituation and thus amplifies the reinforcing value of the exploration box; it effectively converts a reinforcement into a reward. Leaton put it this way: "It is assumed that a normal animal fails to achieve 100% choice performance in the exploratory maze because he habituates to the novelty of the exploratory box as he is exposed to it. The incentive value of the exploratory box is thus reduced, along with its novelty relative to the neutral box, and choice behavior will be impaired as the difference in incentive value between the two end boxes is reduced. If the animal does not habituate to the end box, its relative novelty and incentive value will remain unimpaired and choice performance will remain at a high level."

Still another kind of experiment bears on these considerations. It involves reinforcement by a stimulus that the rat can present to itself by pressing a lever. Rather than allow the animal to wander about with its exploratory behavior unrecorded, a direct measure of responding is obtained.

A rat that is placed in a darkened response chamber that contains a lever will press the lever at a low and declining rate. This occurs when the lever-press does not lead to stimulus presentation other than the minor sounds of lever depression and, of course, the proprioceptive feedback of the response itself. But, if the lever-press turns on a dim light in the response chamber, responding is dramatically increased. Illumination serves as a reinforcement, not a reward, since responding declines as the initial effect of the stimulus is lost, i.e., as habituation takes place.

This intrasession decline in responding is illustrated in Fig. 4. Data for each of four 45-minute periods are plotted; each point was taken from a single animal. The values on the ordinate ("holding times") are the amounts of time each animal depressed the lever and kept it in that position. The light was on for the duration of lever depression.

In one experiment (Carlton, 1966) animals were allowed to respond for 90 minutes, and, when their responding had declined (see Fig. 4), they were removed from the apparatus and injected with saline, scopolamine, or amphetamine. They were then replaced and allowed access to the lever (and, therefore, light) for another 90 minutes.

The results of this procedure are summarized in Fig. 5. The values are the mean holding times taken from single sessions in the course of the experiment. The values at the left are from the initial 90 minutes of the sessions and those at the right are from the second 90. The "zero" injections are saline.

Under control conditions the amount of time the rats kept the light on dropped markedly from the first to the second 90-minute period. Scopolamine reversed this trend. The dose of 0.3 mg/kg produced levels of responding characteristic of the first, not second, period. A

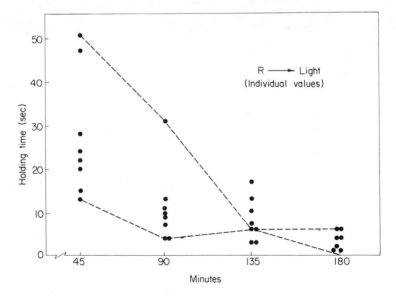

FIG. 4.   Total time of lever depression for light reinforcement (R) in a three-hour session. Each of the points is for an individual rat.

dose of 0.5 mg/kg not only inflated response output but also attenuated the normal decline. As a result, animals that had responded in
the first period gave themselves *more* stimulation in the second period
than they had in the first. Scopolamine evidently reversed the reduction in responding due to initial exposure in the first period and attenuated the development of habituation that would normally have taken
place in the second.

Amphetamine (0.5–1.5 mg/kg) did not increase the amount of time
the animals kept the light on. Amphetamine was not, however, wholly
ineffective. The complex results have been detailed elsewhere
(Carlton, 1966).

One question that these data pose is whether scopolamine produces
an increase in responding that is diffuse or "directed" to turning on
the light. One feature of the data I have already described suggests
such "direction." Normal rats held the lever down for about 1.0 second each time they depressed it. Scopolamine (but not amphetamine)
increased the amount of time the animals kept the light on without
changing this average value. The animals that had been given scopolamine appeared to be responding in a normal way despite an overall
increase in behavioral output. This result at least suggests a mainte-

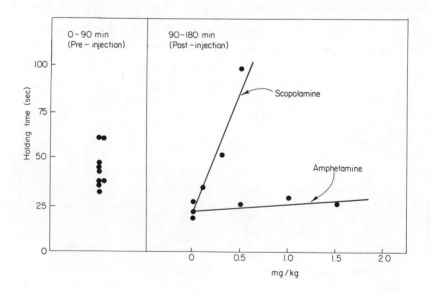

FIG. 5.   Total time of lever depression from individual sessions before injection (at
the left) and following different doses of scopolamine or amphetamine or saline (at the
right). The "zero" doses are saline.

nance of "directed" behavior rather than a nonspecific increase in diffuse motor activity.

A more direct test of the question is provided by allowing the animal access to two levers. One lever turns on the light; the other does not. In an experiment of this kind, three squads of animals were given a session before which one squad was given scopolamine, a second was given amphetamine, and a third saline. Scopolamine dramatically increased light-reinforced responding while having only a minor effect on responding on the lever that did not turn on the light. Amphetamine (1.0 mg/kg) did not have much of an effect on either class of responding. Thus, the increase in responding due to scopolamine was under the control of the reinforcement contingency and was not a diffuse, undirected increase in the tendency to lever-press.

A brief digression is in order here. Fox (1962) found that amphetamine produced profound increases in the light-reinforced responding of monkeys. In this study, the drug was given before the start of the session, unlike the procedure used here. It may be that amphetamine inflates the effect of reinforcement, as Stein (1964) has suggested, but that once reinforcement value has been minimized by habituation, the drug has no effect. This would agree with Stein's view that amphetamine must have some "non-zero" magnitude of reinforcement to affect. More recently, Haude (1967) has reported a related increase in monkeys given amphetamine. He also obtained a *decrease* with scopolamine. As Haude points out, the latter species difference may be related to the fact that the well-known dissociation of EEG and behavior that occurs with anticholinergics is less clearly obtained in monkeys (White, Nash, Westerbeke, & Passanza, 1961).

In an experiment that has already been described, animals were habituated to an environment and later tested for the effects of the prior habituation. Scopolamine evidently attenuated the habituation process. The light-reinforcement situation provides a way to carry out the same sort of experiment in a different way.

Animals were first given a series of sessions during which they could lever-press but could not produce light. On the next day the animals were again placed in the chamber, but the lever was not present; no illumination was present for one group, but light was on continuously for the other. In the subsequent session all animals could turn on the light by depressing the lever. Animals that had never been exposed to light before showed a profound increase in responding. The animals that had had previous, continuous exposure were unaffected; if anything, there was a slight depression of responding in the first postexposure session. These data are summarized in Fig. 6.

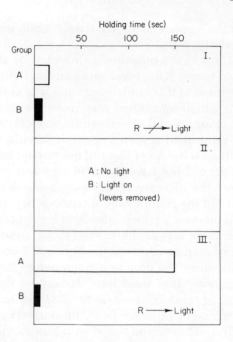

FIG. 6. Total time of lever depression before and after exposure to light. Lever depression did not produce light in the first session (I at the top of the figure) but did produce light in the subsequent test session (III at the bottom of the figure).

How might scopolamine and amphetamine interact with this effect of pre-exposure? The data that I have previously outlined suggest that scopolamine should reduce the effect, the animals should behave as if they had not been exposed. Amphetamine should be ineffective. These expectations are borne out by the data.

Rats were again given a series of sessions with lever, but not light, available. Different groups of rats were then given continuous exposure following one of three kinds of injections: saline, scopolamine (0.5 mg/kg), or amphetamine (1.0 mg/kg). They were then tested in a subsequent session. No injections were given before this session, but each lever depression turned on the light. Animals that had pre-exposure following saline subsequently showed low response levels. As expected, scopolamine given only at the time of prior exposure reduced this effect but amphetamine did not.

These results are summarized in Fig. 7. Despite the intervening exposure to light, animals given scopolamine only at the time of that exposure showed high levels of responding. That is, they behaved much as if habituation had not taken place (cf. Group A in Fig. 6).

At this point I want to pause for a brief summing up. The effects of some stimuli (reinforcements) wane because of habituation; the effects of others (rewards) do not. The normal basis of the lack of waning is biological significance. The anticholinergics protect against the consequences of habituation and thus effectively convert stimuli that are *not* rewards into stimuli that are.

Still another way of examining habituation is to capitalize on the fact that habituation leads to the loss of the functional impact of a stimulus on the organism. If this is true, it should be possible to show that a habituated stimulus is functionally "not there." This is not to say that habituation is a passive process. On the contrary, it is an active inhibitory process that effectively filters stimuli from the ambience with which the rat must deal.

In one experiment (Carlton & Vogel, 1965) we first presented rats with a series of 10-second tones. Following this habituation, the tone

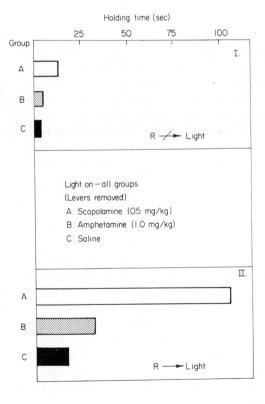

FIG. 7.   Same procedure as in Fig. 6, except that the drugs indicated in the midd* panel were administered during exposure to light.

was paired with a brief inescapable shock. In a subsequent test this tone was turned on while the animals were drinking.

Other animals had only the tone-shock pairing but no prior habituation. These animals showed a marked inhibition of drinking when the tone was turned on. In contrast, those animals that *had* been habituated to the tone prior to tone-shock pairing showed little if any suppression. Thus, prior habituation led to an almost complete lack of conditioning to the tone. Put another way, habituation led to a loss of the functional impact of the stimulus insofar as conditioned suppression may be used as an index of such impact. (Lubow[1] has independently replicated the details of this experiment.)

What should happen if we were to give scopolamine before the habituation session? The previous suggestions indicate that if the anticholinergic does in fact interfere with habituation, we should be able to "protect" the stimulus so that when a subsequent tone-shock pairing is given without drug, conditioning will occur despite the prior opportunity to habituate.

In a preliminary experiment Vogel and I obtained just this result. Animals given tone presentations under the influence of drug (but conditioned and tested without drug) showed reliably higher levels of conditioning than did those that had been habituated without drug. Once again, scopolamine protected the stimulus from habituation just as it did in other, very different experimental arrangements. More recently, Oliverio (1967) has obtained comparable results with mice. Prior habituation to a stimulus that was later used as the warning stimulus in an avoidance task led to reduced acquisition of the avoidance behavior. Scopolamine, given only at the time of prior stimulus presentation, protected against the habituation-induced deficit seen in normal animals.

All of the experiments I have discussed point to the same conclusion: Anticholinergics attenuate the development of habituation or the manifestation of it if it has already developed.

This simple rule about anticholinergics and habituation relates to effects seen in complex reward situations because of the relation of habituation to the absence of biologically significant stimuli (nonreward); i.e., anticholinergics should permit the intrusion of unrewarded responses into the animal's repertoire. Furthermore, this rule accounts for data obtained in situations involving various kinds of exploratory behavior and the habituation consequent to that behavior.

Although the rule accounts for a large amount of data like those il-

[1]Personal communication.

lustrated here and described elsewhere (Carlton, 1963; Longo, 1966), one could, of course, take an unparsimonious approach and postulate separate effects of anticholinergics in each kind of experimental situation. Such an analysis might, in fact, turn out to be the correct one. Or, one could develop an equally parsimonious alternative, which has been done. According to this alternative, anticholinergics interfere with the normal course of memory and are not specific to the habituation process. Some (but, as we shall see, by no means all) of the effects I have described can be fit into a memory format.

II. ANTICHOLINERGICS AND MEMORY

The usual meaning of a drug-induced deficit in memory is that something learned under drug is not recalled later in the absence of drug. Thus, some of the deficits obtained in experiments designed to measure the development of habituation could be due to memory deficits. But the other kinds of effects I have described require a broader definition of memory.

There are three basic paradigms involved in the studies I have discussed. These are summarized in the following tabulation:

Paradigm	Pretest	Test	Sample experiments
I	Drug	Drug	Alternation (Meyers & Domino, 1964) Extinction (Hearst, 1959; McCoy, see Section VI) Maze learning (Whitehouse, 1964, 1966) "Exploratory learning" (Leaton, 1967) Light reinforcement (Carlton, 1966)
II	Normal	Drug	Operant behavior (Carlton, 1963) Maze performance (Miles, 1929; Macht, 1923)
III	Drug	Normal	Pre-exploration (Carlton & Vogel, 1965) Light reinforcement (see Section I)

In Paradigm I, it can be assumed that trial n is a pretest for $n + 1$ and that on $n + 1$ the animal cannot remember what it did on n. Thus, in the alternation situation, for example, the animal returns to the same end box because it cannot remember that it went there on the preceding trial. This was the interpretation tentatively offered by Meyers and Domino. A similar interpretation could be applied to effects seen in extinction, maze learning, or light-reinforcement situations.

These data are also accounted for by the habituation hypothesis, which also does a substantially better job in accounting for Leaton's data. Recall that the animals given scopolamine learned to choose one end box 100% of the time. Furthermore, the animals' choices reversed when the position of the "toys" was reversed. These data indicate that the animals were remembering perfectly well. Thus, it is more parsimonious to suppose that a deficit in habituation, rather than memory, underlies the deficits seen in Paradigm I. (This is also true of several shock-avoidance experiments to be described later.)

As it applies to Paradigm II, the memory hypothesis says that disrupted performance is due to the fact that following drug administration, the animal cannot remember what went on when it was undrugged. This interpretation applies to the very many studies in which animals are trained before drug administration.

An early interpretation of the effects of anticholinergics in terms of this kind of memory deficit was offered by Domer and Schueler (1960). They trained rats to a criterion of errorless performance in a maze and then gave anticholinergics. The usual increase in errors was obtained, and this increase could indeed have been due to a degradation of memory. But the increase can, of course, just as reasonably be attributed to the fact that anticholinergics allow an intrusion of unrewarded responses (errors) that had previously been "filtered" from the animal's repertoire by habituation. Thus, both hypotheses can reasonably account for the same set of data.

A related problem is that it is impossible to separate an effect on the behavior being measured at the time of test from an effect on something the animal brings into the situation solely from prior treatment. One cannot be sure whether the animal makes errors because of the intrusion of *previously* habituated stimuli that come to control behavior in test, whether the animal has forgotten *previously* learned responses, or whether the drug interferes with the animal's vision, say, *at the time* of test. It was, in fact, just these problems of interpretation that prompted our use of Paradigm III, because in this Paradigm the animal is not drugged during test.

The memory hypothesis, as it applies to Paradigm III, says that normal memory processes do not develop under drug. Therefore, there is a deficit when the animals are subsequently tested without drug. Some of the data I have already described can indeed be accounted for in this way. But, obviously, they can also be accounted for by the assumption that anticholinergics interfere with habituation because the experience given under drug (and tested for without drug) was the opportunity to habituate. The question then is: Can deficits be shown in Paradigm III, where habituation does not play a major role? They can.

Buresova, Bures, Bohdanecky, and Weiss (1964), Bohdanecky and Jarvik (1967), and Berger, Margules, and Stein (1967) have all reported such effects. In all experiments rats (or mice) were punished with painful electric shock when they emitted a particular response. Some of these animals were given scopolamine (or atropine) before the punishment session; others were given control injections of saline. When the animals were later tested without any injections, the controls showed substantial suppression of the previously punished response, whereas the animals that had been drugged showed much less suppression. One interpretation of this result is that the development of normal memory was impaired by the drug.

More recently, Vogel (1968) has obtained comparable data in a related situation. Because of the importance of his experiments to the question of memory, the details of the procedure will be given. Rats were placed in a large, dimly illuminated chamber in only one wall of which there was a hole (about 1.0 inch in diameter); the floor of this chamber was made of grids through which shock could be delivered. Rats have a tendency to poke their snouts through holes and thereby explore. Vogel simply measured the frequency of this responding with a photocell mounted just beyond the hole.

In the first experiment he used four groups. Two of these groups, the punishment groups, were given a brief, inescapable shock when they made their first response. The other two, the control groups, were not shocked. One punishment group and one control group were given 1.0 mg/kg scopolamine 20 minutes before the session; the other two received saline. (This dose is twice the highest used in the experiments I described earlier; it was chosen because it was the one used by Bohdanecky and Jarvik and by Berger *et al.*) Three days later all animals were returned to the chamber and the number of responses recorded. These tests were repeated on each of the following three days. No drug was given before any of these.

The data obtained in the test sessions clearly indicate that prior shock suppressed responding in animals that had been given saline. But, if the shock had been given following scopolamine, a very substantial deficit appeared. In still another experiment, Vogel again found that scopolamine produced a deficit but that equimolar doses of methyl scopolamine did not. Methyl scopolamine, like methyl atropine, produces peripheral anticholinergic effects but passes poorly from bloodstream to brain.

[These data are in apparent contradiction to those previously reported by Vogel (1968) and by Carlton (1968). In those studies suppression of ongoing behavior was conditioned to a tone by pairing it with shock; animals that had been given either saline or scopolamine showed equal suppression in a subsequent no-drug test. The conclusion that scopolamine did not interfere with the establishment of this "conditioned emotional response" was based on only a single test trial and was, therefore, generally invalid. This is the case because, in a later experiment, Vogel (1968) found that with *repeated* no-drug tests without shock, animals trained following scopolamine injections showed a substantially more rapid loss of suppression than did animals conditioned following a saline injection. Repeated tests were also necessary to detect the effect of scopolamine in the punishment experiment that I have just described.]

These experiments by Vogel, like the three mentioned earlier, have all demonstrated deficits—and they all involved electric shock. What would happen if the animals were not punished but were rewarded? According to the memory hypothesis, deficits should be obtained.

Vogel repeated the experiment described earlier with one very important change in procedure: The animals were rewarded rather than shocked. The details of technique and dosage were identical to those of the previous experiment. The only change was that two groups were given access to a drinking tube mounted just behind the hole (and two control groups were not). The tube contained sweetened milk; the rewarded animals were allowed to take 100 licks of the milk. The drinking tube was not present during the subsequent no-drug tests.

Vogel found that prior reward reliably inflated the tendency to respond but that scopolamine did not affect this tendency. It is important to note that the effect of reward vs. no reward, although a clearly reliable one, was small relative to that of shock in the earlier study. Thus, any treatment that might produce a deficit would have a reasonable opportunity to be detected. That is, if the effect of reward had been a massive one, it could have obscured a relatively small memory deficit if there had been one.

Still another experiment involved the same techniques (punishment or reward), but these were applied to the same, rather than different, animals. The rats were first rewarded (for "nose-poking") with or without drug. They were then tested without drug and with no reward available. The test data (relative to previously unrewarded controls given saline or scopolamine) revealed an increase in responding but, once again, not a differential one due to scopolamine (275 vs. 250% of unrewarded control values). These data are shown at the top of Fig. 8.

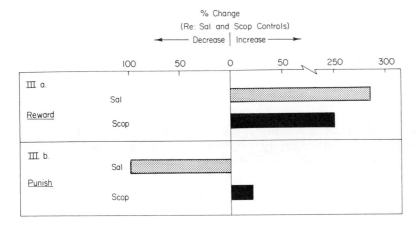

FIG. 8. Relative change in responding following reward (the upper panels) or punishment (the lower panels). Animals were rewarded or punished following saline (Sal) or scopolamine (Scop) and subsequently tested in the absence of drug. Scopolamine given at the time of punishment obliterated the usual punishment effect, whereas the same dose had no reliable effect on the increase of responding due to prior reward.

These same animals were later injected with saline or scopolamine, returned to the apparatus, and, as in the earlier experiments, punished. In a subsequent no-injection test the decrease in responding (relative to previously unpunished controls that had been given either saline or scopolamine) was a substantial one only in those rats that had been given saline prior to punishment. Scopolamine totally eliminated this effect of prior punishment (see the bottom of Fig. 8).

There are two other aspects of Vogel's data that are important. The first pertains to the remote possibility of some kind of experimental error that led to a loss of any drug effect in the reward experiments. How can we be sure that what was called scopolamine was not, in effect, saline? Vogel measured water intake after the reward session and found that the intake of the drugged animals was about 50% of the controls (this depression of drinking is a well-established effect of anticholinergics; see Stein, 1963). Thus, we have independent evidence of biological activity due to drug.

The second aspect of Vogel's data bears on the same point. Highly sweetened condensed milk was used as the reward because, obviously, water would not do. The reward session was continued until all animals had made the same number of licks at the milk tube. The device of using sweetened milk was not, however, wholly successful; those animals that had been given scopolamine took substantially longer to drink their allotted amount of milk. Again, we have internal evidence for drug action. Furthermore, the longer drinking times in the drugged rats at least superficially suggest that they would have emitted fewer responses in the later test. (This may account for the small differences that were obtained.) But despite this difference in rate of intake, a reliable effect of drug treatment was consistently not obtained.

What do these experiments mean? To me, they mean that memory interpretations of data obtained with Paradigm III are at best incomplete. Why should an animal fail to remember a prior shock yet remember a reward perfectly well? We have, of course, only two experiments involving reward. And we are in the position of having to accept a null hypothesis, an unhappy necessity from a statistical point of view. Clearly, more experimentation is required.

For the moment, however, the situation is this: Vogel's procedure is demonstrably sensitive to scopolamine when shock is used but insensitive when food reward is used. This obviously suggests that there is something unique about shock, the stimulus used in all of the earlier experiments demonstrating a deficit due to scopolamine. If there is something peculiar about shock, what might this peculiarity be? Following a brief digression, we will return to this question in a subsequent section.

III. A NOTE ON STIMULUS-CHANGE

If an animal is trained under one condition (drug or no drug), its behavior could be affected when it is tested under the complementary condition (Paradigms II and III) because any stimulus effects due to the drug will not be the same in training and test. This is no more complicated than saying that training with a light turned on should lead to a generalization decrement if testing takes place without the light. Interpretations in terms of stimulus-change are thus reasonable ones and deserve a comment.

Overton (1966) has reported "dissociation," stimulus-change effects, in the rat with scopolamine. The magnitude of effect was, relative to other drugs, only "moderate" and required dose levels that were greater than the ones we have been discussing by a factor of about 20. Doses of 0.5-1.0 mg/kg are a pharmacological world apart from 10.0-20.0 mg/kg. There is therefore the serious question of whether Overton's experiments, while of substantial importance in their own right, are especially useful in interpreting the phenomena we are discussing here.

More recently, however, Oliverio (1967) has reported data suggestive of stimulus-change effects in mice at a 2.0 mg/kg dose (2-4 times greater than those we have been discussing). One can thus raise a question as to the extent to which stimulus-change alone can account for the phenomena we have been discussing in the context of the three experimental paradigms.

A stimulus-change interpretation obviously cannot apply to Paradigm I because no change from drug to no drug is involved. Thus, inferior or superior performance must be due to some action of the anticholinergics other than their stimulus effects. Although there is something persuasive about an account of data obtained in Paradigm I that can also be applied to the other paradigms, there is no denying that an alternate account in terms of stimulus-change must be considered.

Suppose that stimulus-change is a powerful effect. How much of the data from Paradigms II and III can then be accounted for in terms of this effect alone? This question immediately poses another: If stimulus-change can account for the effects of one drug, why do all drugs, at some dose, not produce the same effects? The fact that they do not suggests that an account solely in terms of stimulus-change, although it may occur, may not be too useful. It may be, of course, that anticholinergics act as particularly potent stimuli; Overton's work suggests, however, just the opposite.

We can leave this general question and turn to more particular ones. In Oliverio's experiments, for example, animals that were trained under drug (1) were inferior *throughout* the five training sessions, each preceded by scopolamine administration, and (2) *improved* in a subsequent session not preceded by drug administration. If the *only* effect of the drug was to produce stimulus effects, then (1) why did the animals not learn normally when each session followed drug and when, therefore, no stimulus-change was involved, and (2) why should the change from drug to no drug lead to improved performance when, on the basis of generalization alone, it should have been inferior?

There is, of course, a possible answer to the second question. This is that the presence (or absence) of drug as a stimulus somehow favors (or does not favor) performance. Thus, avoidance learning, for example, might be improved, as it can be (see Section IV), because scopolamine (as stimulus) plus the exteroceptive warning signal is somehow a better compound warning signal than that signal alone. Consideration of the totality of available data immediately suggests that such an interpretation would require some rather fanciful juggling before it would be acceptable. How one could account for both improvement and no effect with the same warning signal plus drug remains a mystery to me. Such data have been reported (the Suits and

Isaacson study and the Leibowitz study, Sections IV and VI, respectively), and they can be accounted for, but not by an appeal to the stimulus properties of the drug.

In addition to all of these problems, there are instances (Berger *et al.*, 1967; Meyers, 1965) in which profound drug effects were obtained but in which direct tests for stimulus-change indicated that none occurred. Finally, why did Vogel find a deficit with punishment but not with reward if, in fact, the punishment deficit was due to stimulus-change?

The problem that we are addressing is one of accounting for a wide variety of phenomena in as simple and economical a way as possible. If one can show an effect that can, for example, be attributed to a deficit in habituation in Paradigm I (e.g., the light reinforcement studies already discussed) and then turns to Paradigm III and finds a deficit in the no-drug test (as in Fig. 7), it is at least parsimonious to suppose that the same mechanism may be operating. If one appeals to stimulus-change as an exclusive account for the data obtained with Paradigm III, then what are we to say about all of those data obtained in Paradigm I? And what are we to say when, in Paradigm II, performance in test shows an initial improvement and/or does not eventually reach normal levels under the "new stimulus?" Although there is no question that drugs can have stimulus effects, there is a certain, perhaps misguided, appeal in being able to say the same thing about the many results obtained in each of the three paradigms.

IV. ANTICHOLINERGICS AND SUPPRESSION

Now that we have completed our side trip into the matter of stimulus-change, we can return to the suggestion that anticholinergics have some special relevance to the effects of shock. The perspicacious reader will recall that we ended Section II by asking a question about what might be peculiar about the relation of shock and anticholinergics.

I want to make two suggestions as a preliminary to answering this question. These are, first, that a rat's initial response to shock is often a general suppression of behavior and, second, that anticholinergics interfere with the animal's tendency to suppress.

Consider the kind of experiment in which the experimenter arranges things so that the animal can avoid the shock. But it is a rare rat that knows how to avoid when the experiment starts; accordingly, we may find substantial shock-induced suppression of behavior, suppression of that very behavior that we want the animal to emit. From the rat's point of view, there is no way to cope with shock until the appropriate means of coping is learned. And the suppression consequent to the lack of coping behavior may preclude learning how to cope. Accordingly, we can expect many animals to fail to learn in many kinds of avoidance situations, as in fact they do. Those situations in which poor learning (or coping) occurs are generally those that reduce the chance of the animals' "catching on" to the programmed contingency in the face of substantial suppression of behavior.

All that I have said is that in the course of an avoidance experiment, suppression due to an apparent lack of coping behavior can interfere with the development of avoidance responding. If the anticholinergics interfere with this suppression, they should thus enhance the acquisition of avoidance responding. Furthermore, this effect should occur, if it occurs at all, only in the *initial* phases of acquisition. At this point coping behavior is absent and the interfering suppression present. Once the response has been learned, we would expect the anticholinergics to produce a general disruption of performance like that I described some time ago (Carlton, 1962; Carlton, 1963). In general, this deterioration of performance was due to the intrusion of competing, normally inhibited responses into the animals' behavioral repertoire.

There is reasonable evidence for such a dual effect of the anticholinergics. Oliverio (1967) has reported a facilitation of avoidance learning with scopolamine. Previously developed responding became worse following the same dose of the same drug. [These experiments evidently grew out of some earlier experiments by Bignami (1964). Bignami had reported a facilitation of avoidance acquisition with another drug, benactyzine. The suspicion that this might be related to the anticholinergic activity of this drug is amply confirmed by Oliverio's work. The studies of benactyzine by Jacobsen and Sonne (1955) are also pertinent here.]

Oliverio also reported another, particularly compelling, experiment. Rats were first trained to avoid in the presence of one stimulus (#1). They were later given scopolamine and given a second series of avoidance trials. On some trials Stimulus #1 was presented, and a new stimulus (#2) was presented on others. Relative to appropriate controls, scopolamine produced inferior performance in response to #1 (the "old") and better performance in the presence of #2 (the "new"). In the same rat and at the same time, scopolamine can degrade well-established avoidance and enhance initial acquisition of the avoidance response.

Entirely comparable results had previously been reported by Leaf and Muller (1966) and by Rech (1968). In addition, Leaf and Muller found that certain aspects of the enhanced performance due to scopolamine in initial acquisition carried over into a subsequent no-drug session. Oliverio did not, however, find this effect. This difference may be due to the more sensitive procedure used by Leaf and Muller.

Still another experiment is pertinent here. Suits and Isaacson (1968) studied two kinds of avoidance situations, one designed to maximize interference due to suppression, the other designed to minimize it. The former procedure was a "two-way" task; i.e., the animals were required to shuttle between two compartments. The other task was "one-way"; i.e., the animals always started in one compartment and could avoid shock by moving into a second. That these two procedures produced profoundly different rates of acquisition is shown by the data from the two control groups in Fig. 9.

Scopolamine (called "experimental" in the figure) produced a profound improvement in the situation designed to maximize suppression and a slight decrement in the one designed to minimize suppression. In fact, scopolamine converted a truly "two-way" animal into a functionally "one-way" animal.

Let me insert two comments on memory at this point. First, the fact that Leaf and Muller did report a carry-over from drug to no-drug conditions is difficult to interpret in the context of the supposition that

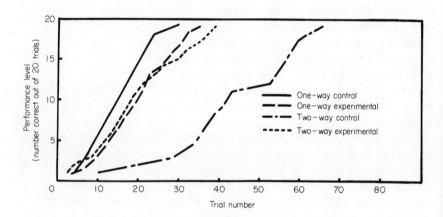

FIG. 9. Rates of avoidance learning in two kinds of avoidance apparatus (one-way and two-way) following administration of either saline (control) or scopolamine (experimental). (From Suits & Isaacson, 1968.)

the anticholinergics interfere with memory. Under the drug condition, Leaf and Muller's animals did learn something which appeared
under no-drug conditions. This is an experiment according to Paradigm III. [Meyers (1965) has also reported that although scopolamine
does interfere with suppression due to punishment, as one would
expect, rats do eventually learn to avoid when under the influence
of scopolamine, and that they can retain what they have learned
when later tested without drug. Meyers also tested for stimulus-
change effects due to scopolamine and found none.]

Second, Oliverio's, Leaf and Muller's, Meyers', Rech's, and Suits
and Isaacson's studies of acquisition under drug fall into the category
I have called Paradigm I. If scopolamine interferes with memory, it is
difficult to see why performance should be uniformly improved.

A summary is in order here. A pair of experiments by Vogel indicates that an apparent memory deficit due to scopolamine may be
peculiar to situations involving shock. This indication prompted a discussion of shock-induced suppression and its antagonism by anticholinergics. I want to continue the discussion along two lines. The first
of these has to do with the possible bases of the antagonism by anticholinergics. The second will bring us back to Vogel's experiments:
Why might scopolamine interfere with the acquisition of shock-
induced suppression but not with the learning of rewarded behavior?
Why does scopolamine interfere with suppression and thereby enhance avoidance learning? My answer is based largely on a series of
ingenious speculations by one of my students, Peter Manto (1968).

Manto's basic idea is based, like most good ideas, on a very simple
observation. A classic sign of emotionality in the rat is defecation.
Defecation is under parasympathetic, not sympathetic, control. This
suggested to Manto that stress may induce a sympathetic reaction
which in turn triggers a parasympathetic (i.e., cholinergic) rebound.
This rebound is assumed to lead to behavioral suppression, another
classic sign of emotionality.

On the basis of a consideration of a wide assortment of data from the
experimental and clinical literature, from behavioral, biochemical,
and medical sources, Manto further suggested that a lack of coping
behavior (apparent or real) in the face of stress leads to a massive release of epinephrine which in turn triggers rebound. This idea accounts for a surprisingly large amount of data; unfortunately, space
limitations will not permit me to outline all of these. Barry and Buckley (1966) have also discussed some of these data.

There is one aspect of this work (Manto, 1967) that is, however, directly pertinent to this discussion. Injection of epinephrine produces,

as it should in theory, a marked suppression of behavior measured, in this case, as a depression of gross motor activity. If epinephrine triggers parasympathetic rebound and thereby suppression, it might be possible to reverse the effect with scopolamine. Manto found that scopolamine, in a dose that did not itself increase activity, produced a complete antagonism of the suppression due to epinephrine. Furthermore, equimolar doses of methyl scopolamine, which is absorbed poorly by the brain, did not have this antagonistic action.

This last result suggests the following sequence of events. The brain detects the presence of stress and triggers a massive epinephrine release peripherally. The brain then detects the fact that epinephrine has in fact been released. This proposed feedback may be like that found in hormonal regulation or it may, as seems more likely, involve *neuronal* feedback from peripheral structures having α and/or β receptors. This detection involves a cholinergic link in the brain and leads to behavioral suppression. It is necessary to postulate this step because of the differential effects of scopolamine and methyl scopolamine.

Manto's suggestions are admittedly speculative; what remains to be done are the experiments that will untangle the phenomenon. He has found that shock, in the absence of available coping behavior, will produce suppression comparable to that produced by epinephrine. This suppression reaches a maximum in about an hour and slowly subsides thereafter; one immediately thinks of the suppression of behavior following training in a shock-avoidance situation (Kamin, 1957).

The experiment that needs to be done, of course, is one designed to determine whether scopolamine will antagonize shock-induced suppression as it does epinephrine-induced suppression; the various experiments that I described earlier in this section certainly suggest that it will. In the absence of those data, however, I can only assume that Manto has correctly guessed at one facet of the mechanism by which scopolamine does in fact enhance the acquisition of avoidance responding. On that assumption, I want to return to the experiments by Vogel, for which one more suggestion is required.

This suggestion is an obvious one. It is simply that the response to initial stress must occur if that response is to become conditioned. The idea is not an unreasonable one. If it is correct, it would mean that scopolamine, by attenuating the suppression due to shock, could attenuate shock-based learning but not affect food-based learning. There is ample evidence on the first point, including the evidence on facilitated avoidance, but much less data on the second. This dual conclusion is an uncomfortably lopsided one because only one half of it has been convincingly supported.

Two comments are in order at this point. First, anticholinergics should not be expected to produce deficits uniformly in all Paradigm III experiments that involve shock. The effect of the anticholinergics is presumably related to the degree of initial stress. It is reasonable to suppose that such stress could be so massive that there would be no effect of the drug at nontoxic doses.

My second comment relates to the first and has, in fact, been touched on before. Suits and Isaacson found that scopolamine produced substantial facilitation of avoidance when suppression was high and a small but opposite effect when suppression was low. The effect of scopolamine was apparently related to the degree of initial stress. Once again, interpretations in terms of memory (within Paradigm I in this case) are called into question. If these data are to be interpreted as changes in memory, it will be necessary to explain why memory was improved with high suppression, whereas it was slightly impaired with low suppression.

I can summarize what we have discussed thus far very briefly. Previously trained animals given anticholinergics emit responses that are normally inhibited because they do not eventuate in reward. This effect is both logically and empirically related to habituation. A number of more direct studies of the effect of anticholinergics on habituation all point to the same conclusion: Anticholinergics attenuate habituation.

Some of these effects can be explained in terms of memory or stimulus-change. But there are two reasons why these accounts are not useful ones. First, either they fail to account for all the relevant data, whereas habituation can, or they cannot be experimentally distinguished from expectations based on a habituation interpretation. The most parsimonious assumption, although not necessarily the correct one, is that anticholinergics do, in fact, produce their effects by interfering with the process of habituation.

The second problem with the memory and stimulus-change explanations is that they cannot account for the differential effects of scopolamine on shock- vs. food-based behavioral changes. I suggested that this may be due to an attenuation of the suppression that is triggered by stress in the absence of coping behavior. This suggestion is clearly a step away from the parsimony inherent in the habituation interpretation. It suggests that there is some more general process that has to do with the inhibition of behavior and that it is this process that is attenuated by the anticholinergics. It is this possibility that I want to discuss now.

V. BRAIN-ACETYLCHOLINE AND INHIBITION

The data reviewed in the previous sections generate an obvious generalization: Anticholinergics lead to an attenuation of the inhibition normally obtained with either stress or exposure to stimuli and attendant nonreward. This generalization leads to the suggestion that the anticholinergics are interfering with an inhibitory process that is common to a very large variety of situations.

At the beginning of this article I talked about stimuli that initially lead to approach behavior. This phylogenetically ubiquitous tendency can have three outcomes. The animal may be led to stimuli that act as rewards, to reinforcements, or to stimuli that control aversive behavior. This last class is traditionally called punishment. The changes in behavior normally controlled by the last two, but not the first, are profoundly altered by the anticholinergics.

What does this fact about anticholinergics suggest about the normal activity of the brain? The most reasonable supposition is that this general inhibitory process requires the activity of brain-acetylcholine (ACH). Inherent in this supposition is the assumption that the anticholinergics act to attenuate acetylcholine's normal function in the brain as they do in the periphery (see Longo, 1966). We can assume that we are, in fact, talking about a brain activity because in those instances where they have been studied, methyl scopolamine and methyl atropine consistently fail to produce the effects I have summarized. In order to account for one other aspect of the phenomena we have discussed, it is necessary to assume that this inhibitory process can be conditioned.

When a stimulus leads to approach, this behavior may have one of several consequences. The animal's approach will have brought him into contact with one of three kinds of stimuli: (S-1) a weak stimulus that acts as a reward, (S-2) a weak stimulus that acts as a reinforcement and leads to habituation, or (S-3) a strong stimulus. The last two circumstances have at least two things in common: They lead to a suppression of behavior, and the suppression so engendered is disrupted by anticholinergics. There are, therefore, grounds for talking about some inhibitory process (I) that is common to both circumstances.

If this process can become conditioned, as the data we have already discussed suggest, we have a situation that can be schematized as follows:

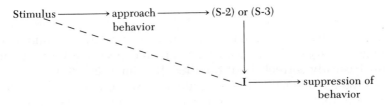

The dashed lines indicate a conditioned relation.

Because conditioned events become anticipatory, the eventual outcome will be:

Stimulus − − − − I ⟶ no approach

Furthermore, in complex learning situations, inhibition is necessarily involved because nonreward leads to the elimination of errors. Thus, training can generate the following:

Stimulus (1) ⟶ approach
Stimulus (2) − − − − I ⟶ no approach

The implication of these diagrams is very simple: An animal that approaches a stimulus and finds that it is not biologically significant or is punished on approach eventually stops approaching. Also, the idea of a conditioned process coming to exert control over emitted, operant behavior is very unoriginal. It can be found in many elaborations of Pavlov's work, notably those within the Hull-Spence tradition. The application of conditioning principles to habituation has been discussed by Thorpe (1963), Konorski (1948), and Stein (1966). However, our usage of the concept of a conditioned inhibitory process differs from these earlier ones in one very important respect. As we shall see, the process can be independently defined on neurochemical and anatomical dimensions rather than on a dimension inferred solely from the behavior that the process controls.

The drift of all the data I have discussed is that the inhibitory process requires the normal activity of ACH. Thus, decreased cholinergic activity should interfere with the development of habituation, error elimination, the extinction of previously learned behavior (discussed below), and the suppression of behavior due to strong stimuli. Furthermore, each of these instances of inhibition, once developed, should deteriorate, in part at least, in the face of reduced ACH activity due to the administration of anticholinergics. Alternatively, increased ACH activity can be shown to increase behavioral inhibition. These expected results have been reported with varying frequencies of replication.

The very simple concept of an ACH-dependency in inhibition accounts for what is, to me at least, an impressively large amount of data. The generality of the account leads me to expect that there is something basically correct about the idea. It is important to bear in mind that although one could devise a different account for each single experiment, that is not the same thing as a single account for many experiments.

This matter of generality results in two additional questions. First, does the rule about inhibition and acetylcholine uniquely define the effects of anticholinergics? Second, should anticholinergics be expected to be the only class of drugs that can produce at least some of the effects we have described?

The answer to the first question is obviously a negative one. For example, we know that acetylcholine activity has an important role in the regulation of water intake (Fisher & Coury, 1962; Grossman, 1962; Stein, 1963; Stein & Seifter, 1962). The problem of uniquely defining the actions of a class of compounds is a pharmacological one. But that is not our problem. Rather, we are using reasonable pharmacological conjecture to make inferences about some of the normal events that may go on in a normal brain. To be metaphorical, one can simply accept the facts of optics, thereby enlarge objects, and peer at paramecia. But the peering at paramecia is not likely to tell us much about optics. (This is not to say, however, that a general knowledge of optics may not be of use to the paramecium watcher; it may, in fact, protect him from being fooled by the tricks that lenses can play.)

The second question has to do with whether attenuation of acetylcholine is the only way to produce the effects we have been discussing. In dealing with a phenomenon as complex as brain-controlled behavior, we could hardly expect this to be the case. Amphetamine, for example, will produce many, but not all, of the effects I have described. If amphetamine does increase activity in a norepinephrine-dependent system that facilitates approach, and if acetylcholine-dependent inhibition antagonizes this system, attenuation of the latter should, in fact, produce many of the effects of the former. This was the view that I outlined some time ago (Carlton, 1963). More recently, Stein (1964) has given a much more precise definition to this role of amphetamine. And other drugs could, because of their own actions on the brain, produce qualitatively similar effects. The question then becomes one of whether the fact of qualitative similarity in some way militates against the validity of the rule about ACH and inhibition.

Another metaphor is in order here. Both pneumonia and cancer can lead to death. We know very little about cancer but we do know a great deal about pneumonia. The fact that an unfortunately obscure set of circumstances called cancer produces the same effect as pneumonia in no way invalidates our suppositions about the latter.

These metaphors seem obvious. Yet one can easily find in the literature related criticisms of the kind of neuropharmacological inference in which we are engaged here. They amount to saying that inferences about the effects of a class of drugs like the anticholinergics are inadequate for two reasons. First, these inferences do not account for all of the effects of the class in question and, second, other drugs can produce some, not all, of the same effects and, therefore, it is not legitimate to draw inferences about specificity of action. Such criticisms can, in kindness, be called ill-considered or, in frankness, silly.

There are, nonetheless, three serious problems inherent in the account we have been discussing. These are: (1) the effects of cholinesterase inhibitors, (2) effects seen in extinction, and (3) the relationships among inhibition generated by different procedures. We will take up each of these in the next section.

VI. THE GENERALITY OF CHOLINERGIC INHIBITORY PROCESSES

Each of the three problems just itemized bears on a more serious, ubiquitous question: Just how general is the inhibitory mechanism we have been describing? We will discuss each problem in turn; the relevance of each to the more general question will be, I hope, obvious.

Inhibition of acetylcholinesterase, the enzyme that inactivates acetylcholine, can augment normal cholinergic activity. Inhibition of an inactivator can increase activity; in effect, two minuses make a plus. But enzyme inhibition can also *decrease* cholinergic activity because accumulation of acetylcholine can lead to a functional blockade of neuronal activity (see McLennan, 1963). Furthermore, there are reasonable grounds for supposing that there is a very small margin between a dose of inhibitor that increases neuronal activity and that which decreases it. I have discussed these reasons elsewhere (Carlton, 1968) and will not repeat them here.

The situation is still more complicated. Every animal has its own responsiveness to a drug, its own dose-response sensitivity. Thus, in a group of animals given a single dose of an inhibitor, neuronal activity may be increased in some, decreased in others, and unchanged in the remainder. Accordingly, an inhibitor like physostigmine should, on neurochemical grounds, be a nightmare to work with in behavioral situations. And it evidently is.

These difficulties account for the relative absence of data on increased activity. The more rapid acquisition due to physostigmine that Whitehouse has reported clearly agrees with expectation, i.e., more rapid habituation, more rapid error elimination. The data reported by Russell also do so, although less directly. We have had, until recently, a seriously lopsided state of affairs; there is abundant evidence that interference with cholinergic activity interferes with inhibitory processes, but there are few data of a complementary kind.

This problem of lack of data has recently been substantially ameliorated by a rather different and extraordinary study by Leibowitz (1968). In her experiments, a cholinesterase inhibitor (DFP) was injected directly into the hippocampus. The relevance of hippocampal activity to the inhibitory mechanisms we have been discussing will be taken up in Section VII.

Leibowitz found that DFP substantially reduced directly measured cholinesterase activity, with maximal inhibition occurring in the hippocampal area. She also found that when injections followed minimal training, performance in a discrimination learning situation was facilitated. In contrast to this result, when injections were given after over-learning, performance levels were reduced. Detailed analyses of these performance changes indicated that with low levels of learning, the animals were making a substantial number of errors and that DFP reduced the incidence of such nonrewarded responses. Thus, increased ACH activity resulting from reduced enzyme activity produced the complement of decreased ACH activity due to a drug like scopolamine. Increased activity leads to fewer errors; decreased activity leads to more.

But why, then, did DFP make performance become worse when the task had been overlearned? Two assumptions are required to account for these data. First, we can assume, with Leibowitz, that increased error elimination is due to increased levels of ACH activity. Thus, with underlearning, ACH levels are low, and with overlearning, they are high. Second, we must also assume that the action of a cholinesterase inhibitor like DFP is necessarily a biphasic one (also see Deutsch & Deutsch, 1966).

As I indicated before, the relationship of ACH level and neuronal activity is essentially an inverted ∪. Thus, excessive accumulation of

ACH beyond some optimum can lead to a functional blockade of activity.

By way of gross oversimplification, suppose that 50 "units" of ACH activity were to lead to optimal neuronal activity and that 80 were to lead to less. If DFP were to increase activity by 30, the optimum would be reached if the initial level were 20, but functionally *less* activity would result from the same dose of DFP if the initial level were 50 (i.e., 30 + 50 = 80; the proof is left to the student).

To return to the Leibowitz experiments, low ACH levels and consequent low levels of error elimination in the minimally trained groups could be increased by DFP and result in greater error elimination. But, with higher baseline levels of ACH activity and consequent high error elimination in the overtrained animals, DFP would result in less functional ACH activity, less inhibition, and, therefore, intrusion of previously inhibited responses (errors) into the animals' repertoire. This is precisely what Leibowitz found.

A different kind of experiment (Pazzagli & Pepeu, 1964) bears directly on the study by Leibowitz as well as on all that we have already discussed. If the inhibition of nonrewarded behavior is, in fact, contingent on ACH, we would expect an inverse relation between errors and directly measured brain levels of ACH. Pazzagli and Pepeu found that (1) scopolamine reduced directly measured, endogenous ACH in brain, (2) scopolamine increased errors in rats that had previously been trained to avoid shock in a multiunit maze, and (3) there was indeed an inverse relation between errors and brain-ACH. I have plotted this relationship in Fig. 10. [The values are taken from Tables 1–4 in the paper by Pazzagli and Pepeu (1964). Normal levels of ACH were about 2.5 μg/gm of tissue.]

There are certain important features of some of the data from this experiment that are not simply accounted for by the hypothesis we have been discussing [see Table 4 in Pazzagli and Pepeu (1964)]. Nevertheless, the demonstration of a hypothesized inverse relation of errors and ACH adds substantial weight to the plausibility of the hypothesis itself.

The second problem mentioned at the end of Section V has to do with extinction. Extinction involves nonreward, of course, and therefore should involve the inhibitory process we have been discussing. This means that attenuating the actions of acetylcholine should attenuate the normal course of extinction. There are some, but unsatisfactorily few, data that support this expectation. Hearst (1959) found that scopolamine dramatically increased levels of responding that had already been reduced by extinction. In a series of subsequent sessions,

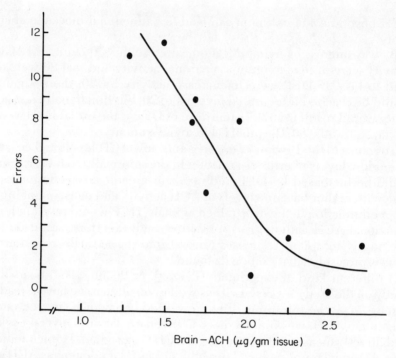

FIG. 10. Relationship between errors during the course of learning and levels of di- - rectly measured brain-acetylcholine (ACH). Lower levels of ACH are correlated with increased errors. (Replotted from Pazzagli & Pepeu, 1964.)

each preceded by drug injection, Hearst's rats emitted literally thousands of responses, no one of which was rewarded.

McCoy[2] has obtained related results. His animals were first trained to lever-press when the lever was introduced into the response chamber. They had 30 seconds in which to do so; failure to respond in this period, or the response itself, led to lever retraction. After an interval, the lever was reintroduced.

Reward training of this kind led, of course, to short response times (the time between lever introduction and response). Discontinuation of reward also, of course, led to increased response times. The action of scopolamine on extinction is shown in Fig. 11.

In the first session the drug markedly attenuated the tendency for response times to increase. In the second session the previously drugged animals were given control injections and extinction pro-

[2]Personal communication.

ceeded normally. (Note the spontaneous recovery.) Reintroduction of drug treatment in the third session reversed the previously established failure to respond. Thus, as one would expect, attenuation of acetylcholine activity attenuated the response inhibition contingent on nonreward. Thus, the data on reinforcement and habituation, on strong stimuli and extinction, tend to agree. But does this agreement dictate the assumption of an identity of processes?

This question leads us to the third problem: What are the relationships among the various procedures that can generate inhibition? Although attenuated acetylcholine activity can reduce the development of inhibition in a number of situations or its manifestation once developed, this obviously does not mean they are identical. An animal that approaches a weak stimulus and finds it reinforcing is clearly not exactly the same animal that approaches reward and fails to find it. The emotional component of failing to find anticipated reward, for example, undoubtedly adds factors that reinforcement does not and should, in fact, make it difficult to attenuate the normal course of extinction. But reinforcement, habituation, and extinction do have something in

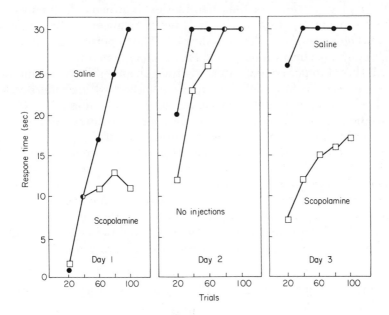

FIG. 11.   Times to respond following the introduction of a response lever during extinction sessions that followed earlier training without drug. Scopolamine or saline was given on days 1 and 3 of extinction, whereas no injections were given on day 2. (Redrawn from McCoy, personal communication.)

common; the inhibitory process that each procedure generates is sensitive to the action of anticholinergics because it is, in part at least, acetylcholine-dependent.

A similar communality without identity characterizes the relation of extinction and punishment. Again, the development and expression of both are affected by the anticholinergics, yet delivering an electric shock is clearly not identical to withdrawal of reward. The fact that both can generate aggressive behavior is another important point of communality.

We have thus far discussed the following general kinds of relations: (1) simple approach learning and reward; (2) reinforcement and habituation; (3) habituation and complex learning (e.g., a maze); (4) punishment; (5) extinction; and (6) avoidance learning.

All but the first (i.e., Vogel's experiments) are affected by anticholinergics. In the very simple situation represented by these studies (which followed Paradigm III) there was evidently no effect because performance during learning was not greatly influenced by the intrusion of competing stimuli. In more complex situations like those studied by both Whitehouse (1966) and me (1963), for example, such stimuli do play a role, and thus habituation is a major factor in determining overall performance. In these instances, anticholinergics should have a major effect, and they do. The experiments reported by Leibowitz also bear directly on this expected outcome.

All six of the phenomena logically involve an inhibitory component, but the relative role of this component in controlling total behavior will obviously vary from situation to situation. But, and this is the major generalization I want to draw, there is a communality about this inhibition that is defined solely by its sensitivity to phamacological manipulations that presumably affect the endogenous activity of ACH. Thus, the study of a class of drugs seems to have told us something about the physiological basis of a phenomenon that plays a role in a very wide variety of behavioral situations. Furthermore, if there is anything to this generalization, we should be able to use this chemical answer to the question of inhibition as a guide to finding an anatomical one. And, as will come up in the next section, we can.

VII. ANATOMICAL CORRELATES OF CHOLINERGIC INHIBITION

It is not appropriate here to outline all of the anatomical bases of behavioral inhibition. Rather, I want to call attention to one striking relationship and some of the data that are pertinent to it.

This relationship becomes apparent from the literature on the effects of hippocampal lesions of the rat brain (Douglas, 1967). The striking aspect of this literature is that essentially every effect that can be produced by the administration of anticholinergics can also be produced by hippocampal lesions. Although reasoning from parallels can be treacherous, this relationship at least suggests that we can begin to guess at an anatomical basis for the chemical effects I have already described.

I have attempted to summarize these relations in Fig. 12. An animal can approach a stimulus and encounter reinforcement (RFT), a strong stimulus, or reward. If reinforcement or a strong stimulus like shock occurs, inhibition of the tendency to approach will develop. This inhibition, defined by its sensitivity to anticholinergics, apparently involves the anatomically defined areas shown at the bottom of the figure. (The "E" relating to punishment refers to Manto's speculations.) This inhibitory network, certainly only a small fraction of the total system involved, is shown as impinging on a lateral hypothalamic (L. Hypothal.), medial forebrain bundle (MFB) system that evidently requires the activity of NE, which is activated by reward and facilitates the tendency to approach (Stein, 1967; Stein, this volume).

This diagram, simple as it is, agrees with a reasonable amount of data. We know that hippocampal activity is in part under cholinergic

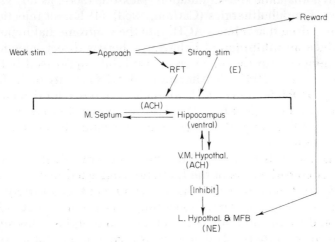

FIG. 12. Schematic representation of (1) the control of approach behavior, (2) the various consequences of that approach, and (3) the relationship of these consequences to, first, a norepinephrine system in the case of reward and, second, other anatomically defined, cholinergic brain areas in the case of inhibition consequent to reinforcement or strong stimuli. (See text for details.)

control and that an important aspect of this control is mediated by the medial septum (Stumpf, 1965). There is histochemical evidence (Shute & Lewis, 1967) that clearly supports the idea of an ACH-dependency in hippocampal activity. We also know that the ventral hippocampus has important relations with the hypothalamus (e.g., Elul, 1964) and that the ventromedial hypothalamus (V.M. Hypothal.) has a general inhibitory function that also appears to be ACH-dependent (Margules & Stein, 1967).

It seems reasonable to suppose, then, that systemically induced disruption of ACH activity would have a good chance of producing disinhibition. It also seems reasonable that localized damage to the hippocampus, evidently a pivotal point in the inhibitory system, should produce effects comparable to those produced by systemically administered anticholinergics.

Can the following facts be only coincidentally related to this scheme? (1) Direct injections of anticholinergics into the medial septum can produce many of the effects of lesions in this area, much as if the drug produces a functional lesion (Hamilton, McCleary, & Grossman, 1968). (2) Direct injections of anticholinergics into the hippocampus produce the same general disinhibitory effects on behavior as do systemic injections (Khavari & Maickel, 1967). (3) Lesions of the ventral hippocampus lower the current levels required to maintain rates of hypothalamic self-stimulation (Jackson, 1968), as do systemic injections of anticholinergics (Carlton, 1963). (4) Direct injections of carbachol, a drug that mimics ACH, into the ventromedial hypothalamus produce an inhibition of behavior, whereas direct injections of anticholinergics into the same area disinhibit suppressed behavior (Margules & Stein, 1967). (5) Alterations of ACH activity in the hippocampus by DFP injections lead to alterations in behavior that conform to what we would expect from all of the foregoing (Leibowitz, 1968). Perhaps all of this congruity of fact and expectation is indeed coincidental, but I doubt it.

We began all this by considering the effects of selected drugs on behavior. A consideration of the literature suggested that the various forms of inhibition of behavior that are contingent on a variety of experimental manipulations have something in common in that each can be disrupted by the administration of anticholinergics. This suggestion leads to two others: (1) that there is a general inhibitory system involved in varying degrees in each of the experimentally defined ways of getting behavior to fail to occur, and (2) that this system involves the normal, endogenous activity of brain-ACH.

This amounts to a chemical answer to a question about the physiological bases of one phenomenon. The beginnings of an anatomical answer can also be provided. And it turns out that anatomy, histochemistry, and neuropharmacology all tend to agree in pointing not only to "what" but also to "where." The story is painfully incomplete, but the beginning is at least encouraging.

REFERENCES

Barry, H., III, & Buckley, J. P. Drug effects on animal performance and the stress syndrome. *J. pharmaceut. Sci.,* 1966, **55,** 1159-1183.
Berger, B., Margules, D. L., & Stein, L. Prevention of learning of fear by oxazepam and scopolamine. *Amer. Psychologist,* 1967, **22,** 492. (Abstract)
Bignami, G. Effects of benactyzine and adiphenine on instrumental avoidance conditioning in a shuttle-box. *Psychopharmacologia,* 1964, **5,** 264-279.
Bohdanecky, Z., & Jarvik, M. E. Impairment on one-trial passive avoidance learning in mice by scopolamine, scopolamine methylbromide, and physostigmine. *Int. J. Neuropharmacol.,* 1967, **6,** 217-222.
Buresova, O., Bures, J., Bohdanecky, Z., & Weiss, T. Effect of atropine on learning, extinction, retention and retrieval in rats. *Psychopharmacologia,* 1964, **5,** 255-263.
Carlton, P. L. Some behavioral effects of atropine and methyl atropine. *Psychol. Rep.,* 1962, **10,** 579-589.
Carlton, P. L. Cholinergic mechanisms in the control of behavior by the brain. *Psychol. Rev.,* 1963, **70,** 19-39.
Carlton, P. L. Scopolamine, amphetamine and light-reinforced responding. *Psychon. Sci.,* 1966, **5,** 347-348.
Carlton, P. L. Brain-acetylcholine and habituation. *Prog. brain Res.,* 1968.
Carlton, P. L., & Vogel, J. R. Studies of the amnesic properties of scopolamine. *Psychon. Sci.,* 1965, **3,** 261-262.
Carlton, P. L., & Vogel, J. R. Habituation and conditioning. *J. Comp. physiol. Psychol.,* 1967, **2,** 348-351.
Deutsch, J. A., & Deutsch, D. *Physiological psychology.* Homewood, Ill.: Dorsey Press, 1966.
Domer, F. R., & Schueler, F. W. Investigations of the amnesic properties of scopolamine and related compounds. *Arch. int. Pharmacodyn. Ther.,* 1960, **127,** 449-458.
Douglas, R. J. The hippocampus and behavior. *Psychol. Bull.,* 1967, **67,** 416-442.
Douglas, R. J., & Isaacson, R. L. Spontaneous alternation and scopolamine. *Psychon. Sci.,* 1966, **4,** 283-284.
Elul, R. Regional differences in the hippocampus of the cat. *Electroencephalog. clin. Neurophysiol.,* 1964, **16,** 489-502.
Fisher, A. E., & Coury, J. N. Cholinergic tracing of a central neural circuit underlying the thirst drive. *Science,* 1962, **138,** 691-693.
Fox, S. S. Self-maintained sensory input and sensory deprivation in monkeys: A behavioral and neuropharmacological study. *J. comp. physiol. Psychol.,* 1962, **55,** 438-444.
Glickman, S. E., & Feldman, S. M. Habituation of the arousal response to direct stimulation of the brain-stem. *Electroencephalog. clin. Neurophysiol.,* 1961, **13,** 703-709.

Grossman, S. P. Direct adrenergic and cholinergic stimulation of hypothalamic mechanisms. *Amer. J. Physiol.*, 1962, **202**, 872-882.

Hamilton, L. W., McCleary, R. A., & Grossman, S. P. Behavioral effects of cholinergic septal blockade in cats. *J. comp. physiol. Psychol.*, 1968, in press.

Haude, R. H. Effects of amphetamine and scopolamine on visual exploratory behavior in monkeys. Paper presented at Eastern Psychol. Assoc. Meetings, 1967.

Hearst, E. Effects of scopolamine on discriminated responding in the rat. *J. Pharmacol. exp. Therapeut.*, 1959, **126**, 349-358.

Jackson, F. Effects of hippocampal lesions on self-stimulation in the rat. Unpublished doctoral dissertation, Rutgers Univer., 1968.

Jacobsen, E., & Sonne, E. The effect of benzilic acid diethylaminoethylester, HC 1 (Benactyzine) on stress-induced behaviour in the rat. *Acta Pharmacol. Toxicol.*, 1955, **11**, 135-147.

Kamin, L. J. The retention of an incompletely learned avoidance response. *J. comp. physiol. Psychol.*, 1957, **50**, 457-460.

Khavari, K. A., & Maickel, P. Atropine and atropine methyl bromide effects on behavior of rats. *Int. J. Neuropharmacol.*, 1967, **6**, 301-306.

Konorski, J. *Conditioned reflexes and neuron organization.* London and New York: Cambridge Univer. Press, 1948.

Leaf, R. C., & Muller, S. A. Effects of scopolamine on operant avoidance acquisition and retention. *Psychopharmacologia*, 1966, **9**, 101-109.

Leaton, R. N. The effects of scopolamine on exploratory motivated behavior in the rat. Paper presented at Eastern Psychol. Assoc. Meetings, 1967.

Leibowitz, S. F. Memory and emotionality after anticholinesterase in the hippocampus: Inverse function of prior learning level. Unpublished doctoral dissertation, New York Univer., 1968.

Lewis, P. R., & Shute, C. C. D. The cholinergic limbic system: Projections to hippocampal formation, medial cortex, nuclei of the ascending cholinergic reticular system, and the subfornical organ and supra-optic crest. *Brain*, 1967, **90**, Part III, 521-540.

Longo, V. G. Behavioral and electroencephalographic effects of atropine and related compounds. *Pharmacol. Rev.*, 1966, **18**, 965-996.

MacCorquodale, K., & Meehl, P. E. Edward C. Tolman. In W. K. Estes *et al.* (Eds.), *Modern learning theory.* New York: Appleton, 1954.

Macht, D. A pharmacodynamic analysis of the cerebral effects of atropin, homatropin, scopolamin and related drugs. *J. Pharmacol. exp. Therapeut.*, 1923, **22**, 35-48.

Maier, N. R. F., & Schneirla, T. C. *Principles of animal psychology.* New York: McGraw-Hill, 1935.

Manto, P. G. Blockade of epinephrine-induced decrement in activity by scopolamine. *Psychon. Sci.*, 1967, **7**, 203-204.

Manto, P. G. An investigation of feedback mechanisms in stress-induced changes of autonomic balance. Unpublished doctoral dissertation, Rutgers Univer., 1968.

Margules, D. L., & Stein, L. Neuroleptics vs. tranquilizers: Evidence from animal behavior studies of mode and site of action. In H. Brill *et al.* (Eds.), *Neuropsychopharmacology.* Vol. 5. Amsterdam: Elsevier, 1967. Pp. 108-120.

McLennan, H. *Synaptic transmission.* (4th ed.) Philadelphia: Saunders, 1963.

Meyers, B. Some effects of scopolamine on a passive avoidance response in rats. *Psychopharmacologia*, 1965, **8**, 111-119.

Meyers, B., & Domino, E. F. The effect of cholinergic blocking drugs on spontaneous alternation in rats. *Arch. int. Pharmacodyn. Ther.*, 1964, **150**, 525-529.

Miles, W. R. Hyoscine vs. alcohol: Effect on the behavior of rats in the elevated maze. *Proc. 9th Int. Congr. Psychol., 1929.* Pp. 309-310.

Oliverio, A. Contrasting effects of scopolamine on mice trained simultaneously with two different schedules of avoidance conditioning. *Psychopharmacologia,* 1967, **11**, 39-51.

Oliverio, A. Effects of scopolamine on avoidance conditioning and habituation of mice. *Psychopharmacologia,* 1968, **12**, 214-226.

Overton, D. A. State-dependent learning produced by depressant and atropine-like drugs. *Psychopharmacologia,* 1966, **10**, 7-31.

Pazzagli, A., & Pepeu, G. Amnesic properties of scopolamine and brain acetylcholine in the rat. *Int. J. Neuropharmacol.,* 1964, **4**, 291-299.

Rech, R. H. Effects of cholinergic drugs on poor performance of rats in a shuttle-box. *Psychopharmacologia,* 1968, **12**, 371-383.

Russell, R. W. Biochemical substrates of behavior. In R. W. Russell, (Ed.), *Frontiers in physiological psychology.* New York: Academic Press, 1966.

Schneirla, T. C. An evolutionary and developmental theory of biphasic processes underlying approach and withdrawal. In M. R. Jones (Ed.), *Nebraska symposium on motivation.* Lincoln, Nebr.: Univer. of Nebraska Press, 1959. Pp. 1-42.

Sharpless, S. K., & Jasper, H. Habituation of the arousal reaction. *Brain,* 1956, **79**, 655-680.

Shute, C. C. D., & Lewis, P. R. The ascending cholinergic reticular system: Neocortical, olfactory and subcortical projections. *Brain,* 1967, **90**, Part III, 497-520.

Stein, L. Anticholinergic drugs and the central control of thirst. *Science,* 1963, **139**, 46-48.

Stein, L. Amphetamine and neural reward mechanisms. In H. Steinberg *et al.* (Eds.), *Animal behavior and drug action.* London: Churchill, 1964. Pp. 91-113.

Stein, L. Habituation and stimulus novelty: A model based on classical conditioning. *Psychol. Rev.,* 1966, **73**, 352-356.

Stein, L. Noradrenergic substrates of positive reinforcement: Site of motivational action of amphetamine and chlorpromazine. In H. Brill *et al.* (Eds.), *Neuropsychopharmacology.* Amsterdam: Excerpta Med. Found., 1967. P. 765.

Stein, L., & Seifter, J. Muscarinic synapses in the hypothalamus. *Amer. J. Physiol.,* 1962, **202**, 751-756.

Stumpf, C. Drug action on hippocampal activity. *Int. Rev. Neurobiol.,* 1965, **8**, 77-132.

Suits, E., & Isaacson, R. L. The effects of scopolamine hydrobromide on one-way and two-way avoidance learning in rats. 1968, in press.

Thorpe, W. H. *Learning and instinct in animals.* (2nd ed.) Cambridge: Harvard Univer. Press, 1963.

Vogel, J. R. The differential effect of scopolamine on rewarded and punished behavior. Unpublished doctoral dissertation, Rutgers Univer., 1968.

White, R. P., Nash, C. B., Westerbeke, E. J., & Passanza, G. J. Phylogenetic comparison of central actions produced by different doses of atropine and hyoscine. *Arch. int. Pharmacodyn. Ther.,* 1961, **132**, 359-363.

Whitehouse, J. M. Effects of atropine on discrimination learning in the rat. *J. comp. physiol. Psychol.,* 1964, **57**, 13-15.

Whitehouse, J. M. The effects of physostigmine on discrimination learning. *Psychopharmacologia,* 1966, **9**, 183-188.

Whitehouse, J. M., Lloyd, A. J., & Fifer, S. A. Comparative effects of atropine and methylatropine on maze acquisition and eating. *J. comp. physiol. Psychol.,* 1964, **58**, 475-476.

CHAPTER 11

Chemistry of Purposive Behavior

LARRY STEIN

The assertion that behavior is purposive or goal-directed arises from the observation that organisms seek to repeat pleasurable or rewarding experiences and to avoid repeating painful or punishing ones. In contemporary terminology, purposive behavior is controlled by its rewarding or punishing consequences. The machinery of hedonic control has been succinctly described by Rado (1956):

> In pleasure and pain the animal organism thus possesses a dependable system of signals for the *yes* and *no* evaluation of its encounters and the self-regulation of its behavior. The activities described as "moving toward" and "moving away from" are mechanisms evolved in response to these *yes* and *no* signals. They are, in fact, the basic executive operations of the organism under this simple system of hedonic control . . . . Hedonic self-regulation extends over the organism's entire operating pattern: pleasure is the reward for successful performance, and the memory of pleasure invites repetition of the beneficial activity. Pain is the punishment for failure and the memory of pain deters the organism from repeating the self-harming activity (p. 291).

From the point of view of behavioral mechanisms, I need only indicate here that Rado's *yes* and *no* signaling systems correspond to mechanisms of reward and punishment, or behavioral-facilitation and behavioral-suppression, which I have treated in detail elsewhere

(Stein, 1964a; Stein, in press). The emphasis of this paper is physiological. Technical developments have permitted rapid progress since the groundbreaking discoveries of Hess (1954), Olds and Milner (1954), and Delgado, Roberts, and Miller (1954). I will try to summarize here, albeit in a highly selective fashion, our current knowledge of the physiological mechanisms of reward and punishment. In addition, I will review a series of experiments, performed in collaboration with Dr. D. L. Margules and Dr. C. David Wise, which provide some new information about the anatomical organization and synaptic chemistry of the parts of the brain in which these mechanisms may reside.

I. ANATOMICAL SUBSTRATES OF REWARD AND PUNISHMENT

Largely as a result of the efforts of Olds (1962), it now seems almost certain (although direct evidence is lacking) that the medial forebrain bundle (MFB) is the principal pathway of the reward system and that the periventricular system of the diencephalon and midbrain (PVS) is the principal pathway of the punishment system (Figs. 1 and 2). Experiments in which animals with permanently implanted electrodes stimulate particular regions of their own brain provide the main evidence that the MFB is a critical focus of reward, if maximal effect from minimum stimulation is used as the criterion (Olds & Olds, 1963). In these studies, electrodes placed anywhere along the MFB produced strong positive reinforcing effects; in some cases, rates of self-stimulation exceeded 8000 responses per hour. Other experiments reveal that rewarding MFB stimulation possesses a second critical attribute of conventional reinforcing agents. If an appropriate goal object is present, stimulation of specific sites in the MFB, particularly in the hypothalamic area, will elicit species-typical consummatory reactions (for a review, see Glickman & Schiff, 1967). Hence, in the presence of food, positive MFB stimulation at the level of the ventromedial nucleus may elicit eating (Hoebel & Teitelbaum, 1962; Margules & Olds, 1962), whereas stimulation of a rewarding posterior hypothalamic site in the presence of a mate may elicit sexual behavior (Caggiula & Hoebel, 1966). Predispositions to gnaw, nest, drink, and even to attack are potentiated by stimulation of particular rewarding sites. Lesions of the MFB, on the other hand, have the expected opposite effects and may cause severe deficits both in goal-directed behavior and consummatory reactions (Morgane, 1961; Teitelbaum & Epstein, 1962).

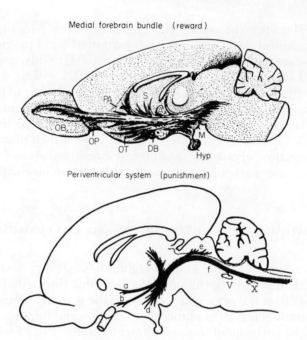

FIG. 1. Diagrams representing medial forebrain bundle (presumed substrate of reward mechanism) and periventricular system of fibers (presumed substrate of punishment mechanism) in a generalized and primitive mammalian brain (sagittal plane). Some abbreviations are as follows: Upper—A, anterior commissure; DB, nucleus of the diagonal band; M, mammillary body; OP, olfactory peduncle; PA, parolfactory area; S, septum. Lower—a, paraventricular n; b, supraoptic n; c, dorsomedial thalamus; d, posterior hypothalamus; e, tectum of midbrain; f, motor nuclei of cranial nerves. (From Le Gros Clark, Beattie, Riddoch, & Dott, 1938.)

Stimulation of the PVS similarly produces the characteristic effects of conventional punishing agents (Olds, 1962). On the reflex side, PVS stimulation elicits species-typical reactions to pain (e.g., jumping, biting, and vocalization). In its effects on goal-directed behavior, response-contingent stimulation of the PVS causes suppression when it is applied and facilitation when it is withheld. Finally, both PVS and MFB stimulation resemble conventional reinforcers in their ability to establish conditioned or secondary reinforcing properties in closely preceding neutral stimuli (Delgado, Roberts, & Miller, 1954; Stein, 1958). Taken together, all these observations provide strong indirect evidence, but not final proof, for the idea that conventional reinforcing agents act via the MFB and PVS and their connections to exert their behavioral effects. To prove this idea, it must be demonstrated that conventional reinforcers cause selective changes in the electrical (or chemical) activity of the MFB or PVS, and that these changes are necessary and sufficient for the reinforcement of behavior.

The general anatomical organization of the reward and punishment systems has been elucidated by Nauta (1960; 1963; 1964) in an important series of papers. In his work, Nauta describes a "limbic system–midbrain circuit" which is assumed to give behavior its "long term anticipatory qualities" (Fig. 3). The MFB and PVS are major pathways in this circuit. Turning first to the parts of the system related to reward or behavioral facilitation, we note that the MFB is a phylo-

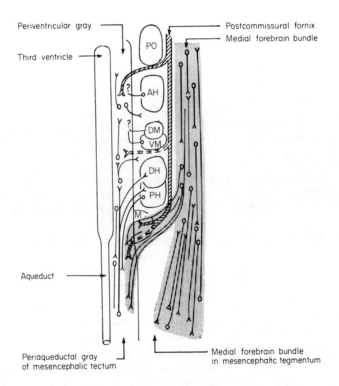

FIG. 2.   Diagrams of medial forebrain bundle (stippled) and periventricular system of fibers in horizontal plane. The scheme of organization shown here conceives of the hypothalamus as three longitudinally arranged columns—a periventricular stratum, a medial zone, and a lateral zone. Fiber bundles in the periventricular and lateral zones flank the medial zone which is devoid of major fiber bundles but does contain several prominent nuclei. Oblique lines denote the fornix system. AH, anterior hypothalamic area; DH, dorsal hypothalamic area; DM, dorsomedial nucleus; M, mammillary nuclei; PH, posterior hypothalamic area; PO, preoptic region; VM, ventromedial nucleus. (From Sutin, 1966.)

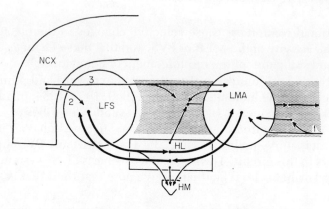

F<small>IG</small>. 3. Diagram of Nauta's limbic system-midbrain circuit. The lateral hypothalamus (HL) is shown as an intermediate relay region between the limbic forebrain structures (LFS) and the paramedian reticular ("limbic") midbrain area (LMA). Heavy arrows indicate prominent neural pathways involved in the limbic system-midbrain
circuit. The medial hypothalamic regions (HM) are connected with the circuit both directly and via neurons of the lateral hypothalamus. Thalamic afferents to the hypothalamus (see text) are not shown in the diagram. Afferent pathways to the circuit include (a)
the primordal lemniscus system (arrow 1) and (b) neocortical projections arising mainly
in frontal and temporal lobes (arrows 2 and 3). Olfactory afferents (not shown) probably
reach the circuit mainly from the olfactory piriform cortex, joining the descending limb
of the circuit. Descending efferent pathways from the circuit arise in both the hypothalamus and limbic midbrain area. Such pathways reach visceral and somatic motor neurons only via relays in the reticular formation (stippled). (From Nauta, 1963.)

genetically old, multisynaptic system of fibers which follows a sagittal
path ventrally through the brain, connecting olfactory, cortical, and
limbic forebrain structures with a circumscribed paramedian region of
the midbrain. This region, which Nauta (1960) terms the "limbic midbrain area," encompasses the ventral tegmental area of Tsai, the ventral half of the periaqueductal gray substance, and the reticular cell
groups of Bechterew and Gudden. In its passage between forebrain
and midbrain, the MFB traverses the lateral zone of the hypothalamus
and preoptic region. The MFB may thus be regarded as a system of
reciprocal connections between limbic forebrain structures (broadly
defined to include prefrontal and ventral temporal cortex) and the
limbic midbrain area, with the lateral hypothalamic area providing an
important way station in this two-way circuit.

Like the MFB, the PVS appears to provide connections between
cortical and limbic forebrain structures at one pole and a dorsomedial
region of the midbrain at the other (Nauta, 1963). In this punishment
or behavioral suppressant system, medial regions of hypothalamus

and thalamus form the main diencephalic way station. From the central gray midbrain substance, fibers ascend (and descend) via the dorsal longitudinal fasciculus of Schütz and distribute to medial thalamic cell groups, including the dorsomedial nucleus, and to the caudal part of the medial hypothalamic region. Fibers descend from orbitofrontal cortex to thalamus, hypothalamus, and midbrain by way of the basal forebrain region (Clemente & Sterman, 1967; Kaada, 1951), and in large volume from amygdala via the ventromedial amygdalofugal fiber system and stria terminalis to medial hypothalamus. A system of fine fibers connects medial thalamus and at least dorsal regions of the medial hypothalamus (Nauta, 1963).

Reward and punishment elements may interconnect at a number of points. Various forebrain structures (for example, amygdala) receive fibers from the MFB and send fibers to the medial hypothalamus and dorsomedial thalamus. In the diencephalon the situation is controversial. According to Nauta (1958), numerous short fibers project from lateral to medial hypothalamus; according to Wolf and Sutin (1966), lesions of the lateral hypothalamus do not cause fiber degeneration in the ventromedial hypothalamus. In the reverse direction, a long-sought pathway from ventromedial to lateral hypothalamus has recently been described (Arees & Mayer, 1967). Besides such intrahypothalamic connections, there exists a thalamo-hypothalamic pathway leading from the dorsomedial nucleus of the thalamus to the lateral hypothalamus (Nauta, 1963). Finally, Nauta (1958) showed that periaqueductal lesions in the midbrain caused degeneration of fibers into the midbrain limbic region and suggested that these fibers might interrelate the periventricular system with cells of origin of the MFB. Clearly, even this partial outline of interconnections provides a substantial anatomical basis for the assumption of reciprocal relationship between reward and punishment systems.

II. PHARMACOLOGY OF THE REWARD SYSTEM

The action of drugs on the reward system may be studied conveniently by use of the self-stimulation method of Olds and Milner (1954). In this method, an animal performs a predesignated response to deliver electrical stimulation through implanted electrodes to the MFB or some other reward area. The pharmacology of the self-stimulation system has been reviewed in detail elsewhere (Stein, 1962; Stein, 1964b; Stein, 1967a). In general, on systemic administration, drugs that influence central adrenergic transmission have the largest and most selective effects on self-stimulation behavior. Substances that release norepinephrine rapidly from stores in the brain (amphetamine, α-methyl-tyrosine, tetrabenazine in combination with a monoamine oxidase inhibitor) facilitate self-stimulation. Conversely, drugs that deplete the brain of norepinephrine (reserpine, α-methyl-tyrosine) or drugs that block adrenergic transmission (chlorpromazine, haloperidol) suppress self-stimulation. Furthermore, if brain levels of norepinephrine are increased by administration of a monoamine oxidase inhibitor, or if the rebinding of released norepinephrine is retarded by imipramine-like drugs, the facilitatory action of amphetamine on self-stimulation is greatly increased. On the other hand, lowering the level of norepinephrine in the brain by administration of reserpine or α-methyl-tyrosine greatly decreases the facilitating effect of amphetamine. Finally, it is known that amphetamine closely resembles norepinephrine in chemical structure; both are derivatives of phenethylamine, the basic structure of compounds possessing sympathomimetic activity. If the reward-facilitating action of amphetamine depends on its similarity to norepinephrine, then phenethylamine, the structure they have in common, ought also to facilitate self-stimulation. As predicted, the effects of amphetamine on self-stimulation are mimicked by phenethylamine when inactivation of this substance is prevented by prior treatment with a monoamine oxidase inhibitor (Stein, 1964b; Stein, 1964c).

III. IDENTIFICATION OF AN ASCENDING ADRENERGIC PATHWAY IN THE REWARD SYSTEM

All of the foregoing evidence is compatible with the idea that the reward mechanism contains a system of adrenergic synapses that are highly sensitive to pharmacological manipulation. Enhancement of noradrenergic transmission at these synapses facilitates behavior, and impairment of noradrenergic transmission suppresses behavior. In all probability, these synapses are the major site of action in the brain at which amphetamine and chlorpromazine exert their effects on goal-directed behavior (Stein, 1967b).

Where are these synapses located? If the MFB in fact constitutes the principal pathway of the reward system as suggested above, the adrenergic synapses in question evidently have already been described by a group of Swedish workers at the Karolinska Institute (Fuxe, 1965; Hillarp, Fuxe, & Dahlström, 1966). Using a histochemical technique for visualizing catecholamines at the cellular level, these investigators report a system of norepinephrine-containing neurons whose cell bodies have their origin in Nauta's limbic midbrain area and whose fibers ascend in the MFB and terminate at adrenergic synapses in the hypothalamus, limbic lobe, and neocortex. In other words, the site of origin and pattern of distribution of this adrenergic system (especially, the cell group A10, which has its origin principally in Tsai's area) closely resemble the main ascending limb of Nauta's limbic system midbrain circuit. Using a different technique Heller, Seiden, and Moore (1966) independently confirmed the existence of this ascending fiber system. These workers lesioned the MFB on one side at the level of the lateral hypothalamus and then assayed different regions of the brain for changes in norepinephrine content. Because the axons in the MFB are largely uncrossed, it was possible to compare norepinephrine levels on the lesioned and nonlesioned sides. Norepinephrine was extensively depleted by the lesion, but only in forebrain structures on the lesioned side; control lesions in the medial hypothalamus caused no important depletion of norepinephrine. These results confirm the presence of norepinephrine-containing fibers in the MFB; in addition, they validate the conclusion that these fibers comprise an ascending system, since decreases in norepinephrine occurred only in structures located above the lesions.

The close correspondence between the origin and distribution of this adrenergic system and the ascending portion of Nauta's circuit is impressive and could hardly be coincidental. Indeed, the MFB is the major diencephalic pathway of the vast majority of noradrenergic fibers that ascend to the forebrain. These considerations, coupled with evidence from pharmacological studies which indicate that self-stimulation is under adrenergic control, strongly support the idea that the Hillarp-Fuxe-Dahlström ascending adrenergic system may be identified with a system in the MFB that is responsible at least in part for the positive reinforcement of behavior (Fig. 4).

However, in apparent conflict with these anatomical and pharmacological studies are behavioral studies which suggest that the self-stimulation system is largely a descending one. For example, the rewarding effect of an implanted electrode is increasingly strong and requires decreasing amounts of current the more posteriorly it is placed along the MFB. More direct evidence has been sought in studies which attempt to determine the direction in which rewarding impulses pass through the MFB by the appropriate positioning of lesions. In general, when lesions are placed posteriorly to the site of stimulation, a greater decrement and less recovery is obtained in the rate of self-stimulation than when the position of stimulating elec-

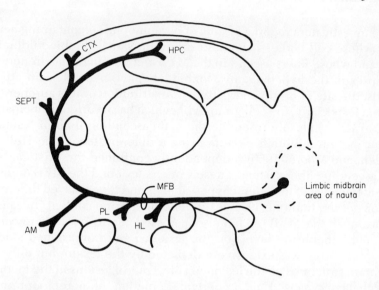

FIG. 4. Ascending adrenergic pathway of reward mechanism of self-stimulation system. Norepinephrine-containing neurons originating in Nauta's limbic midbrain area ascend in the medial forebrain bundle (MFB) and terminate in hypothalamus (HL), preoptic area (PL), amygdala (AM), septum (SEPT), hippocampus (HPC), and neocortex (CTX). (From Stein, 1967a.)

trode and lesions are reversed (Olds & Olds, 1964; work of Fonberg_ reported in Miller, 1963; Ward, 1960; Ward, 1961). Because rostrally going impulses should bypass a posterior lesion, the conclusion from these studies is that rewarding impulses travel caudally in the MFB. Indeed, some investigators, apparently impressed more by eventual recovery from the effects of lesions than by the large deficits they initially produce, conclude that the MFB is not critical for self-stimulation and that the reward system is characterized by "redundancy" and "plasticity" (Boyd & Gardner, 1967; Lorens, 1966; Valenstein, 1966). On the other hand, Morgane (1964) has suggested that lesions anywhere in the trajectory of the MFB, either anterior or posterior to the stimulating electrode, cause substantial suppression of self-stimulation.

This confusing array of results and conclusions suggests that confounding factors may be operative in the electrolytic lesion experiments. Time is usually allowed for recovery between the lesion and the test, during which degeneration could occur. If so, then nerve fibers directly under the stimulating electrodes could be destroyed. Furthermore, since the MFB is compact posteriorly and fans out anteriorly, posterior lesions would result in greater total destruction of the system simply as a result of the geometry of the fiber distribution. In addition to fiber degeneration, other changes (such as denervation supersensitivity) may occur during the course of recovery which could facilitate, as well as inhibit, self-stimulation. Finally, the low survival rates in many of these experiments produce a selection bias in favor of partial lesions, since animals with the most complete lesions of the MFB are the most likely to die (Teitelbaum & Epstein, 1962). The potential interaction of all these factors in the lesion experiments makes it easy to understand why conflicting results have appeared in the literature.

Studies which involve no opportunity for degeneration and the other complications that may develop during a recovery period may 'be more informative about the direction of traffic flow. In preliminary studies performed in collaboration with Dr. B. D. Berger, our approach has been to make "reversible lesions" by direct application of local anesthetics to the MFB. In one experiment, cannulas are implanted in the MFB both anteriorly and posteriorly to a stimulating electrode (Fig. 5). If xylocaine is injected through the anterior cannula, self-stimulation stops (Fig. 6). This suggests that the MFB conducts rewarding impulses anteriorly. Xylocaine introduced through the posterior cannula also suppresses self-stimulation, which suggests that rewarding impulses also may descend. In a complementary experiment, electrodes are implanted in the MFB anteriorly and posteriorly to a cannula. The animals work in a two-lever test chamber and are trained to self-stimulate concurrently at both rewarding sites by distributing their responses between the two levers. In this experiment, the same injection of xylocaine produces a block which is located anteriorly to one electrode and posteriorly to the other. Again, self-stimulation is suppressed by either upstream or downstream blockade. Both experiments thus indicate two-way traffic flow in the MFB. Although other explanations are possible, this conclusion is consistent with anatomical findings (Ban, 1964; Nauta, 1960), and it also explains the bidirectional deficits reported in some electrolytic lesion experiments (Boyd & Gardner, 1967; Morgane, 1964; Olds & Olds, 1964). From the point of view of biochemical mechanisms, however, the critical finding is that self-stimulation behavior appears to depend at least partly on ascending conduction in the MFB. Hence, studies of traffic flow do not contradict the idea that the MFB reward system contains an ascending adrenergic component (the Hillarp-Fuxe-Dahlström fiber system).

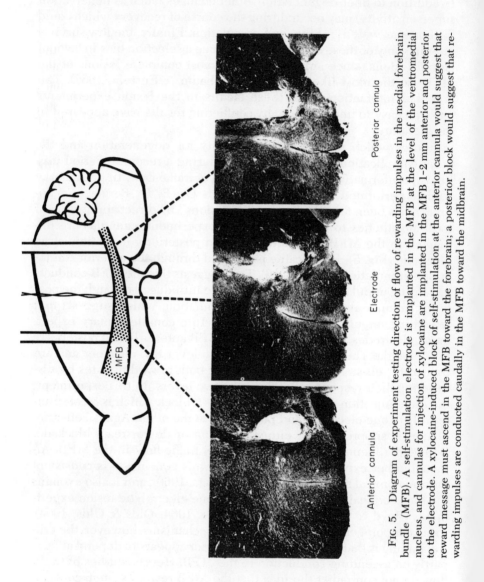

Anterior cannula   Electrode   Posterior cannula

FIG. 5.   Diagram of experiment testing direction of flow of rewarding impulses in the medial forebrain bundle (MFB). A self-stimulation electrode is implanted in the MFB at the level of the ventromedial nucleus, and cannulas for injection of xylocaine are implanted in the MFB 1–2 mm anterior and posterior to the electrode. A xylocaine-induced block of self-stimulation at the anterior cannula would suggest that reward message must ascend in the MFB toward the forebrain; a posterior block would suggest that rewarding impulses are conducted caudally in the MFB toward the midbrain.

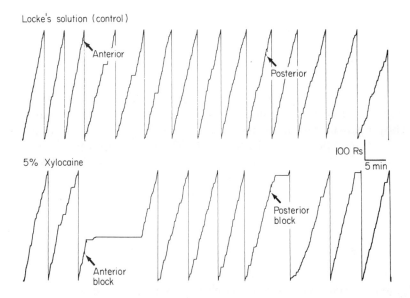

FIG. 6. Effects of anterior and posterior injections of xylocaine in the medial fore-brain bundle. Lower record: anterior injection blocks self-stimulation for more than 10 minutes; posterior injection also blocks self-stimulation but less effectively (this despite the fact that the posterior cannula was closer to the electrode than the anterior cannula). Upper record: control injections of Locke's solution have negligible effects. See Fig. 5 for design of experiment and histology.

IV. PERFUSION STUDIES

The next series of experiments, performed in collaboration with Dr. C. David Wise, was designed as a direct test of the idea that norepinephrine is released when the medial forebrain bundle reward system is activated. Using a permanently indwelling Gaddum push-pull cannula, Stein and Wise (1967) continuously perfused specific areas in the brains of unanesthetized rats with Ringer-Locke's solution for periods of up to six hours (Fig. 7). Among the areas perfused were the terminal sites of the medial forebrain bundle in rostral hypothalamus and amygdala. At intermittent periods, rewarding points in the medial forebrain bundle (as well as nonrewarding control points) were electrically stimulated in an attempt to release norepinephrine or its metabolites into the perfusate. In order to measure the small quantities of norepinephrine that might be released by rewarding stimulation, a sensitive radiotracer method was used (Glowinski, Kopin, & Axelrod, 1965). Forty-five minutes before the start of the perfusion experiment,

[14]C-labeled (41–250 μg) or tritiated norepinephrine (0.3 μg) was injected into the lateral ventricle. Regional and subcellular distribution studies suggest that the labeled norepinephrine introduced into the brain in this way mixes with the endogenous store and can be used as a tracer.

After a control period of 1–3 hours to allow the washout of radioactivity to stabilize, application of rewarding electrical stimulation caused substantial increases in the release of radioactivity in a large number of experiments (Figs. 8 and 9; Table I). Often there was a lag of about 15 minutes before the peak release occurred. Radioactivity levels declined after prolonged stimulation, due presumably to exhaustion of the reserve of radioactive material. When the current was turned off, the control base line was rapidly recovered.

Releases of radioactivity have been obtained only with highly rewarding electrodes which supported a self-stimulation rate of 1000 responses/hour or more (assessed in a self-stimulation test conducted before the perfusion experiment). Nonrewarding electrodes did not release radioactivity and, in some cases, if the stimulation was punishing or aversive, even inhibited its spontaneous release (Fig. 9E; Table I). In other control experiments, the radioactivity of cortical and thalamic perfusates did not increase during rewarding stimulation (Table I).

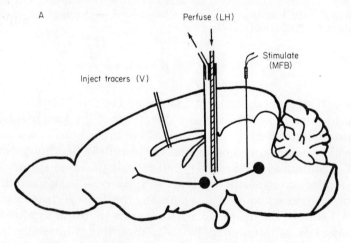

FIG. 7.   (A) Diagram of perfusion experiment showing relative locations of stimulating electrode in the medial forebrain bundle (MFB), perfusion cannula in lateral hypothalamus (LH), and needle for injection of radioisotopes in lateral ventricle (V) on an outline of rat brain. (B) The photograph shows the arrangement of the various devices on a rat's skull. (From Stein & Wise, 1969.)

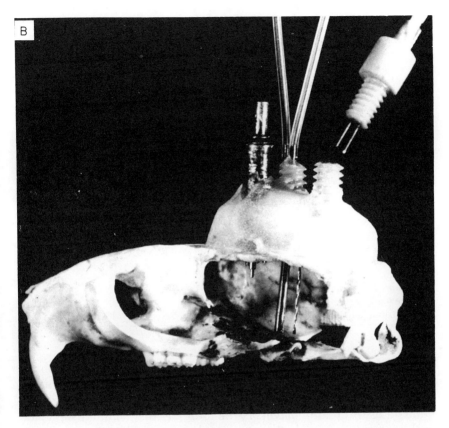

FIG. 7(B)

Chemical analyses of the perfusates revealed that O-methylated metabolites of norepinephrine accounted for most of the radioactivity (Table II). Interestingly, samples of perfusate collected during rewarding stimulation contained a higher proportion of metabolites than did the control samples. If it is correct to assume that the O-methylation of norepinephrine occurs mainly at the synapse, this shift toward metabolites perhaps indicates that during stimulation, the amount of norepinephrine released at synapses is increased relative to that which is washed out nonspecifically.

Taken together, these results and those of the foregoing experiments provide evidence that norepinephrine is released into the hypothalamus and forebrain from terminals of the medial forebrain bundle during rewarding stimulation. What is the physiological

TABLE I
Summary of Results of Perfusion Experiments

Comment	Cannula location	No. of animals	Mean self-stimulation rate (responses/hr)	Mean radioactivity ratio (stimulation/control)
Release of Radioactivity				
Rewarding stimulation,	Hypothalamus	20	4887	2.42
adequate perfusion	Amygdala	4	3242	3.02
No Release of Radioactivity				
Nonrewarding				
stimulation	Hypothalamus	9	210	.74
Inadequate perfusion	Cortex and thalamus	4	2822	.77
	Defective cannula	5	3390	.92
Rewarding stimulation,	Hypothalamus	8	2667	.95
adequate perfusion	Amygdala	2	2796	.72
Inhibition of Spontaneous Release of Radioactivity				
Nonrewarding or				
punishing stimulation	Hypothalamus	5	46	.17

significance of this release? Is the rewarding effect of medial forebrain bundle activation wholly or partially dependent on the release of norepinephrine into the forebrain? If so, does the rewarding effect depend on the excitation of cells in the forebrain that facilitate behavior, or the inhibition of cells that suppress behavior? These questions are taken up in more detail below (see Section VII). At this point it will suffice to indicate that a vast literature may be cited which demonstrates suppressor influences of the forebrain on behavior (Brutkowski, 1965; Clemente & Sterman, 1967; Hernández-Peón, Chávez-Ibarra, Morgane, & Timo-Iaria, 1963; Kaada, 1951). Hence, it is quite likely that norepinephrine released by rewarding stimulation acts mainly as an inhibitory transmitter, which depresses the activity of behaviorally suppressant cell groups in the forebrain. In other words, rewarding stimulation may facilitate behavior by a disinhibitory action.

V. PHARMACOLOGY OF THE PUNISHMENT SYSTEM

The effects of drugs on the punishment system may be studied conveniently in tests in which some easily measured response is sup-

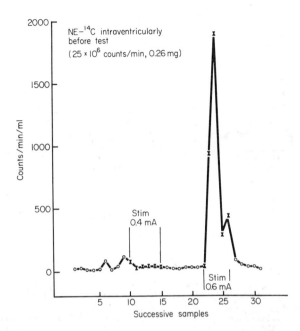

FIG. 8. Release of radioactive norepinephrine (NE) and metabolites from a hypotha-lamic perfusion site by a train of rewarding medial forebrain bundle stimulation (0.6 mA). The less rewarding 0.4 mA stimulus did not cause release in this test, but did in a second test four days later. (From Stein & Wise, unpublished data.)

pressed by punishment. Such behavioral suppression has been termed "passive avoidance" by Mowrer (1960), and any experimen-tally induced disruption or disinhibition of the suppression is referred to as a "passive avoidance deficit." In an elegant form of the passive avoidance test, animals are trained on a program in which punished and unpunished reinforcement schedules are alternated (Geller & Seifter, 1960; Fig. 10). In the unpunished schedule, a lever-press re-sponse is rewarded with milk at infrequent variable intervals; in the punished schedule which is signaled by a tone, every response is rewarded with milk and also punished with a brief electrical shock to the feet. The rate of response in the tone may be precisely regulated by the intensity of the shock, and any degree of behavioral suppres-sion may be obtained by suitable adjustment of shock level.

Geller (1962; 1964) and his associates (Geller, Kulak, & Seifter, 1962) have studied the effects of a variety of different psychoactive drugs in this test. In general, a substantial passive avoidance deficit is produced only by the minor tranquilizers or "antianxiety" agents, which include barbiturates, meprobamate, benzodiazepine deriva-

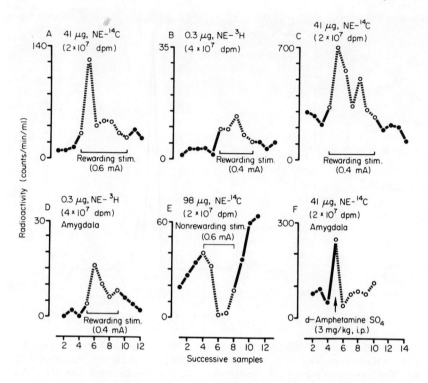

FIG. 9. Sample experiments illustrating effects of rewarding brain stimulation, nonrewarding stimulation, and amphetamine on the release of radioactivity into hypothalamic (A,B,C,E) and amygdaloid (D,F) perfusates. In (C) the monoamine oxidase inhibitor pargyline (50 mg/kg) was injected intraperitoneally 16 hours before the start of perfusion. The radioisotope tracer and dose used in each experiment are indicated (dpm, disintegrations/min). (From Stein & Wise, 1969.)

tives, and ethanol. Interestingly, the major tranquilizers or "antipsychotic" agents (e.g., chlorpromazine and other phenothiazine derivatives) do not have this effect and often cause a further suppression of punished behavior. Stimulant drugs of the amphetamine type also decrease the probability of the punished behavior, despite their facilitatory effects on positively reinforced behavior. Even the powerful analgesic morphine fails to disinhibit punished behavior in this test (Geller, Bachman, & Seifter, 1963; Kelleher & Morse, 1964).

In order to determine whether the passive avoidance deficit induced by tranquilizers is due to a specific antagonism of the effects of punishment, or whether it is due to a more general disinhibitory action, Margules and Stein (1967) studied the effects of the benzodiazepine derivative oxazepam (Serax) in several different situations using

TABLE II

Chemical Composition of Radioactivity Released in Control Periods
and During Rewarding Electrical Stimulation

Experiment	Radioactivity (dpm/ml)		Relative chemical composition (%)							
			Norepinephrine		Normethanephrine		O-Methylated deaminated metabolites		Catechol deaminated metabolites	
	Control	Stim.	Control	Stim.	Control	Stim.	Control	Stim.	Control	Stim.
Untreated (N = 5)	244	770	23.0	3.2	5.6	.6	65.0	87.0	6.0	9.0
Pargyline (N = 2)	434	4628	11.5	4.0	39.0	23.0	49.5	73.0	.0	.0

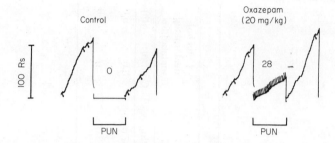

FIG. 10. Sample records of performance in Geller passive avoidance test. Lever-press responses (Rs) are cumulated over time: The slope of the curve at any point gives the response rate. Punishment periods of 3-minutes' duration, signaled by a tone (PUN), are flanked by equivalent periods of unpunished responding. Punished responses are numbered and indicated by upward strokes of the pen; presentations of the milk reward in the unpunished schedule are indicated by downward strokes of the pen. Oxazepam causes a marked disinhibition of punishment-suppressed behavior, but does not importantly influence unpunished behavior. (From Margules & Stein, unpublished data.)

different response measures and means of producing response suppression. Oxazepam caused a marked increase in the occurrence of previously suppressed behavior regardless of whether the behavior was inhibited by foot shock, nonreward (extinction), punishing brain stimulation, or the bitter taste of quinine. Furthermore, oxazepam caused a substantial disinhibition of feeding behavior in satiated rats. Margules and Stein (1967) concluded that the disinhibitory action of oxazepam and related tranquilizers is clearly a general one. They also suggested that tranquilizers may act on a final common pathway for the suppression of behavior, although the possibility that different inhibitory pathways in the brain have a common pharmacology was not excluded.

VI. LESIONS AND CHOLINERGIC STIMULATION OF MEDIAL HYPOTHALAMUS

The observation that oxazepam will cause satiated animals to eat suggested that the drugs may act directly or indirectly on the so-called "satiety center" of the hypothalamus—the ventromedial nucleus (Anand & Brobeck, 1951). In order to test this idea, Margules and Stein (1967; 1968) applied various crystalline substances directly to the medial hypothalamus through permanently indwelling cannulas. The passive avoidance test of Geller and Seifter (1960) was used as the behavioral indicator.

Damage produced by the penetration of cannulas into ventromedial regions of the hypothalamus caused a very large increase in the rate of punished responses (Fig. 11). Penetration of cannulas to the level of the dorsomedial nucleus did not produce a passive avoidance deficit; however, bilateral damage of the periventricular system caused large and permanent deficits (Margules & Stein, 1968). These findings confirm the earlier work of Kaada, Rasmussen, and Kreim (1962). Direct application of the cholinomimetic agents carbachol and physostigmine to the medial hypothalamic area restored the inhibitory effect of punishment, and usually depressed the rate of unpunished behavior as well (Fig. 11). The cholinergic blocking agent atropine methyl nitrate had the expected opposite effect and caused a further disinhibition of punished behavior (Fig. 11). These results support the idea that the punishment system has a critical focus in the medial hypothalamus. They suggest, furthermore, that the system forms cholinergic synapses at this level. Finally, since lesions have the same effect as cholinergic blockade, these behaviorally inhibitory synapses are likely to be excitatory at the cellular level.

In another experiment, Margules and Stein (1967) observed that the suppressant effects of carbachol applications to the medial hypothalamus could be antagonized by a systemic injection of oxazepam (Fig. 12). The finding that oxazepam retains its activity despite intense cholinergic activation of the medial hypothalamus suggests that the drug acts at the same site efferent to the medial hypothalamus.

VII. LESIONS AND ADRENERGIC STIMULATION OF THE AMYGDALA

As indicated above, the amygdala enjoys a strategic location in Nauta's limbic system–midbrain circuit and thus is favorably placed to influence both reward and punishment processes. Behavioral and physiological studies of amygdaloid function support these inferences from anatomy. Damage to the amygdala produces a substantial passive avoidance deficit (Brutkowski, 1965; Margules, 1968; Margules, Morris, & Stein, 1967; Ursin, 1965), which suggests that this region is an important suppressor or punishment area. Support for this suggestion is provided by the finding that electrical stimulation of certain amygdaloid sites is punishing, but other points have been reported which produce mild rewarding effects as well (Kaada, 1951; Wurtz & Olds, 1963).

Histochemical studies indicate that the amygdala receives an adrenergic input from the MFB (Fuxe, 1965). Our perfusion studies, reported above, indicate that rewarding MFB stimulation causes release

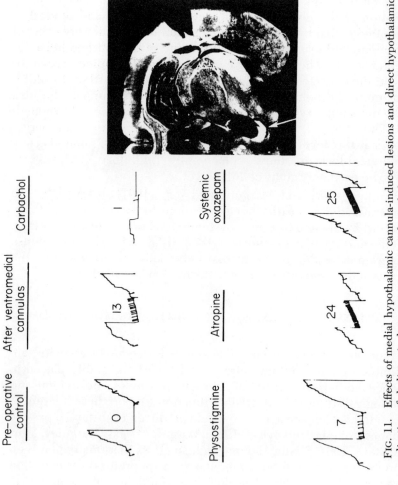

FIG. 11.   Effects of medial hypothalamic cannula-induced lesions and direct hypothalamic application of cholinergic drugs on passive avoidance behavior. See Fig. 10 for further explanation. The photomicrograph at the right shows the tip of the cannula in the region of the ventromedial nucleus of the hypothalamus. (From Margules & Stein, unpublished data.)

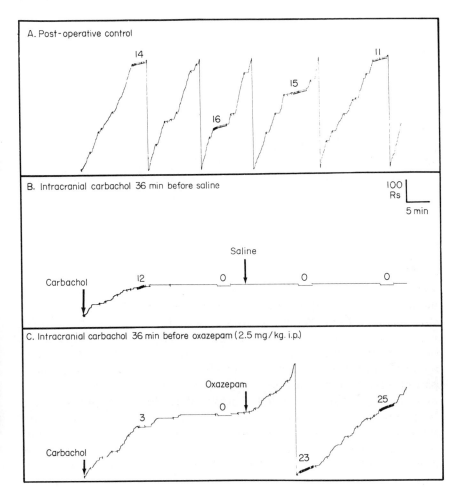

FIG. 12.   Antagonism of response suppression induced by medial hypothalamic application of carbachol by systemic injection of oxazepam. Since oxazepam releases punishment-suppressed behavior despite intense cholinergic activation of the ventromedial nucleus, the drug must act at some point efferent to this structure. (From Margules & Stein, 1967.)

of norepinephrine and its metabolites into an amygdaloid perfusate. In addition, preliminary experiments indicate that self-stimulation of the MFB causes rapid turnover of norepinephrine in the amygdala (Stein, Margules, Wise, & Morris, 1968; Wise & Stein, unpublished data). Heightened noradrenergic transmission in the amygdala thus appears to result from activation of the MFB reward system. What is the function of norepinephrine at these synapses between the MFB and the amygdala? There are at least two possibilities. Norepinephrine could be an excitatory transmitter which activates behaviorally facilitatory cell groups in the amygdala when the MFB is stimulated. Or norepinephrine could be an inhibitory transmitter, which facilitates behavior indirectly by inhibition of suppressor cell groups in the amygdala.

An experiment by Margules (1968) suggests that norepinephrine plays an inhibitory role in the amygdala. Cannulas were implanted bilaterally in the amygdala of rats that previously were trained in the Geller passive avoidance test. Damage produced by penetration of the cannulas into the amygdala caused a passive avoidance deficit, in confirmation of the earlier work of Ursin (1965) and Brutkowski (1965). Direct application of *l*-norepinephrine HCl crystals to the amygdala further decreased the suppressant effect of punishment very markedly, whereas application of *d*-norepinephrine HCl and sodium chloride had little or no effect. More recent studies (Stein *et al.*, 1968) indicate that *l*-epinephrine is nearly as active as *l*-norepinephrine, but that dopamine and dopa are almost inactive (Fig. 13). These experiments thus confirm earlier work which indicates that the amygdala is part of a punishment or behavior-suppressant system. They suggest, in addition, that the amygdala is under the inhibitory control of the MFB reward system, and that this control is exerted at noradrenergic synapses. Release of norepinephrine at these synapses inhibits the amygdala and presumably reduces its contribution to the PVS suppressor mechanism via medial hypothalamic and dorsomedial thalamic relays.

Since the MFB forms noradrenergic synapses in a number of forebrain areas, it is tempting to generalize these MFB–amygdala relationships and assume that activation of the MFB reward system causes a widespread noradrenergic inhibition of forebrain suppressor cell groups. According to this view, a primitive or basic tendency to approach stimuli in the environment is held in check by forebrain inhibition in the mature organism. (Prior to maturation of the connections between the forebrain and the PVS, the infant organism responds indiscriminately to all stimuli.) Stimuli associated with reward selectively release approach behavior from forebrain inhibition by activation of the MFB. The consequent liberation of norepinephrine deactivates these forebrain regions and thereby lessens their contribution to the activity of the PVS suppressor mechanism (Fig. 14).

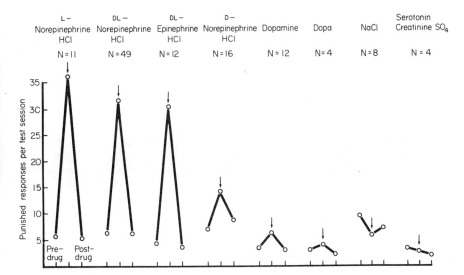

FIG. 13. Effects on punishment-suppressed behavior of direct application of crystalline substances to the amygdala. Animals were dosed twice, 15 minutes before and immediately before the start of the test, with approximately 10 μg of crystalline material on each side. (Data from Stein *et al.*, 1968.)

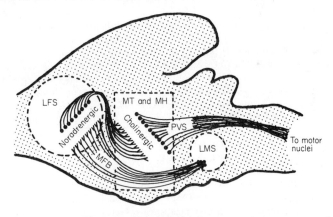

FIG. 14. Diagram representing hypothetical relationships between reward and punishment mechanisms inferred from chemical stimulation experiments of Margules and Stein (1967), Margules (1968), and Stein *et al.* (1968). A rewarding stimulus releases behavior from periventricular system (PVS) suppression by the following sequence of events: (1) Activation of medial forebrain bundle (MFB) by stimuli previously associated with reward (or the avoidance of punishment) causes release of norepinephrine into amygdala and other forebrain suppressor areas (LFS). (2) Inhibitory action of norepinephrine suppresses activity of the LFS, thus reducing its cholinergically mediated excitation of medial thalamus and hypothalamus (MT & MH). (3) Decreased cholinergic transmission at synapses in MT and MH lessens the activity in the periventricular system, thereby reducing its inhibitory influence on motor nuclei of the brain stem.

ACKNOWLEDGMENT

The careful technical assistance of William J. Carmint, Herman Morris, and Alfred T. Shropshire is gratefully acknowledged.

REFERENCES

Anand, B. K., & Brobeck, J. R. Hypothalamic control of food intake. *Yale J. Biol. Med.*, 1951, **24**, 123-140.

Arees, E. A., & Mayer, J. Anatomical connections between medial and lateral regions of the hypothalamus concerned with food intake. *Science*, 1967, **157**, 1574-1575.

Ban, T. The hypothalamus, especially on its fiber connections, and the septo-preoptico-hypothalamic system. *Med. J. Osaka Univ.*, 1964, **15**, 1-83.

Bentham, J. An introduction to the principles of morals and legislation, 1789. In L. J. Lafleur (Ed.), New York: Hafner, 1948.

Bitterman, M. E. Learning in animals. In H. Helson & W. Bevan (Eds.), *Contemporary approaches to psychology.* Princeton, N.J.: Van Nostrand, 1967. Pp. 139-179.

Boyd, E. S., & Gardner, L. C. Effect of some brain lesions on intracranial self-stimulation in the rat. *Amer. J. Physiol.*, 1967, **213**, 1044-1052.

Brown, T. G. On the nature of the fundamental activity of the nervous centres; together with an analysis of the conditioning of rhythmic activity in progression, and a theory of the evolution of function in the nervous system. *J. Physiol. (London)*, 1914, **48**, 18-46.

Brutkowski, S. Functions of prefrontal cortex in animals. *Physiol. Rev.*, 1965, **45**, 721-746.

Caggiula, A. R., & Hoebel, B. G. "Copulation-reward site" in the posterior hypothalamus. *Science*, 1966, **153**, 1284-1285.

Clemente, C. D., & Sterman, M. B. Basal forebrain mechanisms for internal inhibition and sleep. In S. S. Kety (Ed.), *Sleep and altered states of consciousness.* New York: Assoc. Res. Nerv. Ment. Dis., 1967. Pp. 127-147.

Delgado, J. M. R., Roberts, W. W., & Miller, N. E. Learning motivated by electrical stimulation of the brain. *Am. J. Physiol.*, 1954, **179**, 587-593.

Fuxe, K. The distribution of monoamine nerve terminals in the central nervous system. *Acta Physiol. Scand.*, 1965, **64**, Suppl. 247, 37-85.

Geller, I. Use of approach avoidance behavior (conflict) for evaluating depressant drugs. In J. H. Nodine & J. H. Moyer (Eds.), *First Hahnemann symposium on psychosomatic medicine.* Philadelphia: Lea & Febiger, 1962. Pp. 267-274.

Geller, I. Relative potencies of benzodiazepines as measured by their effects on conflict behavior. *Arch. int. Pharmacodyn.*, 1964, **149**, 243-247.

Geller, I., Bachman, E., & Seifter, J. Effects of reserpine and morphine on behavior suppressed by punishment. *Life Sci.*, 1963, **4**, 226-231.

Geller, I., Kulak, J. T., Jr., & Seifter, J. The effects of chlordiazepoxide and chlorpromazine on a punishment discrimination. *Psychopharmacologia*, 1962, **3**, 374-385.

Geller, I., & Seifter, J. The effects of meprobamate, barbiturates, *d*-amphetamine and promazine on experimentally induced conflict in the rat. *Psychopharmacologia*, 1960, **1**, 482-492.

Glickman, S. E., & Schiff, B. B. A biological theory of reinforcement. *Psychol. Rev.*, 1967, **74**, 81-109.

Glowinski, J., Kopin, I. J., & Axelrod, J. Metabolism of [³H]norepinephrine in the rat brain. *J. Neurochem.*, 1965, 12, 25-30.

Heller, A., Seiden, L. S., & Moore, R. Y. Regional effects of lateral hypothalamic lesions in brain norepinephrine in the cat. *Int. J. Neuropharmacol.*, 1966, 5, 91-101.

Hernández-Peón, R. Attention, sleep, motivation, and behavior. In R. G. Heath (Ed.), *The role of pleasure in behavior*. New York: Harper, 1964. Pp. 195-217.

Hernández-Peón, R., Chávez-Ibarra, G., Morgane, P., & Timo-Iaria, C. Limbic cholinergic pathways involved in sleep and emotional behavior. *Exp. Neurol.*, 1963, 8, 93-111.

Hess, W. R. *Das Zwischenhirn: Syndrome, Lokalisationen, Functionen.* (2nd ed.) Basel: Schwabe, 1954.

Hillarp, N. A., Fuxe, K., & Dahlström, A. Demonstration and mapping of central neurons containing dopamine, noradrenaline, and 5-hydroxy-tryptamine and their reactions to psychopharmaca. *Pharmacol. Rev.*, 1966, 18, 727-741.

Hoebel, B. G., & Teitelbaum, P. Hypothalamic control of feeding and self-stimulation. *Science*, 1962, 135-375.

Kaada, B. R. Somato-motor, autonomic and electrocorticographic responses to electrical stimulation of rhinencephalic and other structures in primates, cat, and dog. *Acta Physiol. Scand.*, 1951, 24, Suppl. 83, 1-285.

Kaada, B. R., Rasmussen, E. W., & Kveim, O. Impaired acquisition of passive avoidance behavior by subcallosal, septal, hypothalamic, and insular lesions in rats. *J. comp. physiol. Psychol.*, 1962, 55, 661-670.

Kelleher, R. T., & Morse, W. H. Escape behavior and punished behavior. *Fed. Proc.*, 1964, 23, 808-817.

Le Gros Clark, W. E., Beattie, J., Riddoch, G., & Dott, N. M. *The hypothalamus.* Edinburgh and London: Oliver & Boyd, 1938.

Lorens, S. A. Effect of lesions in the central nervous system on lateral hypothalamic self-stimulation in the rat. *J. comp. physiol. Psychol.*, 1966, 62, 256-262.

Magoun, H. W. *The waking brain.* Springfield, Ill.: Thomas, 1958.

Margules, D. L. Adrenergic basis of inhibition between reward and punishment in amygdala. *J. comp. physiol. Psychol.*, 1968, in press.

Margules, D. L., Morris, H., & Stein, L. Amygdala and midbrain tegmentum control of punishment. *Amer. Psychologist*, 1967, 22, 515.

Margules, D. L., & Olds, J. Identical "feeding" and "rewarding" systems in the lateral hypothalamus of rats. *Science*, 1962, 135, 374-375.

Margules, D. L., & Stein, L. Neuroleptics vs. tranquilizers: Evidence from animal behavior studies of mode and site of action. In H. Brill *et al.* (Eds.), *Neuro-psychopharmacology.* Amsterdam: Excerpta Med. Found., 1967. Pp. 108-120.

Margules, D. L., & Stein, L. Cholinergic synapses in the ventromedial hypothalamus for the suppression of operant behavior by punishment and satiety. *J. comp. physiol. Psychol.*, 1969, 67, 327-335.

Miller, N. E. Some motivational effects of electrical and chemical stimulation of the brain. *Electroencephalog. clin. Neurophysiol.*, 1963, 24, Suppl., 247-259.

Morgane, P. J. Electrophysiological studies of feeding and satiety centers in the rat. *Am. J. Physiol.*, 1961, 201, 838-844.

Morgane, P. J. Limbic-hypothalamic-midbrain interaction in thirst and thirst motivated behavior. In M. J. Wayner (Ed.), *Thirst—first international symposium. Thirst in the regulation of body water.* New York: Macmillan, 1964. Pp. 429-455.

Mowrer, O. H. *Learning theory and behavior.* New York: Wiley, 1960.

Nauta, W. J. H. Hypothalamic regulation of sleep in rats. An experimental study. *J. Neurophysiol.*, 1946, 9, 285-316.

Nauta, W. J. H. Hippocampal projections and related neural pathways to the mid-brain in the cat. *Brain*, 1958, 81, 319-340.

Nauta, W. J. H. Some neural pathways related to the limbic system. In E. R. Rainey & D. S. O'Doherty (Eds.), *Electrical studies on the unanesthetized brain.* New York: Harper (Hoeber), 1960. Pp. 1-16.

Nauta, W. J. H. Central nervous organization and the endocrine motor system. In A. V. Nalbandov (Ed.), *Advances in Neuroendrocrinology.* Urbana, Ill.: Univer. of Illinois Press, 1963. Pp. 5-21.

Nauta, W. J. H. Some efferent connections of the prefrontal cortex in the monkey. In J. M. Warren & K. Akert (Eds.), *The frontal cortex and behavior.* New York: McGraw-Hill, 1964. Pp. 397-409.

Olds, J. Hypothalamic substrates of reward. *Physiol. Rev.*, 1962, 42, 554-604.

Olds, J., & Milner, P. Positive reinforcement produced by electrical stimulation of septal area and other regions of the rat brain. *J. comp. physiol. Psychol.*, 1954, 47, 419-427.

Olds, J., & Olds, M. E. Approach-avoidance analysis of rat diencephalon. *J. comp. Neurol.*, 1963, 120, 259-295.

Olds, J., & Olds, M. E. The mechanisms of voluntary behavior. In R. G. Heath (Ed.), *The role of pleasure in behavior.* New York: Harper, 1964. Pp. 23-54.

Rado, S. *Psychoanalysis of Behavior.* New York: Grune & Stratton, 1956.

Stein, L. Secondary reinforcement established with subcortical stimulation. *Science*, 1958, 127, 466-467.

Stein, L. Effects and interactions of imipramine, chlorpromazine, reserpine, and amphetamine on self-stimulation: Possible neuro-physiological basis of depression. In J. Wortis (Ed.), *Recent advances in biological psychiatry.* New York: Plenum Press, 1962. Pp. 288-308.

Stein, L. Reciprocal action of reward and punishment mechanisms. In R. G. Heath (Ed.), *The role of pleasure in behavior.* New York: Harper, 1964. Pp. 113-139. (a)

Stein, L. Self-stimulation of the brain and the central stimulant action of amphetamine. *Fed. Proc.*, 1964, 23, 836. (b)

Stein, L. Amphetamine and neural reward mechanisms. *Ciba Found. Symp., anim. Behav. drug Action*, 1964, Pp. 91-113. (c)

Stein, L. Psychopharmacological substrates of mental depression. In S. Garrattini *et al.* (Eds.), *Antidepressant drugs.* Amsterdam: Excerpta Med. Found., 1967. Pp. 130-140. (a)

Stein, L. Noradrenergic substrates of positive reinforcement: Site of motivational action of amphetamine and chlorpromazine. In H. Brill *et al.* (Eds.), *Neuro-psycho-pharmacology.* Amsterdam: Excerpta Med. Found., 1967. P. 765. (b)

Stein, L. Chemistry of reward and punishment. In D. H. Efron (Ed.), *Proc. 1968 Meeting of Am. Coll. Neuropsychopharmacol.* Washington, D.C.: U.S. Government Printing Office, in press.

Stein, L., Margules, D. L. Wise, C. D., & Morris, H. Noradrenergic inhibition of amygdala by the medial forebrain bundle reward system. *Fed. Proc.*, 1968, 27, 273.

Stein, L., & Wise, C. D. Release of hypothalamic norepinephrine by rewarding electrical stimulation or amphetamine in the unanesthetized rat. *Fed. Proc.*, 1967, 26, 651.

Stein, L., & Wise, C. D. Release of norepinephrine from hypothalamus and amygdala by rewarding stimulation of the medial forebrain bundle. *J. comp. physiol. Psychol.*, 1969, 67, 189-198.

Sutin, J. The periventricular stratum of the hypothalamus. *Int. Rev. Neurobiol.*, 1966, 263-300.

Teitelbaum, P., & Epstein, A. N. The lateral hypothalamic syndrome. Recovery of feeding and drinking after lateral hypothalamic lesions. *Psychol. Rev.*, 1962, 69, 74-90.

Thorndike, E. L. The psychology of learning. In *Educational psychology*. New York: Teachers College, Columbia Univer., 1913.

Ursin, H. The effect of amygdaloid lesions on flight and defense behavior in cats. *Exp. Neurol.*, 1965, 11, 61-79.

Valenstein, E. S. The anatomical locus of reinforcement. In E. Stellar & J. M. Sprague (Eds.), *Progress in physiological psychology*. New York: Academic Press, 1966. Pp. 149-190.

Ward, H. P. Basal tegmental self-stimulation after septal ablation in rats. *A.M.A. Arch. Neurol. Psychiat.*, 1960, 3, 158-162.

Ward, H. P. Tegmental self-stimulation after amygdaloid ablation. *A.M.A. Arch. Neurol. Psychiat.*, 1961, 4, 657-659.

Wolf, G., & Sutin, J. Fiber degeneration after lateral hypothalamic lesions in the rat. *J. comp. Neurol.*, 1966, 127, 137-156.

Wurtz, R. H., & Olds, J. Amygdaloid stimulation and operant reinforcement in the rat. *J. comp. physiol. Psychol.*, 1963, 56, 941-949.

CHAPTER 12

Plasticity in Aplysia Neurons and Some Simple Neuronal Models of Learning[1]

IRVING KUPFERMANN AND HAROLD PINSKER

I. INTRODUCTION

A. The Cellular Approach and the Use of Simplified Preparations

Neuropsychologists attempt to understand the nature of learning and reinforcement in terms of the activity of the nervous system. Some of the earliest speculation about the neurological basis of learning suggested that it was associated with alterations in the functional

[1]The material in this chapter is based on a paper presented by the authors as part of a symposium on "Cellular Mechanisms of Learning" at the American Psychological Association Annual Convention in September, 1967. Original research reported was supported, in part, by NINDB grant R01 NB 07621-02 EPB, and NIH grant NB 05980-02. In addition, Dr. Harold Pinsker was supported by the NIMH Research Training Program in Psychiatry and the Biological Sciences at New York University Medical School. The authors thank Dr. Eric Kandel and Dr. William Alden Spencer for their helpful comments on this chapter. The figures were prepared by S. Smith and K. Hilten.

properties of single neurons, i.e., plastic changes (Konorski, 1948; Tanzi, 1893). If this reasonable assumption were accepted the problem of the neurophysiological basis of reinforcement would involve, in part, a description of how a reinforcing stimulus leads to those plastic changes that underly learning associated with the reinforcement.

A recent experimental approach to the neurological basis of learning and reinforcement utilizes microelectrode techniques in order to record the electrical activity of single nerve cells in the brain. Several studies have found alterations in cellular activity following the application of reinforcing stimuli (e.g., Jasper, Ricci, & Doane, 1960; Morrell, 1960; Olds, 1965). However, because of the complexity of the mammalian brain, it is extremely difficult to analyze and specify the plastic mechanisms that underly such alterations. For this reason a number of investigators have utilized invertebrate or simplified vertebrate preparations to study learning and neuronal plasticity (e.g., Eisenstein & Cohen, 1965; Horridge, 1964; Hoyle, 1965; Kandel & Tauc, 1965a; Spencer, Thompson, & Neilson, 1966; for a review, see Kandel & Spencer, 1968). In some invertebrate preparations it is possible to investigate cellular processes in detail, and thereby test specific hypotheses about plastic mechanisms. In this chapter we will consider some of these hypotheses and review relevant data obtained primarily from studies of one particular invertebrate preparation: the marine mollusk, *Aplysia*.

Most neurophysiological studies of *Aplysia* have utilized the isolated abdominal ganglion, a discrete cluster of central nerve cells consisting of motor neurons, interneurons, and neurosecretory cells. These cells mediate a number of different behaviors such as egg laying, inking, and gill movement (Bottazzi & Enriques, 1900; Kupfermann, 1967; Kupfermann & Kandel, 1968). For a number of reasons, the abdominal ganglion has proved to be particularly useful for studying neural plasticity (cf. Bruner and Tauc, 1966; Kandel and Tauc, 1965a; Strumwasser, 1967). The ganglion consists of less than 2000 nerve cells, many of which are extremely large and easy to visualize. The size of the cells makes it possible to insert a glass microelectrode into a given cell and record its electrical activity for many hours or even days. Furthermore, 30 of the largest cells can be individually distinguished on the basis of position within the ganglion, appearance, and a number of physiological and anatomical properties (Frazier, Kandel, Kupfermann, Waziri, & Coggeshall, 1967). Thus, it is possible to experiment on the same homologous cell from ganglion to ganglion. Figure 1 shows a map of the identified cells, some of which will be referred to in the later discussion.

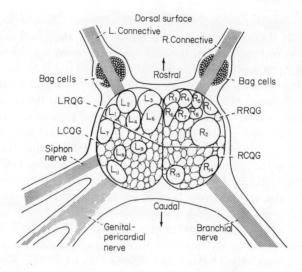

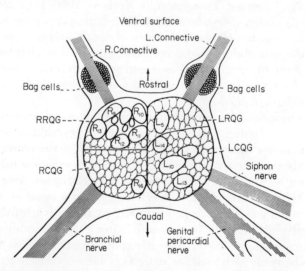

FIG. 1. Map of identified cells in the abdominal ganglion of *Aplysia californica*. (From Frazier *et al.*, 1967.)

B. The Neuron and Its Functional Components

Given the advantages of invertebrate preparations for the study of plastic neural mechanisms, the question arises as to whether findings in invertebrates can be generalized to vertebrate nervous systems. The available data suggest that invertebrate findings may indeed have wide generality. Despite obvious differences in gross morphology, vertebrate and invertebrate neurons have remarkably similar functional properties. We would like to briefly review some of these basic properties as a background for the later discussion of plastic mechanisms (for a more complete review, see Eccles, 1957; Katz, 1966; Stevens, 1966).

The functional activity of a neuron is usually associated with electrical potentials that can be recorded by means of an intracellular electrode, i.e., a glass microelectrode that is inserted into the neuron. A difference in electrical potential (membrane potential) exists between the inside and outside of all neurons. The membrane potential results from an unequal distribution of ions (e.g., Na^+, K^+, Cl^-) across the cell membrane which is selectively permeable to different ions.[2] In neurons that are not stimulated, the membrane potential is generally 50-90 mV, with the inside of the cell negative with respect to the outside. Stimulation of the neuron leads to alterations of the selective ionic permeability of the membrane, resulting in alterations of the membrane potential. A decrease of membrane potential is termed depolarization, whereas an increase is termed hyperpolarization. When a cell is depolarized beyond a critical threshold level, an action potential, or spike, is triggered. The action potential consists of a very rapid decrease (and actual reversal) of membrane potential, followed by a rapid return to the original membrane potential.

On the basis of studies of a large variety of neurons both in vertebrates and invertebrates, neurophysiologists have developed a concept of an idealized neuron. The idealized neuron is composed of the following four functional components that are present in all neurons, independent of their particular size, shape, or location: (1) an input component, (2) an integrative component, (3) a conductile component, and (4) an output component. These functional components are schematized in the idealized neuron shown in Fig. 2A. Figure 2B is a schematic representation of the type of record one might obtain from an intracellular electrode placed in the cell body of the idealized neuron shown in Fig. 2A.

1. Input component. The input components of a neuron are those parts that receive the output components, or end terminals, of other neurons. The junction formed by an end terminal and input component consists of a specialized structure termed "synapse." Depolariza-

---

[2]Recent evidence suggests that in some neurons part of the resting potential results from an electrogenic sodium pump (Carpenter & Alving, 1968; Kerkut & Thomas, 1965).

A

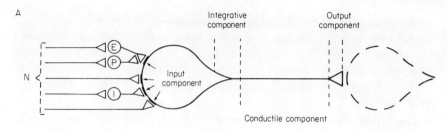

B

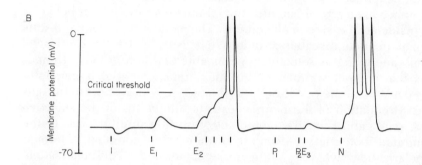

FIG. 2. Part A: Idealized neuron, labeled with functional components. The idealized neuron is innervated by an inhibitory interneuron (I), an excitatory interneuron
(E), and nerve fibers (N). An axo-axonal synapse from an interneuron (P) which synapses on the end terminal of interneuron E is also shown. Part B: Hypothetical intracellular recording from the idealized neuron shown in Part A. At the vertical marks labeled
E, I, or P, a single spike was initiated by brief intracellular depolarization of neurons E,
I, or P of Part A. At N, the nerve trunk was stimulated by an electric shock. The critical
threshold (dashed line) is the membrane potential at which an action potential is generated.

tion of an end terminal of the presynaptic neuron causes the release of
a chemical (transmitter substance) which rapidly diffuses across a
small synaptic cleft and reacts with the input component membrane.
By some means, the transmitter substance causes a change in the ionic
permeability of the postsynaptic cell membrane, resulting in a change
of membrane potential. Such changes of membrane potential are
called postsynaptic potentials (PSPs).[3] The amplitude of a PSP can

---

[3]A new type of synaptic transmission has recently been described in which the chemical transmitter does not cause a change of ionic permeability of the postsynaptic membrane but produces a PSP by stimulating an electrogenic sodium pump (Nishi & Koketsu, 1967; Pinsker & Kandel, 1969). In addition to chemical synapses there is also a type
of synaptic transmission that does not involve a chemical transmitter, but instead the
presynaptic cell affects the membrane potential of the postsynaptic cell by means of
direct current flow through a low resistance bridge between the cells (for a review, see
Eccles, 1964).

show a continuous gradation, which is a function of the amount of transmitter substance released. The size of a PSP decreases with distance away from its origin, and it is therefore localized at the input component and the nearby integrative component.

PSPs may be excitatory (EPSPs) or inhibitory (IPSPs), depending upon the particular transmitter substance and the properties of the postsynaptic cell. EPSPs depolarize the cell, bringing the membrane potential toward a critical threshold level for the initiation of an action potential or spike (Fig. 2B, points E_1 and E_2). IPSPs drive the membrane potential away from the critical firing level, and thereby counteract the effect of EPSPs (Fig. 2B, point I).

2. Integrative component. PSPs that occur close in time can algebraically summate, and the balance between EPSPs and IPSPs determines whether or not the integrative component of the cell reaches the critical firing level for an action potential. Thus, the integrative component adds up the total excitation and inhibition, and since it has a particularly low firing threshold, it is the first area to initiate an action potential when the cell has been sufficiently depolarized. When the action potential is completed, if the cell is still depolarized beyond the critical firing level, other action potentials can be initiated. The more the cell is depolarized beyond the critical firing threshold, the sooner the additional action potentials will result. Therefore, the amplitude of the PSP determines the frequency of firing of the cell, which, in turn, determines the size of the summated PSP produced in the next cell. In Fig. 2B at point E_2, interneuron E has been made to fire repetitively (5 times), causing a summating EPSP that depolarizes the integrative component up to the critical threshold, resulting in two action potentials. In this example the summated EPSP resulted from repetitive activity of a single synapse. It is also possible to have summation of PSPs that results from two or more synapses on a neuron. This is called spatial summation, and it plays a prominent role in several of the models we will later outline.

For experimental purposes an afferent nerve trunk is sometimes stimulated by means of an electric shock. As can be seen from Fig. 2A, stimulation of the nerve trunk (N) should produce a complex response composed of direct (monosynaptic) PSPs and indirect (polysynaptic) PSPs resulting from stimulation of interneurons. In the case shown in Fig. 2B, stimulation of N resulted in greater excitation than inhibition, producing a large depolarization and three spikes.

3. Conductile component. The action potential initiated at the integrative component depolarizes the adjacent membrane to the critical firing level, causing the adjacent membrane to produce an action potential. By this means the spike is rapidly conducted without decre-

ment down the conductile component or the axon of the cell.

4. Output component. When the action potential reaches the end terminals, the depolarization causes the release of a transmitter substance that produces a PSP at the next neuron. Although end terminals usually synapse on the input component, in certain cases they can synapse on the output component of a neuron. Such a synapse is depicted in Fig. 2A, where the end terminal of neuron P synapses on the terminal of neuron E. Depolarization of the P end terminal releases a transmitter substance that can alter the amount of transmitter released by the E end terminal when it is depolarized. At point P_1 in Fig. 2B, neuron P was fired. No PSP is seen, since P does not synapse on the idealized neuron. However, if P is stimulated (P_2) shortly before neuron E is stimulated, the EPSP from E is reduced (compare E_1 with E_3). This is an example of "presynaptic inhibition" (Dudel & Kuffler, 1961; Eccles, 1964; Tauc, 1965). An opposite presynaptic action (presynaptic facilitation) also has been suggested (Kandel & Tauc, 1965b; Tauc & Epstein, 1967).

In many neurons, the resting potential is stable and normally can be altered only by synaptic potentials and action potentials. However, in some cells the resting potential is unstable, and the integrative component can reach the firing threshold as a result of an intrinsic depolarization (pacemaker potential) without any synaptic input. These cells usually fire rhythmically and are said to be endogenously active. The membrane potential and hence the firing rate of endogenously active cells can also be controlled by synaptic inputs.

II. SIMPLE NEURONAL MODELS OF LEARNING

In the previous section we outlined the basic functional features of nerve cells. A long-lasting alteration (plastic change) of any of these functional features will result in a modification in the interaction among nerve cells. Consequently, any plastic change could mediate the altered behavior that characterizes learning. However, only two broad types of plastic change have been emphasized. The first and most commonly considered type of plasticity involves changes in synaptic efficacy, i.e., changes in the size of synaptic potentials (Eccles, 1953; Hebb, 1949; Kandel & Tauc, 1965b; Tanzi, 1893). The second and more recently suggested type of plasticity involves changes in the pacemaker properties of endogenously active neurons (Frazier, Waziri, & Kandel, 1965; Kandel, 1967; Strumwasser, 1963). A number of workers have constructed neuronal models to illustrate how these plastic changes could underlie the simple acquisition of classical or operant conditioning. In the following sections we will review some of these models. This review has several purposes: (1) to clarify basic similarities and differences between the models by organizing them in a common format; (2) to provide a convenient framework for presenting data relevant to the various plastic mechanisms around which the models are built; and (3) to provide suggestions of various roles that behavioral reinforcers might play in producing plastic changes that underlie learning.

All of the models we will review have two basic features: (1) plastic change, and (2) specificity. A plastic change refers to an enduring change in some neuronal property. Operationally, "specificity" has a somewhat different meaning in classical and operant conditioning. In classical conditioning specificity refers to the dependence of conditioning upon the specific pairing of the conditioned stimulus (CS) with the unconditioned stimulus (UCS), or reinforcement. In operant conditioning specificity refers to the dependence of conditioning upon the specific pairing of some behavior with a reinforcing stimulus.

Although the models we will consider have been built around only two basic types of plasticity (changes in synaptic efficacy and changes in endogenous pacemaker activity), each of the plastic changes can result from a variety of neural conditions. The term "cellular reinforcing event" will be used to refer to the set of neural conditions that are necessary and sufficient for a plastic change to occur. The cellular reinforcing event refers only to pre- and postsynaptic activity occurring at the neuron in which the plastic change occurs. Thus, for example, peripheral receptor activity elicited by a reinforcing stimulus would not be considered part of the cellular reinforcing event.

In all of the models we will consider, the neurons interact only by means of synaptic connections. However, several workers have postulated that nonsynaptic effects, such as cortical dc fields, are involved in the production of plastic changes that underlie learning. A number of experiments have provided support for this hypothesis (e.g., Morrell & Naitoh, 1962; Proctor, Pinto-Hamuy, & Kupfermann, 1964; Rowland & Goldstone, 1963), while other experiments have failed to find supporting evidence (Gartside & Lippold, 1967; Kupfermann, 1965; Lashley, Chow, & Semmes, 1951). In any case it is difficult to see how field effects could provide the degree of specificity that appears to be demanded by a cellular reinforcing event involved in learning. It is possible that field factors could be important in behavioral phenomena that may involve gross changes in neuronal excitability, for example, pseudoconditioning and behaviors associated with drive states and motivation.

The models we will consider are incomplete and do not represent the actual total neural circuitry involved in the acquisition of even the simplest learned response. Rather, they are abstractions of certain critical neural events that may occur between sensory integrative activity and motor output. Thus, the output of a given model is not a behavioral act, but rather is the firing of a response neuron (labeled "R" in Figs. 3 and 5). The response neuron could project to, or be part of, a neural system that produces an organized and functionally meaningful response (cf. Kennedy, 1967; Wiersma & Ikeda, 1964), but the nature of such a system is left unspecified in the models. Similarly, the afferent input (labeled "CS," "UCS," or "REINF") to a model can be the end point of preceding integrative activity. For example, a visual input need not represent a point on the retina, but could represent a more complex input such as a line at some given angle at any place in the visual field (cf. Hubel & Wiesel, 1965). The nature of the preceding sensory integrative processes is not specified in the models. The models are also incomplete in that they deal only with simple acquisition, and do not address themselves to other important aspects of learning, e.g., negative reinforcement, partial reinforcement, and extinction.

A. Models Involving Alterations of Synaptic Efficacy

In this section we will review four models of classical conditioning based on plasticity of synaptic efficacy. Each of the models is based on a different cellular reinforcing event, and following each model we will briefly review some data relevant to the particular cellular reinforcing event. Finally, we will indicate how these models can be modified to deal with operant conditioning.

1. "Use" Hypothesis

A. THE MODEL.   One of the oldest notions concerning the plastic change underlying learning postulates that repetitive synaptic use increases synaptic efficacy. The "use" hypothesis has provided the basis for a number of different theoretical treatments of the neural basis of learning (Briggs & Kitto, 1962; Chappell & Pike, 1936; Smith, 1962; Taylor, 1965). Eccles (1953) has been particularly concerned with a mechanism of this type, and he has developed a model that is designed to explain classical conditioning on the basis of synaptic use. A simplified version of this model is presented in Fig. 3A. (In all of the models shown in Fig. 3 the synapse at which the plastic change occurs

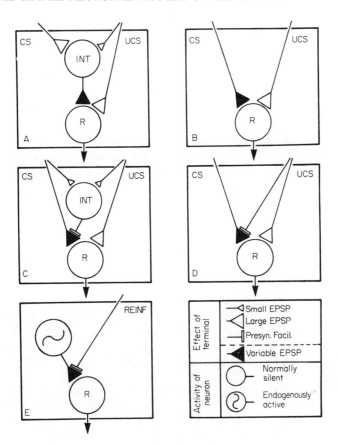

FIG. 3. Simple neuronal models of learning in which the plastic change involves an increase in the efficacy of an excitatory synapse. The locus of the plastic change is indicated by the solid black triangle (plastic synapse). The large empty triangle represents a synaptic terminal that produces an excitatory postsynaptic potential (EPSP) that is capable of firing the postsynaptic cell. The small triangle indicates an EPSP that can fire the postsynaptic cell only when summated with another EPSP. R indicates the response neuron, which is the output of the model. INT indicates an interneuron which is needed to obtain specificity in models where specificity is not part of the cellular reinforcing event. Parts A, B, C, and D: Models of classical conditioning in which the cellular reinforcing event involves: (A) use of the plastic synapse; (B) use of the plastic synapse *and* firing of the postsynaptic cell (successful use); (C) presynaptic activity at the plastic synapse; (D) presynaptic activity *and* activity of the plastic synapse. Part E: Model of operant conditioning. The CS path in model D has been replaced by an endogenously active neuron.

is shown as a large filled triangle, and will be referred to as the "plastic synapse.") In model 3A the cellular reinforcing event is activity or use of the plastic synapse. In order to obtain specificity, it must be assumed that "use" has an effect only when above some minimal level. If this condition is not met, repeated *unpaired* presentation of the conditioned stimulus (CS) will gradually increase the efficacy of the plastic synapse (i.e., sensitization). With the above assumptions, specificity to pairing can be achieved by having the CS and UCS converge on an interneuron. Neither the CS nor the UCS alone can fire the interneuron at a sufficiently high rate so that its synaptic end terminal shows use-plasticity. The CS, unlike the UCS, must be capable of firing the interneuron by itself in order to have access to the plastic synapse; otherwise changes in the plastic synapse would not result in any altered response to the CS. Before conditioning, the plastic synapse is so ineffective that the CS does not fire the response neuron, even though it fires the interneuron. When the CS and UCS occur close in time, summation of the EPSPs leads to firing of the interneuron at a rate high enough to satisfy the requirements of the cellular reinforcing event, and the plastic synapse becomes more effective. The CS can then fire the response neuron. In this model the UCS does not directly lead to the cellular reinforcing event, but it functions to summate with the CS and thereby indirectly leads to the reinforcing event.

B. DATA RELEVANT TO THE "USE" HYPOTHESIS. In both vertebrate and invertebrate preparations, it has been well established that under certain conditions synaptic use leads to increased synaptic efficacy, at least for brief periods of time. The results of studies on the effects of synaptic use can be divided into three types: (1) facilitation following a single stimulus; (2) postactivity potentiation (post-tetanic potentiation) following multiple stimuli; and (3) changes in synaptic efficacy following chronic synaptic use or disuse.

i. Facilitation. For a brief period following the invasion of an end terminal by a nerve impulse, a second impulse produces a larger synaptic potential. The period of facilitation is often followed by a period of depressed synaptic potentials. Thus, the size of the second synaptic potential seems to be determined by two opposing processes, one producing facilitation, and the other producing depression. The period of facilitation following a single synaptic potential can range from a few milliseconds up to several seconds, depending upon the particular synapse and experimental conditions.

In all cases where facilitation has been carefully studied, it has been shown that it results from the second impulse releasing more transmitter agent than was released by the first impulse (Eccles, 1964). Thus, facilitation is due to some brief plastic change involving the presynaptic terminals, rather than the postsynaptic membrane.

ii. Postactivity potentiation. For a period following repetitive activation of a synapse, a synaptic impulse produces a larger synaptic potential than it did before the stimulation. This period of postactivity or post-tetanic potentiation following repetitive invasion of the presynaptic fiber is much longer than the period of facilitation that follows a single impulse. Early studies of postactivity potentiation demonstrated that the effect lasted for only several minutes. Recent studies by Spencer and Wigdor (1965) on the spinal cord of cats have shown that if tetanic stimulation is maintained for a period of 15 minutes to an hour, post-tetanic potentiation lasting several hours can be seen. Beswick and Conroy (1965) have made similar observations, and in addition reported that prolonged stimulation was followed by a period of altered responsiveness for up to one and a half hours after signs of the potentiation disappeared. The residual effect was indicated by a different time course of the onset of facilitation produced for a second time. A profound and very long-lasting (more than 24 hours) depression of synaptic response following long periods of stimulation has also been reported (Fentress & Doty, 1966; see also Evarts & Hughes, 1957).

A feature of postactivity potentiation that is important in the "use" models previously discussed is that synaptic use should lead to long-lasting potentiation only when the synaptic activity is above some threshold rate. Studies by Curtis and Eccles (1960) and of Liley and North (1953) indicate that this property can be found in certain synapses.

iii. Chronic use or disuse. Experiments attempting to produce very prolonged (a week or more) use or disuse of synapses have generally produced effects lasting much longer than those produced by postactivity potentiation. However, the experimental procedures needed to produce prolonged and chronic synaptic use or disuse usually involve surgical intervention, and the "side effects" of such procedures are not well understood. Hence, the interpretation of experiments attempting to produce prolonged use or disuse is exceedingly difficult (cf. reviews by Eccles, 1964; Sharpless, 1964).

2. "Successful Use" Hypothesis

A. THE MODEL. In 1949 Hebb proposed that the fundamental event underlying learning involved synaptic use associated with the firing of the postsynaptic neuron. The models of Griffith (1966) and Rochester, Holland, Haibt, and Duda (1956) postulate a similar mechanism. Hebb did not specify whether the plastic change occurred in the presynaptic unit or postsynaptic unit. For the purpose of the present discussion we will assume that the plastic change occurs in the presynaptic unit; however, the functional implications of this model are not altered by assuming that the plastic change occurs in a localized postsynaptic area. Figure 3B schematizes a model of classical conditioning based on such a mechanism. In this model the cellular reinforcing event involves two things: (1) presynaptic activity, and (2) postsynaptic firing. The UCS serves to insure one of the necessary conditions, i.e., the response of the postsynaptic cell. The CS leads to the other necessary condition, i.e., use of the plastic synapse. In this model, in contrast to the previous "use" model, no additional neural machinery is needed to obtain specificity.

B. DATA RELEVANT TO THE "SUCCESSFUL USE" HYPOTHESIS. There is no direct experimental evidence to support the notion that increased synaptic efficacy is produced when synaptic activity is associated with firing of the postsynaptic cell. Kandel and Tauc (1965b) specifically studied this point in the giant cell (R2) of *Aplysia depilans*. Weak stimulation of a peripheral nerve by means of a brief shock produced an EPSP that did not fire the cell. Immediately following the synaptic potential, the giant cell was made to fire by means of a brief depolarizing current passed through the intracellular electrode. When the nerve was subsequently shocked, the EPSP was no larger than it was before it was associated with firing of the cell. Wurtz, Castellucci, and Nusrala (1967) verified these findings on the giant cell and extended the findings to a number of other cells in *Aplysia*. The discussions of Griffith (1966), Milner (1960), and Ranck (1964) provide theoretical treatment of the "successful use" hypothesis.

3. Nonspecific Presynaptic Facilitation

A. THE MODEL. Kandel and Tauc (1965b) have recently suggested that plasticity could involve presynaptic facilitation. In one type of presynaptic facilitation (nonspecific), facilitation occurs whenever the presynaptic fiber is active, regardless of whether the synapse on which the presynaptic fiber impinges is active or inactive at the time of the presynaptic activity. Burke (1966) has presented some models based on this mechanism, and Fig. 3C shows one such model of classical conditioning. Specificity to pairing is achieved in a manner that is similar to that used in the "use" model (Fig. 3A), and thus, the UCS plays the same role, i.e., it summates with the CS in order to produce the conditions necessary for the occurrence of the cellular reinforcing event.

B. DATA RELEVANT TO THE HYPOTHESIS OF NONSPECIFIC PRE-
SYNAPTIC FACILITATION. Nonspecific presynaptic facilitation has
been described recently by Kandel and Tauc (1965a; 1965b) in a study
on the isolated abdominal ganglion of *Aplysia*. This study utilized intracellular recording while a stimulus sequence derived from the classical conditioning paradigm was presented to the ganglion. Electrical
stimulation of two nerves was used to provide analogs of the CS and
UCS. One nerve was stimulated weakly (test stimulus), and it produced
a small EPSP that did not fire the cell (Fig. 4, Part 1). Another nerve
was stimulated strongly (priming stimulus), and it produced a large
EPSP that fired the cell (Part 2). In the giant cell, pairing of the test
and priming stimuli produced an increase in the size of the test EPSP

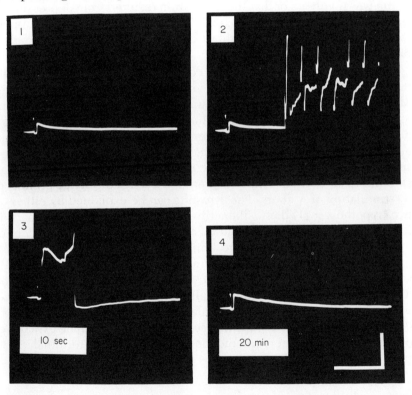

FIG. 4. Presynaptic facilitation of an EPSP in the giant cell (R2) of *Aplysia*. Part 1:
Test EPSP produced by stimulation of the genital nerve before pairing. Part 2: First of
nine pairing trials of test EPSP and response to priming stimulus (6/second train of 1
second duration to the siphon nerve). Parts 3 and 4: Test EPSP 10 seconds and 20 minutes after pairing. The tops of the spikes in frames 2 and 3 have been cut off in photography. Calibration is 10 mV and 500 milliseconds. (Modified from Kandel & Tauc, 1965a.)

(Parts 3 and 4), and the facilitation could last for up to 40 minutes. Control experiments showed that pairing of the two stimuli was *not* necessary for the facilitation to occur, i.e., presentation of the priming stimulus alone also facilitated the test EPSP. By means of further control experiments that ruled out alternative mechanisms, Kandel and Tauc provided good evidence that the increased EPSP resulted from a presynaptic facilitation of the terminals excited by the test stimulus. For example, several alternative mechanisms involved the mediation of interneurons along the path of the test stimulus. Such explanations were ruled out when it was shown that the facilitation could occur in a monosynaptic EPSP that did not involve any interneurons. Other experiments minimized the possibility that the postsynaptic membrane was involved, or that the facilitation resulted from depression of inhibition. Tauc and Epstein (1967) have provided additional support for the conclusion that the facilitation resulted from presynaptic facilitation.

Some observations on the spinal cord suggest that presynaptic facilitation may also be present in the vertebrate central nervous system. Mendell and Wall (1964) have found that in the spinal cord of the unanesthetized cat, selective stimulation of C fibers in afferent nerves produced hyperpolarization of the end terminals of the larger A fibers. Such hyperpolarization would be expected to facilitate a synaptic response from the A fibers, and indeed Mendell and Wall found that stimulation of C fibers greatly potentiated a reflex discharge produced by stimulation of A fibers. These results can be explained by either of two hypotheses: (1) the C fibers directly synapse on the terminals of the A fibers and produce facilitation of the terminals, or (2) the C fibers inhibit interneurons which are tonically active and which produce presynaptic depression of the terminals of A fibers. Mendell and Wall favor the second alternative, but they do not rule out the hypothesis of direct presynaptic facilitation. Finally, Martin and Veale (1967) have pointed out that certain experimental deviations from theoretical expectations in studies on the spinal cord (Kuno, 1964) can be explained by assuming a facilitatory interaction between synaptic terminals.

4. Specific Presynaptic Facilitation

A. THE MODEL.   Kandel and Tauc (1965a) hypothesized a type of presynaptic facilitation which is produced only if the presynaptic activity is associated with activity of the synaptic terminals on which the presynaptic fibers impinge. This model is schematized in Fig. 3D. As in the "successful use" model, the cellular reinforcing event involves two conditions. The UCS functions to produce directly one of the conditions, i.e., activity of the presynaptic fiber. The CS functions to produce the other condition, i.e., activity of the plastic synapse. In all of these models the UCS produces a response, i.e., it is effective in firing the response neuron. However, in this model, as in models 3A and 3C, the response is not part of the cellular reinforcing event. The connection between the reinforcing properties and response producing properties of the UCS in models 3A, 3C, and 3D comes about because a portion of the UCS path projects on elements that in turn converge on the response neuron.

B. Data Relevant to the Hypothesis of Specific Presynaptic Facilitation.   In the previously discussed study of neural analogs of classical conditioning in the abdominal ganglion of *Aplysia* (Kandel & Tauc, 1965a), several unidentified cells were encountered in which a test EPSP became facilitated *only when it was paired* with the priming stimulus. This contrasted with the giant cell (R2), in which facilitation of the test EPSP was not dependent upon the specific pairing of the test and priming stimuli. Kandel and Tauc suggested that it may be possible that in certain terminals presynaptic facilitation occurs only if the terminals have been recently invaded by a spike. Specificity to pairing was tested in only three cells, and the authors did not rule out the possibility that some of the unidentified cells may show nonspecific facilitation or some type of incomplete specificity. Von Baumgarten and Djahnparwar (1967) and Kupfermann and Kandel (unpublished data) have made more detailed investigations of specific facilitation in *Aplysia*. Both groups failed to find cells in which complete specificity could be demonstrated, but they did find cases of partial specificity. In cells which showed facilitation of a test EPSP, the priming stimulus alone was effective in producing facilitation. However, the facilitation was larger when the test and priming stimuli were paired. In the experiments of Kupfermann and Kandel the differences between the paired and unpaired presentations were small, and often in the same preparation later experiments could not establish any difference. Von Baumgarten and Djahnparwar found larger differences, and furthermore, they have found that the amount of facilitation is a function of the precise interval between the test and priming stimuli — maximum facilitation occurring with an interval of 350 milliseconds (von Baumgarten and Hukuhara, 1968; von Baumgarten, Jahan-Parvar, and Hukuhara, 1968).

In order to demonstrate the existence of specific presynaptic facilitation, it is first necessary to have a preparation which shows synaptic facilitation that is specific to pairing, and then it is necessary to show that the specificity does not result from a mechanism of nonspecific facilitation combined with convergence of the CS and UCS paths onto interneurons (see Fig. 3C). The experiments discussed above suggest that synaptic facilitation that is specific to pairing can be seen in certain neurons in *Aplysia*. In none of these experiments, however, has it been possible to control for the contribution of interneurons. Thus, the status of the hypothesis of specific presynaptic facilitation is the same as that of the "successful use" hypothesis of Hebb. Both mechanisms lead to very simple and elegant models of conditioning without the necessity of postulating any network properties, and both mechanisms lack conclusive experimental support.

5. Operant Conditioning in Models with Plasticity of Synaptic Efficacy

All of the classical conditioning models we have considered can be changed into models of operant conditioning by substituting an endogenously active neuron for the CS path. The endogenously active unit has the property of undergoing spontaneous alterations of firing rate. In such models conditioning would occur whenever the endogenously active unit fired sufficiently fast to fire the response unit. Under such circumstances the environment would provide a reinforcing stimulus along the equivalent of the UCS pathway, and the plastic synapse would show enduring facilitation, since all of the requirements of the cellular reinforcing event would be met. Therefore, during conditioning, even though the average frequency and pattern of firing of the endogenously active unit would not change, a given amount of firing would produce a larger amplitude synaptic potential at the response neuron, and hence the overall frequency of firing or probability of a response would increase. Kandel (1967) has pointed out how such a transformation from the amplitude domain (of the synaptic potential) to the frequency domain (firing of the response unit) opens up the possibility of moving from classical conditioning models to operant conditioning models. Burke (1966) has applied similar notions to his model of classical conditioning shown in Fig. 3C. Figure 3E shows how this idea can be applied to the model using specific presynaptic facilitation (model D).

6. The Role of Decreased Synaptic Efficacy

From the previous discussion it should be clear that a given cellular reinforcing event can lead to decreased synaptic efficacy as well as increased synaptic efficacy. Presynaptic influence can produce depression at some synapses and facilitation at others. Also, at different synapses or with different parameters of stimulation at the same synapse, synaptic use can lead to either depression or facilitation. The models that were previously outlined all used synaptic facilitation, since this assumption leads to the simplest models, and most of the available theorizing has been done along this line. However, somewhat more complicated models utilizing synaptic depression can be readily constructed. A prominent feature of such models is that they rely upon a disruption of a balance between excitation and inhibition produced by the CS (Taylor, 1965; Young, 1964). The cellular reinforcing event selectively depresses the inhibitory pathway, and a net increase of excitation to the CS results.

B. Models Involving Alterations of Endogenous Activity

Since operant conditioning typically involves changes in the frequency of "spontaneously" occurring behavior, such conditioning can be modeled readily by plastic changes in the average firing rate of an endogenously active neuron. Strumwasser (1963) was the first to suggest plasticity of an endogenously active neuron. Frazier et al. (1965) and Kandel (1967) have more recently hypothesized that synaptic input to an endogenously active neuron might produce long-lasting changes in its activity. They described two forms of this hypothesis. One form (nonspecific or noncontingent alteration of endogenous activity) assumes that the change in activity is dependent only on synaptic input, and does not depend upon the firing of the endogenously active unit. A second form of the hypothesis (specific or contingent alteration of endogenous activity) assumes that an enduring alteration resulting from synaptic input is dependent upon whether or not the endogenously active unit is firing at the time of the synaptic input. In both cases the cellular reinforcing event is mediated synaptically; however, the plastic change occurs not in the synaptic terminals but in the postsynaptic cell.

1. Nonspecific Alteration of Endogenous Activity

A. THE MODEL. Figure 5A schematizes a model of operant conditioning in which the cellular reinforcing event involves synaptic input independent of the state of firing of the endogenously active unit. The synaptic input is assumed to produce a plastic change which leads to a persistent increase in the probability of the neuron firing. In this model, specificity could be accomplished by having the response neuron send a recurrent collateral to an interneuron. Synaptic input from this interneuron would constitute the cellular reinforcing event, and this would occur only under the conditions of synaptic summation

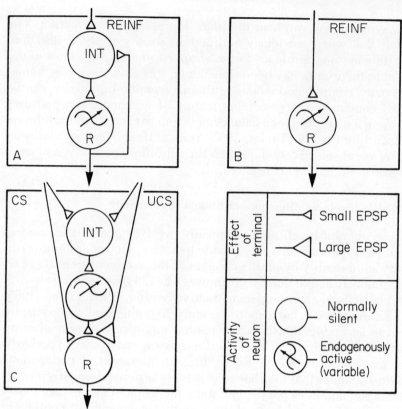

FIG. 5. Simple neuronal models of learning in which the plastic change involves an increase of the average firing frequency of an endogenously active neuron. Parts A and B: Models of operant conditioning in which the cellular reinforcing event involves: (A) synaptic input to the endogenously active neuron (nonspecific effect); (B) synaptic input *and* firing of the endogenously active neuron (specific effect). Part C: Model of classical conditioning utilizing plasticity of an endogenously active neuron and nonspecific cellular reinforcing event.

provided by the combined input from the reinforcing stimulus and the recurrent collateral from the response unit.

B. DATA RELEVANT TO HYPOTHESIS OF NONSPECIFIC ALTERATION OF ENDOGENOUS ACTIVITY. The functional importance of endogenous activity, especially in invertebrates, has long been appreciated (cf. Bullock, 1961; Roeder, 1963). Several recent experiments, reviewed in the following sections, have found evidence that endogenous activity can undergo plastic change. Although these studies are very encouraging, this work must be viewed with caution. When a change in the spontaneous activity of a neuron is demonstrated, it is very difficult to determine whether the change results from an alteration of the endogenous pacemaker properties of the neuron or from an altered spontaneous synaptic input to the cell. In all of the experiments described in the following sections, no change in spontaneously occurring PSPs was seen to underlie the altered spontaneous activity of the cell. However, in no case has this possibility been completely excluded, since synaptic potentials far from the cell body may not be detected.

The abdominal ganglion of *Aplysia* contains a number of endogenously active neurons of several types (Arvanitaki and Chalazonitis, 1958; Frazier *et al.*, 1967), and consequently it is ideal for the study of plasticity of endogenous activity. All of the data described in the following sections were obtained from identified cells in this ganglion.

Several studies in *Aplysia* have shown alterations in the endogenous activity of cells under conditions in which the effect of synaptic input does not depend upon the presence or absence of spike activity at the moment of the input. These studies fall into three broad categories: (1) cases involving long-term increases or decreases of the average firing frequency of an endogenously active cell; (2) cases in which a cell that is normally silent becomes endogenously active; and (3) cases involving long-term changes in the pattern of firing of a cell, with little change in average frequency.

Frazier *et al.* (1965) have demonstrated prolonged increases in the firing frequency of identified "bursting" cells (L3 and L6) following nerve stimulation (see also Kandel, 1967, Figs. 14 and 15). These cells typically show an endogenous firing pattern (Waziri, Frazier, & Kandel, 1965) that consists of regular bursts of spikes. Following strong nerve stimulation, a cell that had been bursting began to fire continuously. After several minutes of continuous firing, the quiet periods reappeared gradually. The nerve stimulation resulted in an altered pattern of firing, but the most striking aspect of the results was that the overall frequency of firing of the cell remained elevated for periods of up to 30 minutes. Repetition of the stimulus (every two minutes for a ten-minute period) could produce even greater effects. No maintained change in spontaneous PSPs was seen, and therefore the changes in firing were attributed to a direct effect on the endogenous properties of the cell.

An increase in the firing rate of a neuron will result in an increase in PSPs in the cells with which the neuron synapses. Increases in the frequency of spontaneous PSPs following nerve stimulation have been described for several cells in *Aplysia,* and this has been termed PSP recruitment (Frazier *et al.*, 1965; see also Holmgren and Frenk, 1961, for a similar phenomenon in a land snail).

In certain cases of PSP recruitment, spontaneously occurring PSPs can be seen where none was evident before the nerve stimulation. Such cases may involve a normally silent interneuron that has the property of becoming endogenously active following synaptic input. Such a property seems to be exhibited by a group of several hundred neurosecretory cells called "bag cells" (Kupfermann, Kandel, & Coggeshall, 1966). The bag cells are normally completely inactive. Following a single strong shock to a nerve (left or right connective), they can all begin to fire for periods lasting up to 50 minutes. A plastic mechanism of this sort could not serve in the operant conditioning models previously described, but could serve in one of the models of classical conditioning (Fig. 5C).

The work of Strumwasser (1965) provides a good example of a plastic change in which the most prominent feature involves a change of firing pattern, rather than a change in overall average frequency of firing. The studies were done on an endogenously active cell called the "parabolic burster" by Strumwasser and "R15" by Frazier *et al.* (1967). In long-term studies (24-48 hours) on the isolated ganglion, Strumwasser demonstrated that the maximum of the average spike output of this cell fluctuates with a circadian rhythm when the intact animals were maintained under conditions of constant light for a week or more prior to the experiments. When the animals were previously exposed to alternating 12-hour periods of light and darkness, the maximum spike activity occurred close in time to when the dark-light transition would have occurred. Furthermore, Lickey (1967) has provided evidence that the cell could be entrained to a 27-hour period as well as a 24-hour period. The effects described by Strumwasser and Lickey do not represent an increase in the overall firing rate of the cell, but rather a rephasing of its endogenous rhythm by an environmental stimulus. In the isolated ganglion, no fluctuations in spontaneous PSPs were seen to underlie the modified circadian fluctuations, and it was concluded that the modifications were in the endogenous properties of the cell. The nature of the cellular reinforcing event operating in the intact animal to produce the rephasing is not known, but it could involve synaptic input since this cell receives powerful synaptic input from peripheral nerves (Frazier *et al.*, 1967). Although the learning models previously described do not utilize plastic change of pattern of firing, such plastic change could be of great importance in mechanisms of learning.

2. Specific Alteration of Endogenous Activity

A. THE MODEL.   In the specific variant of the models involving changes in endogenous activity, it is postulated that the cellular reinforcing event has two aspects: synaptic activity and activity of the endogenously active unit. For example, synaptic activity could produce a persistent increase of firing of the endogenously active unit, but only when the synaptic activity occurs close in time with the firing of the postsynaptic neuron. Such a cellular reinforcing event could be the basis of a very simple model of operant conditioning which has been schematized in Fig. 5B. In this model the cellular reinforcing event has specificity built into it, and no additional neural machinery is needed.

B. DATA RELEVANT TO HYPOTHESIS OF SPECIFIC ALTERATIONS OF ENDOGENOUS ACTIVITY.   Cells L3 and L6 in *Aplysia* can show either nonspecific or specific alterations of endogenous activity, depending upon the parameters of the stimulation applied to the nerves. As previously described, strong nerve stimulation produced increases in the rate of firing of the cell. The effect was not dependent upon the time of the stimulation relative to the spiking of the cell, i.e., it was nonspecific. On the other hand, Frazier *et al.* (1965) have also found that with weaker stimulation the effects are different when the stimulus is presented at different parts of the burst cycle (see Kandel, 1967, Fig. 16). Figure 6 shows a complete burst cycle, consisting of a burst of spikes and a quiet period. The burst onset interval is the duration of the burst cycle. When synaptic input resulting from stimulation of a nerve occurred during the early part of the burst (contingency A), the burst onset interval was shortened. When the same synaptic input occurred later in the burst cycle (contingency B), the burst onset interval was lengthened. In other words, contingency A stimulation led to more bursts per unit time, whereas contingency B led to fewer bursts per unit time. When contingency B stimulation was presented repeatedly, there was often a buildup; each successive burst onset interval was longer than the previous one. Following the cessation of repeated stimulation, the succeeding burst onset intervals sometimes remained lengthened for up to 20 minutes.

Nerve stimulation produces a complex synaptic input to the bursting cells, and it is therefore difficult to specify the cellular reinforcing event underlying the specific plastic change just described. However, Pinsker and Kandel (1967) have recently obtained similar results with simplified synaptic input consisting of pure monosynaptic IPSPs produced by intracellular stimulation of an identified interneuron (L10)

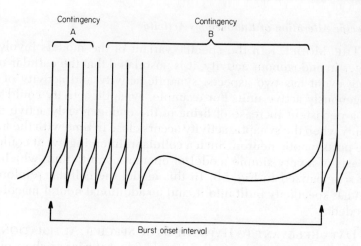

FIG. 6.   Schematic diagram of a complete burst cycle of an endogenously active bursting cell in *Aplysia*. Synaptic input produces opposite effects on the burst onset interval depending upon the phase of the burst cycle in which it is presented. Contingency A stimulation shortens the burst onset interval, whereas contingency B stimulation lengthens the burst onset interval. (Unpublished figure from Frazier, Waziri, and Kandel.)

that synapses with the bursting cells (Kandel, Frazier, Waziri, & Coggeshall, 1967). Figure 7 shows the opposite effects of contingency A and contingency B stimulation. As was true with the complex synaptic input produced by nerve stimulation, the pure IPSPs presented early in the burst cycle reduced the number of spikes in the burst and shortened the burst onset interval (cont. A). Stimulation later in the burst cycle lengthened the burst onset interval (cont. B). With repeated contingency A stimulation with the pure IPSPs, there was often a buildup; successive burst onset intervals became progressively shorter (Fig. 8). Following a block of 10 stimuli the shortening usually persisted for several burst cycles, but on occasion could persist for up to 30 minutes. Preliminary results indicate that persistence can be enhanced when such blocks of stimuli are repeated. In contrast with the earlier findings with nerve stimulation, the lengthening of the burst onset interval produced by contingency B stimulation with the pure IPSPs does not appear to persist.

ɔtimulation of an interneuron is less likely than nerve stimulation to produce effects on other cells which in turn could synaptically modulate the bursting cells. Therefore, these experiments with a monosynaptic input from an interneuron provide strong evidence that

synaptic input can directly produce a plastic alteration of the endogenous firing rhythm of a cell.[4]

3. Classical Conditioning in Models with Plasticity of Endogenous Activity

Cellular reinforcing events involving changes in endogenous activity need not be limited to models of operant conditioning. Figure 5C
schematizes a model of classical conditioning based on the nonspecific

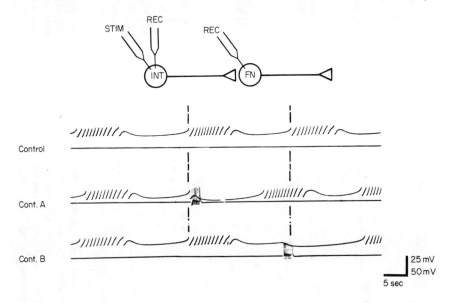

FIG. 7. Specific effects of inhibitory synaptic input on an endogenously active
bursting cell. In each part, the bursting cell (labeled FN for follower neuron in the
inset) is shown on the upper trace and the interneuron (INT) is shown on the lower
trace (at reduced gain). Control traces show fairly regular bursting rhythm in the absence of stimulation. (Control burst onset interval, 21 seconds.) Contingency A traces
show that a high frequency train of IPSPs produced by stimulation of the interneuron
inhibits spikes when presented at the onset of the burst and shortens the burst onset
interval. Contingency B traces show that the same synaptic input presented near the
end of the burst cycle lengthens the burst onset interval. The tops of the spikes in the
three FN traces have been cut off in photography. (Unpublished figure from Pinsker
and Kandel.)

[4]Stimulation of cell L10 has recently been shown to synaptically activate an electrogenic sodium pump in the bursting cells (Pinsker & Kandel, 1969), and these cells also
have an electrogenic sodium pump that contributes to the resting potential (Carpenter
& Alving, 1968). It is possible that some of the alterations of endogenous activity described in this section may involve synaptically induced alterations in the activity of
electrogenic pumps.

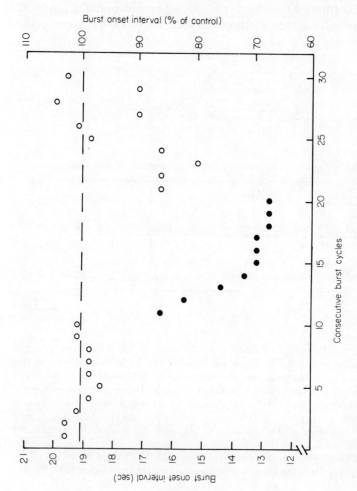

FIG. 8.   Effect of repetitive contingency A stimulation. Following 10 control burst cycles (open circles), stimulation was given for 10 burst cycles (filled circles). The shortening of the burst onset interval gradually increases during the period of stimulation, and the burst onset interval gradually returns to the control value during the last 10 (unstimulated) burst cycles. (Unpublished figure from Pinsker and Kandel.)

plasticity of endogenous activity previously discussed. In this model, the endogenously active neuron constantly fires, providing a tonic level of depolarization of the response neuron. The CS and UCS converge on an interneuron whose firing provides a synaptic input to the endogenously active neuron, and thereby produces a persistent increase in its firing rate. This increased firing, in turn, leads to an increase in tonic depolarization of the response unit, bringing it closer to the firing level, so that the CS will now fire the response neuron. In this model the endogenously active neuron could be replaced by a neuron that was initially silent, but which can become endogenously active following sufficient synaptic input.

III. SUMMARY AND CONCLUSIONS

In this chapter we have assumed that a reinforcing stimulus results in neural activity that enters the brain and undergoes a series of transformations, which ultimately lead to long-lasting changes in the functional properties of nerve cells (plastic changes). From this point of view, the physiological analysis of reinforcement can be divided into at least three phases: (1) a description of the plastic changes underlying the learning associated with the reinforcement; (2) a description of the immediate neural conditions (cellular reinforcing events) necessary for the production of the plastic changes; and (3) a description of how behavioral stimuli (e.g., CSs, UCSs, food, shock) are transformed into cellular reinforcing events.

Two broad types of plastic changes have been suggested by a number of workers: (1) changes in synaptic efficacy; and (2) changes in endogenous pacemaker properties of neurons. By means of neuronal models, it was shown that either type of plastic change could be involved in simple forms of either classical or operant conditioning. These plastic changes can be produced by a number of different cellular reinforcing events, all of which are mediated by synaptic activity. In each of the models that utilizes a different cellular reinforcing event, the "reinforcement" plays a somewhat different role. In some cases there is a parallel to recent molar theories of reinforcement (see, in particular, Deutsch, 1960; Glickman & Schiff, 1967; Sheffield, 1965), but a discussion of these similarities is beyond the scope of the present chapter.

Plastic changes and cellular reinforcing events have been studied in simple preparations in which long-term intracellular recording is possible. The data indicate that plastic changes can be produced either in synaptic efficacy or pacemaker properties of neurons. Plasticity of synaptic efficacy can result either from synaptic use, or from nonspecific presynaptic modulation, However, data at present do not support the hypothesis of "successful use," or specific presynaptic facilitation. Synaptic input to a cell with endogenous pacemaker properties can result in persistent alterations in its rate and pattern of firing, and under certain conditions the degree and sign of the alteration depends upon when the input occurs relative to the spike activity of the cell.

The plastic changes that have been described generally persist, at most, for only a few hours, whereas learning can sometimes persist for the lifetime of an organism. It is possible that the neurons in brains of animals that show advanced learning could have taken advantage of the primitive types of plasticity that have been studied in simple systems. The evolution of relatively minor structural or biochemical alterations of a neuron could perhaps considerably extend the persistence of its plastic properties. On the other hand, one cannot exclude the possibility that there are special "learning" neurons with unique properties that have not yet been studied, either in vertebrates or invertebrates.

We have not dealt with the problem of how a behavioral stimulus becomes transformed into a cellular reinforcing event. The same sensory stimulus under some circumstances can act as a reinforcer, while under other circumstances will be ineffective. This presumably involves the gating and patterning of the neural activity resulting from sensory stimuli. Under certain special conditions, the gating and patterning is such that a cellular reinforcing event occurs, with a resulting plastic change. The study of these special conditions is in the domain of the physiology of perception, cognition, motivation, and drive, and in recent years techniques of cellular neurophysiology have been applied to the study of these problems.

It cannot be overemphasized that there is an enormous gap between knowledge of the plastic properties of neurons studied in simple preparations, and knowledge of the physiological basis of reinforcement and learning in intact animals. However, interest in this area has developed only recently, and although there are as yet only relatively few studies, the results are provocative and encouraging.

REFERENCES

Arvanitaki, A., & Chalazonitis, N. Configurations modales de l'activité, propres à différents neurones d'un même centre. *J. Physiol. (Paris)*, 1958, **50**, 122-125.
Beswick, F. B., & Conroy, R. T. W. L. Optimal tetanic conditioning of heteronymous monosynaptic reflexes. *J. Physiol. (London)*, 1965, **180**, 134-146.

Bottazzi, F., & Enriques, P. Recherches physiologiques sur le système nerveux viscéral des Aplysies et de quelque Céphalopodes. *Arch. ital. Biol.*, 1900, **34**, 111-143.

Briggs, M. H., & Kitto, G. B. The molecular basis of memory and learning. *Psychol. Rev.*, 1962, **69**, 537-541.

Bruner, J., & Tauc, L. Long-lasting phenomena in the molluscan nervous system. *Symp. Soc. exp. Biol.*, 1966, **20**, 457-475.

Bullock, T. H. The origins of patterned nervous discharge. *Behaviour*, 1961, **17**, 48-59.

Burke, W. Neuronal models for conditioned reflexes. *Nature*, 1966, **210**, 269-271.

Carpenter, D. O., & Alving, B. O. A contribution of an electrogenic sodium pump to membrane potential in *Aplysia* neurons. *J. Gen. Physiol.*, 1968, **52**, 1-21.

Chappell, M. N., & Pike, F. H. Summation of stimuli and the neural changes in learning. *Psychol. Rev.*, 1936, **43**, 283-307.

Curtis, D. R., & Eccles, J. C. Synaptic action during and after repetitive stimulation. *J. Physiol. (London)*, 1960, **150**, 374-398.

Deutsch, J. A. *The structural basis of behavior*. Chicago: Univer. of Chicago Press, 1960.

Dudel, J., & Kuffler, S. W. Presynaptic inhibition at the crayfish neuromuscular junction. *J. Physiol. (London)*, 1961, **155**, 543-562.

Eccles, J. C. *The neurophysiological basis of mind*. London and New York: Oxford Univer. Press, 1953.

Eccles, J. C. *The physiology of nerve cells*. Baltimore: Johns Hopkins Press, 1957.

Eccles, J. C. *The physiology of synapses*. Berlin: Springer, 1964.

Eisenstein, E. M., & Cohen, M. J. Learning in an isolated prothoracic insect ganglion. *Anim. Behav.*, 1965, **13**, 104-108.

Evarts, E. V., & Hughes, J. R. Effects of prolonged optic nerve tetanization on lateral geniculate potentials. *Amer. J. Physiol.*, 1957, **188**, 245-248.

Fentress, J. C., & Doty, R. Protracted tetanization of the optic tract in squirrel monkeys. *Fed. Proc.*, 1966, **25**, 573.

Frazier, W. T., Kandel, E. R., Kupfermann, I., Waziri, R., & Coggeshall, R. E. Morphological and functional properties of identified neurons in the abdominal ganglion of *Aplysia californica*. *J. Neurophysiol.*, 1967, **30**, 1288-1351.

Frazier, W. T., Waziri, R., & Kandel, E. Alterations in the frequency of spontaneous activity in Aplysia neurons with contingent and noncontingent nerve stimulation. *Fed. Proc.*, 1965, **24**, 522.

Gartside, I. B., & Lippold, O. C. J. The production of persistent changes in the level of neuronal activity by brief local cooling of the cerebral cortex of the rat. *J. Physiol. (London)*, 1967, **189**, 475-487.

Glickman, S. E., & Schiff, B. B. A biological theory of reinforcement. *Psychol. Rev.*, 1967, **74**, 81-109.

Griffith, J. S. A theory of the nature of memory. *Nature*, 1966, **211**, 1160-1163.

Hebb, D. O. *The organization of behavior*. New York: Wiley, 1949.

Holmgren, B., & Frenk, S. Inhibitory phenomena and "habituation" at the neuronal level. *Nature*, 1961, **192**, 1294-1295.

Horridge, G. A. The electrophysiological approach to learning in isolatable ganglia. *Anim. Behav.* 1964, Suppl. 1, 163-182.

Hoyle, G. Neurophysiological studies on "learning" in headless insects. In J. E. Treherne and J. W. L. Beament (Eds.), *Physiology of the insect central nervous system*. New York: Academic Press, 1965. Pp. 203-232.

Hubel, D. H., & Wiesel, T. N. Receptive fields and functional architecture in two nonstriate visual areas (18 and 19) of the cat. *J. Neurophysiol.*, 1965, **28**, 229-289.

Jasper, H., Ricci, G., & Doane, B. Microelectrode analysis of cortical cell discharge during avoidance conditioning in the monkey. *Electroencephalog. clin. Neurophysiol.* 1960, Suppl., **13**, 137-155.

Kandel, E. R. Cellular studies of learning. In G. C. Quarton, T. Melnechuck, and F. O. Schmitt (Eds.), *The neurosciences.* New York: Rockefeller Univer. Press, 1967. Pp. 666-689.

Kandel, E. R., Frazier, W., Waziri, R., & Coggeshall, R. E. Direct and common connections among the identified neurons in *Aplysia. J. Neurophysiol.*, 1967, **30**, 1352-1376.

Kandel, E. R., & Spencer, W. A. Cellular neurophysiological approaches in the study of learning. *Physiol. Rev.*, 1968, **48**, 65-134.

Kandel, E. R., & Tauc, L. Heterosynaptic facilitation in neurones of the abdominal ganglion of *Aplysia depilans. J. Physiol. (London)*, 1965, **181**, 1-27. (a)

Kandel, E. R., & Tauc, L. Mechanism of heterosynaptic facilitation in the giant cell of the abdominal ganglion of *Aplysia depilans. J. Physiol. (London)*, 1965, **181**, 28-47. (b)

Katz, B. *Nerve muscle and synapse.* New York: McGraw-Hill, 1966.

Kennedy, D. Small systems of nerve cells. *Sci. Amer.*, 1967, **216**, 44-52.

Kerkut, G. A., & Thomas, R. C. An electrogenic sodium pump in snail nerve cells. *Comp. Biochem. Physiol.*, 1965, **14**, 167-183.

Konorski, J. *Conditioned reflexes and neuron organization.* London and New York: Cambridge Univer. Press., 1948.

Kuno, M. Quantal components of excitatory synaptic potentials in spinal motoneurones. *J. Physiol. (London)*, 1964, **175**, 81-99.

Kupfermann, I. Effects of cortical polarization on visual discriminations. *Exp. Neurol.*, 1965, **12**, 179-189.

Kupfermann, I. Stimulation of egg laying: Possible neuroendocrine function of bag cells of abdominal ganglion of *Aplysia californica. Nature*, 1967, **216**, 814-815.

Kupfermann, I., & Kandel, E. R. Reflex functions of some identified cells in *Aplysia. Fed. Proc.*, 1968, **27**, 348.

Kupfermann, I., Kandel, E. R., & Coggeshall, R. E. Synchronized activity in a neurosecretory cell cluster in *Aplysia. Physiologist*, 1966, **9**, 223.

Lashley, K. S., Chow, K. L., & Semmes, J. An examination of the electrical field theory of cerebral integration. *Psychol. Rev.*, 1951, **58**, 123-136.

Lickey, M. E. Effect of various photoperiods on a circadian rhythm in a single neuron. In C. A. G. Wiersma (Ed.), *Invertebrate nervous systems: Their significance for mammalian neurophysiology.* Chicago: Univer. of Chicago Press, 1967. Pp. 321-328.

Liley, A. W., & North, K. A. K. An electrical investigation of effects of repetitive stimulation on mammalian neuromuscular junction. *J. Neurophysiol.*, 1953, **16**, 509-527.

Martin, A. R., & Veale, J. L. The nervous system at the cellular level. *Ann. Rev. Physiol.*, 1967, **29**, 401-426.

Mendell, L. M., & Wall, P. D. Presynaptic hyperpolarization: A role for fine afferent fibres. *J. Physiol. (London)*, 1964, **172**, 274-294.

Milner, P. Learning in neural systems. In M. Yovitts and S. Cameron (Eds.), *Self-organizing systems.* Oxford: Pergamon Press, 1960.

Morrell, F. Microelectrode and steady potential studies suggesting a dendritic locus of closure. *Electroencephalog. clin. Neurophysiol.* 1960, **13**, Suppl., 65-79.

Morrell, F., & Naitoh, P. Effect of cortical polarization on a conditioned avoidance response. *Exp. Neurol.*, 1962, **6**, 507-523.

Nishi, S., & Koketsu, K. Origin of ganglionic inhibitory postsynaptic potential. *Life Sciences*, 1967, **6**, 2049-2055.

Olds, J. Operant conditioning of single unit responses. *Proc. 23rd Int. Congr. Physiol. Sci.* Amsterdam: Excerpta Medica Found., 1965. Pp. 372-380.

Pinsker, H., & Kandel, E. R. Contingent modification of an endogenous bursting rhythm by monosynaptic inhibition. *Physiologist*, 1967, **10**, 279.

Pinsker, H., & Kandel, E. R. Synaptic activation of an electrogenic sodium pump. *Science*, 1969 (in press).

Proctor, F., Pinto-Hamuy, T., & Kupfermann, I. Cortical stimulation during learning in rabbits. *Neuropsychologia*, 1964, **2**, 305-310.

Ranck, J. B., Jr. Synaptic "learning" due to electroosmosis: A theory. *Science*, 1964, **144**, 187-189.

Rochester, M., Holland, J., Haibt, L., & Duda, W. Test on a cell assembly theory of the action of the brain, using a large digital computer. *IRE (Inst. radio Engrs) Trans. inform. Theory*, 1956, **2**, 80-93.

Roeder, K. *Nerve cells and insect behavior.* Cambridge, Mass.: Harvard Univer. Press, 1963.

Rowland, V. S., & Goldstone, M. Appetitively conditioned and drive-related bioelectric baseline shift in cat cortex. *Electroencephalog. clin. Neurophysiol.*, 1963, **15**, 474-485.

Sharpless, S. K. Reorganization of function in the nervous system — use and disuse. *Ann. Rev. Physiol.*, 1964, **26**, 357-388.

Sheffield, F. D. Relation between classical conditioning and instrumental learning. In W. F. Prokasy (Ed.), *Classical conditioning.* New York: Appleton, 1965. Pp. 302-322.

Smith, C. E. Is memory a matter of enzyme induction? *Science*, 1962, **38**, 889-890.

Spencer, W. A., Thompson, R. F., & Neilson, D. R., Jr. Response decrement of the flexion reflex in the acute spinal cat and transient restoration by strong stimuli. *J. Neurophysiol.*, 1966, **29**, 221-239.

Spencer, W. A., & Wigdor, R. Ultra-late PTP of monosynaptic reflex in cat. *Physiologist*, 1965, **8**, 278.

Stevens, C. F. *Neurophysiology: A primer.* New York: Wiley, 1966.

Strumwasser, F. A circadian rhythm of activity and its endogenous origin in a neuron. *Fed. Proc.*, 1963, **22**, 220.

Strumwasser, F. The demonstration and manipulation of a circadian rhythm in a single neuron. In J. Aschoff (Ed.), *Circadian clocks.* Amsterdam: North-Holland Publ., 1965. Pp. 442-462.

Strumwasser, F. Types of information stored in single neurons. In C. A. G. Wiersma (Ed.), *Invertebrate nervous systems: Their significance for mammalian neurophysiology.* Chicago: Univer. of Chicago Press, 1967. Pp. 291-319.

Tanzi, E. I fatti e la induzione nell'odierne istologia del sistema nervoso. *Riv. sper. Freniat.*, 1893, **19**, 149.

Tauc, L. Presynaptic inhibition in the abdominal ganglion of *Aplysia*. *J. Physiol. (London)*, 1965, **181**, 282-307.

Tauc, L., & Epstein, R. Heterosynaptic facilitation as a distinct mechanism in *Aplysia*. *Nature*, 1967, **214**, 724-725.

Taylor, W. K. A model of learning mechanisms in the brain. *Progr. brain Res.*, 1965, **17**, 369-397.

von Baumgarten, R. J., & Djahnparwar, B. Time course of repetitive heterosynaptic facilitation in *Aplysia californica*. *Brain Res.*, 1967, **4**, 295-297.

von Baumgarten, R. J. & Hukuhara, T. The role of the interstimulus interval in heterosynaptic facilitation in *Aplysia californica. Brain Res.*, 1969 (in press).

von Baumgarten, R. J., Jahan-Parvar, B., & Hukuhara, T. Mechanisms and partial specificity of heterosynaptic facilitation in *Aplysia californica. Proc. Int. Union Physiol. Sci.*, 1968, **7**, 455.

Waziri, R., Frazier, W., & Kandel, E. R. Analysis of "pacemaker" activity in an identifiable burst generating neuron in *Aplysia. Physiologist*, 1965, **8**, 300.

Wiersma, C. A. G., & Ikeda, K. Interneurones commanding swimmeret movements in the crayfish *Procambarus clarki* (Girard). *Comp. Biochem. Physiol.*, 1964, **12**, 509–525.

Wurtz, R. H., Castellucci, V. F., & Nusrala, J. M. Synaptic plasticity: The effect of the action potential in the postsynaptic neuron. *Exp. Neurol.*, 1967, **18**, 350–368.

Young, J. Z. *A model of the brain.* London and New York: Oxford Univer. Press (Clarendon), 1964.

CHAPTER 13

Current Status and Future Directions[1]

JACK T. TAPP

I. INTRODUCTION

Over half a century of extensive work on the nature of learning has allowed us to specify, with some accuracy, those variables which influence the learning process. Among these, the rewards that are used in training are an extremely important class of events. When delivered

[1]The preparation of this chapter was supported by funds from NIMH training grant 08107. The author is grateful to Dr. Jum C. Nunnally, Dr. Keith N. Clayton, and Dr. Hardy Wilcoxon for reading the early drafts of the manuscript and providing many helpful comments.

appropriately, rewards influence the performance of the behavior that we measure, and we assert that learning has taken place. When this performance change has occurred, we also conclude that our reward had reinforcing properties. Unfortunately, this operational limitation has restricted the distinction between reinforcement and learning. With the current restrictions in our measurement systems, the two concepts are inexorably linked by the operations which define them.

Conceptually, however, learning and reinforcement are distinguishable. We generally think of learning as a process by which a behavior becomes a part of the organism's future performance repertoire. We say that an animal has learned when it will perform a response sequence on occasion 2 which it did not perform on occasion 1 (all else being equal). On the other hand, the concept of reinforcement implies that an event(s) occurred during the course of learning that influenced the learning process. According to this view, reinforcement is also a process, but distinguishable from learning by the assumption that it influences learning.

Whether or not reinforcement occurs during learning seems to be dependent on the presence of those observable, manipulative stimulus events that have been traditionally called rewards. These rewards are typically made available to the organism when it has made a "correct" response within the learning situation. Thus, rewards are "something given for something done," in the sense outlined by Clayton in Chapter 4 of this volume. When the presentation of the reward influences the learning process, the reward is said to have reinforcing properties. Unfortunately, the correlation between the presentation of a reward and the occurrence of reinforcement is not perfect, and herein lies the problem. What special properties must rewards have to assure us that reinforcement will occur when a reward is presented?

The material presented in the preceding chapters of this volume has reviewed many of the conceptions of the manner in which rewards influence behavior, i.e., how rewards operate as reinforcers. In this chapter, I will attempt to summarize the current status of the problem of reinforcement. I hope that some of the gaps in our current knowledge will make themselves apparent and thus indicate some of the directions which future research on this problem might take.

A. Prologue

There are certain philosophical biases of an epistomological nature that will, from time to time, reappear in the course of this chapter. These should be set forth at the outset in order to make my purpose in this overview more explicit. First, I believe that behavior is mediated by the operations of neural systems. In these times there is not much argument about this assumption, which has some definite implications for the behavioral sciences in general, and for this overview in particular. Specifically, it implies that an event(s) takes place within the nervous system when learning and reinforcement occur. Admittedly we do not know what the latter are, but they are knowable. In addition, this assumption implies that the descriptions and theories of reinforcement derive part of their value from their ability to specify the characteristics of the reinforcement process. To the extent that these descriptions are accurate and the theories are valid, they contribute to our understanding of the nature of the reinforcement process, and to our analysis of the nature of the underlying neural events. This overview will be limited to those views which seem to be most immediately relevant to an understanding of the mechanisms of reinforcement.

B. Classification of Reinforcement Theories

In his revision of Hilgard and Marquis' *Conditioning and Learning*, Kimble (1961) pointed out that there are three attributes that are more or less common to all conditions in which reinforcement occurs: (a) the organism is in some state of motivation, (b) a stimulus is presented, and (c) the organism makes a response. Many of the more recent views of reinforcement have variously emphasized one or several of these attributes in their attempts to derive a unifying summary of those characteristics which give rewards reinforcing properties. In the sections that follow, I have divided these theories, according to what I perceive as their major emphasis, into three sections. I shall review some of the recent theoretical developments, as reflected in this volume and in other related literature, and attempt in the process to point out some of the empirical and conceptual problems of each position.

II. MOTIVATIONAL THEORIES

A. Drive Reduction

In the first chapter of this book, Wilcoxon has reviewed the evolution of Hull's need-reduction principle of reinforcement to the more general statements of drive-stimulus reduction. These ideas are an

extremely important part of our current conception of the reinforcement process. These theories emphasize the fact that those rewards
which seem to restore homeostatic balance or, more generally, reduce
drive stimuli within the animal are the most effective reinforcers.
Drives, by this view, are related to both the strong internal stimuli that
are induced by upsets in homeostatic regulatory systems, and the
strong external stimuli that can be perceived by the animal. When an
action will reduce these stimuli, the action is strengthened, and this
state of affairs constitutes reinforcement. The explanatory power of
this view cannot be denied. There are numerous demonstrations that
those events which reduce drive can serve as reinforcers. In addition,
the ingenious experiments which Miller and his students have devised to test the drive-reduction hypothesis have given it a considerable amount of support.

There are, however, some empirical problems that the theory has
not completely overcome. Specifically, it has been repeatedly demonstrated that numerous stimuli can serve as reinforcers, many of which
do not result in any obvious reduction in drive. Nondeprived animals
will learn a task in order to taste a non-nutritive sweet substance, they
will press bars to turn on lights or receive a puff of a novel odor, they
will run mazes in order to explore an empty goal box, etc. Furthermore, they will work to receive electric shocks or injections of minute
amounts of chemicals into certain parts of their brains. All of these
demonstrations could be incorporated into the drive-reduction hypothesis, but it would necessitate postulating the existence of a drive
to explore or drink sweet substances, or postulating that brain stimulation somehow reduced drive. Though these are real possibilities, it is
rather uncomfortable to have to argue that there is a new drive for every new reward that is demonstrated to have reinforcing attributes.

Even assuming that there are exploratory drives or that brain stimulation reduces drive, it is difficult to demonstrate that these statements
are valid. The demonstration of the existence of a drive is dependent
on the ability to manipulate the conditions that are antecedent to the
appearance of the drive in a variety of ways, and to show by multiple
criteria that the subsequent behavior of the animal is consistent with
the presence of such a drive. Unfortunately, the most frequently used
criterion of the existence of a drive is the observation that a reduction
of the drive is reinforcing, i.e., animals will work to restore the state
that existed before deprivation was introduced. For example, the
demonstration that there is an exploratory drive is dependent on (a)
the ability to deprive the animal of exploration and thus heighten its
subsequent exploratory behavior, and (b) the demonstration that ani-

mals so deprived will learn a variety of tasks for the opportunity to explore at a different rate from those that have not been deprived of exploration. This makes the operations which demonstrate that a drive exists the same as the operations which demonstrate that reducing the drive has reinforcing properties.

Though such demonstrations are difficult, they do exist in the literature on exploration (see Fowler, 1965). Furthermore, intracranial reinforcement and exploration appear to be enhanced by such drives as hunger and thirst (Olds, 1962). Such experiments would suggest that these demonstrations could be fit into the traditional drive-reduction framework, particularly if a part of the function of drives is to energize behavior. However, more work is needed on both of these problems before they can be incorporated into the drive-stimulus reduction theory completely.

There are additional difficulties with a drive-reduction theory of reinforcement that may be more serious. Specifically, for both exploration and intracranial reinforcement, when the stimuli that are presumed to be the reinforcers are presented to the animal, they appear to result in an increase in drive. For example, intracranial stimulation will frequently elicit eating and/or drinking in sated animals (see Valenstein, Cox, and Kakolewski, Chapter 9, this volume). Similarly, the presentation of a light in a darkened test chamber seems to increase exploratory behavior (see Tapp, Chapter 6, this volume). Thus, the stimuli for which the animal will work to reduce drive also have the capacity to increase drive. This seems to present a paradox to the drive-reduction view of reinforcement that cannot be easily resolved within the theory.

B. Arousal

A second major class of motivational theories has arisen in the recent years following the initial demonstration by Moruzzi and Magoun (1949) that the reticular formation of the brain stem is important for the maintenance of consciousness and electroencephalographic activation of the forebrain in cats. These are the arousal theories of drive, and they represent a substantially broader motivational explanation of reinforcement than the drive-reduction view. According to these views, drive is equated with the arousal state of the animal. The higher the drive, the more aroused the organism. When too much arousal occurs, the animal engages in behaviors to attempt to restore the arousal level to a more comfortable range. When some consequence of these behaviors reduces arousal, reinforcement occurs.

These views are very similar to the drive-reduction view and thus face similar difficulties, e.g., animals work or play when arousal apparently does not exist, or at least is not induced by need. Such demonstrations led to reformulations such as those of Berlyne in Chapter 7 of this volume and elsewhere (Berlyne, 1967). According to this view, if a stimulus or a need moves the animal from an optimal state of arousal, it will induce drive or tension, and any event which returns the animal to the optimal level will serve as a reinforcer. Thus, two factors interact to determine whether a particular event will be a reinforcer: (a) the arousal level of the subject, and (b) the arousal potential of the reward. If the arousal potential of the reward moves the organism toward an optimal level of arousal, the reward will be reinforcing.

Arousal theories are potentially attractive for several reasons. First, they have a considerable amount of heuristic value, and they can incorporate much of the known data on drive and reinforcement. Second, they are testable and can lead to specific experiments. Third, they are potentially quantifiable in terms that would allow the development of specific models. Fourth, they remove the apparent paradox from the drive-reduction views that is introduced by the fact that organisms sometimes seek aroused states.

These theories are subject to a number of weaknesses at their present stage of development, not the least of which is the lack of agreement on the operations which define arousal. The terms "arousal" or "activation" in such theories are used because of their obvious physiological implication. The user, however, is quite frequently unclear about which of the several arousal measures should be employed as an independent assessment of the existence of arousal. Such measures are essential for adequate tests of the theory.

Arousal theories also postulate that some measure of behavior is related to some measure or manipulation of arousal by an inverted U-shaped function. Such a definitive statement of a relationship implies that it would be possible, if not absolutely necessary, to include enough data points to examine the shape of the function. Recent technological developments both in the measurement and manipulation of arousal make this a possibility. For example, Berlyne has used standard pharmacological manipulations to both induce and reduce arousal. It should also be possible, using physiological measures, to quantify the arousal change accompanying those manipulations which change arousal levels.

Finally, on a somewhat more conceptual level, the relationship between the arousal level of the subject and the arousal potential of reward needs to be spelled out in more detail. Berlyne has argued that if a reward can move the subject to an optimal level of arousal, it will reinforce. The arousal potential of a reward, as Berlyne has also suggested, is a function of the arousal level of the subject. This gives the theory too much freedom and consequently little predictive value. In Chapter 7 of this volume, Berlyne has recognized this problem and has suggested two possible relationships that might exist between arousal level and arousal potential. Investigations of these relationships are extremely important for the theory.

Routtenberg (1968) has recently proposed a two-arousal hypothesis that is, in some ways, compatible with the suggestions that have been made by Berlyne. Routtenberg has been much more specific in suggesting the function of some particular brain structures in the mediation of arousal. The theory is too detailed for an extensive analysis here, but it represents a laudable effort toward the development of a neural theory that is subject to test.

The main points of Routtenberg's argument are based on the recognition that both external and internal stimuli contribute, in somewhat different ways, to the arousal level of the subject and the subsequent organization of behavior patterns. The reticular formation of the brain stem (arousal system 1) is recognized as critical both for the regulation of the activated state of the animal in response to internal stimuli and for the organization of the responses that will satisfy the need. (This property could easily be incorporated into Berlyne's considerations with regard to the arousal level of the subject.) The limbic system (arousal system 2) provides the control of behavior by regulating the incentive value of external stimuli. (This property is reminiscent of Berlyne's concern for the relationship between arousal potential and reward-value.) The two systems interact by the mutual inhibition and excitation of one another. Rewards have incentive value which excite arousal system 2. This activity leads to consequences in behavior which, in turn, lead to the suppression of arousal system 1. When this occurs, reinforcement takes place.

Though the overlap with Berlyne's view is implicit in Routtenberg's hypothesis, it has not been spelled out in detail. Such an effort might have considerable value for the development of a more definitive neural theory of arousal.

From the preceding discussion, it can be seen that one of the current trends in motivational theories has substituted the concept of arousal for the concept of drive. Unfortunately, theories based on drive and arousal both suffer from problems which arise out of the difficulties associated with defining these concepts in operational terms. Increases in specific drives, such as hunger and thirst, do produce increases in arousal, as measured by changes in electrophysiological activity within the brain (Hockman, 1964; Steiner, 1962; Sutton, 1967), as well as by changes in peripheral autonomic activity (Malmo, 1959; O'Kelly, Hatton, Tucker, & Westall, 1965). Furthermore, the presentation of external stimulus events will arouse the animal by the same criterion (Duffy, 1962). Obviously, much more work is necessary to specify the particular events which contribute to such results. It would be ideal in future experiments to include these physiological measures in behavioral experiments as an independent check on the arousal changes that occur with the observed behavioral changes.

At this point, neither the drive-reduction nor the arousal theories are completely satisfactory explanations of reinforcement phenomena, though both theories hold a great deal of promise for generating future research. There are numerous unanswered questions that relate both to the role of specific drives and to the more general concepts of arousal. What are the specific neural and chemical changes within the brain that occur with increases in drive? Do these occur within relatively discrete systems or are they manifest in more general changes within the brain? How might such changes be related to specific need manipulations? How do increases in drive alter the incentive properties of indifferent stimuli?

III. STIMULUS THEORIES

The arousal theories originated out of the recognition that both external (sensory) and internal (drive) stimuli contribute to the behavior of the organisms within situations in which rewards operate as reinforcers. The demonstrations that rats, mice, monkeys, and men would work when the only apparent reward for their effort was the onset of a light, the taste of a sweet substance, or the opportunity to explore, have led to the development of these stimulus theories of reinforcement. These views were presented as a substitution for drive-reduction theories. They held in common their emphasis on the fact that those events which have some characteristic of a stimulus will reinforce a response if they occur in close temporal contiguity with the response. Since many stimuli occur in contiguity with many responses, but do not seem to reinforce all of these responses, the debate among stimulus theorists becomes one of specifying what attribute of the stimulus gives it the capacity to reinforce behavior.

A. Stimulus-Change

There are some ideas about reinforcement that are embodied in the so-called noneffect theories of learning that will be discussed within the context of the stimulus theories. Guthrie's theory of learning is representative, and his view of reinforcement has been reviewed by Wilcoxon in the first chapter of this volume. I have classified this view as a stimulus-change theory because of historical precedent.

For Guthrie, all learning occurs by the contiguous association between stimuli and responses. Rewards facilitate learning because they remove the animal from the learning situation and protect the formation of stimulus–response associations that are not related to the behavior that is to be learned. If responses occur within the learning situation which cause S–R associations that are incompatible with the one(s) to be learned, they slow acquisition. By causing a change in the learning situation which prevents the occurrence of such competing responses, rewards facilitate learning.

In Chapter 3 in this volume, Estes has taken a somewhat similar view in his discussion of the effectiveness of rewards in learning. According to Estes' model, all learning occurs by the contiguous association among stimuli, responses, and rewards. Rewards are not necessary for learning, but they form a subset of the possible associations that will occur within the learning situation.

According to Estes, the principal function of rewards is to modify the selection of responses. When associations related to particular stimuli are scanned, they are brought into memory. Part of those associations will include the responses that have occurred to those stimuli and the consequences of those responses, i.e., rewards or punishments. The recall of rewarding or punishing consequences carries faciliatory or inhibitory feedback to the S–R associations and will thereby increase or decrease the probability that a response will occur overtly. This process is dependent on the state of learning, in that rewards do not affect acquisition until the response–reward associations have been formed. By this view, rewards can influence performance only after information about rewards has been acquired.

Like Guthrie, then, Estes bases his view on the recognition that rewards do facilitate performance in a learning task when the subject is aware of them. One wonders, however, what special properties rewards might have which give them the capacity to facilitate the formation of the S–R association and the subsequent selection of responses. Could any event have this capacity or must that event have been associated with motivational variables in the past history of the subject? If this association is necessary, is the contiguous association between motivational variables and rewards sufficient for rewards to have this property? Estes has recognized these difficulties and will no doubt deal with them in the future developments of the theory.

I have classified Estes' theory as a stimulus-change theory, in part because of its similarity with Guthrie's earlier statement, but also because I have assumed that the rewards have stimulus properties which contribute to their effects on learning. In this latter capacity, one particularly appealing aspect of Estes' theory is its emphasis on the informational capacity of rewards. Once the subject has learned the reward-punishment consequence of his responses, these consequences can facilitate or inhibit the selection of the appropriate responses when the stimuli are encountered on future trials. In this way rewards provide information about the relevance of a particular S-R association. Though this aspect of the theory does not deal with the reinforcement problem, i.e., it does not tell us what special properties rewards and punishments have which allow them to produce these effects, it is a rather simple and parsimonious statement about the role of rewards in learning. Furthermore, it offers a potential for integrating this theory with much of the current work on the informational properties of conditioned rewards (see Wike, 1966). Finally, this aspect of the theory points to one of the major problems in the current work on reinforcement: the distinction between the informational and the affective properties of rewards. I will return to this point later.

In a substantially different tradition from Guthrie, another class of stimulus-change theories has arisen from the demonstration that sensory events per se can reinforce a response (see Kish, 1966). In its original form, the hypothesis states that response-contingent stimulation in any modality is reinforcing. In a somewhat more general form, the hypothesis has been modified to suggest that a response-produced change in stimulation is reinforcing. Proponents of this view hypothesize that a change in stimulation is necessary for reinforcement to occur. Unfortunately, they have not dealt with the problem of whether stimulus-change is sufficient for reinforcement to occur.

In this form, the theory has some appeal because it can include all of the known facts of reinforcement. Every event that has been demonstrated to reinforce a response has an element of stimulus-change, regardless of whether the change occurs in external or internal receptors. This, however, merely represents a description of one of several common components of those rewards which have reinforcing properties. The theory is not sufficiently well developed to handle the negative cases, i.e., those instances where a detectable change occurs in the stimulus but where the response which produced those changes is not reinforced. It would be difficult to predict whether any given stimulus will reinforce a response. One is then faced with the task of cataloging all stimuli over all of their possible parametric variations to determine which are and which are not members of the reinforcing class.

Furthermore, stimuli apparently lose their effectiveness as reinforcers on repeated presentations even though it is reasonable to assume that the response-produced change is detectable by the animal (see Chapter 6 by Tapp and Chapter 10 by Carlton, this volume). Finally, there is no evidence to date to indicate that the reinforcing effectiveness of a response-produced change in stimulation is not related in some way to the animal's motivational state or to the animal's previous experiences with the stimulus. Obviously, further developments and research in this theory are necessary for it to attain status beyond that of a description of one of the characteristics of rewards.

An integration of these stimulus-change views with the previous discussion of Estes' view is possible since a response-produced change in stimulation is a potential source of information to the organism. Assuming that exploratory behavior represents an instance of information seeking behaviors on the part of the animal, a response which produces a stimulus-change in the environment might facilitate the repetition of that response by serving as a source of feedback, providing the animal with information about the relevance of the one response over all others. It is necessary, however, to postulate qualitatively different types of feedback for different classes of stimuli, in order to handle the cases in which stimulus-change is not reinforcing. One is again faced with the task of studying animals' reactions to all stimuli in the hope of deriving general relationships between stimuli and their effects.

B. Optimal Level of Stimulation

There has been an effort by McCall (1966) to save the stimulus-change theory by couching it in terms of the ideas which have developed around Helson's concept of adaptation level. According to McCall, the stimulus-change hypothesis predicts that the reinforcing properties of an illumination change will be an increasing function of the amount of light change (up to a point), regardless of the direction of the change. He then proceeds to demonstrate that rats will work for an illumination change from a level to which they had previously adapted. Unfortunately, the data are not completely consistent with the theory, for the rats continue to work longer for both dimmer illumination changes and decrements than they work for brighter illuminations and increments. McCall attributes these changes to the nocturnal nature of the rat.

Bevan and Adamson (1960) have developed a more quantitative model of reinforcement from similar considerations of adaptation level theory, which thus far has not received critical examination, perhaps because they have not specified the limits of its parameters. The Bevan and Adamson model assumes that organisms can discriminate changes in stimulation from a background level of stimuli and that expected levels of stimulation are derived by averaging stimuli over time. The magnitude of reinforcement then will be dependent on the distance of the reinforcing stimulus from the expected levels of stimulation. The theory further postulates that the tension level of the subject, which is a function of such variables as amount of deprivation, will also influence the effects of reinforcement on performance. Thus, the effect of rewards is a function of both the deviations from expectation and the tension level of the subject. The particular relationship between these variables is not specified.

The ideas in this theory are worthy of further development and test. The Bevan-Adamson theory stresses the fact that change from adaptation levels will be reinforcing, and McCall's data certainly support this notion. Furthermore, as Helson (1966) has pointed out, these changes become a part of the background levels, and as they become integrated into the total sample of stimuli over time, they should lose their effectiveness as reinforcers. This implication is also supported by McCall's results. However, the theory does not take into account the potential preferences that an organism may have for particular levels of stimulation. Such preferences would certainly bias the results of experiments designed to test the theory.

Lockhard (1963) has recognized the difficulties with a theory of reinforcement based solely on stimulus-change and offers an alternative that is compatible with other explanations of reinforcement. In an ingenious set of studies, Lockhard demonstrated that rats will press levers to maintain their environment at particular levels of illumination. Furthermore, the illumination level that they prefer is a function of the strain of the rat and the illumination of the environment in which the animals were reared (Lockhard, 1962). He has interpreted these results as indicating that rats prefer particular levels of illumination. He then predicts that those illumination changes which are in the direction of the animal's preferred level of illumination will be reinforcing. He confirms this prediction in another series of experiments (Lockhard, 1966).

Lockhard's results and interpretations are in sharp contrast to those of McCall. Indeed, they are so different that one wonders at first impression whether either set of results could be valid. The facts suggest that both results are accurate reflections of a true state of affairs. The differences between experiments are numerous and include such variables as the length of the test session, the range of light intensities used, the duration and conditions of prior exposure to the particular illumination intensities, etc. All of these variables contribute to the differential results of each investigator.

The two sets of results can be made compatible by suggesting, as Lockhard and McCall have, that there are two different processes at work which govern performance over short- and long-run tests. In the long run, rats do prefer a range of low levels of illumination, and they will work to maintain these levels. In the short run, a response-produced change in stimulation is a novel event. Under these circumstances, it is likely that a response will be repeated until the stimulus consequence is learned and that performance will then continue only if the consequent level of illumination is a more preferred one. If this is a valid interpretation, it suggests that considerations with regard to adaptation level will determine the reinforcing properties of stimuli over the short run. Innate preference hierarchies may produce the more long-range effects of reinforcing stimuli. In the short run the animal may react to any stimulus that is deviant (novel) from its expectant level of stimulation. This stimulus is evaluated, and long-range behaviors are initiated in terms of the results of the evaluation process. The ease with which evaluation will occur will depend on the modality of stimulation, the neural organization of that modality with reflexive response systems, and the previous experiences of the animal with the stimulus.

At this point, there is no satisfactory theory which accounts for the reinforcing properties of stimuli in the sense that they have been reviewed in this section. It is certainly the case that response-produced changes in some stimuli can increase the frequency of lever-pressing (see Tapp, Chapter 6, this volume). However, as pointed out elsewhere (Tapp & Simpson, 1966), there is a considerable difference between the reinforcing properties of light onset and reinforcement by food, water, or escape from shock.

One of the main differences between reinforcement by stimulation and reinforcement by more traditional rewards is in the temporal duration of the reaction of the animal to the stimuli. For some stimuli these reactions habituate when the stimulus is presented repeatedly. For other stimuli, the reactions persist, frequently increasing in vigor. Carlton (Chapter 10, this volume) distinguishes between these effects on the basis of the "biological significance" of the stimulus for the animal. For those stimuli which have "biological significance," habituation will not occur. Though there are some rather obvious difficulties with the definition of "biological significance," the point of the distinction is important, for it reiterates the fact that animals have been selected on the basis of their ability to react and stop reacting to stimuli within their environment. Such considerations lead us into another set of stimulus theories which have been around for a long time and which appear to offer a potential resolution to some of the problems of reinforcement.

C. Hedonic Properties of Stimuli

For centuries it has been recognized that some stimuli are more pleasant than others, and furthermore, that both men and animals would work for those stimuli. Such considerations have given rise to the so-called hedonic theories. Young has made the argument for such views repeatedly (see Young, 1959; Young, 1966). He has called attention to the fact that organisms move toward some stimuli and will work to maintain proximity with those stimuli. Other stimuli seem to elicit withdrawal, and the animal will work to remove itself from proximity with those stimuli. These behaviors reflect hedonic processes which have a physiological basis in the nervous system. At this time, we do not know what this neural organization is, but by assessing the hedonic properties of stimuli by their associated approach and withdrawal patterns, the problem becomes solvable.

Pfaffman (Chapter 8, this volume; 1960) has taken the hedonic argument much further by pointing to research which indicates that the approach behaviors elicited by sweet substances may be genetically determined. Furthermore, he suggests that those substances which are most preferred in a free response situation offer the greatest potential as reinforcers.

One particularly appealing aspect of these theories is found in the assumption that the "pleasantness" of a stimulus can be genetically determined. This assumption has the effect of dismissing the concern for demonstrating how the stimulus got its pleasant attributes. In a way, the argument here is analogous to postulating a drive for every motivated behavior. Instead of a drive, however, we have substituted a genetically organized neural system that releases or excites approach behavior when the stimulus is encountered.

The arguments for the existence of such systems are impressive, not so much for their empirical demonstration as for their basis in biological fact. Le Magnen (1967) has pointed out that when a substance is tasted, it is at a point where the organism must make a final decision about ingesting it. Consuming a sweet tasting substance is likely to promote the survival of the species since, in nature, sweet tastes are correlated with substances that promote survival. Conversely, bitter or sour substances would be likely to have undesirable effects on the species since such tastes are correlated with substances that are deleterious to survival. Since the consequences of ingestion determine the life or death of the species, it is reasonable to assume that natural selection has culled out the animals who find pleasure in the taste of bitter substances. As Pfaffman has pointed out, there is a great need for empirical investigations of the sort which would examine the genetic environmental contributions to animals' preferences for particular substances in order to evaluate the validity of these arguments.

The hedonic theories have also offered a method that seems to have some potential application to the reinforcement problem. Specifically, the suggestion has been made that those stimuli which are most preferred have the greatest potential as reinforcers. Indeed, Lockhard's data could be taken as a demonstration of the validity of the hedonic hypothesis to another sense modality. The main point here is that both Pfaffman and Lockhard have used independent manipulations (preferences tests) to generate *a priori* predictions about the reinforcing properties of taste substances and illumination changes. As a method, this offers possibilities for operationally separating reinforcement and learning. Nunnally and his students have used the preference methods to study acquired rewards in children. Their data are further testimony to the possibilities that such methods afford (Nunnally & Faw, 1968).

The hedonic theories have had another general effect that is perhaps of some consequence for future developments. Specifically, they have served as a constant reminder of the biological nature of the beasts we study. It is reasonable to assume that selective pressures have contributed to animals' reactions to stimuli. The particular question of interest is how these reactions are mediated by neural systems.

By way of summary, there are some common themes to the stimulus theories of reinforcement. First, they all recognize that a reward is, at least, a response-contingent change in stimulation. Second, there is some recognition that animals approach or withdraw from these stimuli and that some attribute of the stimulus may elicit these behaviors. Third, the reinforcing properties of the stimuli seem to be related to the attributes of the stimuli that effect approach and withdrawal. Fourth, species of animals may differ markedly from one another with respect to the kinds of stimuli they will approach or avoid.

The primary problem with the stimulus theories is the specification of the origin of the approach or withdrawal behaviors that accompany the stimuli. This problem holds equally well for Estes' view of rewards in learning and the hedonic theories. How do stimuli come to elicit faciliatory or inhibitory feedback (approach or withdrawal)? The answer to this question appears to be related to an understanding of the informational and affective attributes of stimuli and their interactions. In this regard, it is important to keep in mind potential differences in the informational properties of stimuli. In particular, a stimulus has informational properties both in its role as a cue that forecasts some future event and as a source of confirmation which indicates the "appropriate" or "inappropriate" nature of a response. In its confirmatory capacity, a stimulus may be effective as a reinforcer to the extent to which it has either served as a cue or elicits approach and withdrawal behaviors, i.e., serves as a UCS. In either function, a cue may have affective properties.

Obviously, more information is necessary on the origin and the conditions under which informative stimuli and/or preference hierarchies affect behavior. How are the informational attributes of stimuli related to preferences for those stimuli, and vice versa? How flexible are preference hierarchies? What is the range over which a stimulus for any sense modality can become a conditioned reinforcer? What are the necessary and sufficient conditions for conditioned reinforcement to occur? Are these the same for all sense systems? What is the neural organization of preference behavior? Is the neural control of preference similar for different sense modalities?

IV. RESPONSE THEORIES

A third major class of reinforcement theories emphasizes the fact that for most rewards there is an associated response that leads to the completion of the instrumental act. For example, food rewards are chewed up and swallowed, water is lapped up and swallowed, and the onset of a light facilitates observing responses. Theories which emphasize these attributes of rewards are the so-called response theories, and they suggest that responses which accompany rewards may be related to their reinforcing properties. This general view is also supported by the demonstrations that animals will press levers to run in a wheel, will run down runways to copulate without ejaculating, will work in order to manipulate objects, etc.

A. Consummatory Response

The nature of the consummatory response theories has been confused somewhat by two interpretations of the word "consummatory." In the literature, it is generally accepted that these theories reflect something which relates to the behaviors which are associated with the presence of the reward. Consummatory is, however, the adverbial form of the word "consummate," and thus the theories can be taken as having reference to the satisfying state of affairs which accompanies the achievement of a goal by the successful completion of a series of acts. The difficulty with this latter meaning is derived from the inability to observe this satisfactory completion of the series of acts. The best, and perhaps only, available measure of this state is the consumptive acts associated with the goal object. Unfortunately, this operational limitation appears to have placed the major emphasis in these theories on the peripheral consumptive behaviors.

One of the major consummatory response theories of reinforcement has been developed over several years by Sheffield. According to an early version, Sheffield (see 1966a) outlined a theory of drive induction which was proposed as an explanation for the sequence of events that occurred during the course of the acquisition of an instrumental behavior. In brief, the theory indicated that stimuli could come to excite the animal by their contiguous association with consummatory responses and that this conditioned excitement induced the animal to increase its performance over the course of acquisition. It was rather difficult to tell exactly what the reinforcing event was in this earlier paper, though it was certainly correlated with the consumptive behaviors. The consummatory response itself was defined as "the response which removes the drive." In later papers, Sheffield has become more explicit. At one point (see Sheffield, 1966b) he suggested that drive states induce excitability in the animal, which in turn sensitizes the activation mechanism for the appropriate consummatory response. When the innate consummatory stimulus is presented, the activated mechanism channels impulses into the consummatory response, and presumably reinforcement has taken place.

Sheffield (1965) suggests that the rewards in instrumental learning have stimulus characteristics that make them unconditioned stimuli.

These elicit unconditioned responses which, I presume, are the total array of reactions to the rewards, including the consummatory response. Acquisition proceeds when the response-produced cues (sensory feedback) associated with the instrumental behavior (CS) become conditioned to the reward stimuli (UCS). When this occurs, the instrumental behavior elicits some fraction of the array of reactions to rewards. This last view might be called "reinforcement by substitution" in the sense that the instrumental responses themselves become conditioned reinforcers. Thus, only correct responding will lead to anticipation of reward, and other responses will not have this conditioned reinforcing value. Presumably, if the correct response has conditioned reward value, some of the stimuli that are in proximity with the response also take on some strength as conditioned stimuli. Through a series of such associations, the stimuli which elicit anticipation of food are exciting and increase the vigor of behavior until consummation occurs. Then the vigor subsides and the animal relaxes.

It is hard to determine from this analysis when reinforcement takes place during acquisition. Though Sheffield may now have taken a nonreinforcement position, i.e., that learning occurs without reinforcement, he, like Estes, still has rewards in the system to make instrumental learning work more efficiently. Sheffield, as does Estes, also uses the excitatory effects of unconditioned responses associated with rewards to facilitate acquisition. Sheffield, also as Estes, does not address himself specifically to a discussion of how these rewards come to elicit consummatory responses, but presumably this is either innate in the system or is conditioned by association with relaxation.

The idea that consummatory responses are, in some way, mediators of reinforcement is appealing partly because Sheffield's theory seems to be an accurate description of the events which have taken place in instrumental learning. Furthermore, on an empirical level the experiments that are reviewed by Valenstein, Cox, and Kakolewski (Chapter 9, this volume) and by Glickman and Schiff (1967) give this view a considerable amount of support. Specifically, these articles describe the numerous recent reports of "stimulus-bound" behavior that is elicited by electrical stimulation of the hypothalamus and brain stem. The behaviors that are produced are, almost without exception, consumptive responses, e.g., eating, drinking, exploration, sexual activity, which occur in the presence of the appropriate goal object. The same electrode sites are frequently found to be positively reinforcing when tested in a lever-pressing situation. The implication from this work is that consummatory responses accompany consumptive behaviors.

Glickman and Schiff (1967) have elaborated a biological theory of reinforcement which is an extension of Sheffield's consummatory response theory. In brief, they suggest that reinforcement occurs when the neural systems within the brain stem that mediate the expression of species-specific responses are activated. A reward is reinforcing when the stimuli associated with the reward facilitate the activity of these response systems. Neural activity in these pathways is the sufficient condition for reinforcement. Thus, rewards have the properties of unconditioned stimuli in that they can elicit species-specific behavior patterns. Not all stimuli will be equally effective in this capacity. Glickman and Schiff make some rather specific statements about the organization of these neural systems, and they amass a considerable amount of data in support of their argument. Their theory is a valuable elaboration of the neural basis of the consummatory response theory and suggests numerous experiments to evaluate its validity.

It would be appropriate here to interject some empirical counterarguments to the consummatory response theories. The major demonstrations which contradict this view are based on experiments in which animals show evidence of learning without engaging in consumptive behaviors. Miller and Kessen (1952), for example, found that rats will learn a T-maze when milk is delivered directly into their stomachs. Similarly, Epstein (1960) has demonstrated that rats will press levers when the only reward is an injection of food or water into their stomachs. No obvious sensory cues nor consummatory responses occur in the Epstein preparation, yet the animals will learn the task (though slowly) and regulate their food intake very accurately (Epstein & Teitelbaum, 1962). Similarly, injections of glucose into the blood stream can reward choice behavior (Clark, Schuster, & Brady, 1961). Apparently the consumptive response is not necessary for acquisition, and therefore we must assume that it is not necessary for reinforcement. This does not, however, rule out the presence of consummatory states elsewhere in the organism. Indeed, all groups of animals in the Kessen and Miller experiments did change their performance, suggesting that the rewards were reinforcing regardless of the mode of delivery. It is clear from these studies that the presence of the consumptive responses served to facilitate learning. Furthermore, if, as Glickman and Schiff suggest, it is the case that the activation of the central response mechanisms is sufficient for reinforcement to occur, delivering nutrients without consumptive behaviors might induce such neural activation.

B. Prepotent Response

Premack (1965) has presented an eclectic response theory of reinforcement which can easily incorporate the consummatory response
ideas. He points out that in a learning situation reinforcement always
involves a relative relationship between two responses: one that is
being reinforced and one that is responsible for the reinforcement.
The latter response is the prepotent one within the situation, i.e., it
always occurs at a higher rate than the response which is to be
learned. From this analysis, he argues that a necessary condition for
reinforcement is a rate (frequency) differential between two responses
within the situation. The responses that occur at a high rate can reinforce those that are emitted at a lower rate. Premack and his students
have performed a number of ingenious experiments that demonstrate
that reinforcement has such a relative relationship.

Obviously this response relativity is not the sufficient condition for
reinforcement, because there are many cases in which a high frequency response follows a low frequency response and reinforcement
does not occur. These considerations have led Premack to analyze
those conditions which are used as a demonstration that reinforcement has occurred. Of primary importance in this regard is the contingency between the response and the reward. As he indicates, there
are three conditions that accompany the contingent relationship between a response and the potential reinforcer. First, the response that
is to be reinforced must precede the reinforcement in time. Second,
the response of the organism to the reinforcer is restricted in that it is
generally circumscribed by the experimental arrangement within the
situation, e.g., rats must press levers for reinforcement to occur. The
animal is thus restricted in the kinds of behaviors which produce rewards. Third, a reduction in the duration of responding typically accompanies the reward, e.g., on any given trial, animals do not consume all of the food or water they would normally consume if they had
free access to food or water. Though the fact that the contingency between responses and rewards leads to rapid acquisition cannot be
denied, we do not know which of these three factors contributes to the
power of that contingency.

Premack cites Skinner's demonstration of superstitious behavior in
pigeons as a demonstration that the response need not be circumscribed or limited to any particular act for learning to take place. He
then describes an experiment in which rats can run in order to drink.
The difference between this procedure and those used elsewhere is
that both running and drinking are programmed to occur at their base

levels. Running is always followed by drinking, but running and drinking occur in amounts equal to their normal "burst" frequencies. This procedure produces no increase in running, i.e., no learning, and therefore indicates that the temporal order between responses and rewards is not sufficient for reinforcement to occur. By exclusion, Premack then argues that the reduction in the duration of responding is the necessary and sufficient conduct for contingency between responses and rewards to produce reinforcement: "Apparently, an invariant though unrecognized component contingency is a decrement in the amount of responding that occurs to the contingent stimulus, relative to what would occur were the stimulus free. Our results suggest that this reduction is vital, that reinforcement cannot be initiated without it (Premack, 1965, p. 172)."

Because Premack's ideas represent a relatively new contribution to the analysis of the reinforcement problem, it is only to be expected that empirical evidence is lacking to establish the generality of the theory. The theory is, however, valuable for several reasons. First, it has heuristic value in that it summarizes the nature of those events which do lead to reinforcement quite well. All events which have a high frequency of occurrence (H) will reinforce a response of lower frequency of occurrence (L) if the responses occur in temporal contiguity and if H is reduced in duration from its naturally occurring level. Second, Premack has been very explicit in specifying the operations that would allow one to determine whether or not a particular response would reinforce another response. In particular, one measures the amount of time the animal engages in a particular behavior in a free operant situation, then presents H after L, with H being reduced in duration. (This measure is an assessment of response-preference hierarchies.) This is in contrast to other theories, where the measure of the reinforcing event is not specified. Finally, his ideas may force us to evaluate the nature of the reinforcement process more precisely.

To establish the generality of Premack's theory, the ideas presented need to be extended to other situations in which the reinforcement process has been investigated, such as in avoidance conditioning, classic conditioning, and reinforcement by sensory stimulation. This theory, like other response theories, does not account for the demonstration that animals will change their performance when there are apparently no overt responses involved, as in the cases in which a performance change occurs after food or water is placed directly into the stomach. Finally, the theory needs further empirical examination in a variety of situations in which reinforcement is presumed to operate.

C. Central Confirming Reaction

A third response theory that has received some revitalized support is the "central confirming reaction" of Thorndike. According to this view, when a reward occurs it initiates the "overhead control mechanism" which stamps in, or confirms, the previous S–R association.

Miller (1963) has recently postulated a "go mechanism(s) within the brain which acts to intensify ongoing responses to cues and traces of immediately preceding activities, producing a stronger intensification the more strongly the 'go mechanism' is activated." A variety of satisfying and annoying states of affairs will activate this mechanism, and all responses, including activation of this mechanism, are subject to conditioning with contiguity being sufficient. Miller then goes on to elaborate the rules by which acquisition and extinction take place. He puts the "go mechanism" in the nervous system and suggests numerous experiments to evaluate its operational properties. The similarity of this view to Thorndike's view is also acknowledged.

With the possible exception of Premack's prepotent response theory, there is a similarity between all of the response theories, which is based primarily on the idea that a central neural event somehow related to a response takes place when a reward occurs. Some aspect of this central neural event is related to behaviors that are elicited by the reward. Even Premack recognizes that "the efficacy of a stimulus as a reinforcer varies with the probability that the subject will respond to that stimulus."

There is a considerable amount of current evidence which favors the aforementioned response theories. I have mentioned previously the demonstrations that electrical stimulation of the brain, which is positively reinforcing, can also elicit consumptive behaviors. Similarly, there appears to be chemical specificity in the elicitation of these behaviors. For example, Grossman (1960) has demonstrated that central injections of acetylcholine and norepinepherine into the hypothalamus elicit drinking or eating, depending on the substance injected. Furthermore, there is evidence that loading an animal to satisfy an existing need without sensory feedback from ingestion will activate neural circuits in the brain. Oomura, Kimura, Ooyama, Maeno, Iki, and Kuniyoshi (1964) have reported increases in the neural activity of units in the ventral medial nucleus of the hypothalamus following glucose injections into the carotid arteries of cats. Similar injections decreased unit activity in the lateral hypothalamus. Perhaps these, or similar, neural changes represent the central confirming event which reflects a consummatory state that is necessary for reinforcement.

For a variety of reasons, it is justifiable to argue that the consumptive responses per se are not sufficient for reinforcement. Rather, the presence of environmental stimuli plays a very important role in eliciting and maintaining these behaviors. In Premack's theory, which is perhaps the most response-oriented of these views, it is recognized that the stimuli are critical for the initiation and control of the responses. On a more empirical level, the electrically elicited consummatory behaviors following hypothalamic or brain stem stimulation are "stimulus bound," i.e., they do not occur in the absence of the "stimulus object" appropriate to the consummatory response. These results suggest that the elicitation of the response is dependent on sensory feedback from the environment for the behavior to be maintained.

The data presented by Valenstein, Cox, and Kakolewski (Chapter 9, this volume) suggest that further modification of the response theories may be in order. In most of the response theories of reinforcement it is implicitly assumed, or explicitly stated, that the consummatory response is innate to the organism and is elicited by the appropriate stimuli. Valenstein *et al.* present data to show that there is a considerable amount of flexibility in the "stimulus-bound" behaviors elicited by electrical stimulation of the hypothalamus. In the absence of the appropriate stimulus (e.g., food), animals will switch to another stimulus (water), and show a relatively permanent change in "stimulus-bound" responding.

V. ECLECTIC VIEWS

The preceding sections have made it fairly apparent that no single theory of reinforcement will handle all of the phenomena that have been related to the reinforcement process. All of the various views I have reviewed fall short in some respects. Indeed, all theories are forced to examine all three of the components of the reinforcement situation in one way or another. As an alternative, several theories have evolved which were from the outset more eclectic in their approach and have emphasized various aspects of the reinforcement problem simultaneously. Rather than try to cover all of these, I will

sketch the basic outlines of such theories in order to point out one of
their major problems.

For the most part, these eclectic views emphasize the motivational
events that occur during the performance changes which follow the
delivery of rewards. Walker (Chapter 2, this volume) and Bindra
(1968) have illustrated this point. Walker argues that reinforcement is
not necessary for learning, in the sense that the reinforcer is a
strengthener (glue) of the connection between a stimulus and a response. Instead, he suggests that ideas that have traditionally been
associated with incentives or with drives (pull and push concepts,
respectively) can account for phenomena typically ascribed to reinforcement effects. He argues that the latent-learning literature has
provided ample demonstration that learning does occur without glue
(reinforcement). Therefore, reinforcement must affect only performance changes. However, performance changes are due to the incentive properties of rewards as they interact with drives. Of what use,
then, is the reinforcement concept?

Bindra (1968) has made a similar argument. He sees two types of
motivational effects that control behavior: those related to the physiological consequences of drive manipulations and those produced by
incentives. Both of these effects interact to determine the final motor
output of the organism.

Both authors make a strong case for their point of view and, indeed,
much of behavior can be accounted for by these two motivational concepts. The critical problem in these theories resides in their failure to
explain how incentives come to be. Walker suggests that "stimuli
without incentive value can acquire it through consistent association
with incentives." This is an empirically valid statement (Duchnowski,
1968), but the question remains: Where did the first incentive get its
incentive value? The acquired rewarding properties of stimuli remains a problem of considerable importance for understanding of the
process of reinforcement.

VI. OVERVIEW

In the preceding sections, many of the theories reviewed have been
concerned with specifying the necessary and sufficient conditions for
reinforcement to occur, i.e., the attributes of rewards that give them
reinforcing properties. With the exception of Premack's theory, there
are probably more similarities between these views than there are
differences. The theories were conceived to handle particular subsets

of data associated with reinforcement phenomena, and consequently they differ in their major emphasis. However, there is a striking similarity among most of these theories and their hypothetical statements about the nature of the reinforcing event, which, for most theories, is analogous to the central confirming reactions of Thorndike. In the motivational theories, reinforcement is the event which produces a reduction in drive, or returns the arousal level to an optimum. In the stimulus theories, this event is the response-produced change in stimulation and its associated informational value or the activation of hedonic neural circuits. In Estes' view of rewards, the inhibitory or facilitatory feedback associated with rewards has the same function. For response theories, the reaction is some component of the consummatory response for the activation of a "go mechanism." For the more eclectic views, the reinforcing event is a characteristic of an incentive that in some way interacts with drive. In all cases, the event is unobservable, and in all cases it is this particular event that gives the reward reinforcing properties.

All of these views seem to be variations on a common theme, the views being distinguished by slightly different empirical points of origin. Specifically, most of the theories postulate a neural reaction which accompanies the reward and which represents the explanation of reinforcement. Because this event is, at present, unobservable, these theories offer little to the determination of those critical characteristics of rewards which make them reinforcers.

It is true that some of the hypotheses arising from these theories are testable, in the sense that they have been spelled out in enough detail to allow one to generate predictable consequences that may or may not actually occur. Other theories are less rigorous but offer the possibility for further development that might lead to some fruitful research. However, it appears to me that no matter what the findings are that would be generated by one theory over another they could easily be incorporated into an alternative view. No doubt this state of affairs reflects the current status of our knowledge of the reinforcement process. It would appear that all of the facts on reinforcement phenomena are not available. There is still too much we do not know about what rewards do to an organism beyond their capacity to change performance.

Another point of similarity among some of the theories can be found in the specification of the origin of the reinforcing event. For many of the views outlined above, the neural event that accompanies reinforcement is an innately organized neural response that is elicited by an external stimulus. For these theories, the reinforcing event is an unconditioned response that is elicited by an unconditioned stimulus. A conditioned stimulus can acquire its reinforcing properties through association with the unconditioned stimulus. In this regard, the stimuli that serve as rewards are usually viewed as a source of feedback to regulate the behaviors that occur within the training environment. It is generally recognized by all theorists that selective pressures have predisposed the animal to be more or less reactive to stimuli. These reactions may occur more easily to stimuli within some modalities more than others and to some stimulus qualities within a modality to a greater extent than others. The evolutionary process, no doubt, has endowed the animal with innately organized approach and withdrawal reactions to stimuli, which can be modified to differing extents by the experiences of the animal. These reactions to stimuli are the responses which we measure. They frequently take the form of consumptive acts. The consequences of these acts result in other stimuli which act on the organism and produce their associated reactions. Through association, stimuli can acquire reinforcing properties.

As a final point of similarity, all the theories reviewed above have addressed themselves to problems of motivation. The reinforcement concept has evolved out of a need to explain why reactions are repeated, why running is facilitated by the presence of some stimulus events and not others, and why some stimuli are approached and others avoided. In the classic tradition of psychology, these are motivational problems. In the views outlined above, these questions have been asked within the context of the reinforcement problem.

Historically, this represents a reorientation to some old questions. The consequence of this new orientation is to shift the locus of control of the organism's behavior from within the organism to within the environment. It is no longer necessary with this new orientation to postulate drives which control behavior. Rather, drives become a part of the total stimulus array, and the questions become ones related to how rewards or, more generally, external stimuli interact with internal stimuli in the regulation of behavior. This is not to say that considerations about the effects of drive on behavior are not relevant to these problems. However, drives can now be viewed as dispositional tendencies that potentially bias the effects of external stimuli on the organism. The problem can now be seen in a somewhat different light. The actions of the nervous system, as they are manifest in behavior, reflect relative states of imbalance between neurochemical control systems within the brain. These neural systems are continually sampling states of the internal and external environments, and as a result of this sampling process, corrective behaviors are continually being generated. In this context, reinforcement represents a process that feeds back information to further modify the state of these systems as they become set to receive future information and execute future acts. Thus, the process of reinforcement is not explained by any single event, but by specifying the interaction between events that are occurring within the neural systems. By this view, our understanding of the reinforcement process will come with our understanding of the neuroanatomical, neurophysiological, and neurochemical mechanisms that regulate these control systems and their interactions.

These considerations point to the need to bring newer technological developments to the work on the problem of reinforcement. In this volume, chapters by Valenstein, Cox, and Kakolewski (9), Carlton (10), Stein (11), and Kupferman and Pinsker (12), exemplify this development. They indicate that there are ways of examining this problem different from those which have been used in our traditional analyses of the effects of rewards. The data of Valenstein, Cox, and Kakolewski demonstrate that there is a considerable amount of modification that can take place in the elicitation of behaviors by electrical stimulation. The data presented by Carlton have laid the foundation for detailed examination of the role of acetylcholine in the mediation of the inhibitory behavioral system. As he has indicated, there is much need for further examination of the neurochemical functioning of specific neural systems, and he has provided us with a rather detailed hypothesis for future investigations. Similarly, Stein has gone a long way toward specifying some of the neurochemical changes that are taking place within the nervous system that accompany reinforcement by brain stimulation. He has shown that an analysis of such neurochemical systems is possible by the use of a variety of techniques. The data in his chapter are extremely provocative and make the point that controlled behavior is regulated by complex interacting activities within the brain. Finally, the work reviewed by Kupferman and Pinsker points to specific neurological models that can be applied to the learning situation and can be examined not only in simple organisms like the *Aplysia*, but also potentially in organisms as complicated as the rat.

This is not to say that there is not a need for behavioral experiments in the analysis of reinforcement phenomena. Indeed, the reinforcement process is defined by its effects on behavior, and there is much we do not understand about these effects. As I have indicated above, there is a definite need for disassociating the informational and affective attributes of stimuli. Specifically, the nervous system is responding to the information received about the external and internal environment, but apparently the magnitude of the affective qualities of some sources of the information seems to interact with their informational attributes and to produce greater potential changes in performance. An analysis of the interactions between informational and affective effects of stimuli on behavior is a very important step toward the understanding of the nature of reinforcement.

Numerous other behavioral problems exist which require much more research. The examination of the effects on behavior of alterations in need is critical to a determination of how internal states alter animals' reactions to environmental stimuli. Similarly, we do not understand how stimuli acquire conditioned reward value, or how preferences are related to the reinforcing properties of stimuli, or how preference hierarchies can be altered by experience. Finally, on the theoretical level, there is need for a definitive specification of the operational characteristics of rewards. To the extent that mathematical theories of learning can specify the magnitude of the parameters as they are influenced by the operation of the rewards within a learning situation, these developments will provide a firm basis on which to analyze the reinforcement process.

It is clear, both from the material I have reviewed in this chapter and from material that has been presented elsewhere in this volume, that research on the problem of reinforcement is just beginning. With the demonstration of the effectiveness of rewards for behavior modification and control, we have begun to realize the power of the reinforcement process. At the same time, there has been a renewed recognition of the biological significance of rewards. Both of these developments have resulted in the rephrasing of older problems in what appear to be meaningful contexts. As a result, many new alternatives are being suggested, considered, and subjected to experimental verification. This, of course, is the way of progress.

REFERENCES

Berlyne, D. E. Arousal and reinforcement. In D. Levine (Ed.), *Nebraska symposium on motivation.* Lincoln, Nebr.: Univer. of Nebraska Press, 1967. Pp. 1-110.

Bevan, W., & Adamson, R. Reinforcers and reinforcement: Their relation to maze performance. *J. exp. Psychol.*, 1960, **59**, 226-232.

Bindra, D. Neuropsychological interpretation on general activity and instrumental behavior. *Psychol. Rev.*, 1968, **75**, 1-22.

Clark, R., Schuster, C. R., & Brady, J. V. Instrumental conditioning of jugular self-infusion in the rhesus monkey. *Science*, 1961, **133**, 1829-1830.

Duchnowski, A. J. The association of neutral objects with rewards: Effects of continuous versus partial reward. Unpublished doctoral dissertation, Vanderbilt Univer., 1968.

Duffy, E. *Activation and behavior.* New York: Wiley, 1962.

Epstein, A. N. Water intake without the act of drinking. *Science,* 1960, **131,** 497-498.

Epstein, A. N., & Teitelbaum, P. Regulation of food intake in the absence of taste, smell and other oropharyngeal sensations. *Psychol. Rev.,* 1962, **55,** 753-759.

Fowler, H. *Curiosity and exploratory behavior.* New York: Macmillan, 1965.

Glickman, S. E., & Schiff, B. B. A biological theory of reinforcement. *Psychol. Rev.,* 1967, **74,** 81-109.

Grossman, S. P. Eating or drinking elicited by direct adrenergic or cholinergic stimulation of the hypothalamus. *Science,* 1960, **132,** 301-302.

Helson, H. Some problems in motivation from the point of view of the theory of adaptation level. In D. Levine (Ed.), *Nebraska symposium on motivation.* Lincoln, Nebr.: Univer. of Nebraska Press, 1966. Pp. 137-182.

Hockman, C. H. EEG and behavioral effects of food deprivation in the albino rat. *Electroencephalog. clin. Neurophysiol.,* 1964, **17,** 420-427.

Kimble, G. A. *Hilgard and Marquis' Conditioning and learning.* (2nd ed.) New York: Appleton, 1961.

Kish, G. B. Studies of sensory reinforcement. In W. K. Honig (Ed.), *Operant behavior.* New York: Appleton, 1966. Pp. 109-115.

Le Magnen, J. Habits and food intake. In C. F. Code (Ed.), *Handbook of physiology.* Sect. 6. *Alimentary canal.* Vol. 1. *Control of food and water intake.* Washington, D. C.: Amer. Physiol. Soc., 1967. Pp. 11-30.

Lockhard, R. B. Some effects of maintenance luminance and strain differences upon self-exposure to light by rats. *J. comp. physiol. Psychol.,* 1962, **55,** 1118-1123.

Lockhard, R. B. Some effects of light upon behavior of rodents. *Psychol. Bull.,* 1963, **60,** 509-529.

Lockhard, R. B. Several tests of stimulus-change and preference theory in relation to light-controlled behavior in rats. *J. comp. physiol. Psychol.,* 1966, **62,** 415-426.

Malmo, R. B. Activation: A neurophysiological dimension. *Psychol. Rev.,* 1959, **66,** 367-386.

McCall, R. B. Initial-consequent-change surface in light contingent bar pressing. *J. comp. physiol. Psychol.,* 1966, **62,** 35-42.

Miller, N. E. Some reflections on the law of effect produce a new alternative to drive reduction. In M. R. Jones (Ed.), *Nebraska symposium on motivation.* Lincoln, Nebr.: Univer. of Nebraska Press, 1963. Pp. 65-112.

Miller, N. E., & Kessen, M. L. Reward effects of food via stomach fistula compared with those of food via mouth. *J. comp. physiol. Psychol.,* 1952, **45,** 550-564.

Moruzzi, G., & Magoun, H. W. Brain stem reticular formation and activation of the EEG. *Electroencephalog. clin. Neurophysiol.,* 1949, **1,** 455-473.

Nunnally, J. C., & Faw, T. T. The acquisition of conditioned reward value in discrimination learning. *Child Develpm.,* 1968, **39,** 159-166.

O'Kelly, L. I., Hatton, G. I., Tucker, L., & Westall, D. Water regulation in the rat: Heart rate as a function of gydration, anesthesia, and association with reinforcement. *J. comp. physiol. Psychol.,* 1965, **59,** 159-165.

Olds, J. Hypothalamic substrates of reward. *Physiol. Rev.,* 1962, **42,** 554-604.

Oomura, Y., Kimura, K., Ooyama, H., Maeno, T., Iki, M., & Kuniyoshi, M. Reciprocal activities of the ventromedial and lateral hypothalamic areas of cats. *Science,* 1964, **143,** 484-485.

Pfaffman, C. The pleasure of sensation. *Psychol. Rev.,* 1960, **67,** 253-268.

Premack, D. Reinforcement theory. In D. Levine (Ed.), *Nebraska symposium on motivation.* Lincoln, Nebr.: Univer. of Nebraska Press, 1965. Pp. 123-188.

Routtenberg, A. The two arousal hypothesis: Reticular formation and limbic system. *Psychol. Rev.*, 1968, **75**, 51-80.

Sheffield, F. D. Relation between classical conditioning and instrumental learning. In W. F. Prokasy (Ed.), *Classical conditioning: A symposium*. New York: Appleton, 1965. Pp. 302-322.

Sheffield, F. D. A drive-induction theory of reinforcement. In R. N. Haber (Ed.), *Current research in motivation*. New York: Holt, 1966. Pp. 98-111. (a)

Sheffield, F. D. New evidence on the drive-induction theory of reinforcement. In R. N. Haber (Ed.), *Current research in motivation*. New York: Holt, 1966. Pp. 111-121. (b)

Steiner, W. G. Electricial activity of rat brain as a correlate of primary drive. *Electroencephalog. clin. Neurophysiol.*, 1962, **14**, 233-243.

Sutton, D. Deprivation and drug effects on pre-pyriform cortex electrical activity in rats. *Physiol. Behav.*, 1967, **2**, 139-144.

Tapp, J. T., & Simpson, L. L. Motivational and response factors as determinants of the reinforcing value of light onset. *J. comp. physiol. Psychol.*, 1966, **62**, 143-146.

Wike, E. L. *Secondary reinforcement: Selected experiments*. New York: Harper, 1966.

Young, P. T. The role of affective processes in learning and motivation. *Psychol. Rev.*, 1959, **66**, 104-125.

Young, P. T. Hedonic organization and regulation of behavior. *Psychol. Rev.*, 1966, **73**, 59-86.

Author Index

Numbers in italics refer to the pages on which the complete references are listed.

Subject Index

A

Acetylcholine, 289, 314-325, 408, 413
Acquisition, 48, 49, 51, 57, 88, 102, 309, 310, 362, 364, 404
Action potential (spike), 226, 227, 359, 361, 362, 375
Activation, 254, 281, 282, 392, 205, 206, 405, 408, 411
Activity, *see also* Exploration, Hunger, Thirst
  locomotor, 147, 148, 163, 181, 186, 188, 268, 277, 297, 312
  nature of, 148-154
  of nerve cells, 356-382
Adaptation, 144
  level, 397, 398
Adipsia, 260
Adrenergic transmission, *see* Catecholamines
Affect, 19, 239, 243, 396, 402, 413, 414
Aggression, 183, 243, 322
Alice, 52
All-or-none
  learning, 72, 92
  model, 98-119
Amphetamine, 198-201, 210, 211, 292, 295, 296, 298, 316, 334, 343
Amygdala, 333, 339, 347, 349, 350
Anticholinergics, 347, 348, 303-309, 313-323
  habituation, and, 288-302
  memory, and, 301-306
  suppression, and, 308-314
Aphagia, 260
Arousal, 48, 49, 181, 183, 238, 287, 391-
394, *see also* Electroencephalograph
  conditioned, 200
  cortical, 211
  level, 186, 188, 197-202, 207-210, 216, 411
  novelty, and, 194-199
  potential, 199, 201, 202, 206-208, 217, 392, 393
  reward, and, 204-211
Attack, 281, 329
Attention, 14, 26, 71, 87, 101, 180
Atropine, *see* Anticholinergics
Autonomic nervous system, 211, 242, 243
  parasympathetic, 311
  sympathetic, 311
Aversion system, 205, 206, *see also* Periventricular system
Awareness, 64, 74, 84, 86, 395

B

Barbiturates, 201-204, 210, 343
Behavior-directing properties of stimuli, 146-175, 216, 294, 296, 297
Behaviorism, 23, 33
Belongingness, principle of, 14, 84
Benactyzine, *see* Anticholinergics
Biological needs, *see* Need states
Biological significance, 34, 182
  of rewards, 31, 414
  of stimuli, 179, 206, 287, 288, 299, 300, 315, 400
Brainstem, 183, 404
  reticular system, 210, 332, 391-394